CITY
OPEN DOORS

KURT BUSIEK
WRITER

BRENT ERIC ANDERSON
ARTIST

ALEX ROSS
COVERS

ALEX SINCLAIR &
WENDY BROOME
COLORS

JG ROSHELL & COMICRAFT'S
JIMMY BETANCOURT
LETTERING & DESIGN

ASTRO CITY
CREATED BY BUSIEK,
ANDERSON & ROSS

Juke Box Productions

Comicraft Since 1992
RICHARD STARKINGS
Art Director

VERTIGO

Kristy Quinn Editor
Jessica Chen Assistant Editor
Robbin Brosterman Design Director – Books

Shelly Bond Executive Editor – Vertigo
Hank Kanalz Senior VP – Vertigo & Integrated Publishing

Diane Nelson President
Dan DiDio and Jim Lee Co-Publishers
Geoff Johns Chief Creative Officer
Amit Desai Senior VP – Marketing & Franchise Management
Amy Genkins Senior VP – Business & Legal Affairs
Nairi Gardiner Senior VP – Finance
Jeff Boison VP – Publishing Planning
Mark Chiarello VP – Art Direction & Design
John Cunningham VP – Marketing
Terri Cunningham VP – Editorial Administration
Larry Ganem VP – Talent Relations & Services
Alison Gill Senior VP – Manufacturing & Operations
Jay Kogan VP – Business & Legal Affairs, Publishing
Jack Mahan VP – Business Affairs, Talent
Nick Napolitano VP – Manufacturing Administration
Sue Pohja VP – Book Sales
Fred Ruiz VP – Manufacturing Operations
Courtney Simmons Senior VP – Publicity
Bob Wayne Senior VP – Sales

SUSTAINABLE FORESTRY INITIATIVE
Certified Chain of Custody
20% Certified Forest Content, 80% Certified Sourcing
www.sfiprogram.org
SFI-01042
APPLIES TO TEXT STOCK ONLY

Library of Congress Cataloging-in-Publication Data

Busiek, Kurt, author.
Astro City : Through Open Doors / Kurt Busiek ; [illustrated by] Brent Anderson.
pages cm
Summary: "Kurt Busiek and Brent Anderson launch their next epic in the world of Astro City when a mysterious door appears, heralding the arrival of the Ambassador. But when an ordinary man is caught in a cosmic conflict, it is up to favorites like Samaritan and Honor Guard, as well as new heroes, to rise to the occasion and save the world! Astro City #1-6"-- Provided by publisher.
ISBN 978-1-4012-4996-0
1. Graphic novels. I. Anderson, Brent Eric, illustrator. II. Title. III. Title: Through Open Doors.
PN6728.A79B866 2014
741.5'973--dc23

2013049638

ASTRO CITY: THROUGH OPEN DOORS, published by DC Comics, 1700 Broadway, New York, NY 10019.

Printed by RR Donnelley, Salem, VA, USA. 8/15/2014.

DC Comics, a Warner Bros. Entertainment Company.

ISBN: 978-1-4012-4996-0

CONTENTS

1: Through Open Doors, Part One   7

2: Welcome to HumanoGlobal   33

3: Mistakes   59

4: On the Sidelines   85

5: Thumbtacks & Yarn   111

6: Through Open Doors, Part Two   137

Sketchbook   163

About the Creators   176

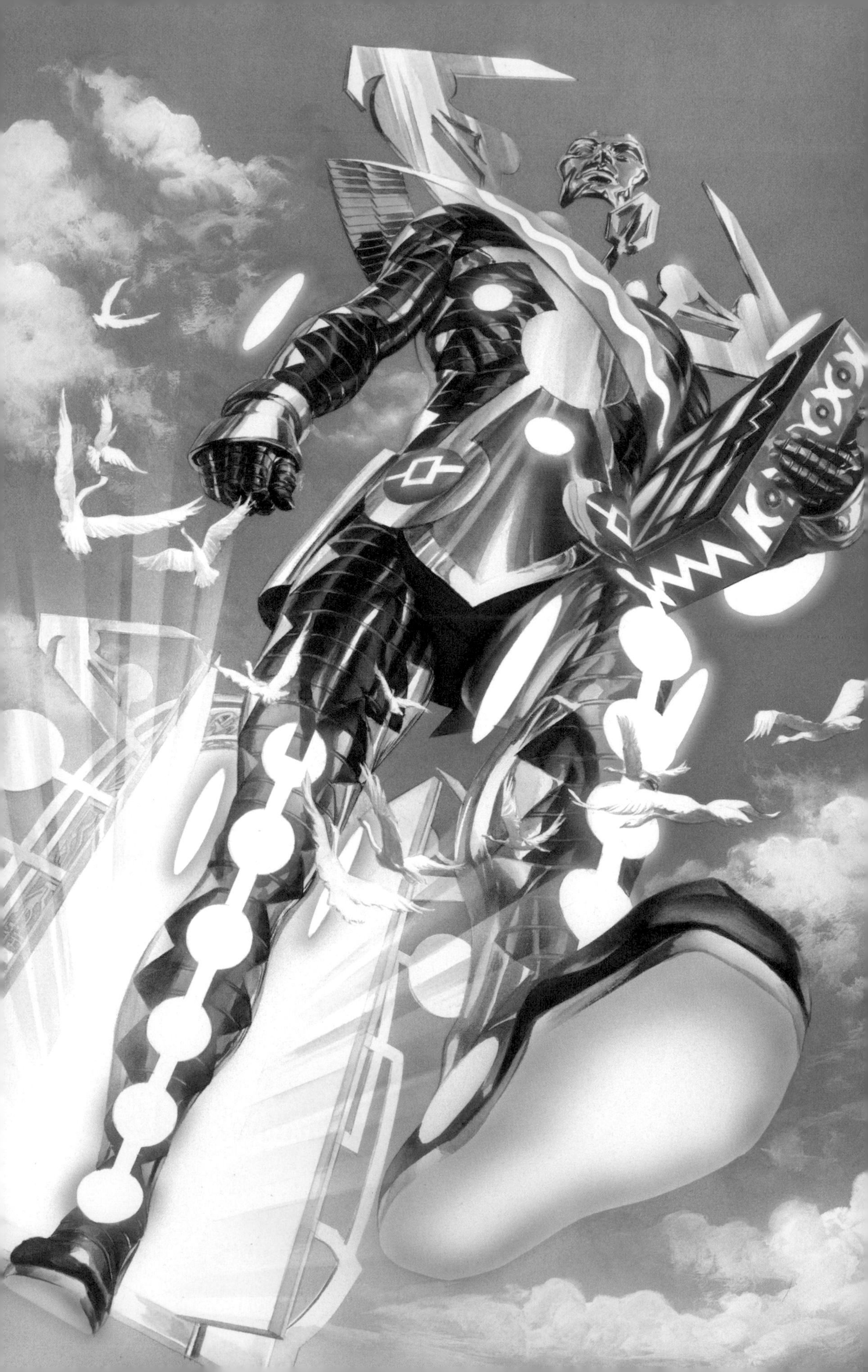

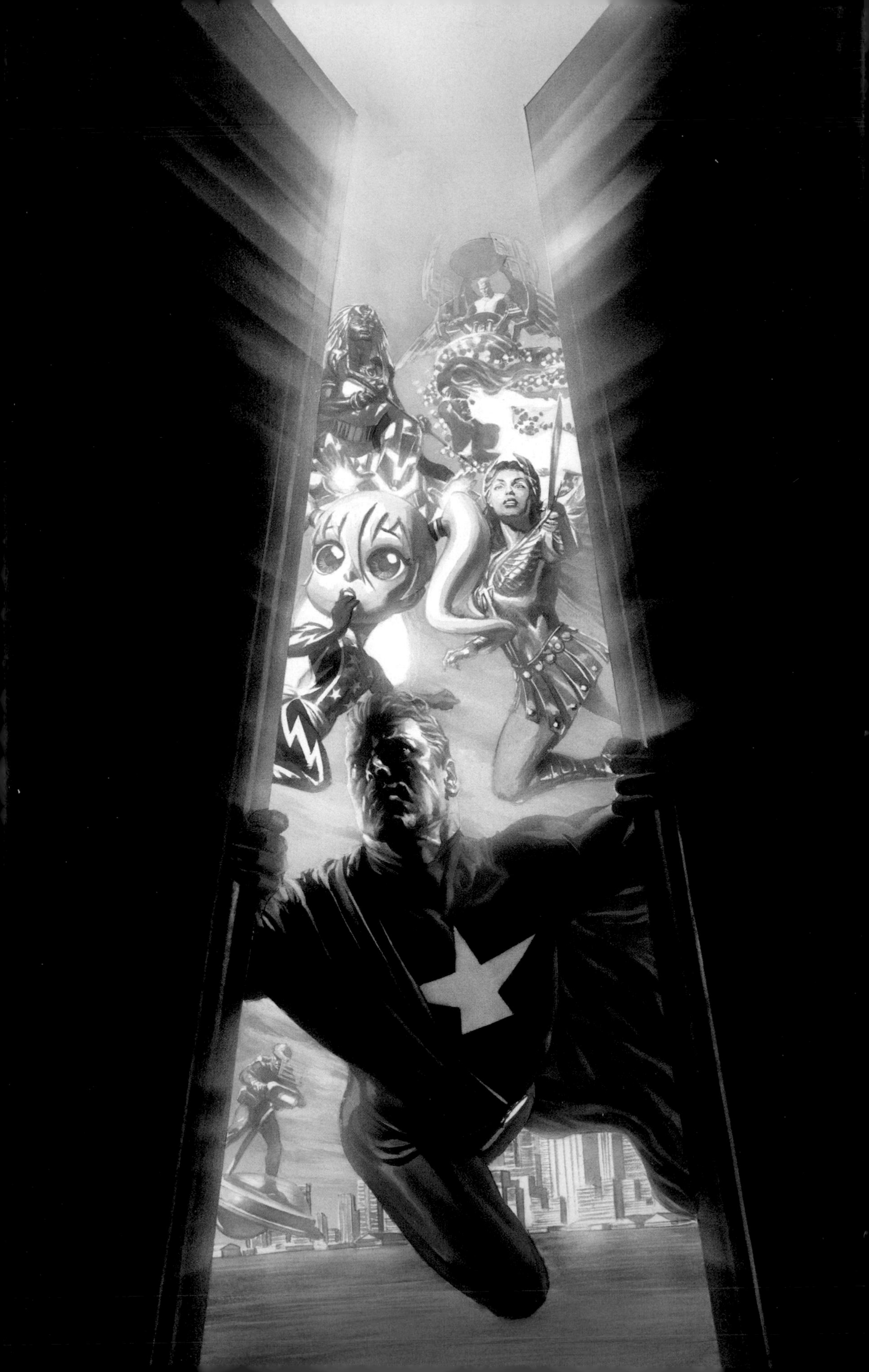

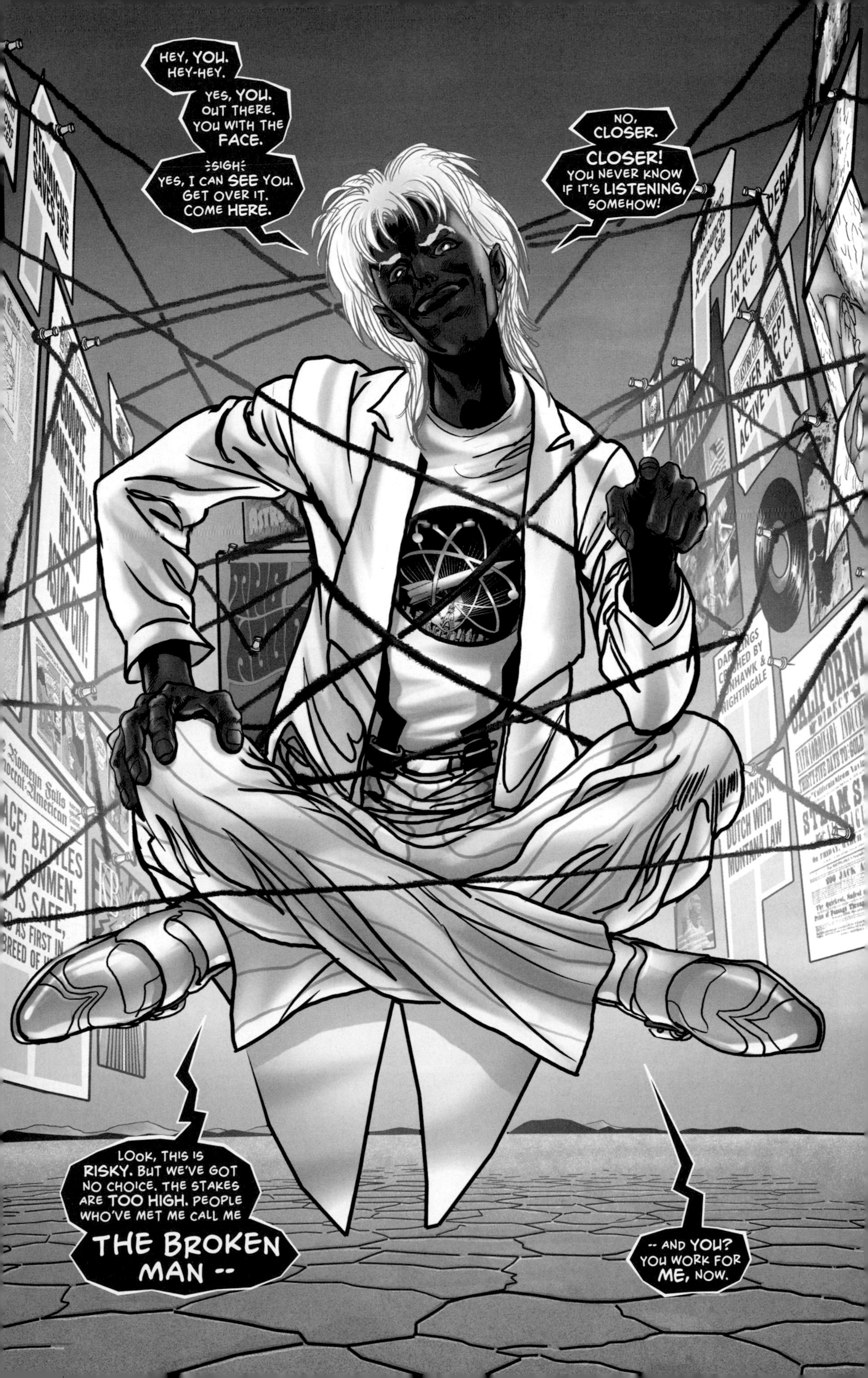
HEY, YOU. HEY-HEY.
YES, YOU. OUT THERE. YOU WITH THE FACE.
SIGH YES, I CAN SEE YOU. GET OVER IT. COME HERE.
NO, CLOSER.
CLOSER! YOU NEVER KNOW IF IT'S LISTENING, SOMEHOW!
LOOK, THIS IS RISKY. BUT WE'VE GOT NO CHOICE. THE STAKES ARE TOO HIGH. PEOPLE WHO'VE MET ME CALL ME
THE BROKEN MAN --
-- AND YOU? YOU WORK FOR ME, NOW.

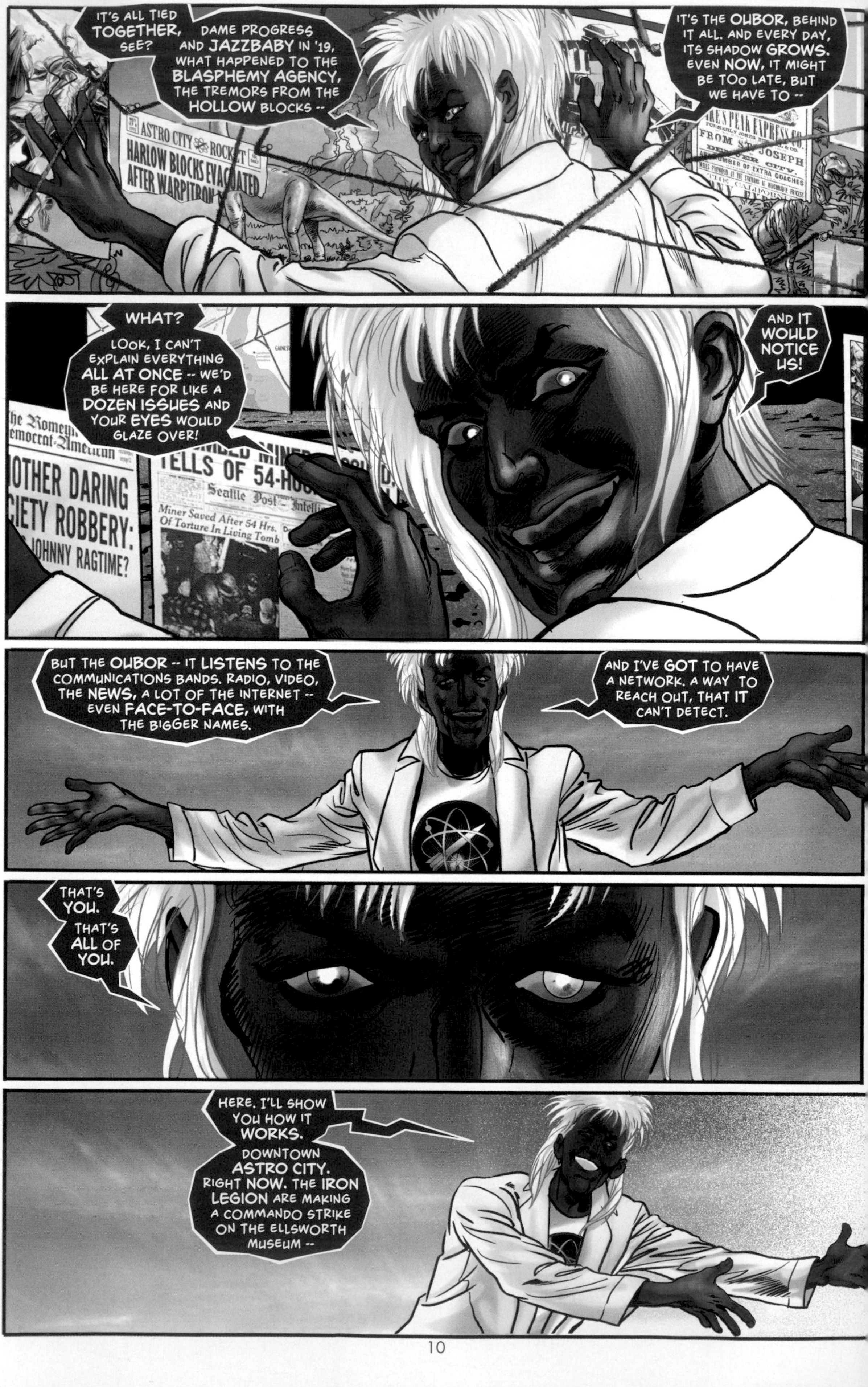
IT'S ALL TIED TOGETHER, SEE?
DAME PROGRESS AND JAZZBABY IN '19, WHAT HAPPENED TO THE BLASPHEMY AGENCY, THE TREMORS FROM THE HOLLOW BLOCKS --
ASTRO CITY ROCKET
HARLOW BLOCKS EVACUATED AFTER WARPITRON
IT'S THE OUBOR, BEHIND IT ALL. AND EVERY DAY, ITS SHADOW GROWS. EVEN NOW, IT MIGHT BE TOO LATE, BUT WE HAVE TO --
WHAT?
LOOK, I CAN'T EXPLAIN EVERYTHING ALL AT ONCE -- WE'D BE HERE FOR LIKE A DOZEN ISSUES AND YOUR EYES WOULD GLAZE OVER!
AND IT WOULD NOTICE US!
OTHER DARING CIETY ROBBERY: JOHNNY RAGTIME?
Seattle Post-Intelli
Miner Saved After 54 Hrs. Of Torture In Living Tomb
BUT THE OUBOR -- IT LISTENS TO THE COMMUNICATIONS BANDS. RADIO, VIDEO, THE NEWS, A LOT OF THE INTERNET -- EVEN FACE-TO-FACE, WITH THE BIGGER NAMES.
AND I'VE GOT TO HAVE A NETWORK. A WAY TO REACH OUT, THAT IT CAN'T DETECT.
THAT'S YOU.
THAT'S ALL OF YOU.
HERE. I'LL SHOW YOU HOW IT WORKS.
DOWNTOWN ASTRO CITY. RIGHT NOW. THE IRON LEGION ARE MAKING A COMMANDO STRIKE ON THE ELLSWORTH MUSEUM --

SPLAMMO!
DID YOU SEE THAT? DID YOU SEE THAT?
YEAH, YOU HAVEN'T SEEN HER BEFORE.
SPEND A FEW YEARS MESSING AROUND WITH STUFF THAT MOSTLY HAPPENED THIRTY YEARS AGO, AND YOU'RE GOING TO MISS A FEW THINGS.
SHE'S CALLED AMERICAN CHIBI.
KRAMM
AH --
UH --
through open doors
part one

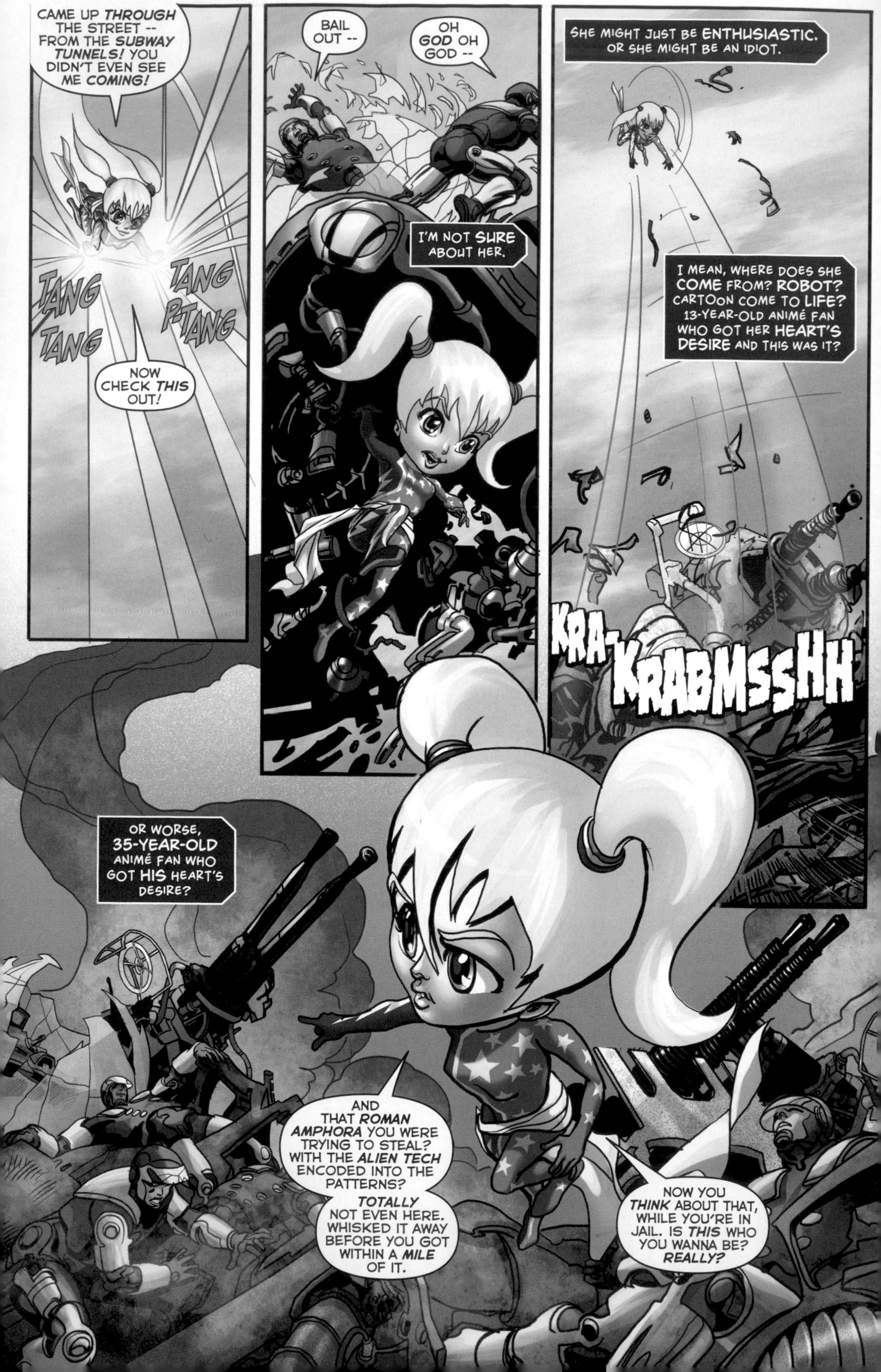

CAME UP THROUGH THE STREET -- FROM THE SUBWAY TUNNELS! YOU DIDN'T EVEN SEE ME COMING!
TANG TANG
TANG PTANG
NOW CHECK THIS OUT!
BAIL OUT --
OH GOD OH GOD --
I'M NOT SURE ABOUT HER.
SHE MIGHT JUST BE ENTHUSIASTIC. OR SHE MIGHT BE AN IDIOT.
I MEAN, WHERE DOES SHE COME FROM? ROBOT? CARTOON COME TO LIFE? 13-YEAR-OLD ANIMÉ FAN WHO GOT HER HEART'S DESIRE AND THIS WAS IT?
KRA-KRABMSSHH
OR WORSE, 35-YEAR-OLD ANIMÉ FAN WHO GOT HIS HEART'S DESIRE?
AND THAT ROMAN AMPHORA YOU WERE TRYING TO STEAL? WITH THE ALIEN TECH ENCODED INTO THE PATTERNS?
TOTALLY NOT EVEN HERE. WHISKED IT AWAY BEFORE YOU GOT WITHIN A MILE OF IT.
NOW YOU THINK ABOUT THAT, WHILE YOU'RE IN JAIL. IS THIS WHO YOU WANNA BE? REALLY?

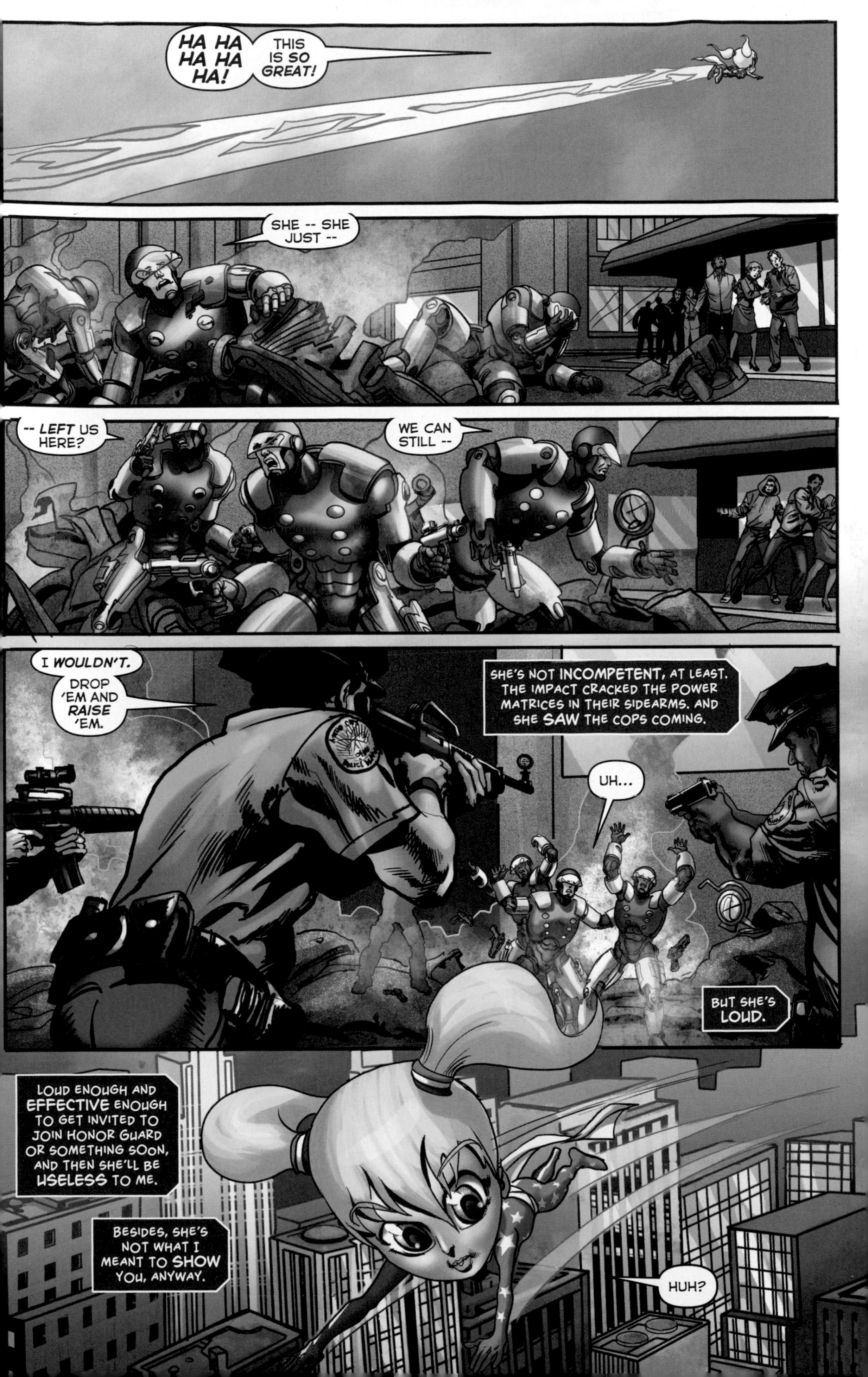
HA HA HA HA HA!
THIS IS SO GREAT!
SHE -- SHE JUST --
-- LEFT US HERE?
WE CAN STILL --
I WOULDN'T.
DROP 'EM AND RAISE 'EM.
SHE'S NOT INCOMPETENT, AT LEAST. THE IMPACT CRACKED THE POWER MATRICES IN THEIR SIDEARMS. AND SHE SAW THE COPS COMING.
UH...
BUT SHE'S LOUD.
LOUD ENOUGH AND EFFECTIVE ENOUGH TO GET INVITED TO JOIN HONOR GUARD OR SOMETHING SOON, AND THEN SHE'LL BE USELESS TO ME.
BESIDES, SHE'S NOT WHAT I MEANT TO SHOW YOU, ANYWAY.
HUH?

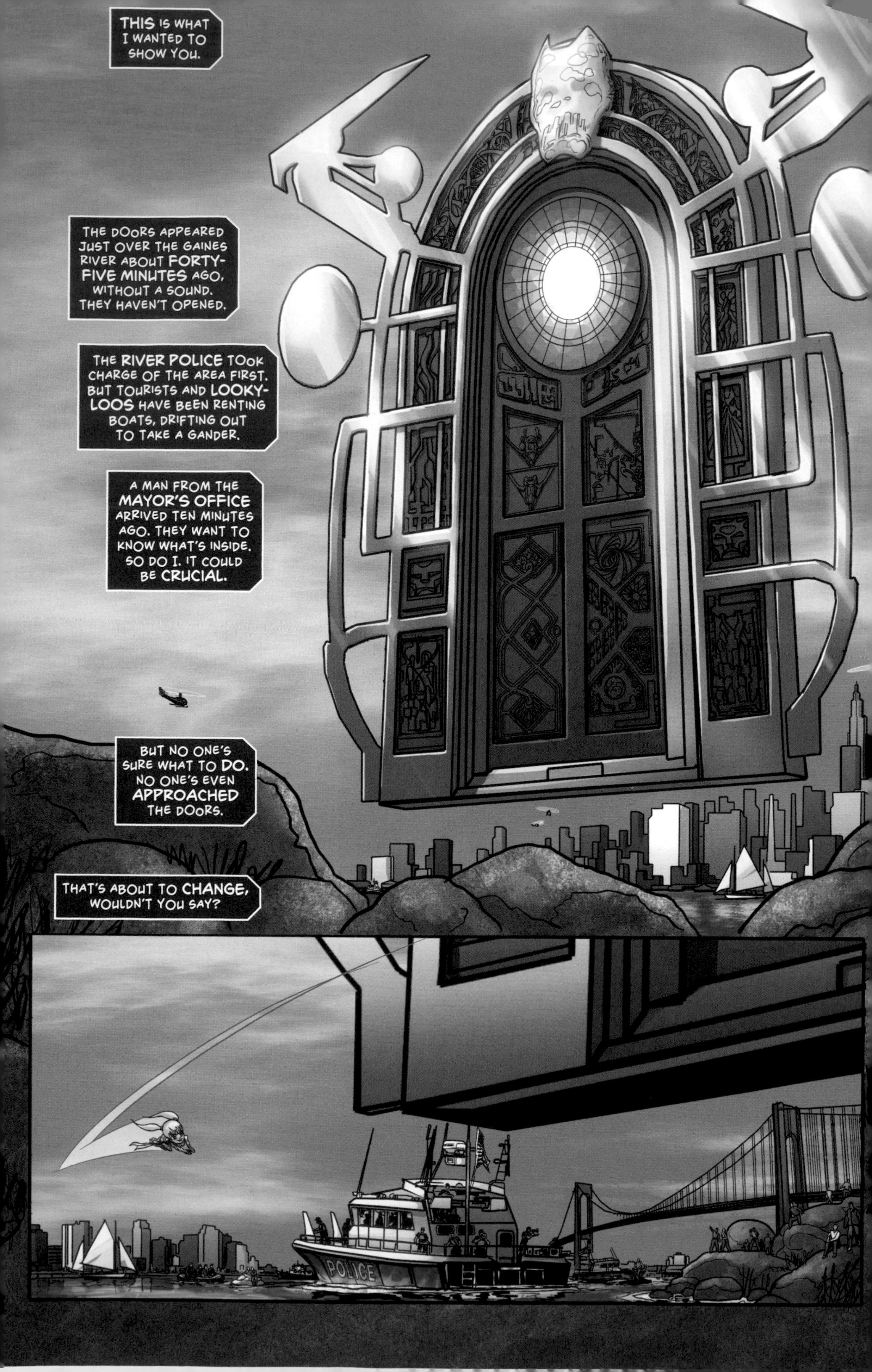
THIS IS WHAT I WANTED TO SHOW YOU.
THE DOORS APPEARED JUST OVER THE GAINES RIVER ABOUT FORTY-FIVE MINUTES AGO, WITHOUT A SOUND. THEY HAVEN'T OPENED.
THE RIVER POLICE TOOK CHARGE OF THE AREA FIRST. BUT TOURISTS AND LOOKY-LOOS HAVE BEEN RENTING BOATS, DRIFTING OUT TO TAKE A GANDER.
A MAN FROM THE MAYOR'S OFFICE ARRIVED TEN MINUTES AGO. THEY WANT TO KNOW WHAT'S INSIDE. SO DO I. IT COULD BE CRUCIAL.
BUT NO ONE'S SURE WHAT TO DO. NO ONE'S EVEN APPROACHED THE DOORS.
THAT'S ABOUT TO CHANGE, WOULDN'T YOU SAY?
POLICE

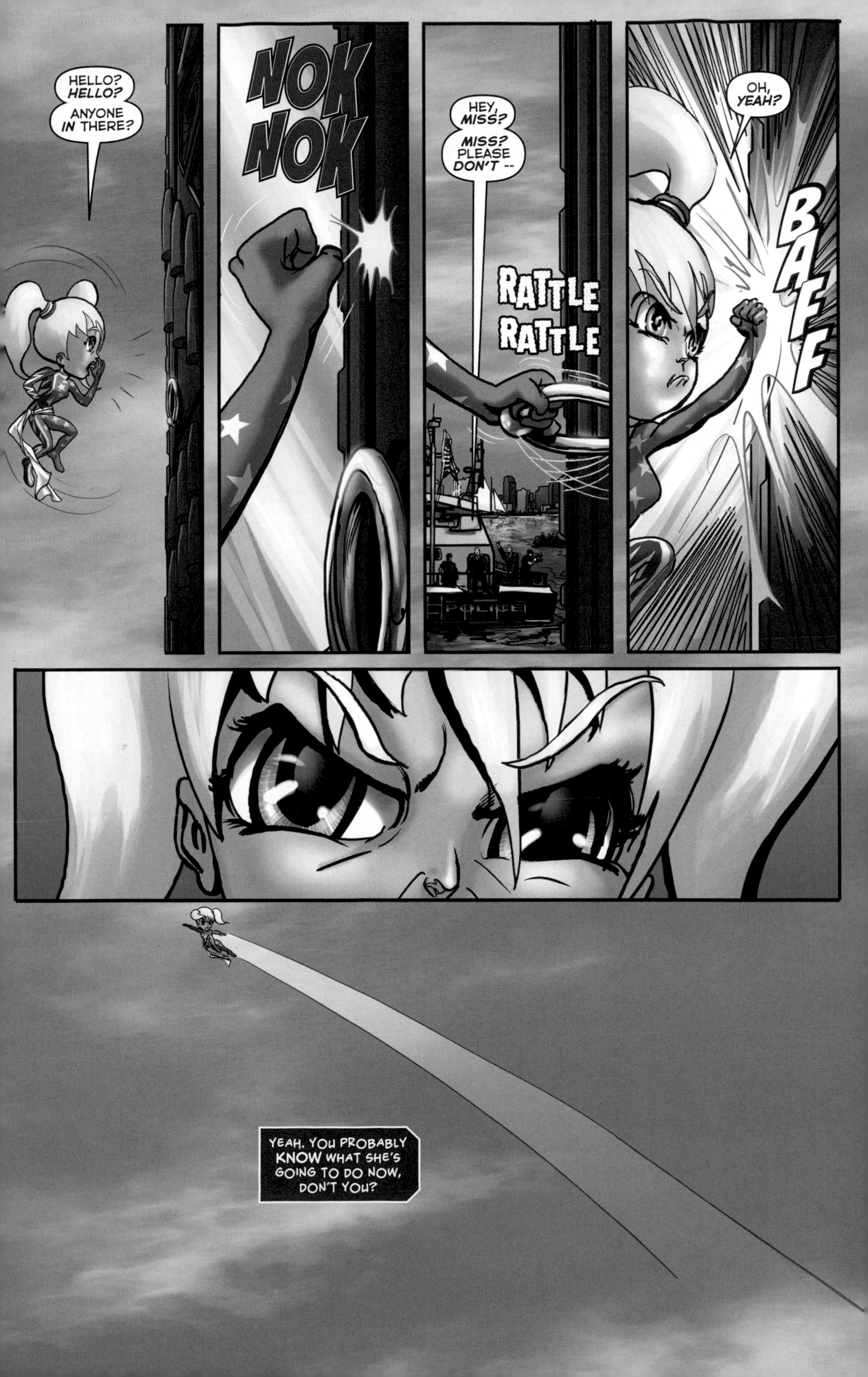
HELLO? HELLO? ANYONE IN THERE?
NOK NOK
HEY, MISS? MISS? PLEASE DON'T --
RATTLE RATTLE
POLICE
OH, YEAH?
BAFF
YEAH. YOU PROBABLY KNOW WHAT SHE'S GOING TO DO NOW, DON'T YOU?

EXACTLY.
SPLAMMMM
SHE WON'T DO. NOT AT ALL.
UHH!
I NEED SOMEONE TO FIND OUT ABOUT THOSE DOORS. BUT SOMEONE SMARTER. QUIETER.
A LOT QUIETER.

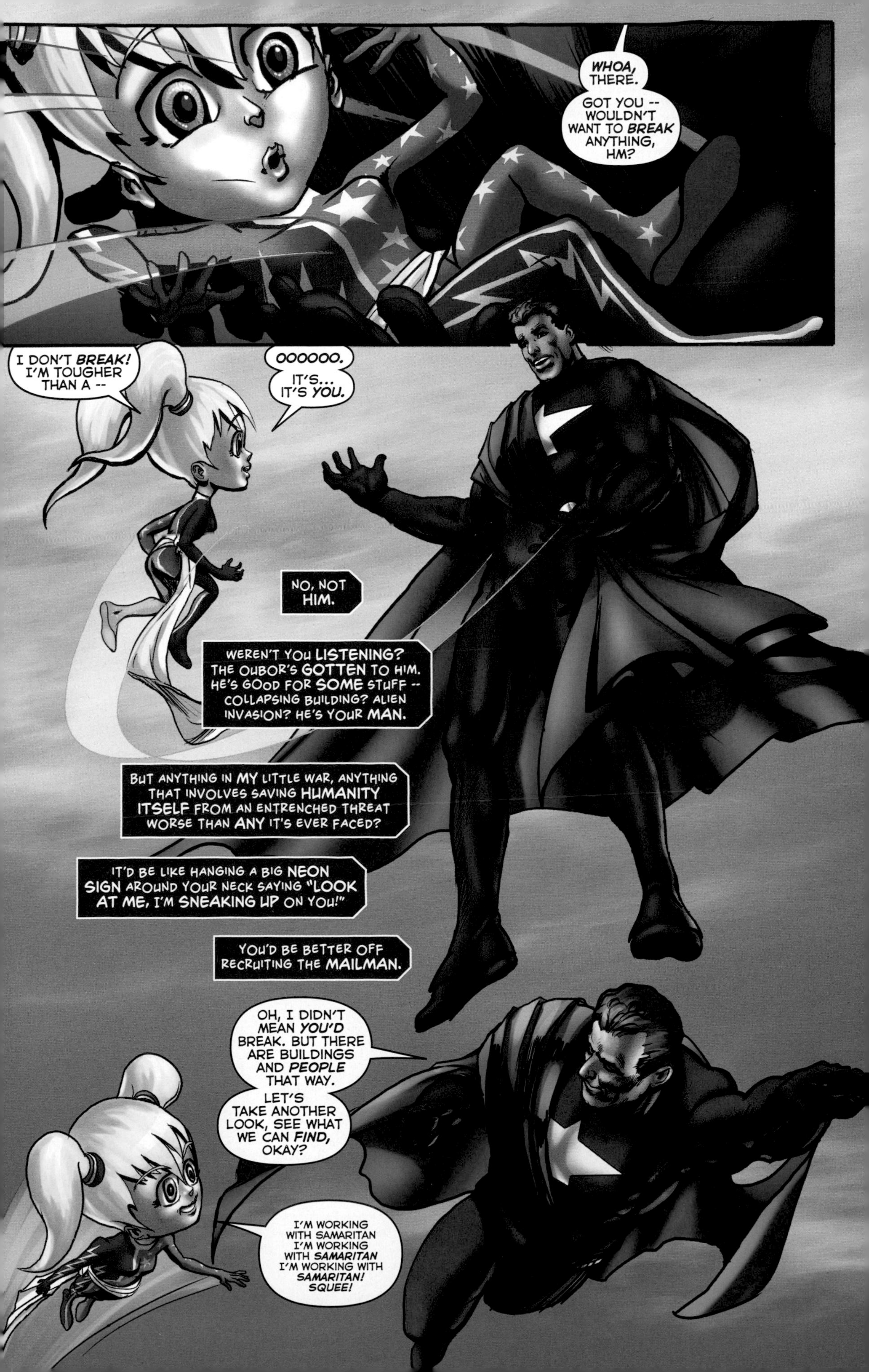
WHOA, THERE.
GOT YOU -- WOULDN'T WANT TO BREAK ANYTHING, HM?
I DON'T BREAK! I'M TOUGHER THAN A --
OOOOOO. IT'S... IT'S YOU.
NO, NOT HIM.
WEREN'T YOU LISTENING? THE OUBOR'S GOTTEN TO HIM. HE'S GOOD FOR SOME STUFF -- COLLAPSING BUILDING? ALIEN INVASION? HE'S YOUR MAN.
BUT ANYTHING IN MY LITTLE WAR, ANYTHING THAT INVOLVES SAVING HUMANITY ITSELF FROM AN ENTRENCHED THREAT WORSE THAN ANY IT'S EVER FACED?
IT'D BE LIKE HANGING A BIG NEON SIGN AROUND YOUR NECK SAYING "LOOK AT ME, I'M SNEAKING UP ON YOU!"
YOU'D BE BETTER OFF RECRUITING THE MAILMAN.
OH, I DIDN'T MEAN YOU'D BREAK. BUT THERE ARE BUILDINGS AND PEOPLE THAT WAY.
LET'S TAKE ANOTHER LOOK, SEE WHAT WE CAN FIND, OKAY?
I'M WORKING WITH SAMARITAN I'M WORKING WITH SAMARITAN I'M WORKING WITH SAMARITAN! SQUEE!

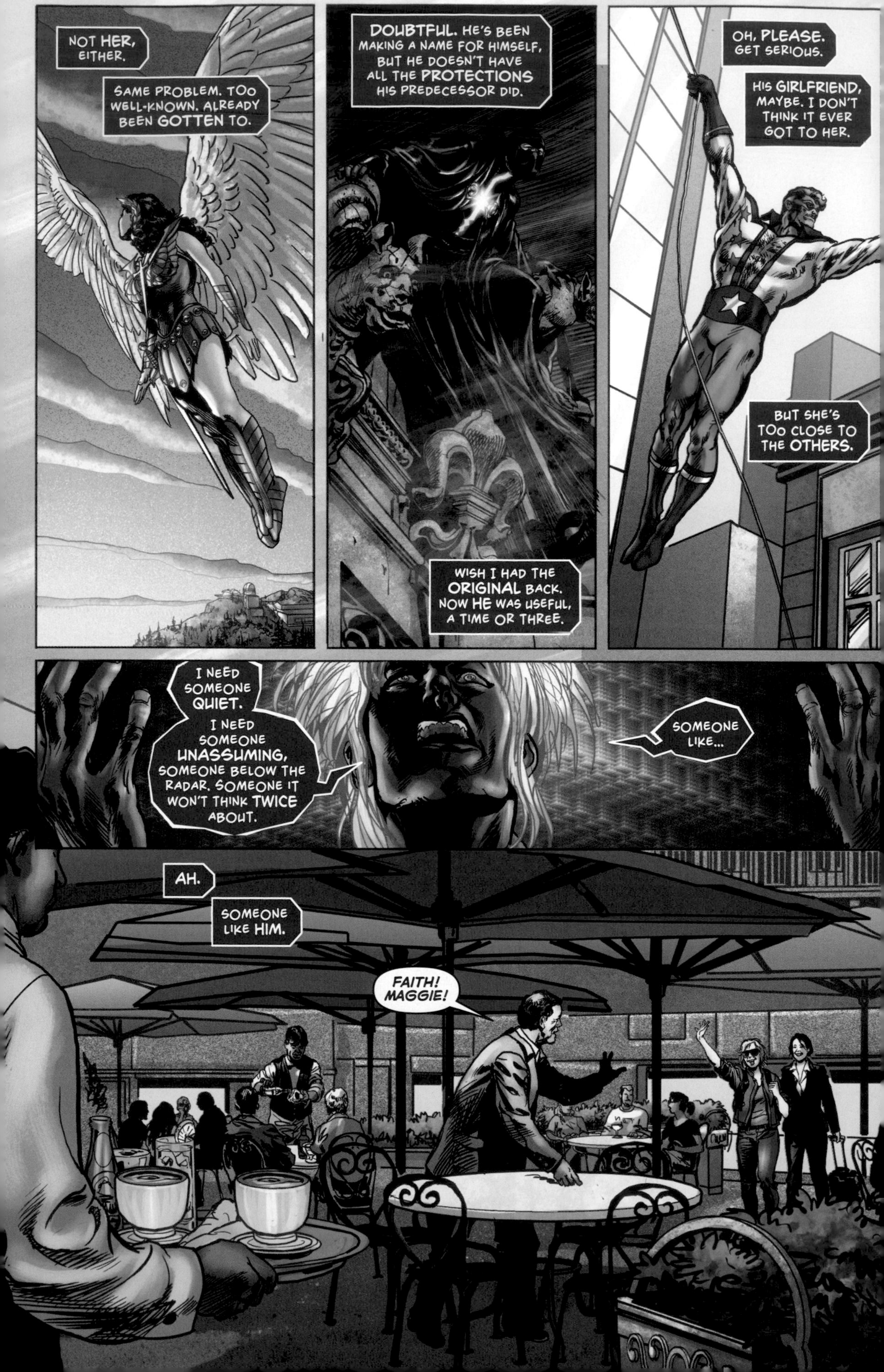
NOT HER, EITHER.
SAME PROBLEM. TOO WELL-KNOWN. ALREADY BEEN GOTTEN TO.
DOUBTFUL. HE'S BEEN MAKING A NAME FOR HIMSELF, BUT HE DOESN'T HAVE ALL THE PROTECTIONS HIS PREDECESSOR DID.
WISH I HAD THE ORIGINAL BACK. NOW HE WAS USEFUL, A TIME OR THREE.
OH, PLEASE. GET SERIOUS.
HIS GIRLFRIEND, MAYBE. I DON'T THINK IT EVER GOT TO HER.
BUT SHE'S TOO CLOSE TO THE OTHERS.
I NEED SOMEONE QUIET.
I NEED SOMEONE UNASSUMING, SOMEONE BELOW THE RADAR. SOMEONE IT WON'T THINK TWICE ABOUT.
SOMEONE LIKE...
AH.
SOMEONE LIKE HIM.
FAITH! MAGGIE!

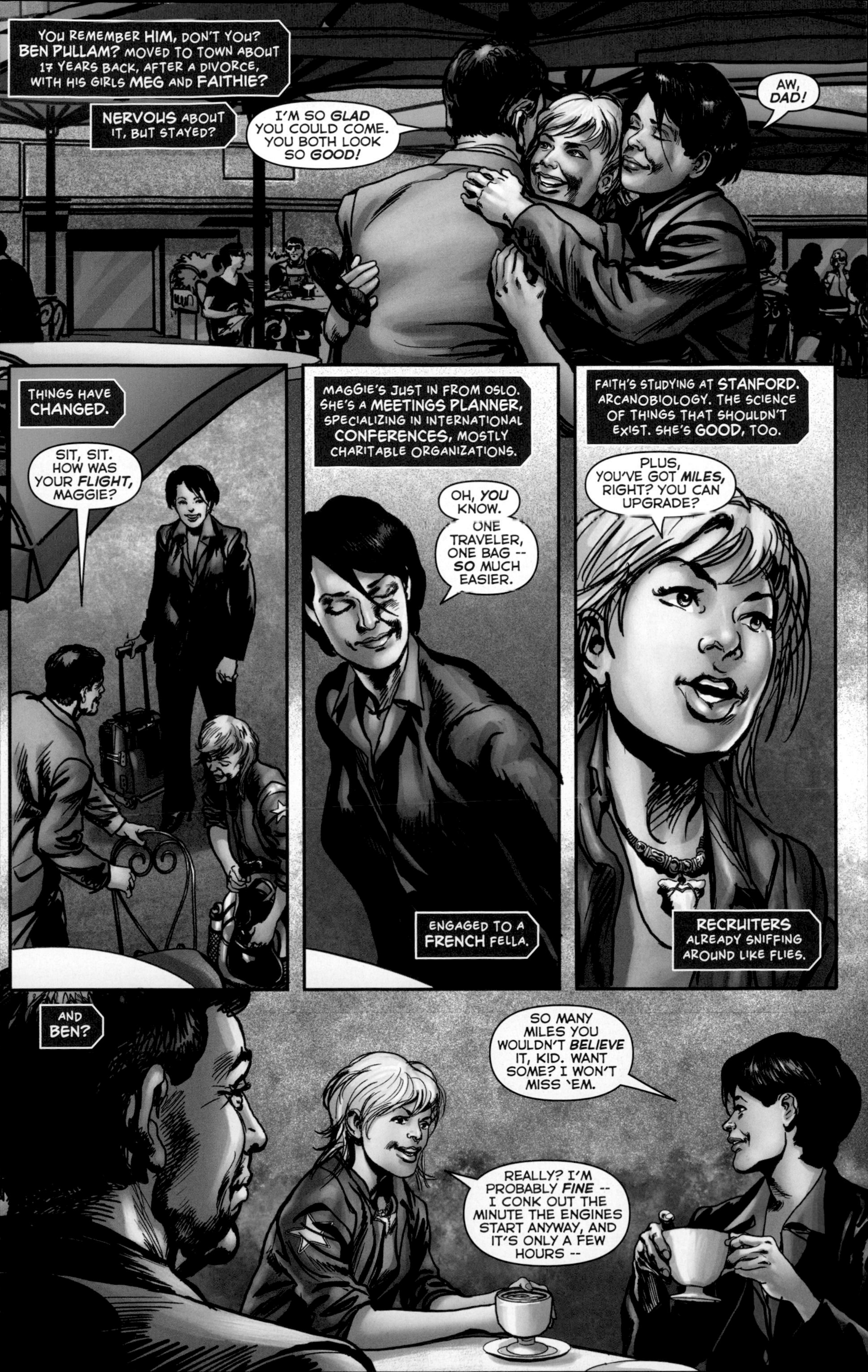
YOU REMEMBER HIM, DON'T YOU? BEN PULLAM? MOVED TO TOWN ABOUT 17 YEARS BACK, AFTER A DIVORCE, WITH HIS GIRLS MEG AND FAITHIE?
NERVOUS ABOUT IT, BUT STAYED?
I'M SO GLAD YOU COULD COME. YOU BOTH LOOK SO GOOD!
AW, DAD!
THINGS HAVE CHANGED.
SIT, SIT. HOW WAS YOUR FLIGHT, MAGGIE?
MAGGIE'S JUST IN FROM OSLO. SHE'S A MEETINGS PLANNER, SPECIALIZING IN INTERNATIONAL CONFERENCES, MOSTLY CHARITABLE ORGANIZATIONS.
OH, YOU KNOW. ONE TRAVELER, ONE BAG -- SO MUCH EASIER.
ENGAGED TO A FRENCH FELLA.
FAITH'S STUDYING AT STANFORD. ARCANOBIOLOGY. THE SCIENCE OF THINGS THAT SHOULDN'T EXIST. SHE'S GOOD, TOO.
PLUS, YOU'VE GOT MILES, RIGHT? YOU CAN UPGRADE?
RECRUITERS ALREADY SNIFFING AROUND LIKE FLIES.
AND BEN?
SO MANY MILES YOU WOULDN'T BELIEVE IT, KID. WANT SOME? I WON'T MISS 'EM.
REALLY? I'M PROBABLY FINE -- I CONK OUT THE MINUTE THE ENGINES START ANYWAY, AND IT'S ONLY A FEW HOURS --

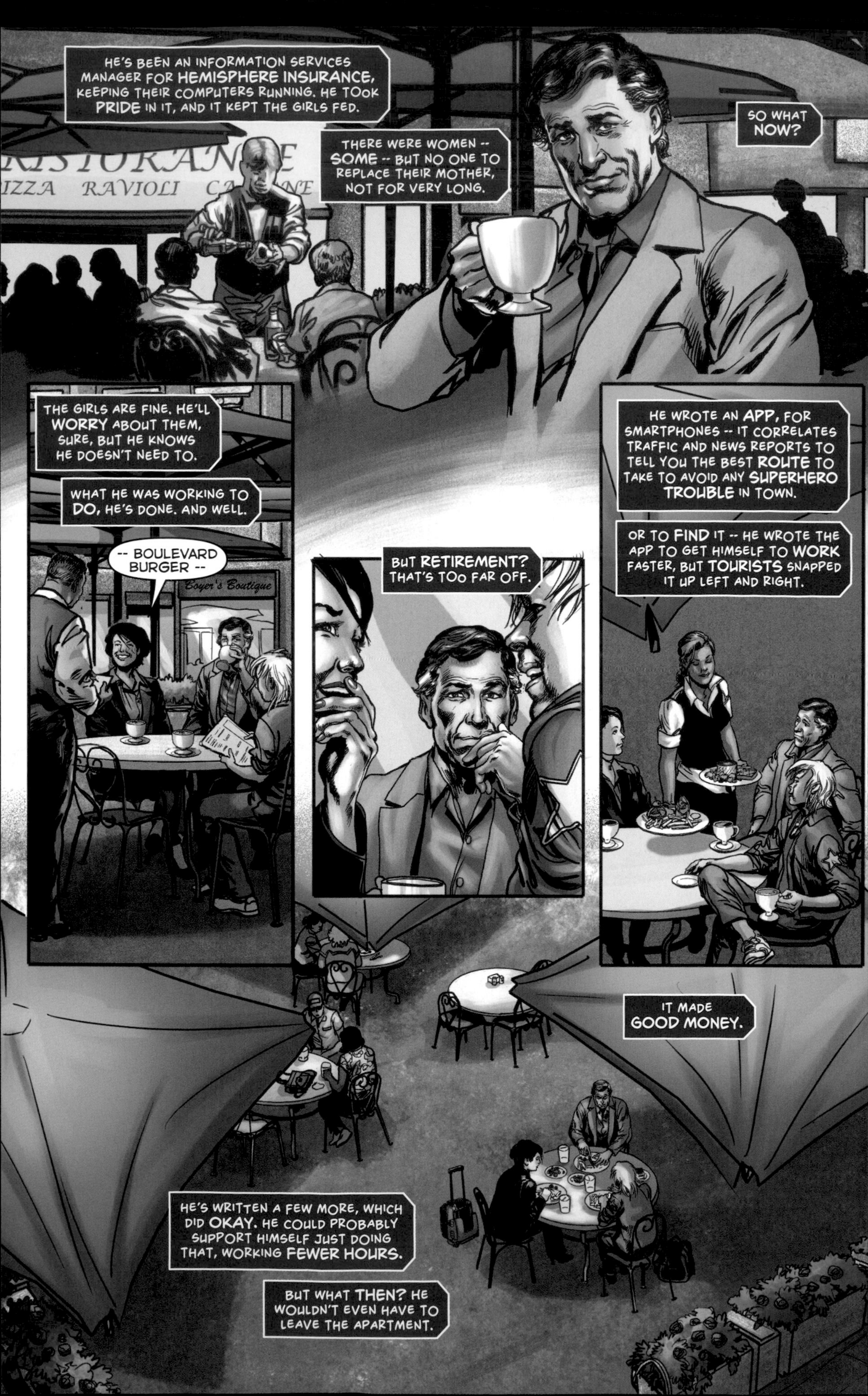

HE'S BEEN AN INFORMATION SERVICES MANAGER FOR HEMISPHERE INSURANCE, KEEPING THEIR COMPUTERS RUNNING. HE TOOK PRIDE IN IT, AND IT KEPT THE GIRLS FED.
THERE WERE WOMEN -- SOME -- BUT NO ONE TO REPLACE THEIR MOTHER, NOT FOR VERY LONG.
SO WHAT NOW?
THE GIRLS ARE FINE. HE'LL WORRY ABOUT THEM, SURE, BUT HE KNOWS HE DOESN'T NEED TO.
WHAT HE WAS WORKING TO DO, HE'S DONE, AND WELL.
-- BOULEVARD BURGER --
Boyer's Boutique
BUT RETIREMENT? THAT'S TOO FAR OFF.
HE WROTE AN APP, FOR SMARTPHONES -- IT CORRELATES TRAFFIC AND NEWS REPORTS TO TELL YOU THE BEST ROUTE TO TAKE TO AVOID ANY SUPERHERO TROUBLE IN TOWN.
OR TO FIND IT -- HE WROTE THE APP TO GET HIMSELF TO WORK FASTER, BUT TOURISTS SNAPPED IT UP LEFT AND RIGHT.
IT MADE GOOD MONEY.
HE'S WRITTEN A FEW MORE, WHICH DID OKAY. HE COULD PROBABLY SUPPORT HIMSELF JUST DOING THAT, WORKING FEWER HOURS.
BUT WHAT THEN? HE WOULDN'T EVEN HAVE TO LEAVE THE APARTMENT.

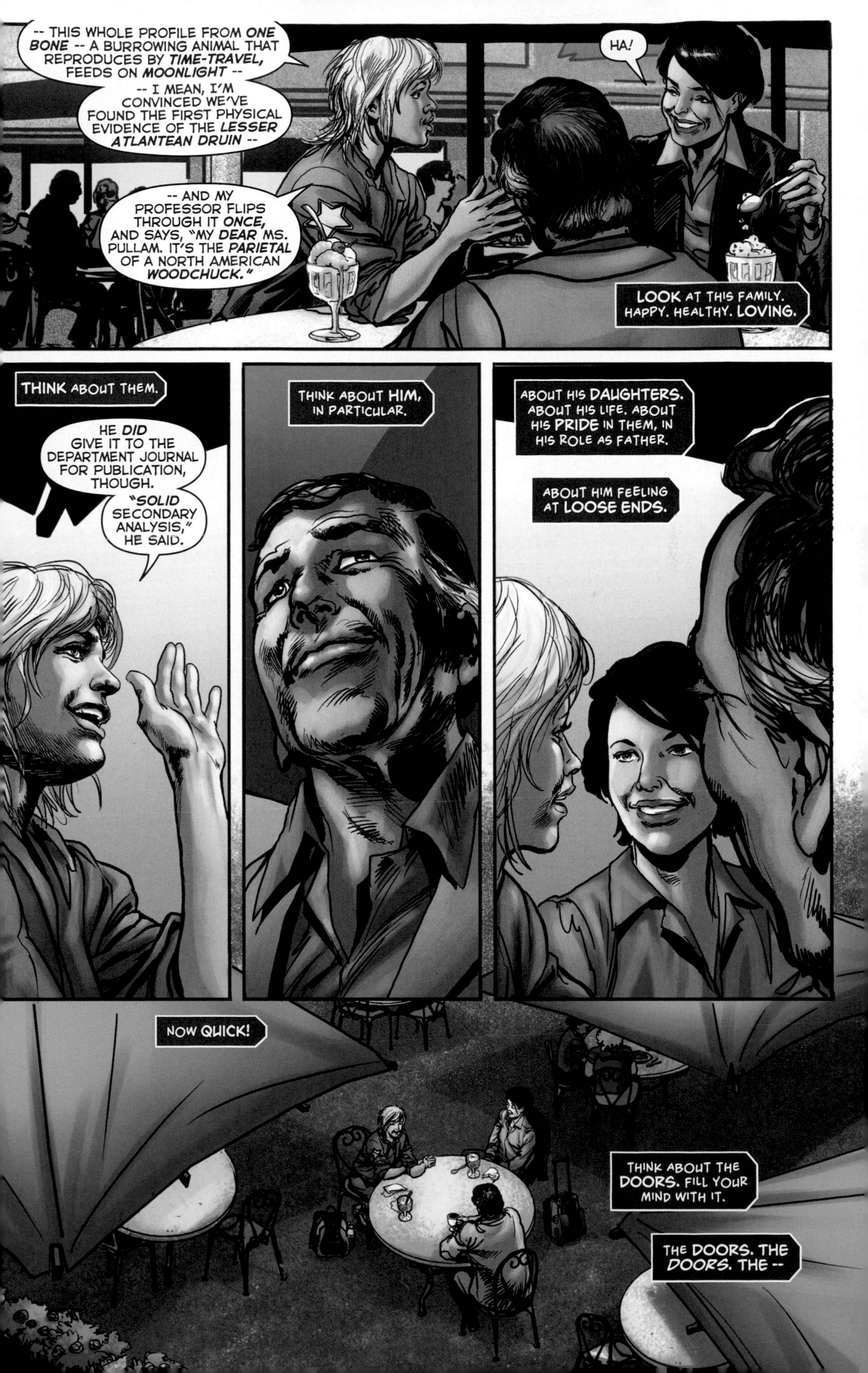
-- THIS WHOLE PROFILE FROM ONE BONE -- A BURROWING ANIMAL THAT REPRODUCES BY TIME-TRAVEL, FEEDS ON MOONLIGHT --
-- I MEAN, I'M CONVINCED WE'VE FOUND THE FIRST PHYSICAL EVIDENCE OF THE LESSER ATLANTEAN DRUIN --
HA!
-- AND MY PROFESSOR FLIPS THROUGH IT ONCE, AND SAYS, "MY DEAR MS. PULLAM. IT'S THE PARIETAL OF A NORTH AMERICAN WOODCHUCK."
LOOK AT THIS FAMILY. HAPPY. HEALTHY. LOVING.
THINK ABOUT THEM.
HE DID GIVE IT TO THE DEPARTMENT JOURNAL FOR PUBLICATION, THOUGH.
"SOLID SECONDARY ANALYSIS," HE SAID.
THINK ABOUT HIM, IN PARTICULAR.
ABOUT HIS DAUGHTERS. ABOUT HIS LIFE. ABOUT HIS PRIDE IN THEM, IN HIS ROLE AS FATHER.
ABOUT HIM FEELING AT LOOSE ENDS.
NOW QUICK!
THINK ABOUT THE DOORS. FILL YOUR MIND WITH IT.
THE DOORS. THE DOORS. THE --

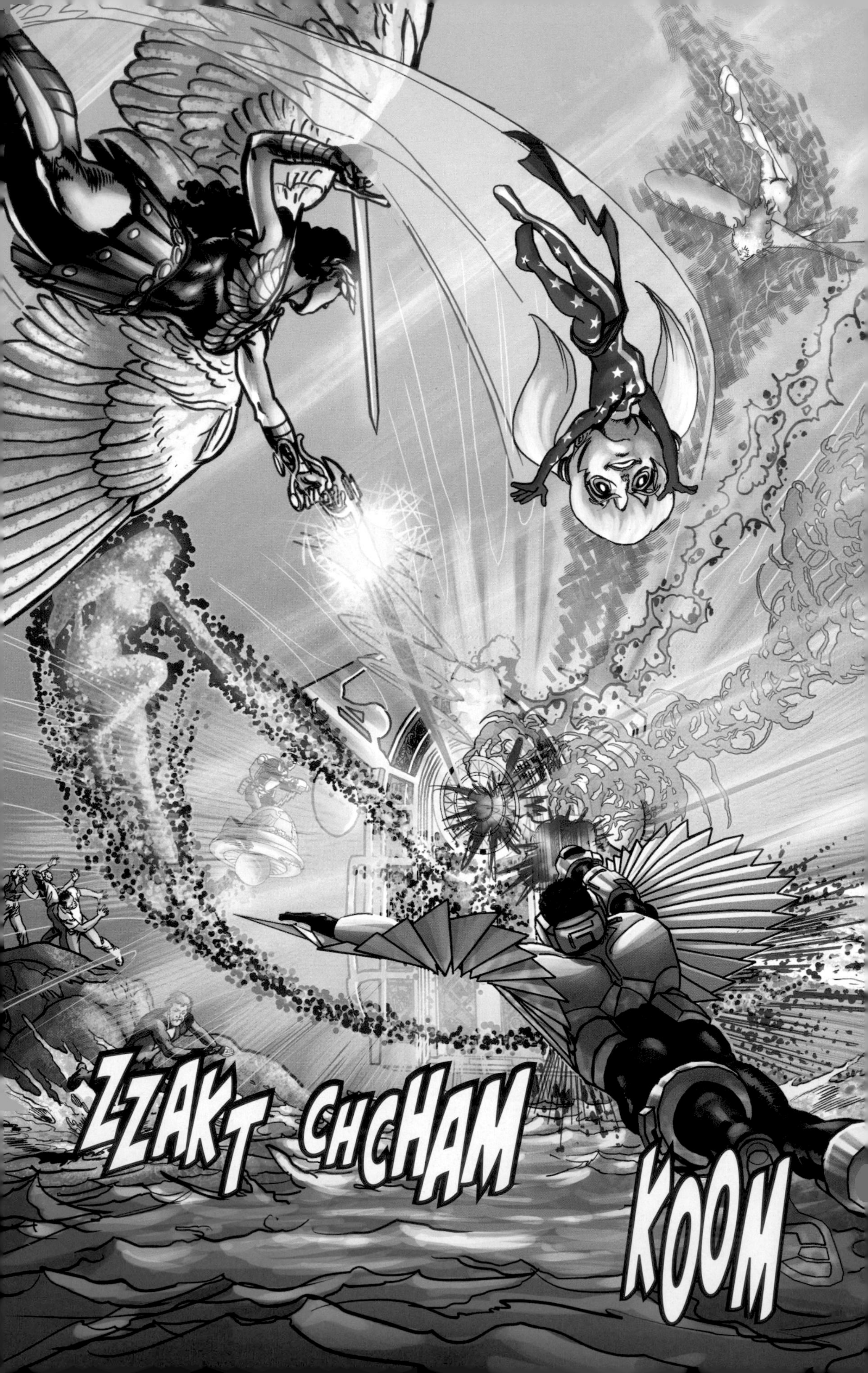
ZZAKT
CHCHAM
KOOM

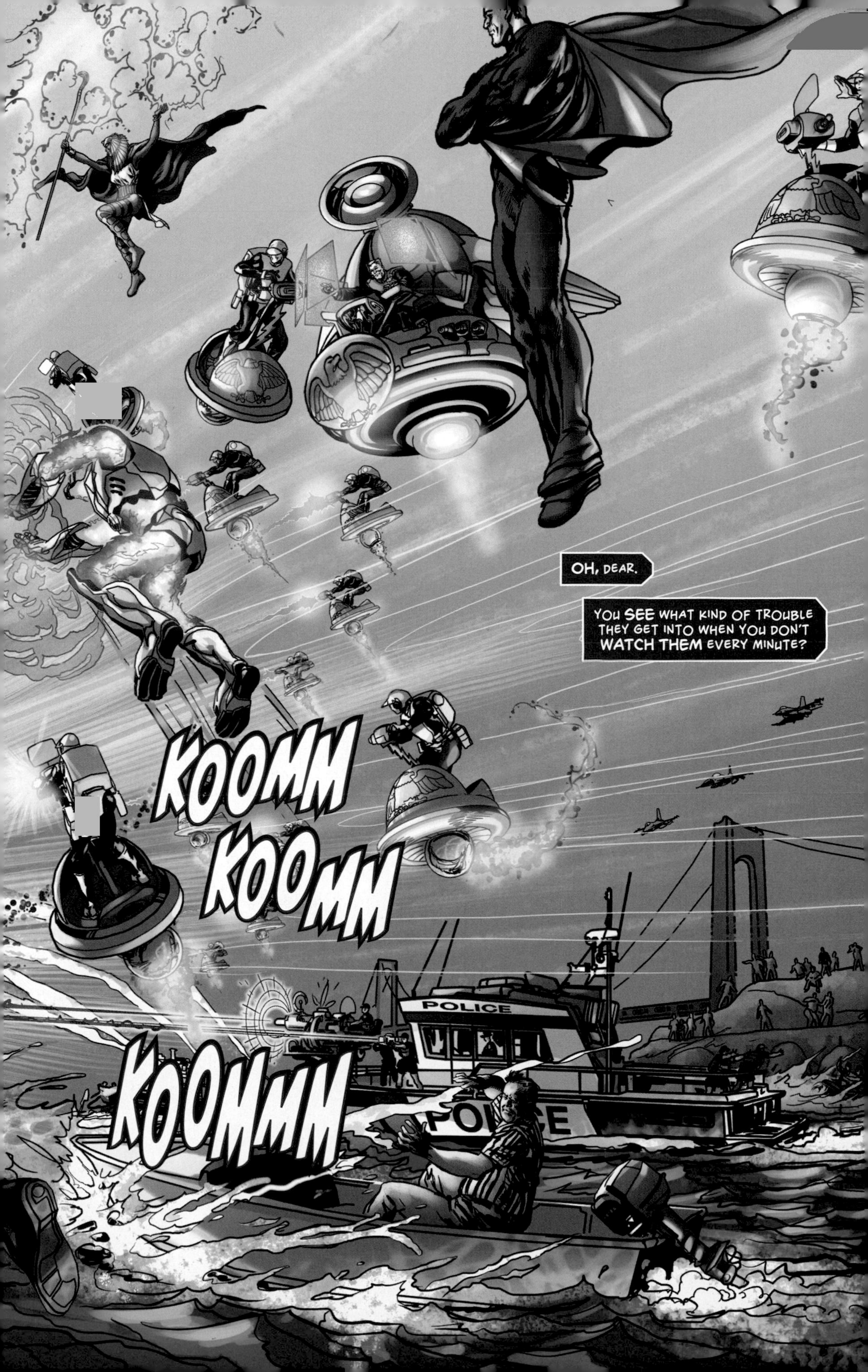
OH, DEAR.
YOU SEE WHAT KIND OF TROUBLE THEY GET INTO WHEN YOU DON'T WATCH THEM EVERY MINUTE?
KOOMM
KOOMM
KOOMMM
POLICE
POLICE

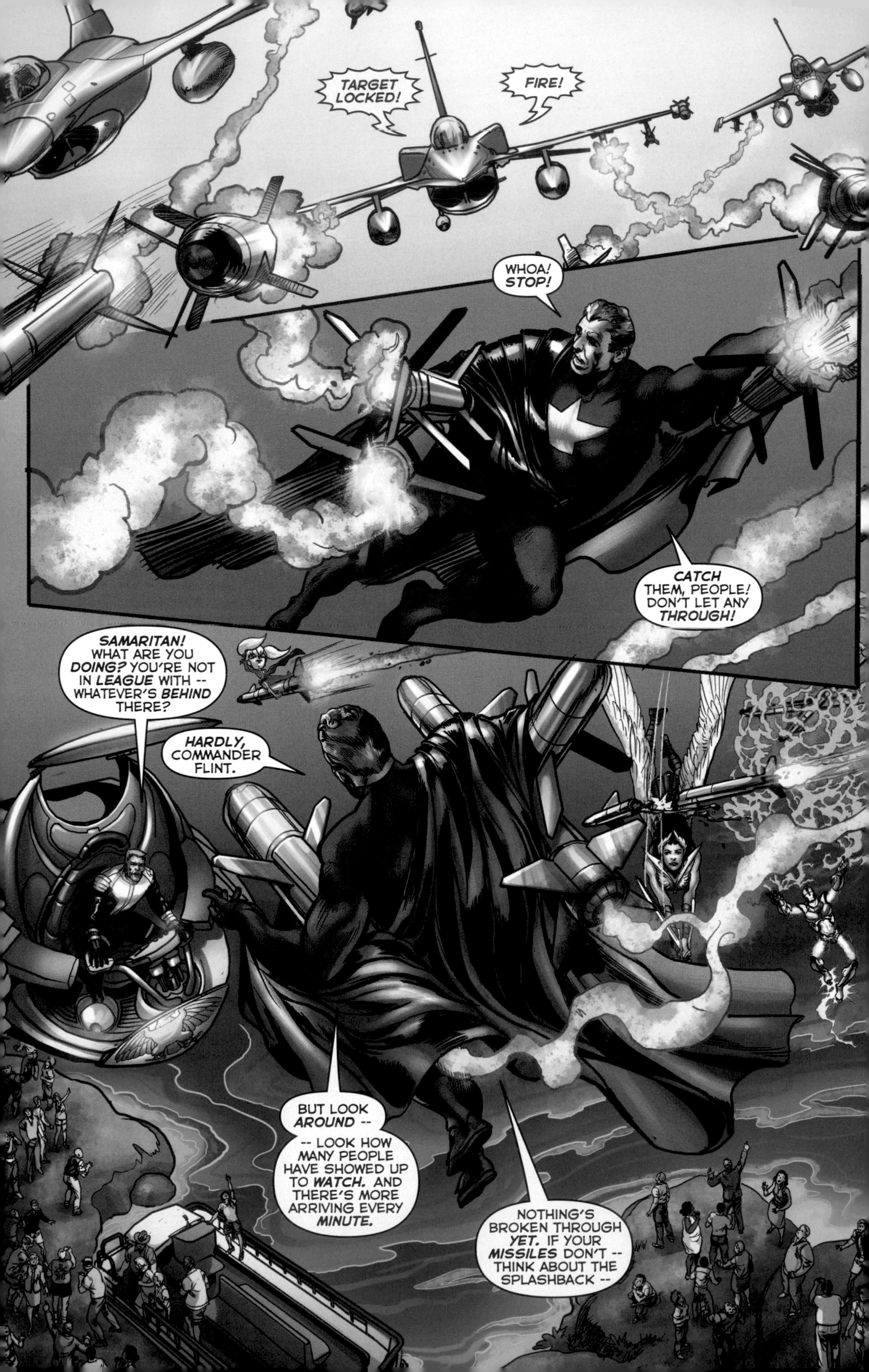
TARGET LOCKED!
FIRE!
WHOA! STOP!
CATCH THEM, PEOPLE! DON'T LET ANY THROUGH!
SAMARITAN! WHAT ARE YOU DOING? YOU'RE NOT IN LEAGUE WITH -- WHATEVER'S BEHIND THERE?
HARDLY, COMMANDER FLINT.
BUT LOOK AROUND --
-- LOOK HOW MANY PEOPLE HAVE SHOWED UP TO WATCH. AND THERE'S MORE ARRIVING EVERY MINUTE.
NOTHING'S BROKEN THROUGH YET. IF YOUR MISSILES DON'T -- THINK ABOUT THE SPLASHBACK --

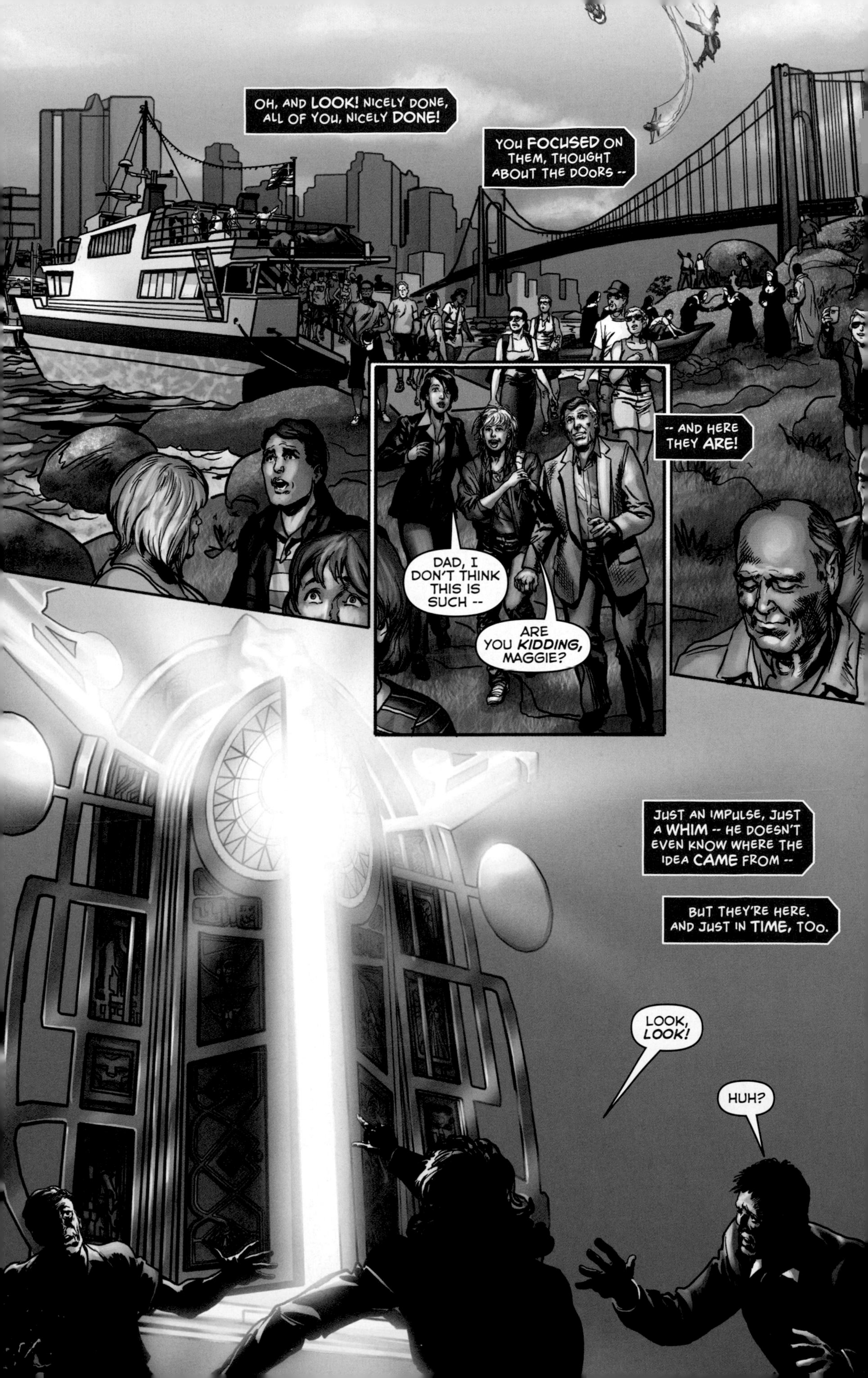
OH, AND LOOK! NICELY DONE, ALL OF YOU, NICELY DONE!
YOU FOCUSED ON THEM, THOUGHT ABOUT THE DOORS --
-- AND HERE THEY ARE!
DAD, I DON'T THINK THIS IS SUCH --
ARE YOU KIDDING, MAGGIE?
JUST AN IMPULSE, JUST A WHIM -- HE DOESN'T EVEN KNOW WHERE THE IDEA CAME FROM --
BUT THEY'RE HERE. AND JUST IN TIME, TOO.
LOOK, LOOK!
HUH?

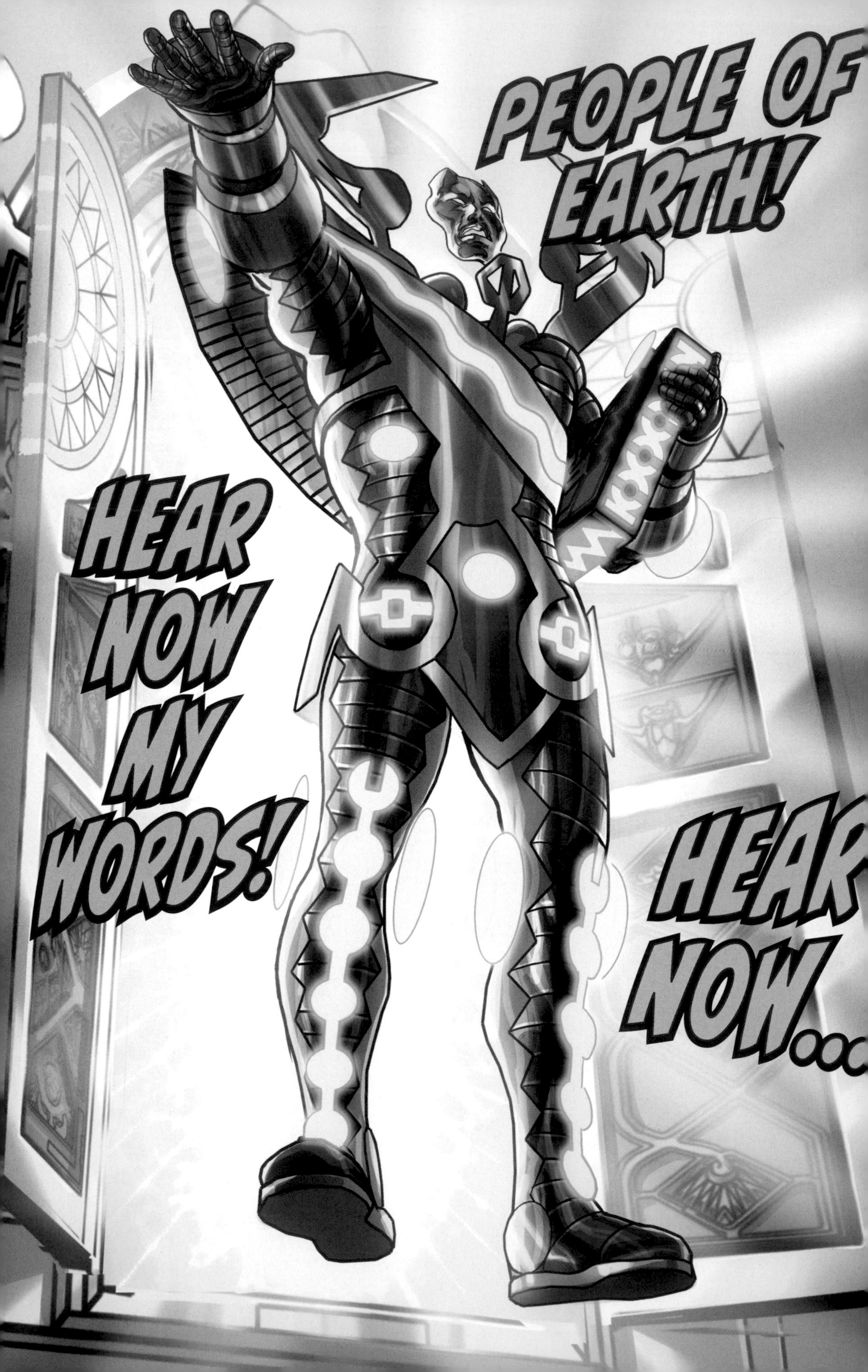
PEOPLE OF EARTH!
HEAR NOW MY WORDS!
HEAR NOW...

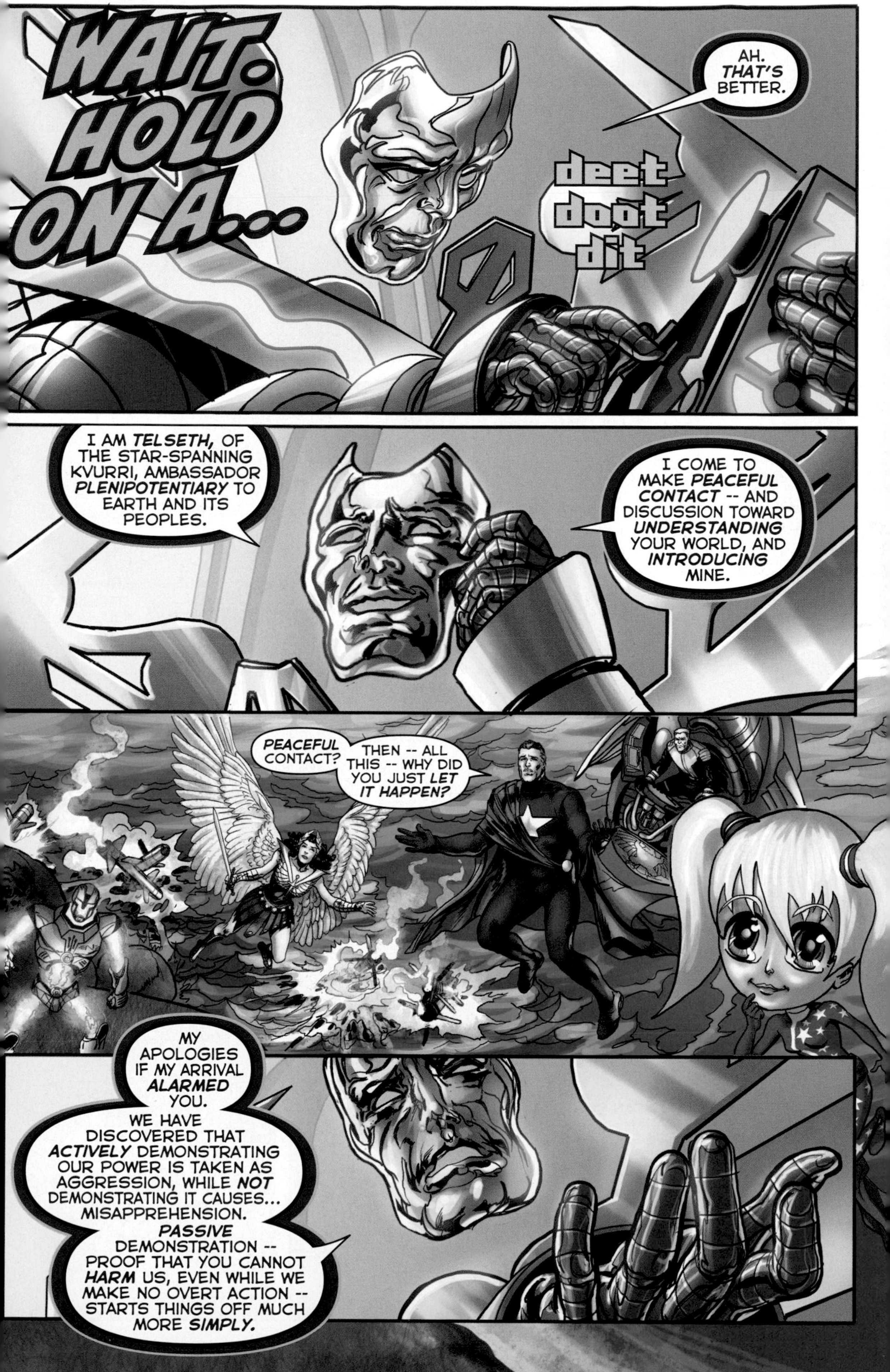
WAIT. HOLD ON A...
AH. THAT'S BETTER.
deet doot dit
I AM TELSETH, OF THE STAR-SPANNING KVURRI, AMBASSADOR PLENIPOTENTIARY TO EARTH AND ITS PEOPLES.
I COME TO MAKE PEACEFUL CONTACT -- AND DISCUSSION TOWARD UNDERSTANDING YOUR WORLD, AND INTRODUCING MINE.
PEACEFUL CONTACT?
THEN -- ALL THIS -- WHY DID YOU JUST LET IT HAPPEN?
MY APOLOGIES IF MY ARRIVAL ALARMED YOU.
WE HAVE DISCOVERED THAT ACTIVELY DEMONSTRATING OUR POWER IS TAKEN AS AGGRESSION, WHILE NOT DEMONSTRATING IT CAUSES... MISAPPREHENSION.
PASSIVE DEMONSTRATION -- PROOF THAT YOU CANNOT HARM US, EVEN WHILE WE MAKE NO OVERT ACTION -- STARTS THINGS OFF MUCH MORE SIMPLY.

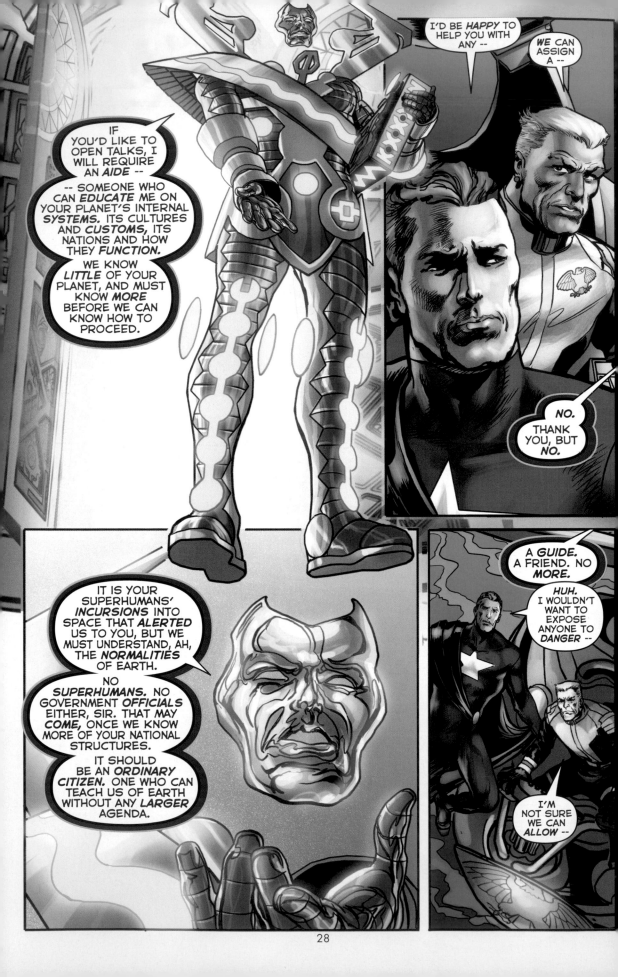

IF YOU'D LIKE TO OPEN TALKS, I WILL REQUIRE AN *AIDE* --

-- SOMEONE WHO CAN *EDUCATE* ME ON YOUR PLANET'S INTERNAL *SYSTEMS*. ITS CULTURES AND *CUSTOMS*, ITS NATIONS AND HOW THEY *FUNCTION*.

WE KNOW *LITTLE* OF YOUR PLANET, AND MUST KNOW *MORE* BEFORE WE CAN KNOW HOW TO PROCEED.

I'D BE *HAPPY* TO HELP YOU WITH ANY --

WE CAN ASSIGN A --

NO. THANK YOU, BUT *NO.*

IT IS YOUR SUPERHUMANS' *INCURSIONS* INTO SPACE THAT *ALERTED* US TO YOU, BUT WE MUST UNDERSTAND, AH, THE *NORMALITIES* OF EARTH.

NO *SUPERHUMANS.* NO GOVERNMENT *OFFICIALS* EITHER, SIR. THAT MAY *COME*, ONCE WE KNOW MORE OF YOUR NATIONAL STRUCTURES.

IT SHOULD BE AN *ORDINARY CITIZEN.* ONE WHO CAN TEACH US OF EARTH WITHOUT ANY *LARGER* AGENDA.

A *GUIDE.* A *FRIEND.* NO *MORE.*

HUH. I WOULDN'T WANT TO EXPOSE ANYONE TO *DANGER* --

I'M NOT SURE WE CAN *ALLOW* --

28

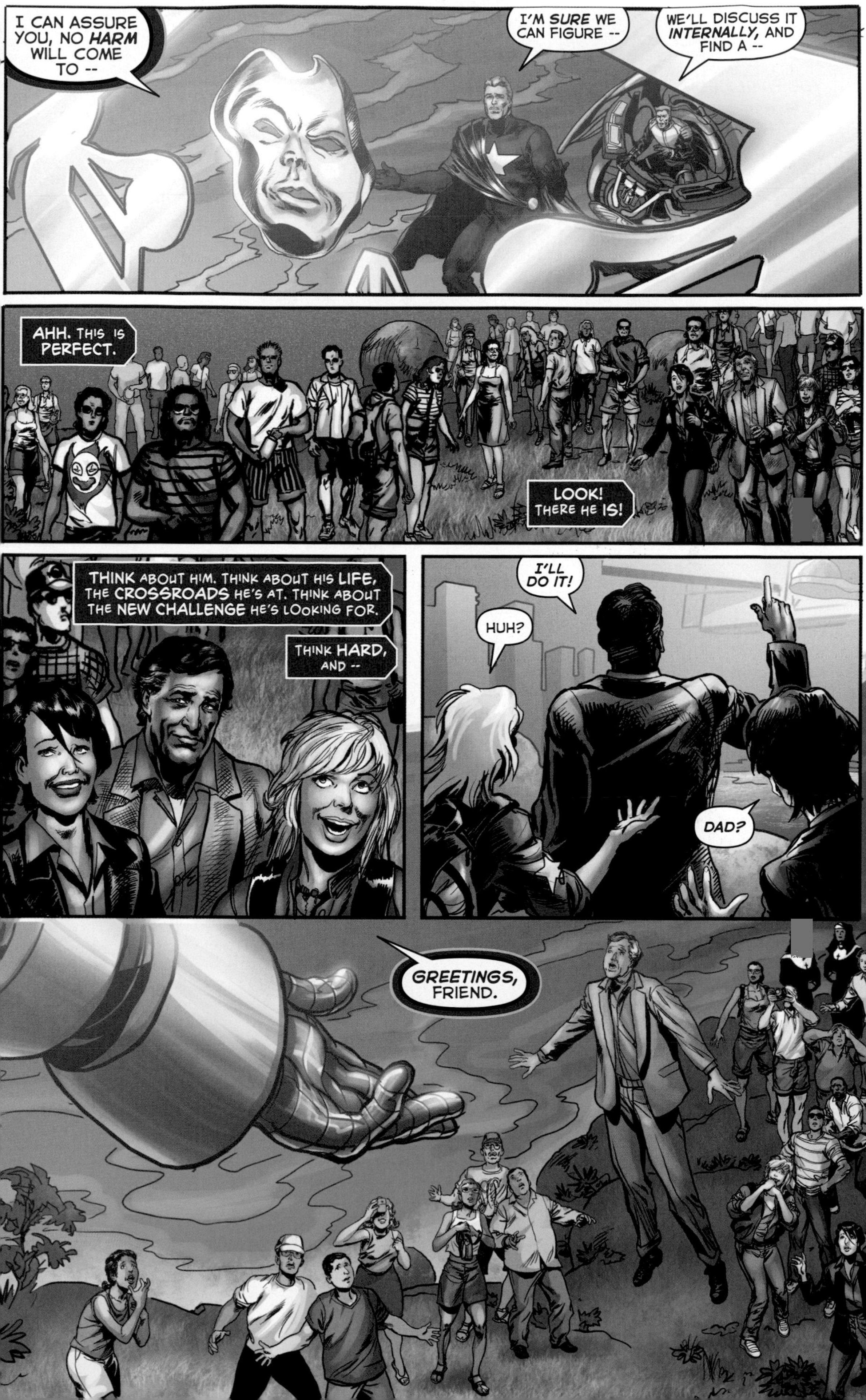
I CAN ASSURE YOU, NO HARM WILL COME TO --
I'M SURE WE CAN FIGURE --
WE'LL DISCUSS IT INTERNALLY, AND FIND A --
AHH. THIS IS PERFECT.
LOOK! THERE HE IS!
THINK ABOUT HIM. THINK ABOUT HIS LIFE, THE CROSSROADS HE'S AT. THINK ABOUT THE NEW CHALLENGE HE'S LOOKING FOR.
THINK HARD, AND --
I'LL DO IT!
HUH?
DAD?
GREETINGS, FRIEND.

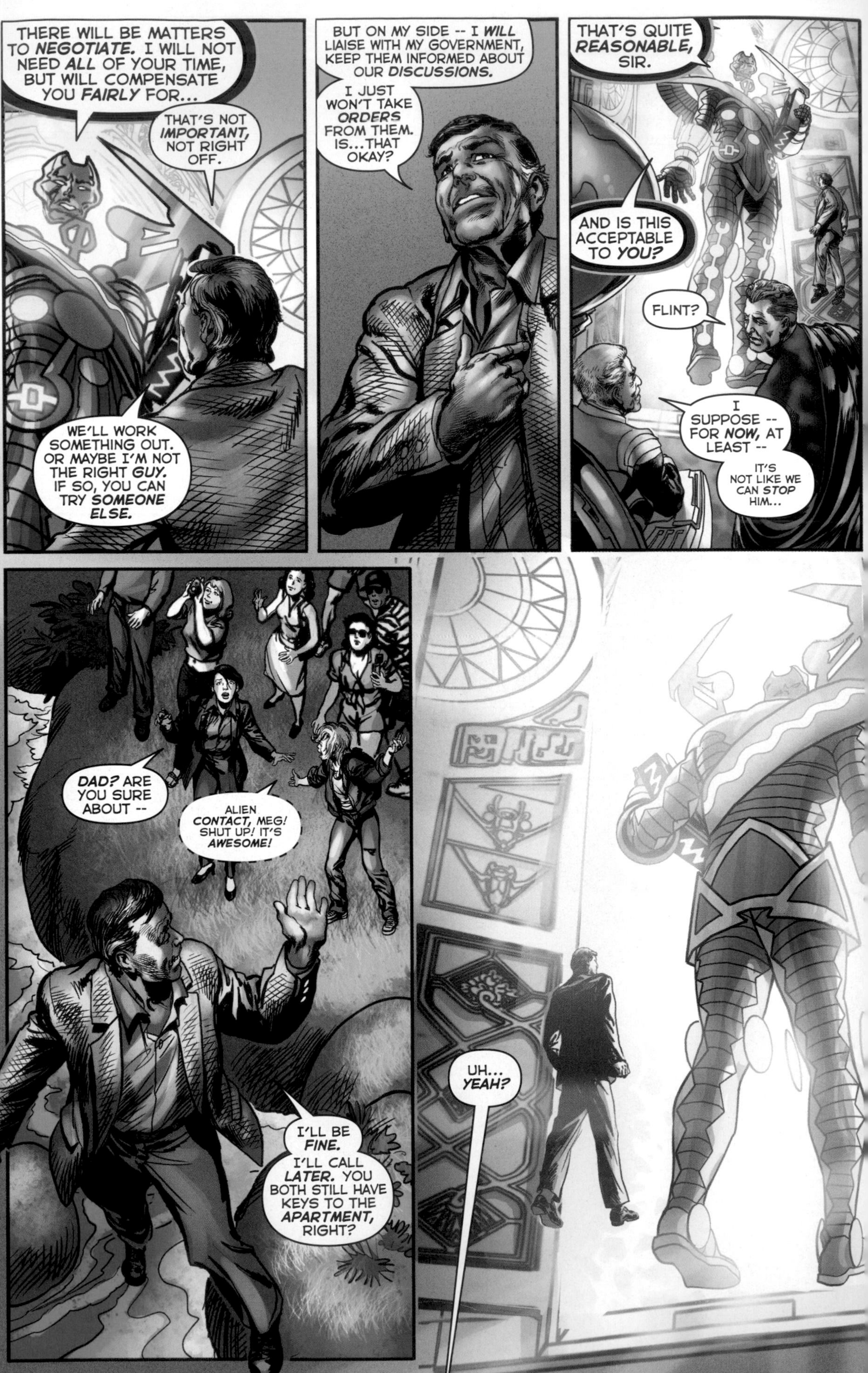
THERE WILL BE MATTERS TO NEGOTIATE. I WILL NOT NEED ALL OF YOUR TIME, BUT WILL COMPENSATE YOU FAIRLY FOR...
THAT'S NOT IMPORTANT, NOT RIGHT OFF.
WE'LL WORK SOMETHING OUT. OR MAYBE I'M NOT THE RIGHT GUY. IF SO, YOU CAN TRY SOMEONE ELSE.
BUT ON MY SIDE -- I WILL LIAISE WITH MY GOVERNMENT, KEEP THEM INFORMED ABOUT OUR DISCUSSIONS.
I JUST WON'T TAKE ORDERS FROM THEM. IS...THAT OKAY?
THAT'S QUITE REASONABLE, SIR.
AND IS THIS ACCEPTABLE TO YOU?
FLINT?
I SUPPOSE -- FOR NOW, AT LEAST --
IT'S NOT LIKE WE CAN STOP HIM...
DAD? ARE YOU SURE ABOUT --
ALIEN CONTACT, MEG! SHUT UP! IT'S AWESOME!
I'LL BE FINE.
I'LL CALL LATER. YOU BOTH STILL HAVE KEYS TO THE APARTMENT, RIGHT?
UH... YEAH?

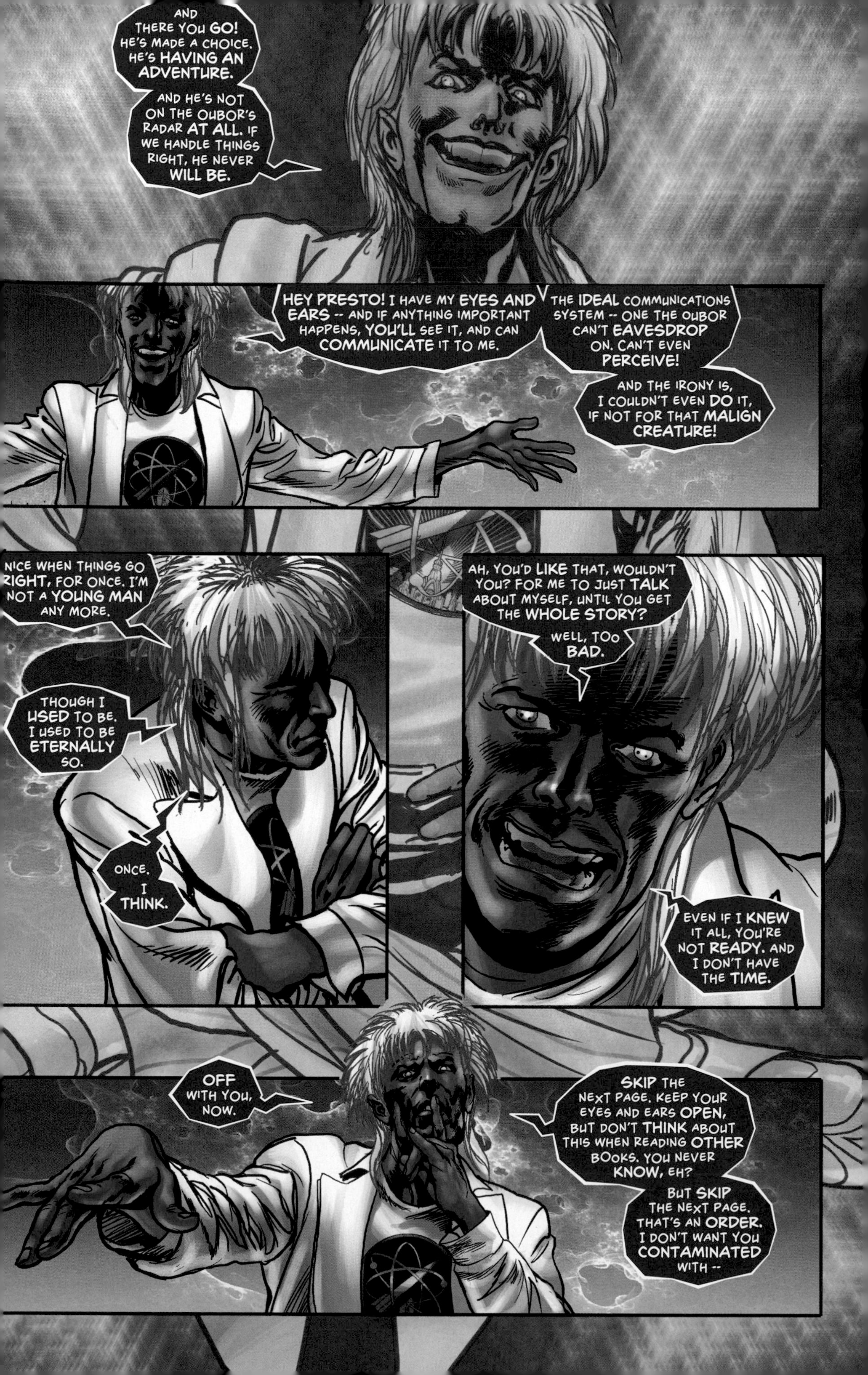

AND THERE YOU GO! HE'S MADE A CHOICE. HE'S HAVING AN ADVENTURE.
AND HE'S NOT ON THE OUBOR'S RADAR AT ALL. IF WE HANDLE THINGS RIGHT, HE NEVER WILL BE.
HEY PRESTO! I HAVE MY EYES AND EARS -- AND IF ANYTHING IMPORTANT HAPPENS, YOU'LL SEE IT, AND CAN COMMUNICATE IT TO ME.
THE IDEAL COMMUNICATIONS SYSTEM -- ONE THE OUBOR CAN'T EAVESDROP ON. CAN'T EVEN PERCEIVE!
AND THE IRONY IS, I COULDN'T EVEN DO IT, IF NOT FOR THAT MALIGN CREATURE!
NICE WHEN THINGS GO RIGHT, FOR ONCE. I'M NOT A YOUNG MAN ANY MORE.
THOUGH I USED TO BE. I USED TO BE ETERNALLY SO.
ONCE.
I THINK.
AH, YOU'D LIKE THAT, WOULDN'T YOU? FOR ME TO JUST TALK ABOUT MYSELF, UNTIL YOU GET THE WHOLE STORY?
WELL, TOO BAD.
EVEN IF I KNEW IT ALL, YOU'RE NOT READY. AND I DON'T HAVE THE TIME.
OFF WITH YOU, NOW.
SKIP THE NEXT PAGE. KEEP YOUR EYES AND EARS OPEN, BUT DON'T THINK ABOUT THIS WHEN READING OTHER BOOKS. YOU NEVER KNOW, EH?
BUT SKIP THE NEXT PAGE. THAT'S AN ORDER. I DON'T WANT YOU CONTAMINATED WITH --

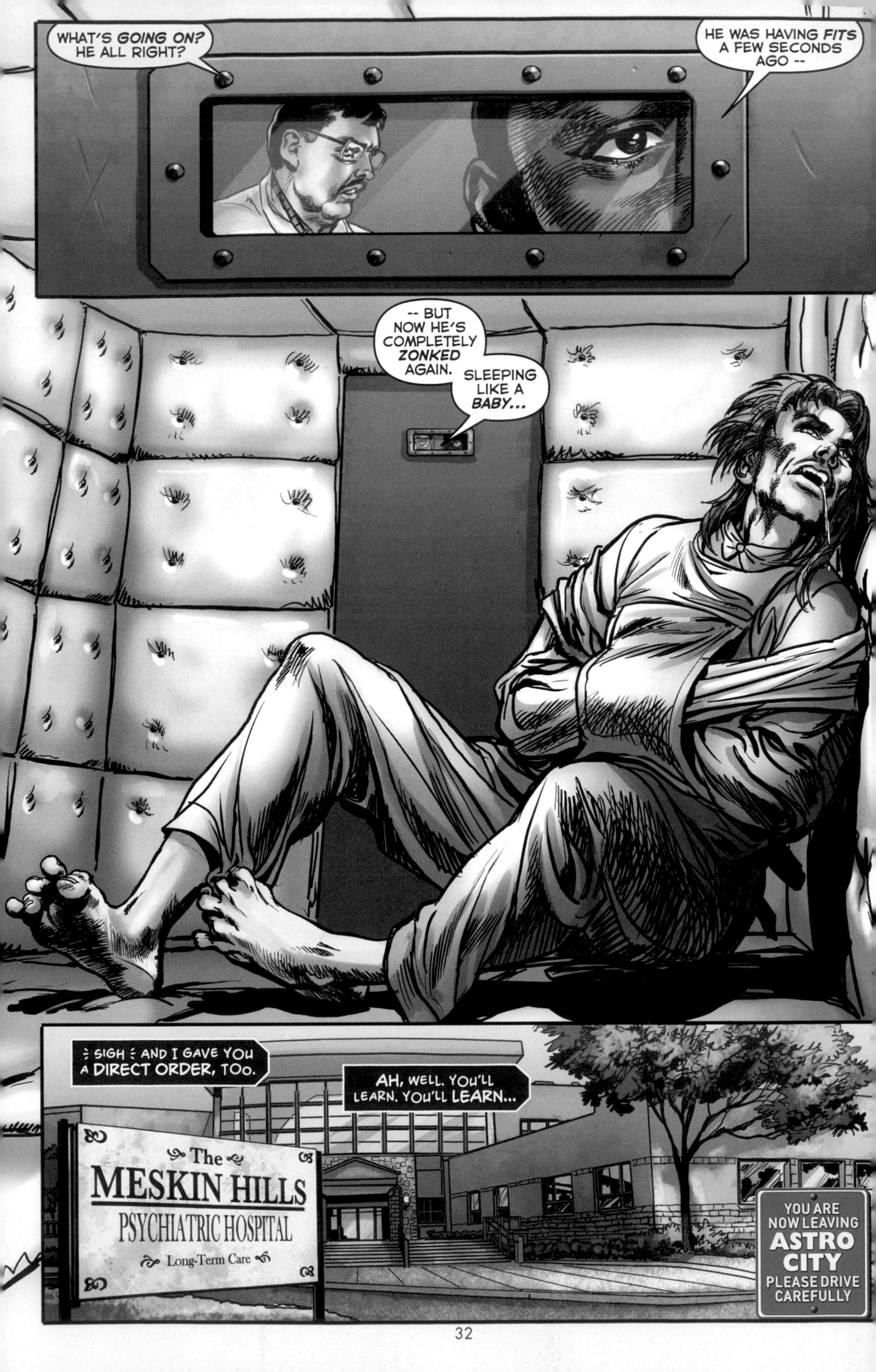
WHAT'S GOING ON? HE ALL RIGHT?
HE WAS HAVING FITS A FEW SECONDS AGO --
-- BUT NOW HE'S COMPLETELY ZONKED AGAIN.
SLEEPING LIKE A BABY...
⁝ SIGH ⁝ AND I GAVE YOU A DIRECT ORDER, TOO.
AH, WELL. YOU'LL LEARN. YOU'LL LEARN...
The MESKIN HILLS PSYCHIATRIC HOSPITAL
Long-Term Care
YOU ARE NOW LEAVING ASTRO CITY PLEASE DRIVE CAREFULLY

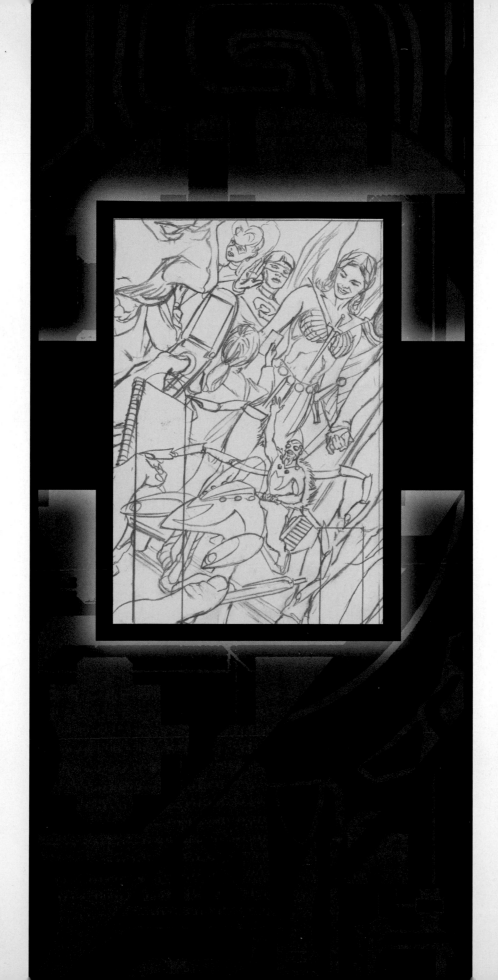

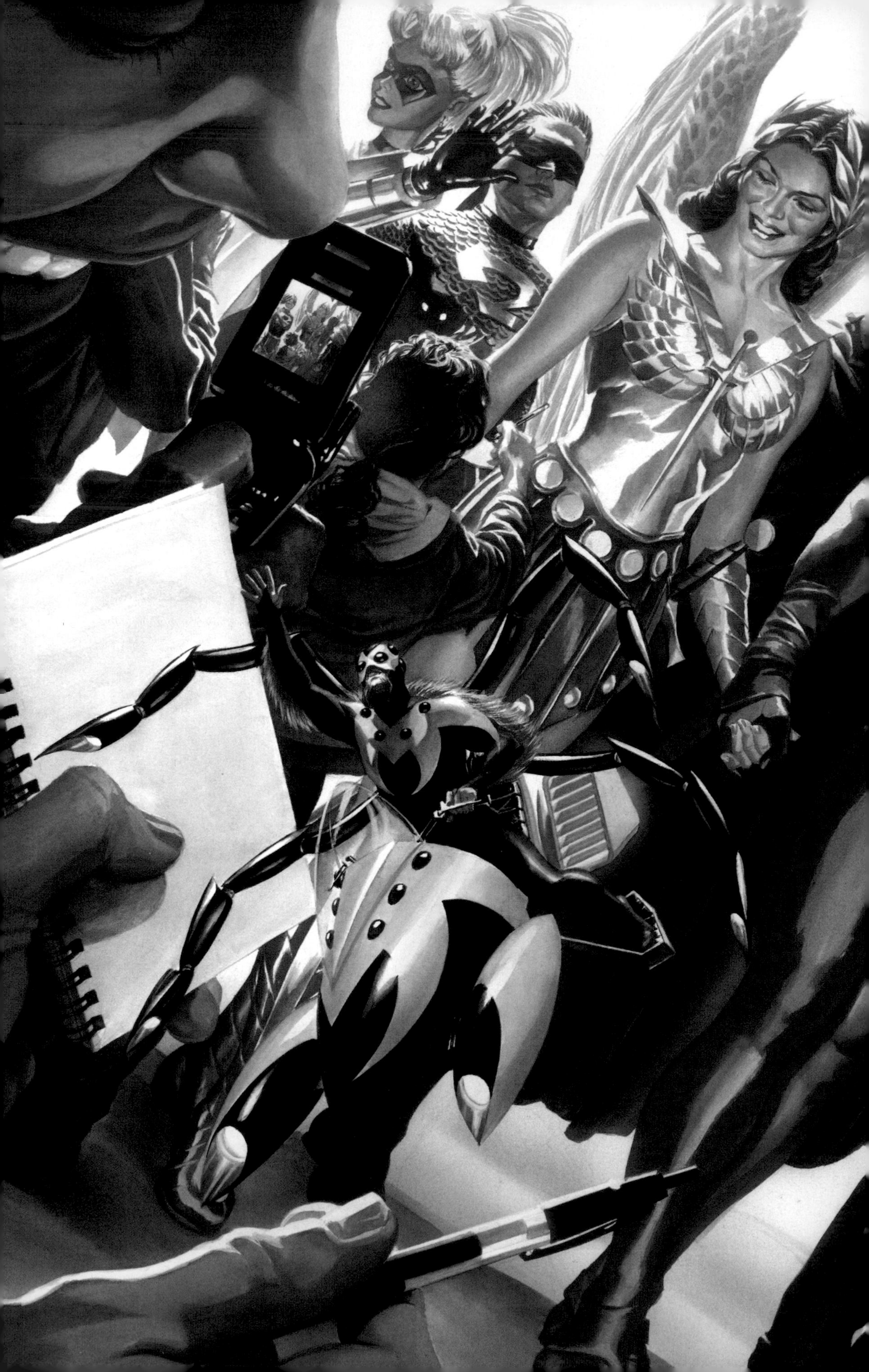

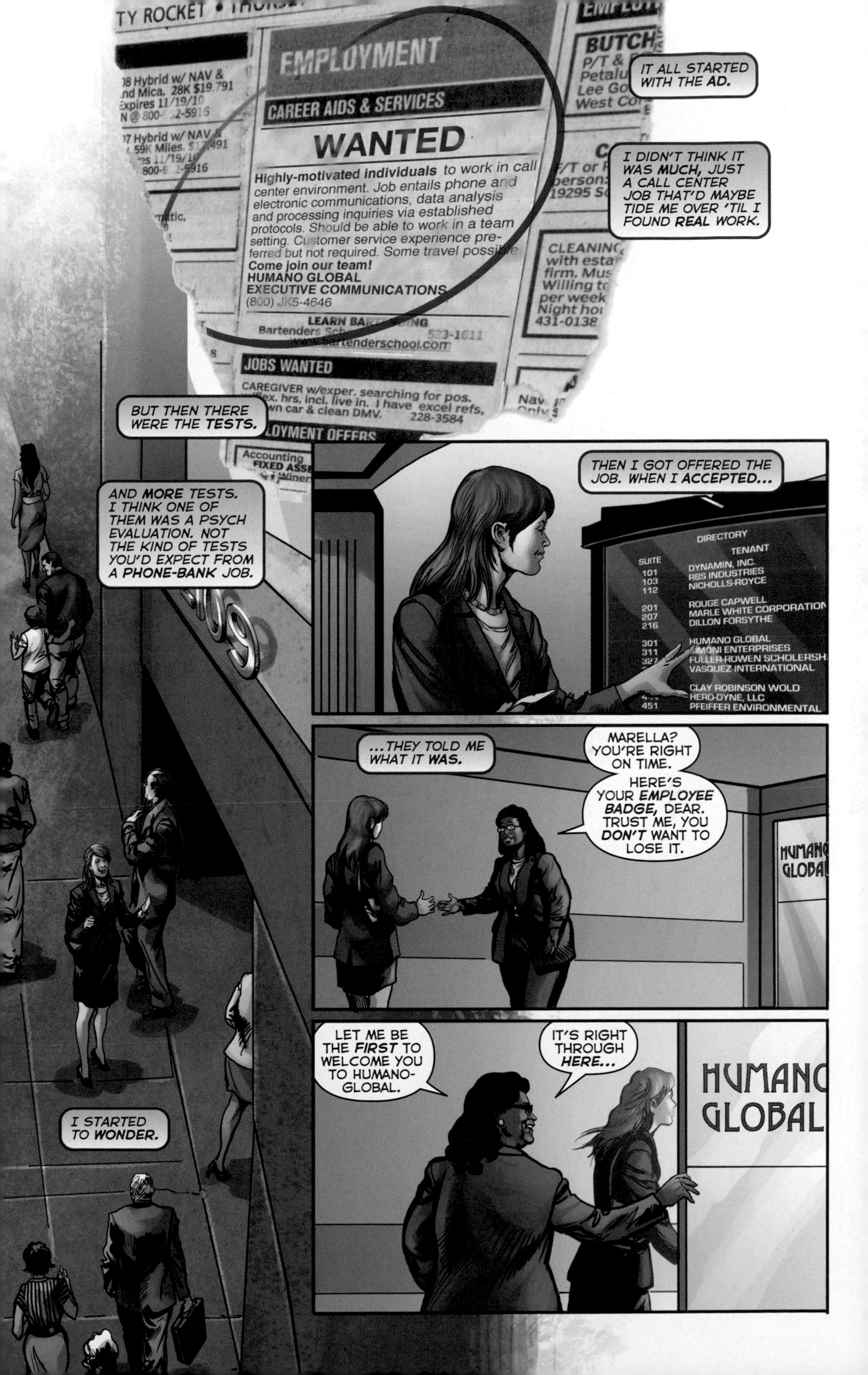
IT ALL STARTED WITH THE AD.
I DIDN'T THINK IT WAS MUCH, JUST A CALL CENTER JOB THAT'D MAYBE TIDE ME OVER 'TIL I FOUND REAL WORK.
EMPLOYMENT
CAREER AIDS & SERVICES
WANTED
Highly-motivated individuals to work in call center environment. Job entails phone and electronic communications, data analysis and processing inquiries via established protocols. Should be able to work in a team setting. Customer service experience preferred but not required. Some travel possible.
Come join our team!
HUMANO GLOBAL
EXECUTIVE COMMUNICATIONS
(800) JK5-4646
JOBS WANTED
BUT THEN THERE WERE THE TESTS.
AND MORE TESTS. I THINK ONE OF THEM WAS A PSYCH EVALUATION. NOT THE KIND OF TESTS YOU'D EXPECT FROM A PHONE-BANK JOB.
I STARTED TO WONDER.
THEN I GOT OFFERED THE JOB. WHEN I ACCEPTED...
DIRECTORY
SUITE TENANT
101 DYNAMIN, INC.
103 RBS INDUSTRIES
112 NICHOLLS-ROYCE
201 ROUGE CAPWELL
207 MARLE WHITE CORPORATION
216 DILLON FORSYTHE
301 HUMANO GLOBAL
311 SIMONI ENTERPRISES
FULLER-ROWEN SCHOLERSHIP
VASQUEZ INTERNATIONAL
CLAY ROBINSON WOLD
HERO-DYNE, LLC
451 PFEIFFER ENVIRONMENTAL
...THEY TOLD ME WHAT IT WAS.
MARELLA? YOU'RE RIGHT ON TIME.
HERE'S YOUR EMPLOYEE BADGE, DEAR. TRUST ME, YOU DON'T WANT TO LOSE IT.
HUMANO GLOBAL
LET ME BE THE FIRST TO WELCOME YOU TO HUMANO-GLOBAL.
IT'S RIGHT THROUGH HERE...
HUMANO GLOBAL

WH -- ?
THE TRAINING HADN'T MENTIONED THIS.
Welcome to
HUMANOGLOBAL

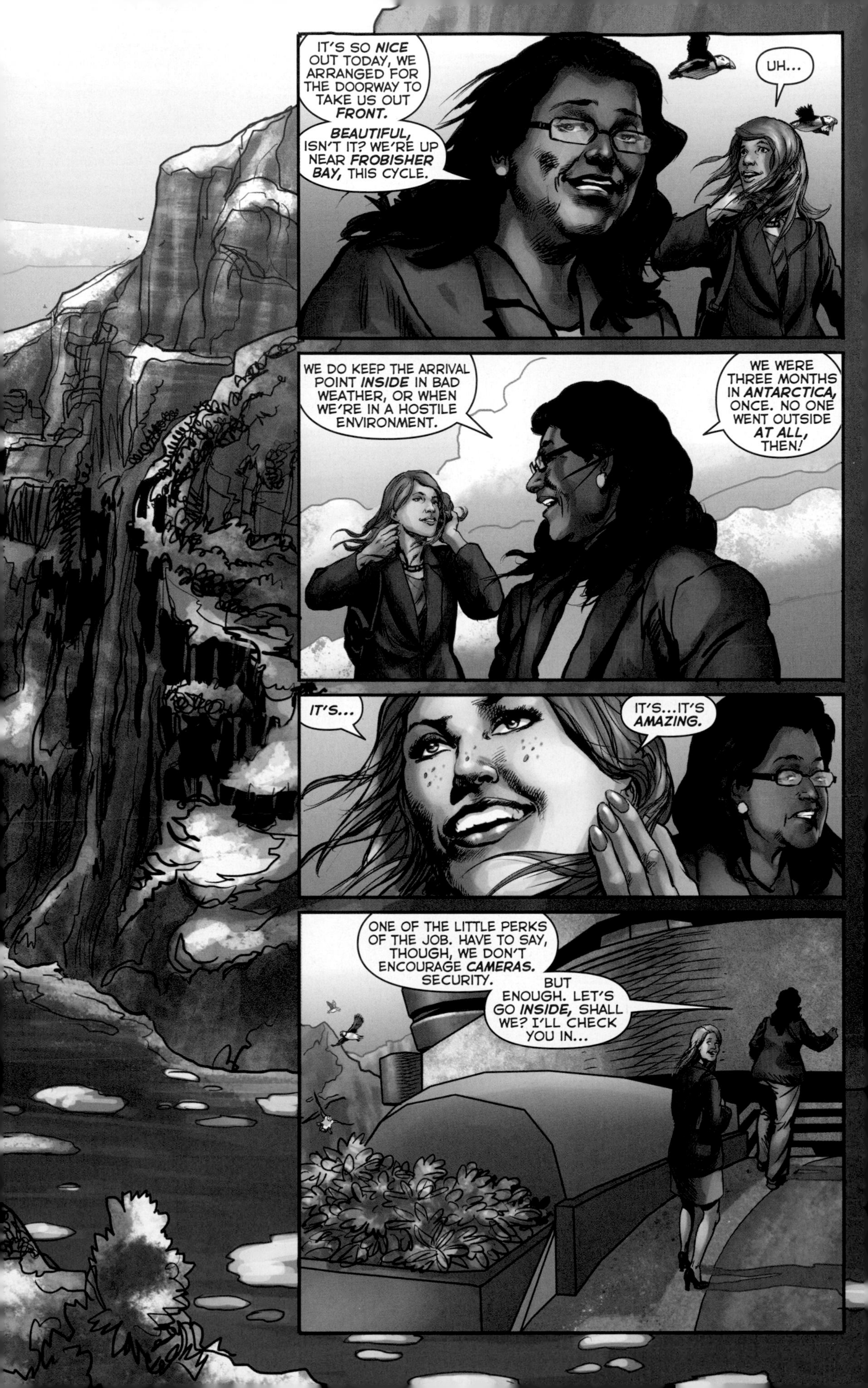
IT'S SO NICE OUT TODAY, WE ARRANGED FOR THE DOORWAY TO TAKE US OUT FRONT.
BEAUTIFUL, ISN'T IT? WE'RE UP NEAR FROBISHER BAY, THIS CYCLE.
UH...
WE DO KEEP THE ARRIVAL POINT INSIDE IN BAD WEATHER, OR WHEN WE'RE IN A HOSTILE ENVIRONMENT.
WE WERE THREE MONTHS IN ANTARCTICA, ONCE. NO ONE WENT OUTSIDE AT ALL, THEN!
IT'S...
IT'S...IT'S AMAZING.
ONE OF THE LITTLE PERKS OF THE JOB. HAVE TO SAY, THOUGH, WE DON'T ENCOURAGE CAMERAS. SECURITY.
BUT ENOUGH. LET'S GO INSIDE, SHALL WE? I'LL CHECK YOU IN...

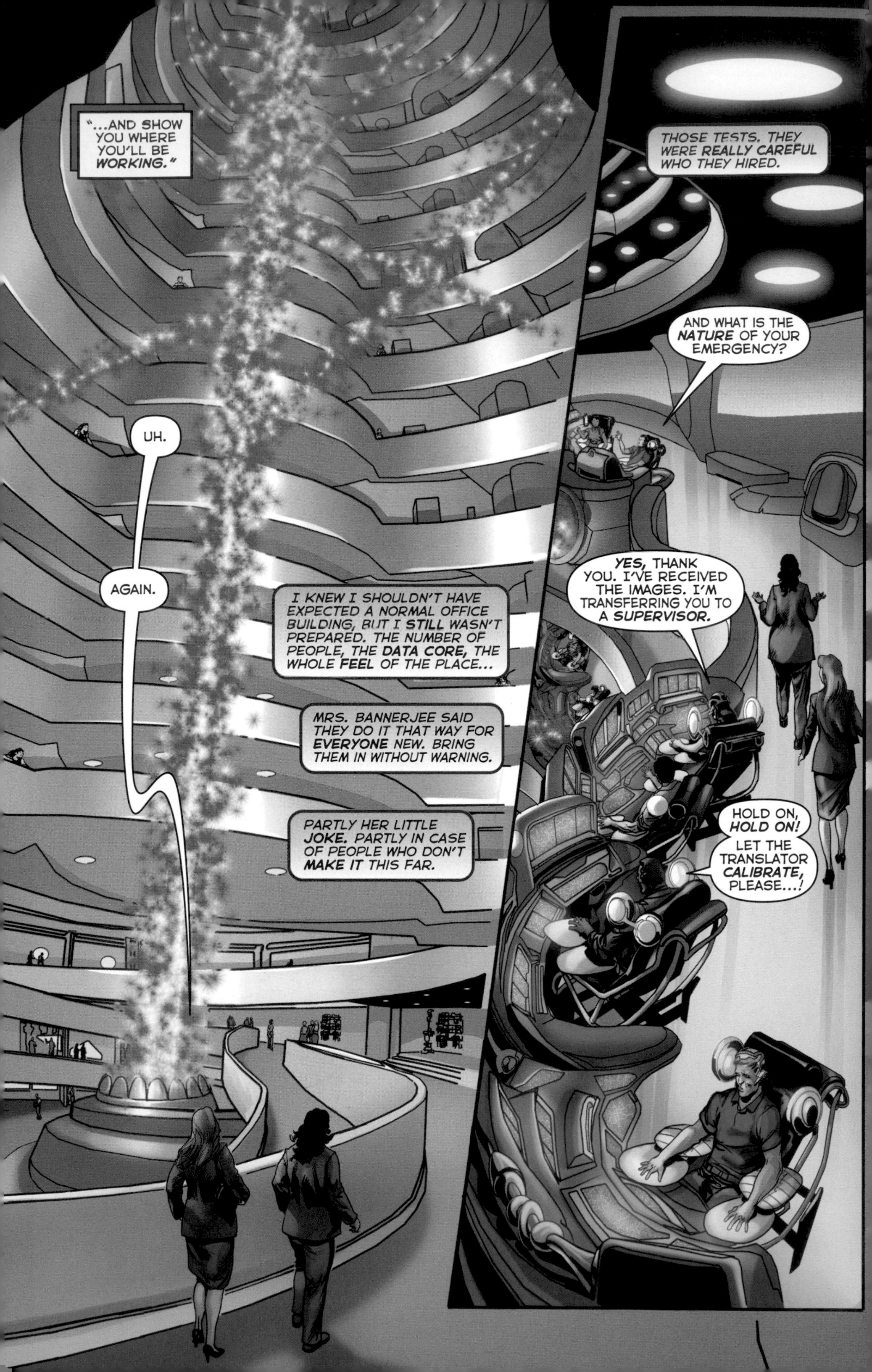
"...AND SHOW YOU WHERE YOU'LL BE WORKING."
UH.
AGAIN.
I KNEW I SHOULDN'T HAVE EXPECTED A NORMAL OFFICE BUILDING, BUT I STILL WASN'T PREPARED. THE NUMBER OF PEOPLE, THE DATA CORE, THE WHOLE FEEL OF THE PLACE...
MRS. BANNERJEE SAID THEY DO IT THAT WAY FOR EVERYONE NEW. BRING THEM IN WITHOUT WARNING.
PARTLY HER LITTLE JOKE. PARTLY IN CASE OF PEOPLE WHO DON'T MAKE IT THIS FAR.
THOSE TESTS. THEY WERE REALLY CAREFUL WHO THEY HIRED.
AND WHAT IS THE NATURE OF YOUR EMERGENCY?
YES, THANK YOU. I'VE RECEIVED THE IMAGES. I'M TRANSFERRING YOU TO A SUPERVISOR.
HOLD ON, HOLD ON! LET THE TRANSLATOR CALIBRATE, PLEASE...!

AND THIS'LL BE YOUR *STATION.*

THE CHAIR SHOULD AUTOMATICALLY *ADJUST* TO YOUR WEIGHT AND POSTURE. LET ME KNOW IF IT *DOESN'T* -- YOU'LL BE IN IT A LOT, AND WE WANT YOU COMFORTABLE.

AND YOU'LL BE SPENDING A LOT OF TIME WITH YOUR *CO-WORKERS*, AS WELL...

AH, NEW *FISH.* I'M JEREMY BAINES.

MICHIKO OHARA.

HEY. *TONI UMTATA.*

NICE -- NICE TO MEET YOU ALL. I'M MARELLA COWPER.

YOU'RE *ALL RIGHT?* READY TO GO?

I... *THINK* SO.

GOOD. BECAUSE YOU ALREADY HAVE YOUR *FIRST CALL.*

OH!

CODE AMBER
Location : Austin, TX
Local time: 09:45
Call Init: 00:11

YOU'RE *CONNECTED.*
AND WHAT IS THE *NATURE* OF YOUR EMERGENCY?

I REALLY, REALLY DIDN'T WANT TO MESS UP. NOT *JUST* BECAUSE IT WAS A NEW JOB...

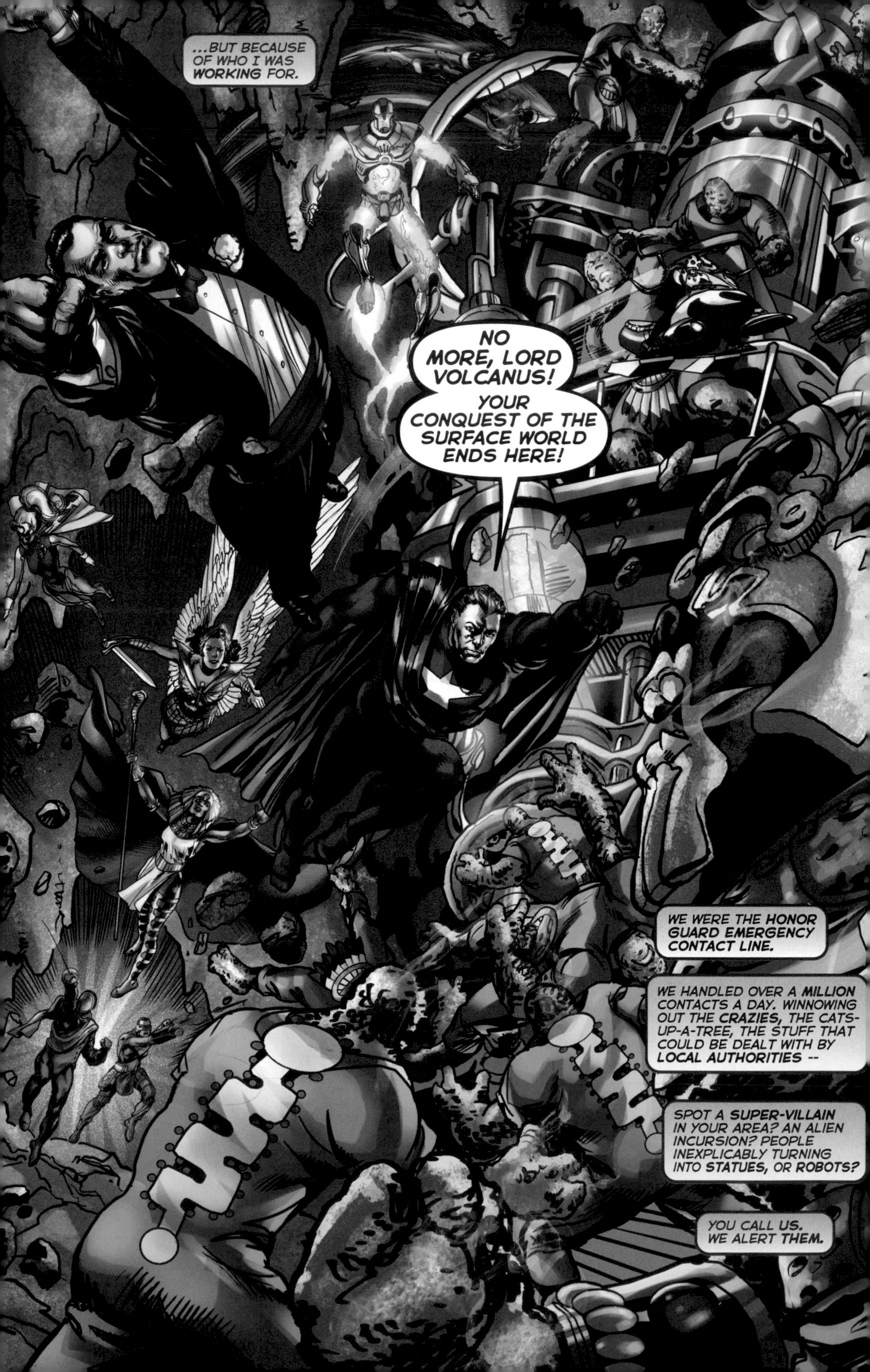
...BUT BECAUSE OF WHO I WAS WORKING FOR.
NO MORE, LORD VOLCANUS! YOUR CONQUEST OF THE SURFACE WORLD ENDS HERE!
WE WERE THE HONOR GUARD EMERGENCY CONTACT LINE.
WE HANDLED OVER A MILLION CONTACTS A DAY. WINNOWING OUT THE CRAZIES, THE CATS-UP-A-TREE, THE STUFF THAT COULD BE DEALT WITH BY LOCAL AUTHORITIES --
SPOT A SUPER-VILLAIN IN YOUR AREA? AN ALIEN INCURSION? PEOPLE INEXPLICABLY TURNING INTO STATUES, OR ROBOTS?
YOU CALL US. WE ALERT THEM.

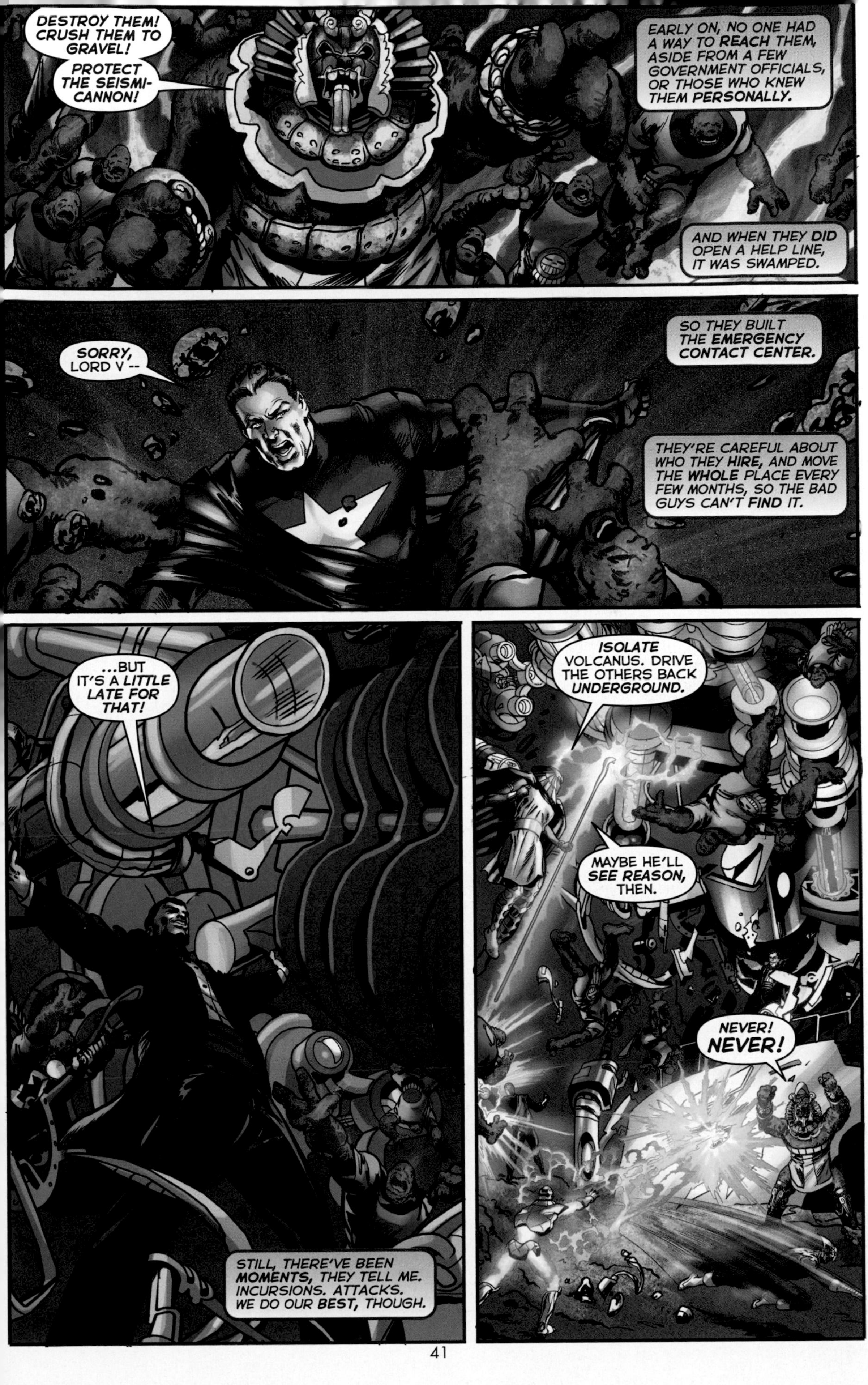
DESTROY THEM! CRUSH THEM TO GRAVEL!
PROTECT THE SEISMI-CANNON!
EARLY ON, NO ONE HAD A WAY TO REACH THEM, ASIDE FROM A FEW GOVERNMENT OFFICIALS, OR THOSE WHO KNEW THEM PERSONALLY.
AND WHEN THEY DID OPEN A HELP LINE, IT WAS SWAMPED.
SO THEY BUILT THE EMERGENCY CONTACT CENTER.
SORRY, LORD V --
THEY'RE CAREFUL ABOUT WHO THEY HIRE, AND MOVE THE WHOLE PLACE EVERY FEW MONTHS, SO THE BAD GUYS CAN'T FIND IT.
...BUT IT'S A LITTLE LATE FOR THAT!
STILL, THERE'VE BEEN MOMENTS, THEY TELL ME. INCURSIONS. ATTACKS. WE DO OUR BEST, THOUGH.
ISOLATE VOLCANUS. DRIVE THE OTHERS BACK UNDERGROUND.
MAYBE HE'LL SEE REASON, THEN.
NEVER! NEVER!

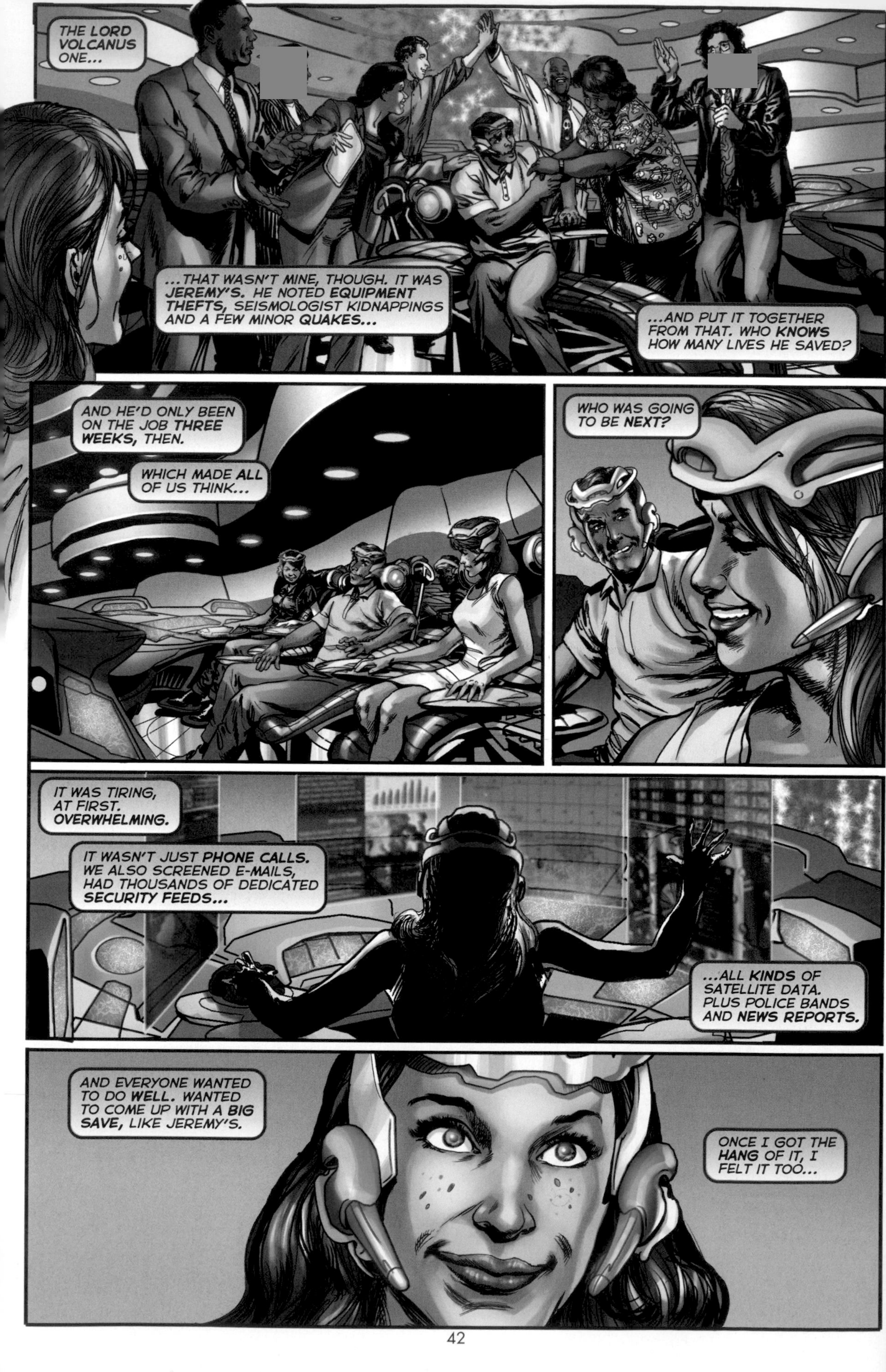

THE LORD VOLCANUS ONE...
...THAT WASN'T MINE, THOUGH. IT WAS JEREMY'S. HE NOTED EQUIPMENT THEFTS, SEISMOLOGIST KIDNAPPINGS AND A FEW MINOR QUAKES...
...AND PUT IT TOGETHER FROM THAT. WHO KNOWS HOW MANY LIVES HE SAVED?
AND HE'D ONLY BEEN ON THE JOB THREE WEEKS, THEN.
WHICH MADE ALL OF US THINK...
WHO WAS GOING TO BE NEXT?
IT WAS TIRING, AT FIRST. OVERWHELMING.
IT WASN'T JUST PHONE CALLS. WE ALSO SCREENED E-MAILS, HAD THOUSANDS OF DEDICATED SECURITY FEEDS...
...ALL KINDS OF SATELLITE DATA. PLUS POLICE BANDS AND NEWS REPORTS.
AND EVERYONE WANTED TO DO WELL. WANTED TO COME UP WITH A BIG SAVE, LIKE JEREMY'S.
ONCE I GOT THE HANG OF IT, I FELT IT TOO...

SO. YOU DON'T TALK ABOUT THE NEW *JOB* MUCH.

SELLING NEWSPAPER SUBSCRIPTIONS REALLY *THAT* BAD? LOTTA YELLING AND *HANG-UPS?*

JESS!

IT'S *OKAY,* MOM.

IT'S NOT THAT KIND OF *CALL CENTER,* JESSIE. IT'S LIKE -- AN *INFORMATION LINE,* REALLY. PEOPLE CALL IN, WITH PROBLEMS --

WE WEREN'T SUPPOSED TO TELL PEOPLE MUCH ABOUT THE JOB. NOT EVEN OUR *FAMILIES,* EARLY ON.

WE DIDN'T HAVE TO *LIE,* NOT IF WE DIDN'T WANT TO. WE WERE JUST...ENCOURAGED TO KEEP IT *VAGUE.*

-- WE *HELP* 'EM IF WE CAN, TRANSFER 'EM TO SOMEONE ELSE IF WE *CAN'T.* PLUS A LOT OF *DATA GATHERING,* AND LIKE THAT.

THERE'D BEEN AN ATTACK, ONCE, WHEN *PYRAMID* FIGURED OUT WHERE THE CENTER WAS. AND OPERATORS -- PEOPLE LIKE ME -- *DIED.*

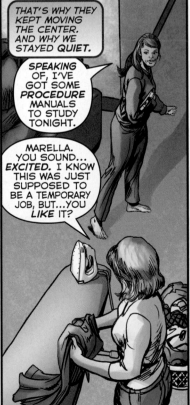

THAT'S WHY THEY KEPT MOVING THE CENTER. AND WHY WE STAYED *QUIET.*

SPEAKING OF, I'VE GOT SOME *PROCEDURE* MANUALS TO STUDY TONIGHT.

MARELLA. YOU SOUND... *EXCITED.* I KNOW THIS WAS JUST SUPPOSED TO BE A TEMPORARY JOB, BUT...YOU *LIKE* IT?

WE *HELP* PEOPLE. THE ORGANIZATION...THEY *CARE,* AND WHAT I DO MATTERS. I REALLY WANT TO BE *GOOD* AT IT, I DON'T WANT TO *MESS UP.*

BUT *YEAH,* MOM... I LIKE IT.

43

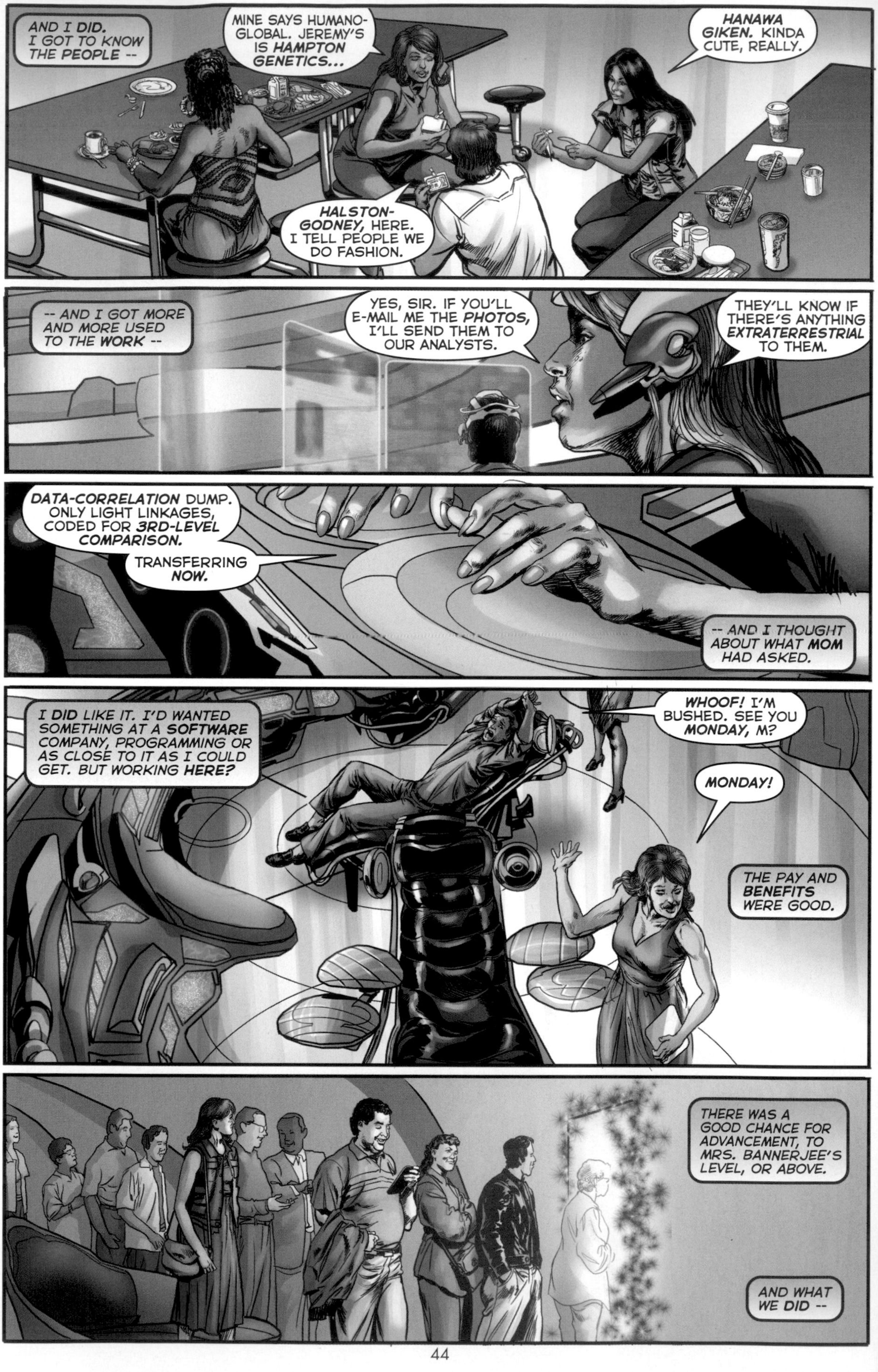
AND I DID. I GOT TO KNOW THE PEOPLE --
MINE SAYS HUMANO-GLOBAL. JEREMY'S IS HAMPTON GENETICS...
HANAWA GIKEN. KINDA CUTE, REALLY.
HALSTON-GODNEY, HERE. I TELL PEOPLE WE DO FASHION.
-- AND I GOT MORE AND MORE USED TO THE WORK --
YES, SIR. IF YOU'LL E-MAIL ME THE PHOTOS, I'LL SEND THEM TO OUR ANALYSTS.
THEY'LL KNOW IF THERE'S ANYTHING EXTRATERRESTRIAL TO THEM.
DATA-CORRELATION DUMP. ONLY LIGHT LINKAGES, CODED FOR 3RD-LEVEL COMPARISON.
TRANSFERRING NOW.
-- AND I THOUGHT ABOUT WHAT MOM HAD ASKED.
I DID LIKE IT. I'D WANTED SOMETHING AT A SOFTWARE COMPANY, PROGRAMMING OR AS CLOSE TO IT AS I COULD GET. BUT WORKING HERE?
WHOOF! I'M BUSHED. SEE YOU MONDAY, M?
MONDAY!
THE PAY AND BENEFITS WERE GOOD.
THERE WAS A GOOD CHANCE FOR ADVANCEMENT, TO MRS. BANNERJEE'S LEVEL, OR ABOVE.
AND WHAT WE DID --

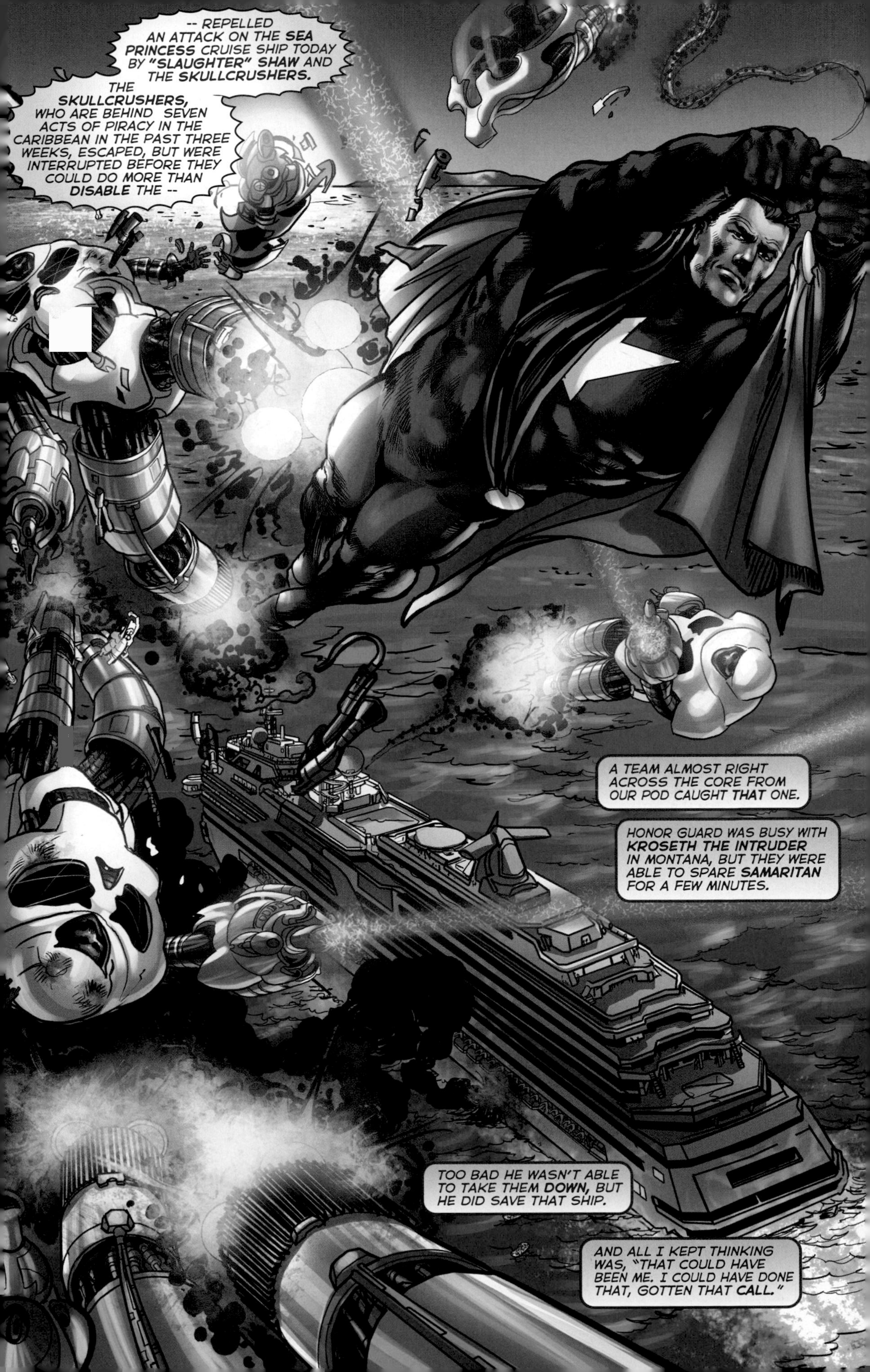
-- REPELLED AN ATTACK ON THE SEA PRINCESS CRUISE SHIP TODAY BY "SLAUGHTER" SHAW AND THE SKULLCRUSHERS.
THE SKULLCRUSHERS, WHO ARE BEHIND SEVEN ACTS OF PIRACY IN THE CARIBBEAN IN THE PAST THREE WEEKS, ESCAPED, BUT WERE INTERRUPTED BEFORE THEY COULD DO MORE THAN DISABLE THE --
A TEAM ALMOST RIGHT ACROSS THE CORE FROM OUR POD CAUGHT THAT ONE.
HONOR GUARD WAS BUSY WITH KROSETH THE INTRUDER IN MONTANA, BUT THEY WERE ABLE TO SPARE SAMARITAN FOR A FEW MINUTES.
TOO BAD HE WASN'T ABLE TO TAKE THEM DOWN, BUT HE DID SAVE THAT SHIP.
AND ALL I KEPT THINKING WAS, "THAT COULD HAVE BEEN ME. I COULD HAVE DONE THAT, GOTTEN THAT CALL."

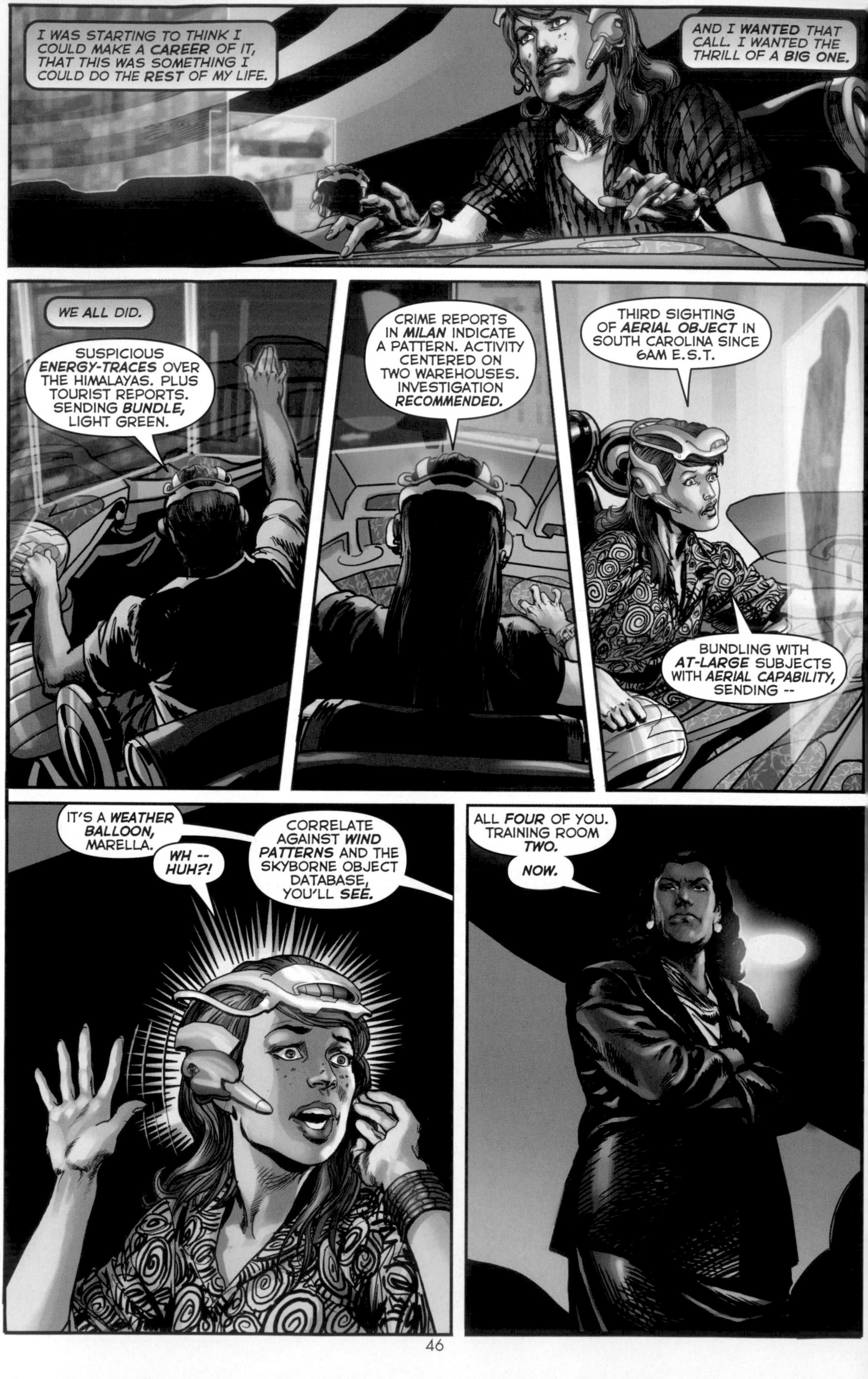
I WAS STARTING TO THINK I COULD MAKE A CAREER OF IT, THAT THIS WAS SOMETHING I COULD DO THE REST OF MY LIFE.
AND I WANTED THAT CALL. I WANTED THE THRILL OF A BIG ONE.
WE ALL DID.
SUSPICIOUS ENERGY-TRACES OVER THE HIMALAYAS. PLUS TOURIST REPORTS. SENDING BUNDLE, LIGHT GREEN.
CRIME REPORTS IN MILAN INDICATE A PATTERN. ACTIVITY CENTERED ON TWO WAREHOUSES. INVESTIGATION RECOMMENDED.
THIRD SIGHTING OF AERIAL OBJECT IN SOUTH CAROLINA SINCE 6AM E.S.T.
BUNDLING WITH AT-LARGE SUBJECTS WITH AERIAL CAPABILITY, SENDING --
IT'S A WEATHER BALLOON, MARELLA.
WH -- HUH?!
CORRELATE AGAINST WIND PATTERNS AND THE SKYBORNE OBJECT DATABASE, YOU'LL SEE.
ALL FOUR OF YOU. TRAINING ROOM TWO.
NOW.

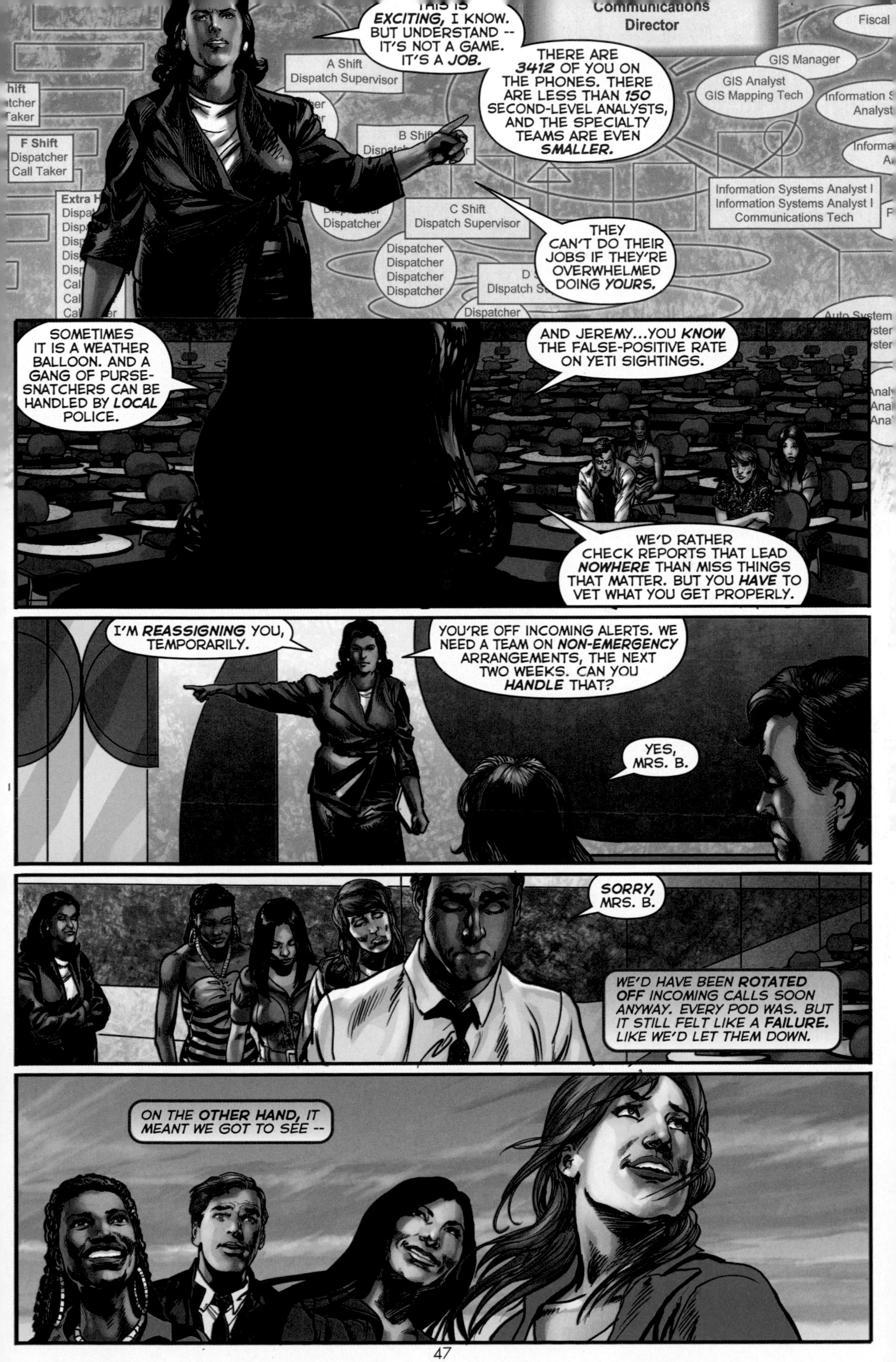
Communications Director
Fiscal
A Shift Dispatch Supervisor
GIS Manager
GIS Analyst GIS Mapping Tech
F Shift Dispatcher Call Taker
C Shift Dispatch Supervisor
Information Systems Analyst I Information Systems Analyst I Communications Tech
Dispatcher Dispatcher Dispatcher Dispatcher
EXCITING, I KNOW. BUT UNDERSTAND -- IT'S NOT A GAME. IT'S A JOB.
THERE ARE 3412 OF YOU ON THE PHONES. THERE ARE LESS THAN 150 SECOND-LEVEL ANALYSTS, AND THE SPECIALTY TEAMS ARE EVEN SMALLER.
THEY CAN'T DO THEIR JOBS IF THEY'RE OVERWHELMED DOING YOURS.
SOMETIMES IT IS A WEATHER BALLOON. AND A GANG OF PURSE-SNATCHERS CAN BE HANDLED BY LOCAL POLICE.
AND JEREMY...YOU KNOW THE FALSE-POSITIVE RATE ON YETI SIGHTINGS.
WE'D RATHER CHECK REPORTS THAT LEAD NOWHERE THAN MISS THINGS THAT MATTER. BUT YOU HAVE TO VET WHAT YOU GET PROPERLY.
I'M REASSIGNING YOU, TEMPORARILY.
YOU'RE OFF INCOMING ALERTS. WE NEED A TEAM ON NON-EMERGENCY ARRANGEMENTS, THE NEXT TWO WEEKS. CAN YOU HANDLE THAT?
YES, MRS. B.
SORRY, MRS. B.
WE'D HAVE BEEN ROTATED OFF INCOMING CALLS SOON ANYWAY. EVERY POD WAS. BUT IT STILL FELT LIKE A FAILURE. LIKE WE'D LET THEM DOWN.
ON THE OTHER HAND, IT MEANT WE GOT TO SEE --

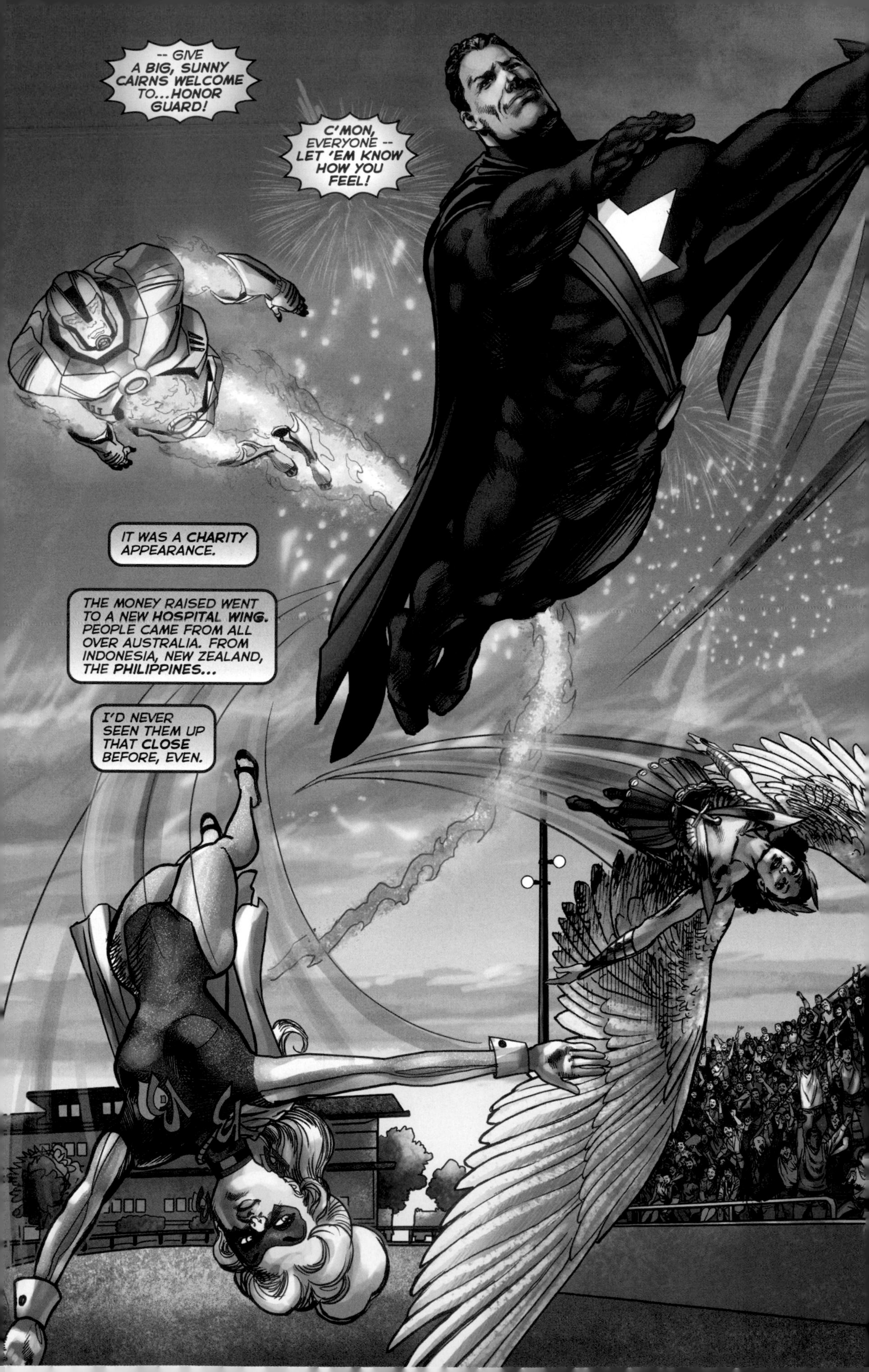
-- GIVE A BIG, SUNNY CAIRNS WELCOME TO...HONOR GUARD!
C'MON, EVERYONE -- LET 'EM KNOW HOW YOU FEEL!
IT WAS A CHARITY APPEARANCE.
THE MONEY RAISED WENT TO A NEW HOSPITAL WING. PEOPLE CAME FROM ALL OVER AUSTRALIA. FROM INDONESIA, NEW ZEALAND, THE PHILIPPINES...
I'D NEVER SEEN THEM UP THAT CLOSE BEFORE, EVEN.

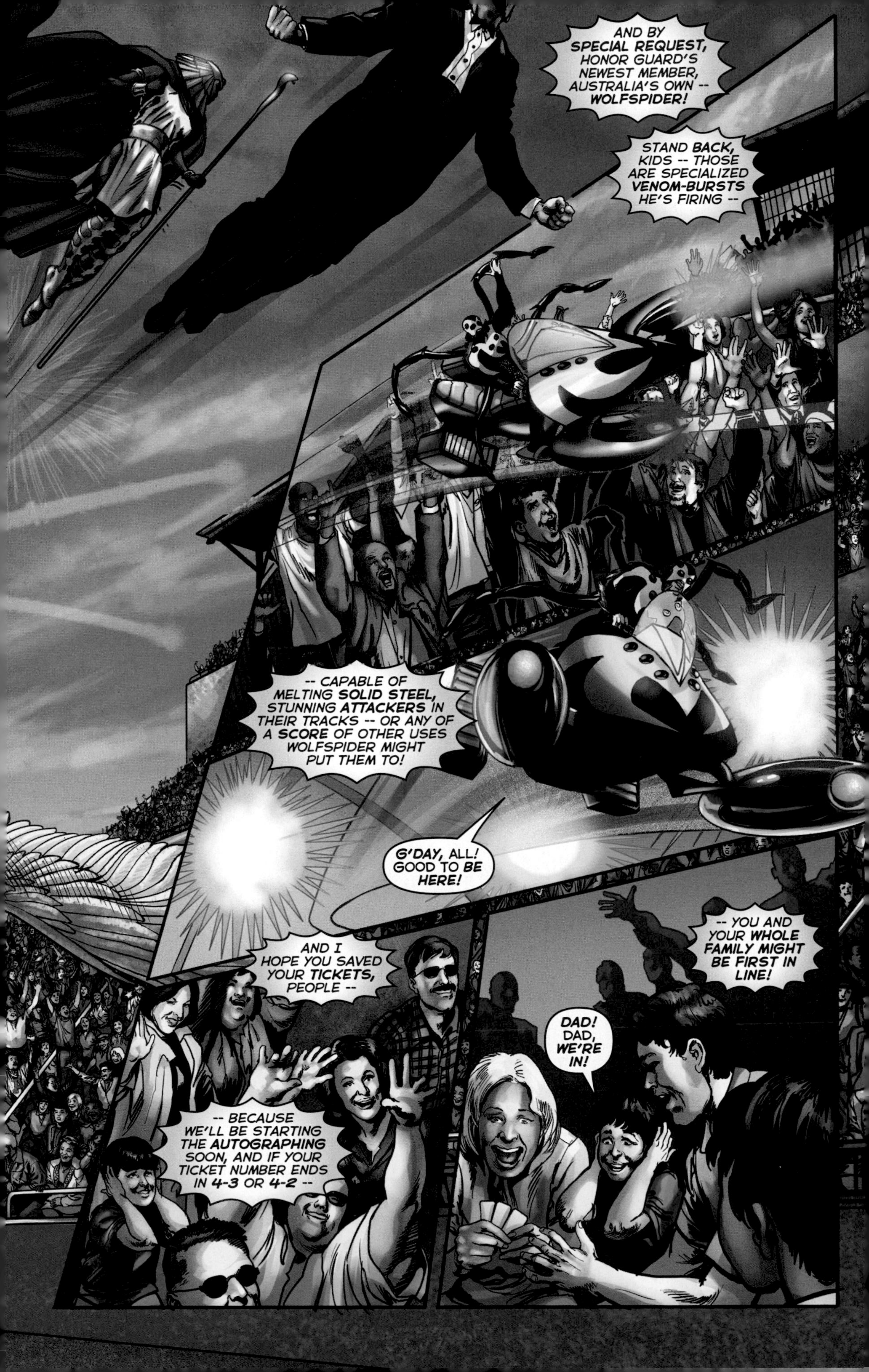
AND BY SPECIAL REQUEST, HONOR GUARD'S NEWEST MEMBER, AUSTRALIA'S OWN -- WOLFSPIDER!
STAND BACK, KIDS -- THOSE ARE SPECIALIZED VENOM-BURSTS HE'S FIRING --
-- CAPABLE OF MELTING SOLID STEEL, STUNNING ATTACKERS IN THEIR TRACKS -- OR ANY OF A SCORE OF OTHER USES WOLFSPIDER MIGHT PUT THEM TO!
G'DAY, ALL! GOOD TO BE HERE!
AND I HOPE YOU SAVED YOUR TICKETS, PEOPLE --
-- BECAUSE WE'LL BE STARTING THE AUTOGRAPHING SOON, AND IF YOUR TICKET NUMBER ENDS IN 4-3 OR 4-2 --
-- YOU AND YOUR WHOLE FAMILY MIGHT BE FIRST IN LINE!
DAD! DAD, WE'RE IN!

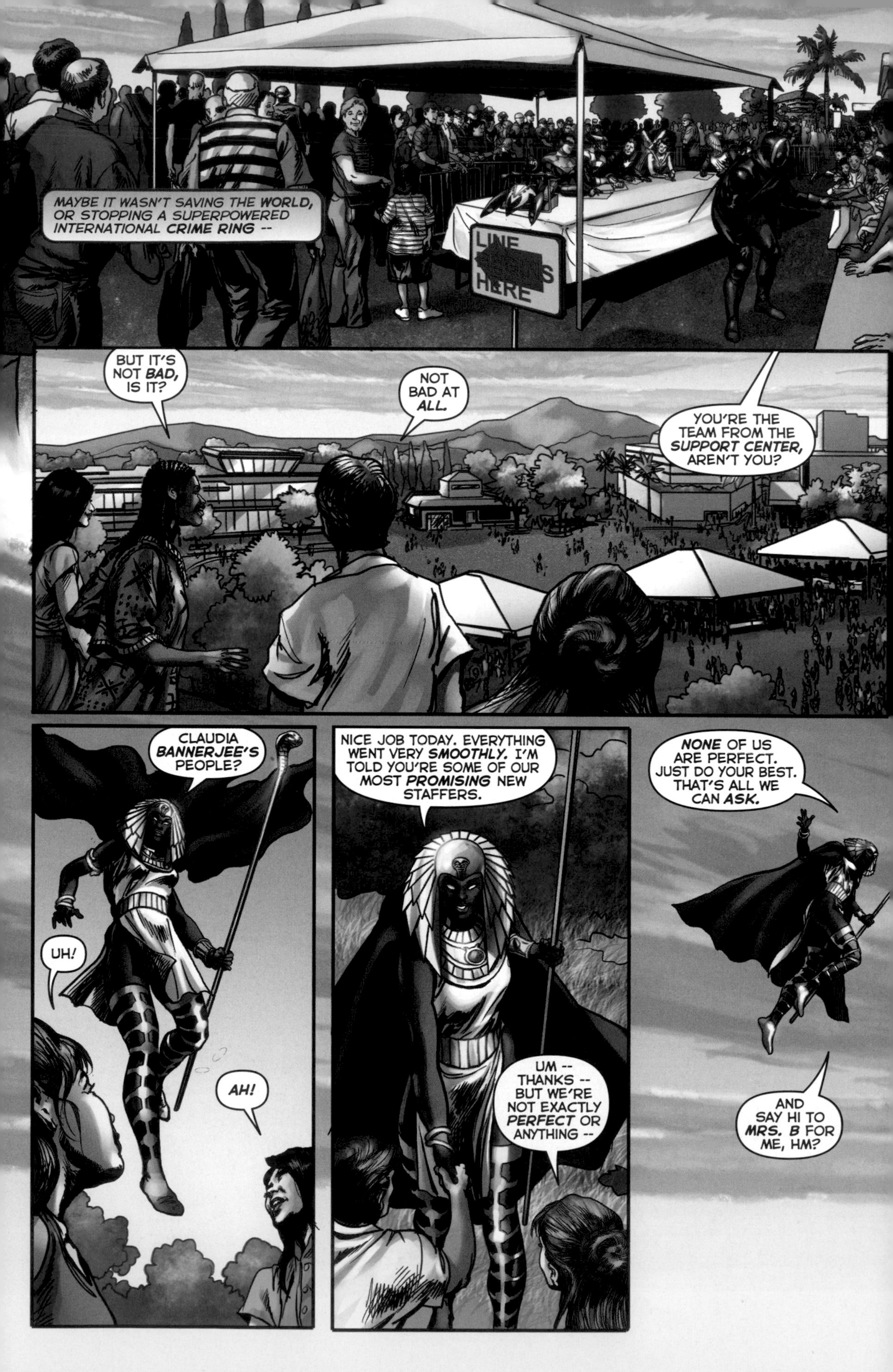
MAYBE IT WASN'T SAVING THE WORLD, OR STOPPING A SUPERPOWERED INTERNATIONAL CRIME RING --
LINE [redacted] HERE
BUT IT'S NOT BAD, IS IT?
NOT BAD AT ALL.
YOU'RE THE TEAM FROM THE SUPPORT CENTER, AREN'T YOU?
CLAUDIA BANNERJEE'S PEOPLE?
UH!
AH!
NICE JOB TODAY. EVERYTHING WENT VERY SMOOTHLY. I'M TOLD YOU'RE SOME OF OUR MOST PROMISING NEW STAFFERS.
UM -- THANKS -- BUT WE'RE NOT EXACTLY PERFECT OR ANYTHING --
NONE OF US ARE PERFECT. JUST DO YOUR BEST. THAT'S ALL WE CAN ASK.
AND SAY HI TO MRS. B FOR ME, HM?

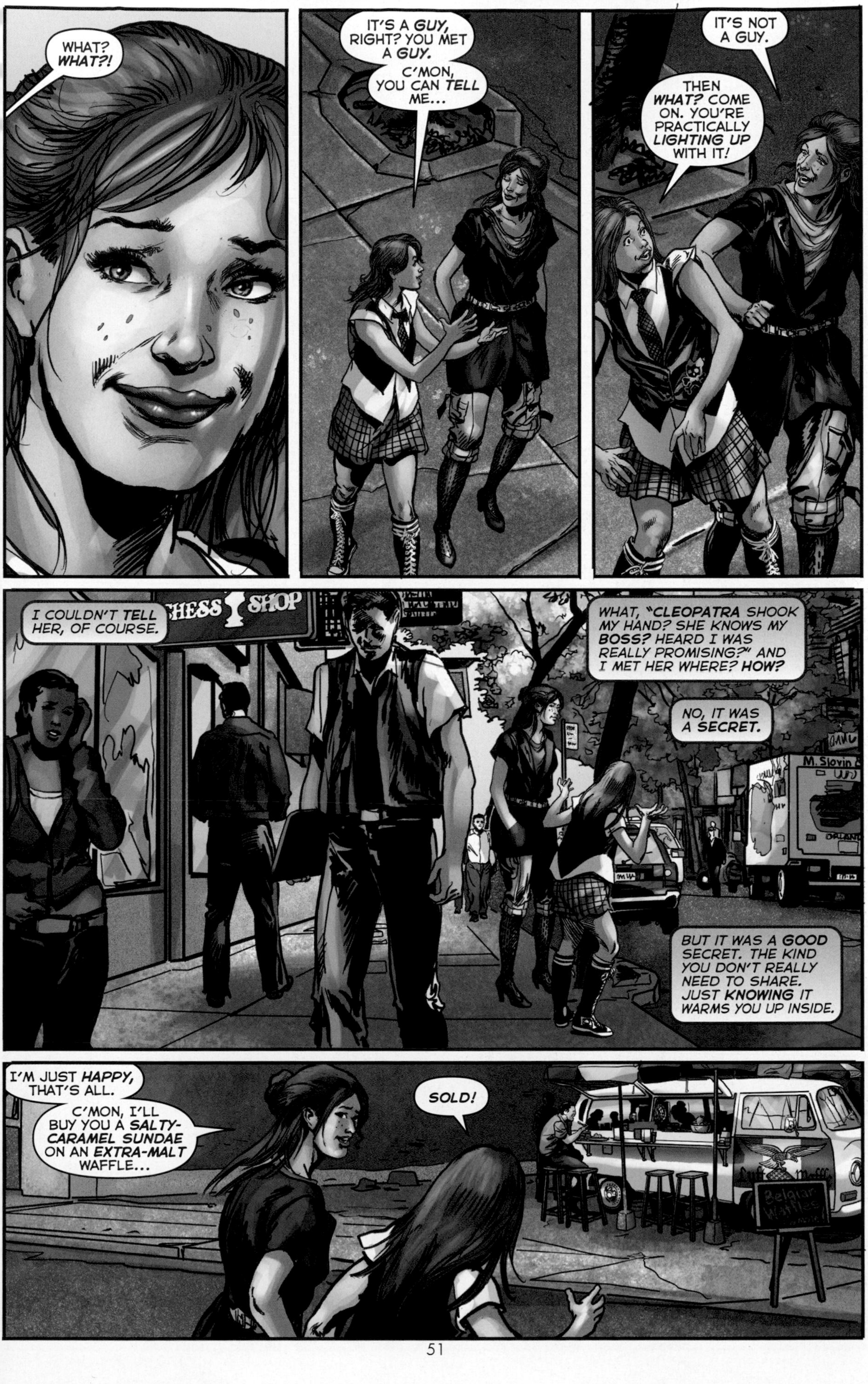
WHAT? WHAT?!
IT'S A GUY, RIGHT? YOU MET A GUY.
C'MON, YOU CAN TELL ME...
IT'S NOT A GUY.
THEN WHAT? COME ON. YOU'RE PRACTICALLY LIGHTING UP WITH IT!
CHESS SHOP
I COULDN'T TELL HER, OF COURSE.
WHAT, "CLEOPATRA SHOOK MY HAND? SHE KNOWS MY BOSS? HEARD I WAS REALLY PROMISING?" AND I MET HER WHERE? HOW?
NO, IT WAS A SECRET.
BUT IT WAS A GOOD SECRET. THE KIND YOU DON'T REALLY NEED TO SHARE. JUST KNOWING IT WARMS YOU UP INSIDE.
I'M JUST HAPPY, THAT'S ALL.
C'MON, I'LL BUY YOU A SALTY-CARAMEL SUNDAE ON AN EXTRA-MALT WAFFLE...
SOLD!

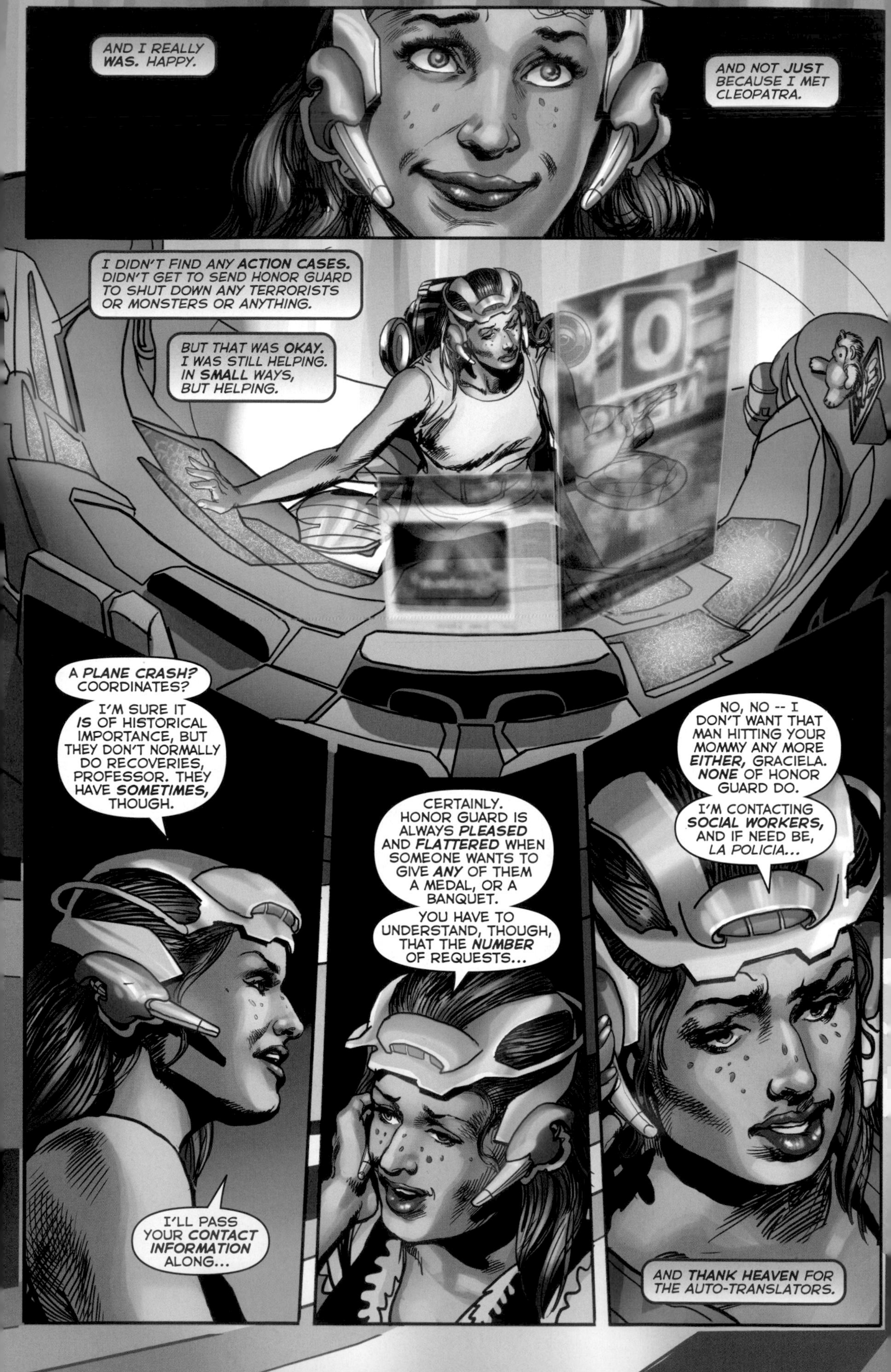
AND I REALLY WAS. HAPPY.
AND NOT JUST BECAUSE I MET CLEOPATRA.
I DIDN'T FIND ANY ACTION CASES. DIDN'T GET TO SEND HONOR GUARD TO SHUT DOWN ANY TERRORISTS OR MONSTERS OR ANYTHING.
BUT THAT WAS OKAY. I WAS STILL HELPING. IN SMALL WAYS, BUT HELPING.
A PLANE CRASH? COORDINATES?
I'M SURE IT IS OF HISTORICAL IMPORTANCE, BUT THEY DON'T NORMALLY DO RECOVERIES, PROFESSOR. THEY HAVE SOMETIMES, THOUGH.
I'LL PASS YOUR CONTACT INFORMATION ALONG...
CERTAINLY. HONOR GUARD IS ALWAYS PLEASED AND FLATTERED WHEN SOMEONE WANTS TO GIVE ANY OF THEM A MEDAL, OR A BANQUET.
YOU HAVE TO UNDERSTAND, THOUGH, THAT THE NUMBER OF REQUESTS...
NO, NO -- I DON'T WANT THAT MAN HITTING YOUR MOMMY ANY MORE EITHER, GRACIELA. NONE OF HONOR GUARD DO.
I'M CONTACTING SOCIAL WORKERS, AND IF NEED BE, LA POLICIA...
AND THANK HEAVEN FOR THE AUTO-TRANSLATORS.

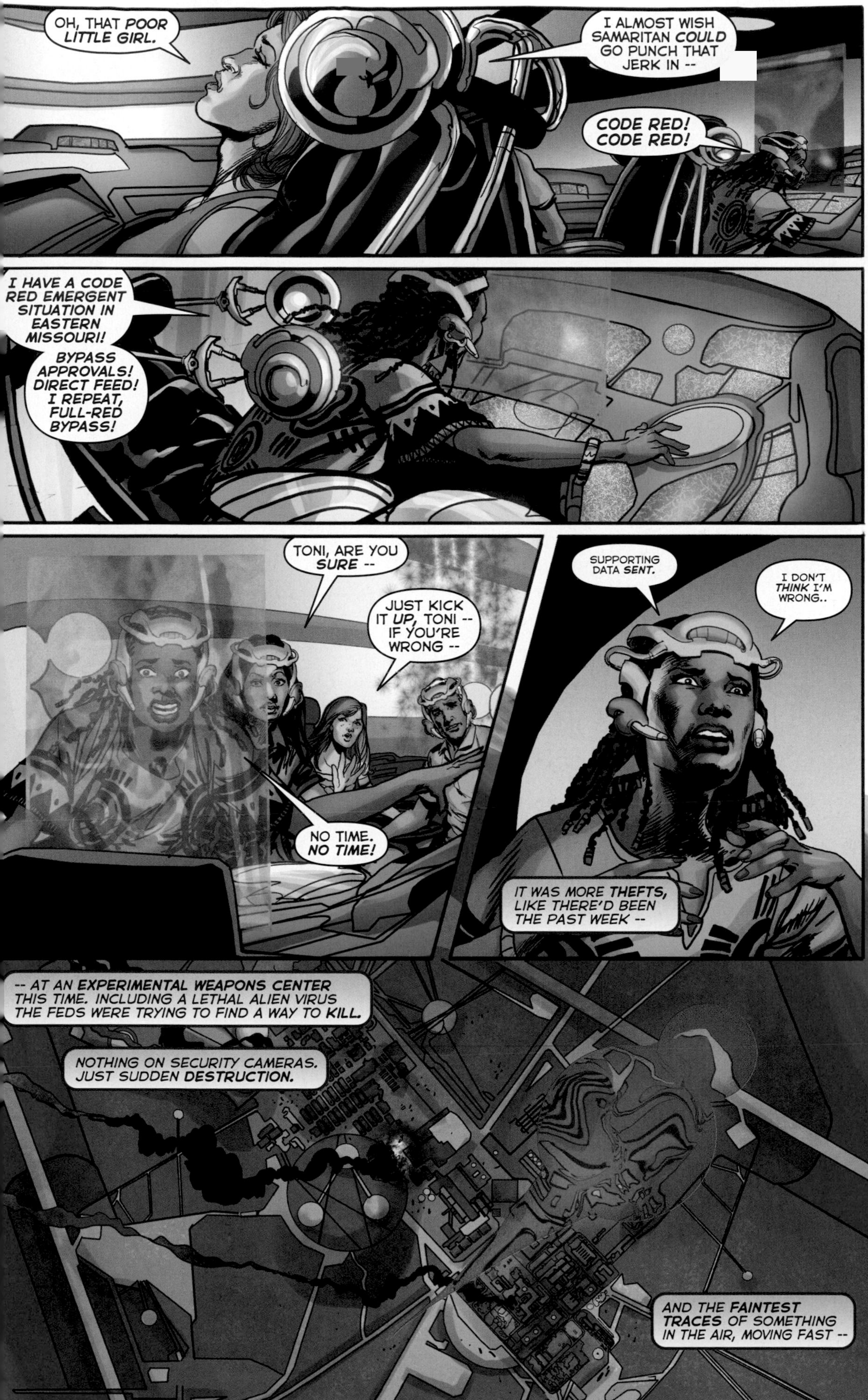
OH, THAT POOR LITTLE GIRL.
I ALMOST WISH SAMARITAN COULD GO PUNCH THAT JERK IN --
CODE RED! CODE RED!
I HAVE A CODE RED EMERGENT SITUATION IN EASTERN MISSOURI!
BYPASS APPROVALS! DIRECT FEED! I REPEAT, FULL-RED BYPASS!
TONI, ARE YOU SURE --
JUST KICK IT UP, TONI -- IF YOU'RE WRONG --
NO TIME. NO TIME!
SUPPORTING DATA SENT.
I DON'T THINK I'M WRONG..
IT WAS MORE THEFTS, LIKE THERE'D BEEN THE PAST WEEK --
-- AT AN EXPERIMENTAL WEAPONS CENTER THIS TIME. INCLUDING A LETHAL ALIEN VIRUS THE FEDS WERE TRYING TO FIND A WAY TO KILL.
NOTHING ON SECURITY CAMERAS. JUST SUDDEN DESTRUCTION.
AND THE FAINTEST TRACES OF SOMETHING IN THE AIR, MOVING FAST --

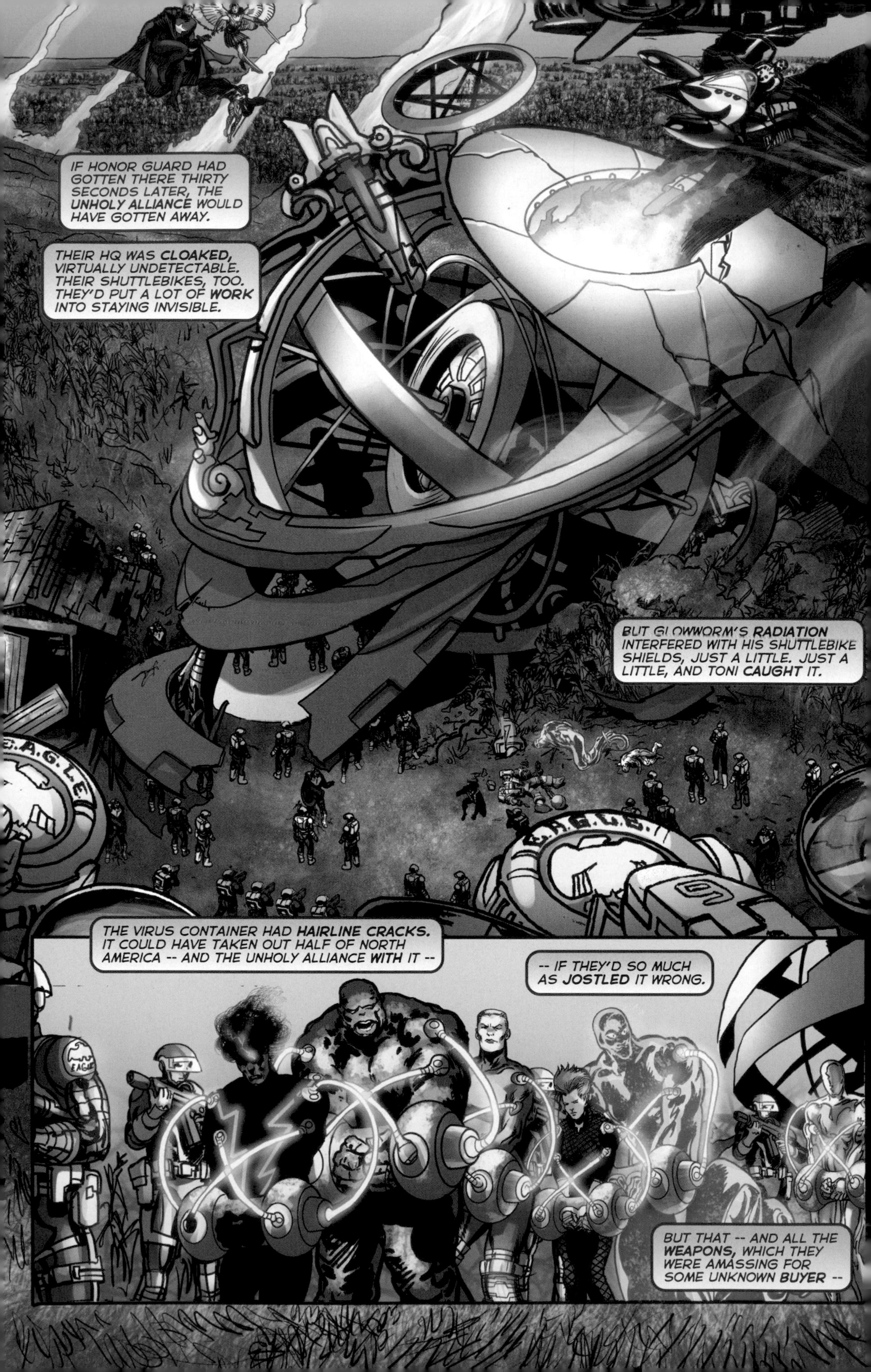
IF HONOR GUARD HAD GOTTEN THERE THIRTY SECONDS LATER, THE UNHOLY ALLIANCE WOULD HAVE GOTTEN AWAY.
THEIR HQ WAS CLOAKED, VIRTUALLY UNDETECTABLE. THEIR SHUTTLEBIKES, TOO. THEY'D PUT A LOT OF WORK INTO STAYING INVISIBLE.
BUT GLOWWORM'S RADIATION INTERFERED WITH HIS SHUTTLEBIKE SHIELDS, JUST A LITTLE. JUST A LITTLE, AND TONI CAUGHT IT.
THE VIRUS CONTAINER HAD HAIRLINE CRACKS. IT COULD HAVE TAKEN OUT HALF OF NORTH AMERICA -- AND THE UNHOLY ALLIANCE WITH IT --
-- IF THEY'D SO MUCH AS JOSTLED IT WRONG.
BUT THAT -- AND ALL THE WEAPONS, WHICH THEY WERE AMASSING FOR SOME UNKNOWN BUYER --

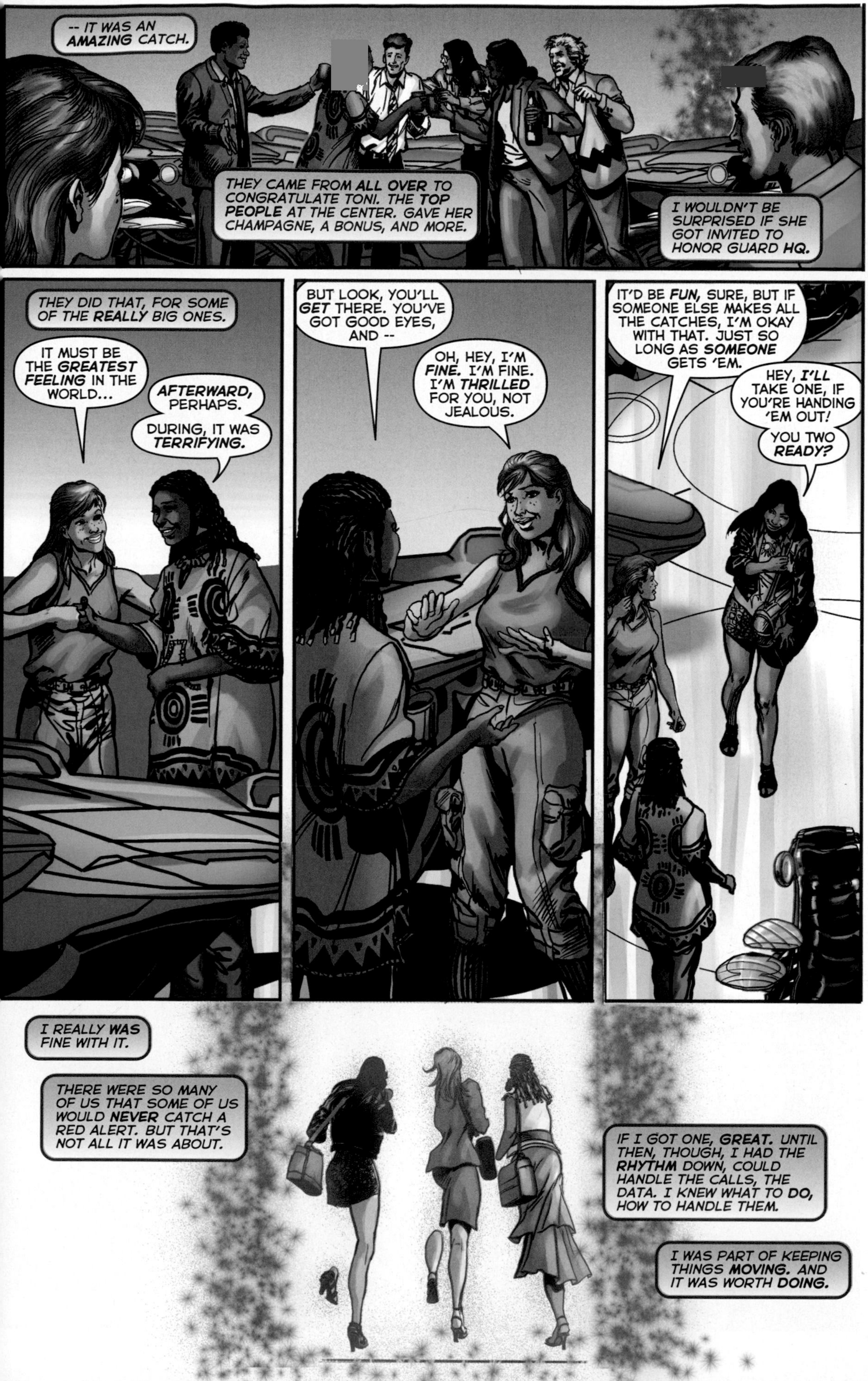
-- IT WAS AN AMAZING CATCH.
THEY CAME FROM ALL OVER TO CONGRATULATE TONI. THE TOP PEOPLE AT THE CENTER. GAVE HER CHAMPAGNE, A BONUS, AND MORE.
I WOULDN'T BE SURPRISED IF SHE GOT INVITED TO HONOR GUARD HQ.
THEY DID THAT, FOR SOME OF THE REALLY BIG ONES.
IT MUST BE THE GREATEST FEELING IN THE WORLD...
AFTERWARD, PERHAPS.
DURING, IT WAS TERRIFYING.
BUT LOOK, YOU'LL GET THERE. YOU'VE GOT GOOD EYES, AND --
OH, HEY, I'M FINE. I'M FINE. I'M THRILLED FOR YOU, NOT JEALOUS.
IT'D BE FUN, SURE, BUT IF SOMEONE ELSE MAKES ALL THE CATCHES, I'M OKAY WITH THAT. JUST SO LONG AS SOMEONE GETS 'EM.
HEY, I'LL TAKE ONE, IF YOU'RE HANDING 'EM OUT!
YOU TWO READY?
I REALLY WAS FINE WITH IT.
THERE WERE SO MANY OF US THAT SOME OF US WOULD NEVER CATCH A RED ALERT. BUT THAT'S NOT ALL IT WAS ABOUT.
IF I GOT ONE, GREAT. UNTIL THEN, THOUGH, I HAD THE RHYTHM DOWN, COULD HANDLE THE CALLS, THE DATA. I KNEW WHAT TO DO, HOW TO HANDLE THEM.
I WAS PART OF KEEPING THINGS MOVING. AND IT WAS WORTH DOING.

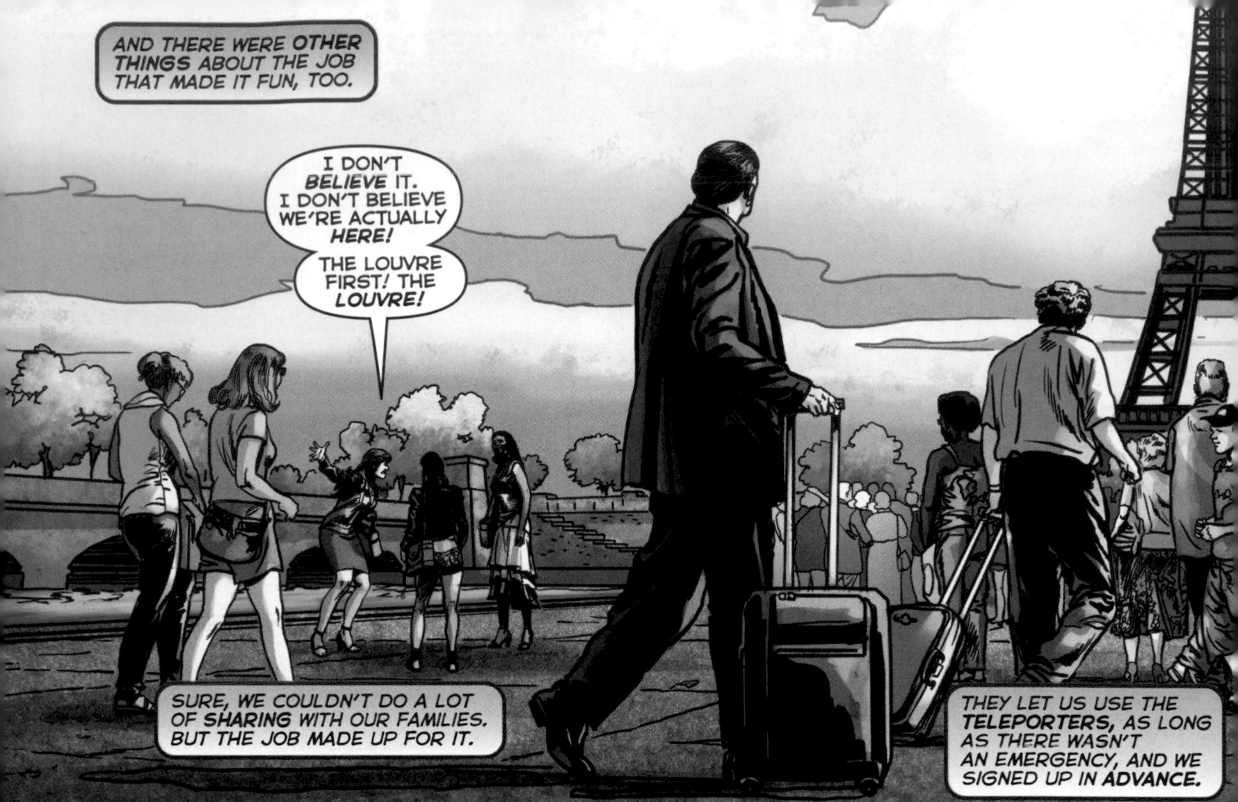
AND THERE WERE OTHER THINGS ABOUT THE JOB THAT MADE IT FUN, TOO.
I DON'T BELIEVE IT. I DON'T BELIEVE WE'RE ACTUALLY HERE!
THE LOUVRE FIRST! THE LOUVRE!
SURE, WE COULDN'T DO A LOT OF SHARING WITH OUR FAMILIES. BUT THE JOB MADE UP FOR IT.
THEY LET US USE THE TELEPORTERS, AS LONG AS THERE WASN'T AN EMERGENCY, AND WE SIGNED UP IN ADVANCE.

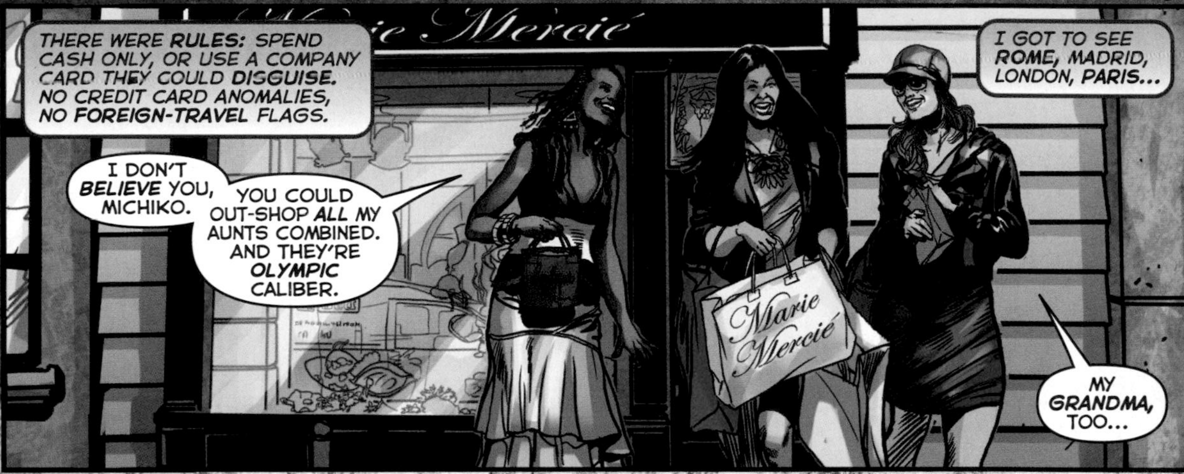
THERE WERE RULES: SPEND CASH ONLY, OR USE A COMPANY CARD THEY COULD DISGUISE. NO CREDIT CARD ANOMALIES, NO FOREIGN-TRAVEL FLAGS.
I GOT TO SEE ROME, MADRID, LONDON, PARIS...
I DON'T BELIEVE YOU, MICHIKO.
YOU COULD OUT-SHOP ALL MY AUNTS COMBINED. AND THEY'RE OLYMPIC CALIBER.
MY GRANDMA, TOO...
Marie Mercié

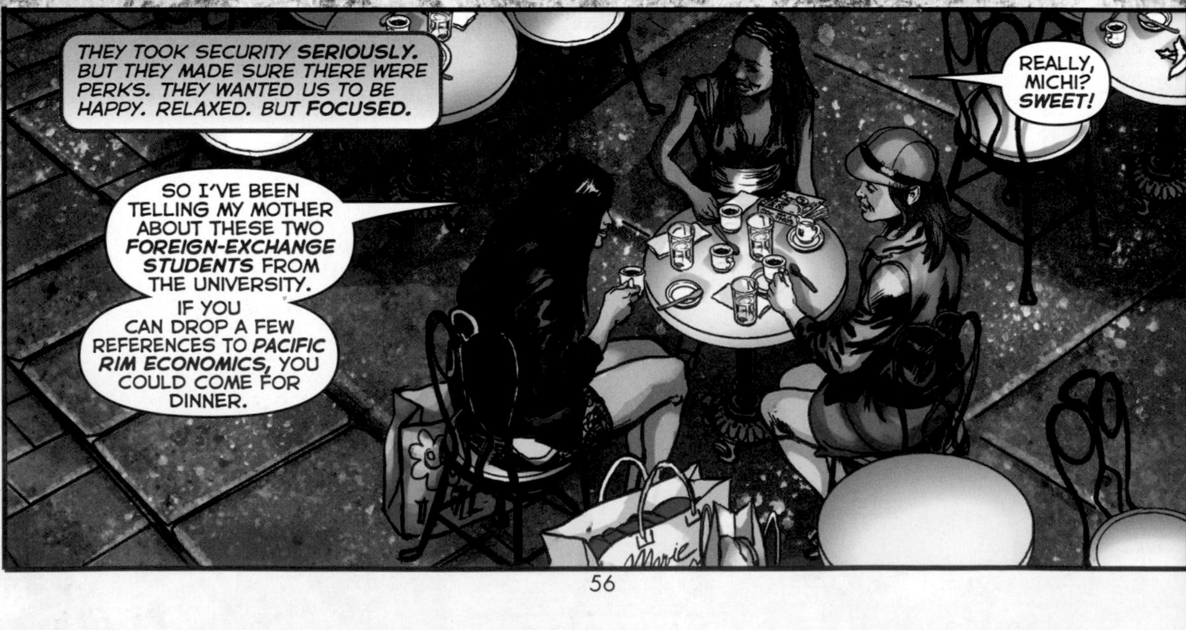
THEY TOOK SECURITY SERIOUSLY. BUT THEY MADE SURE THERE WERE PERKS. THEY WANTED US TO BE HAPPY. RELAXED. BUT FOCUSED.
REALLY, MICHI? SWEET!
SO I'VE BEEN TELLING MY MOTHER ABOUT THESE TWO FOREIGN-EXCHANGE STUDENTS FROM THE UNIVERSITY.
IF YOU CAN DROP A FEW REFERENCES TO PACIFIC RIM ECONOMICS, YOU COULD COME FOR DINNER.

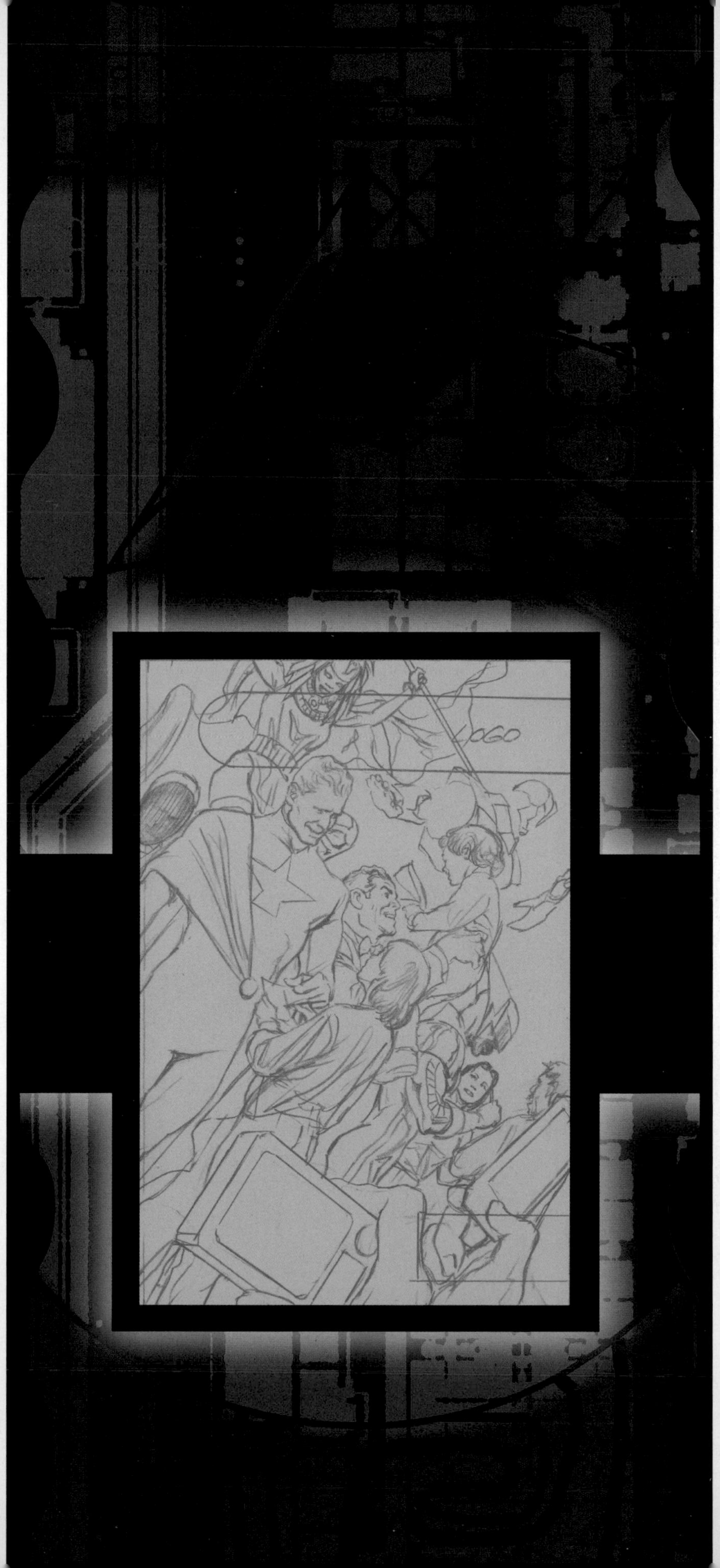
LOGO

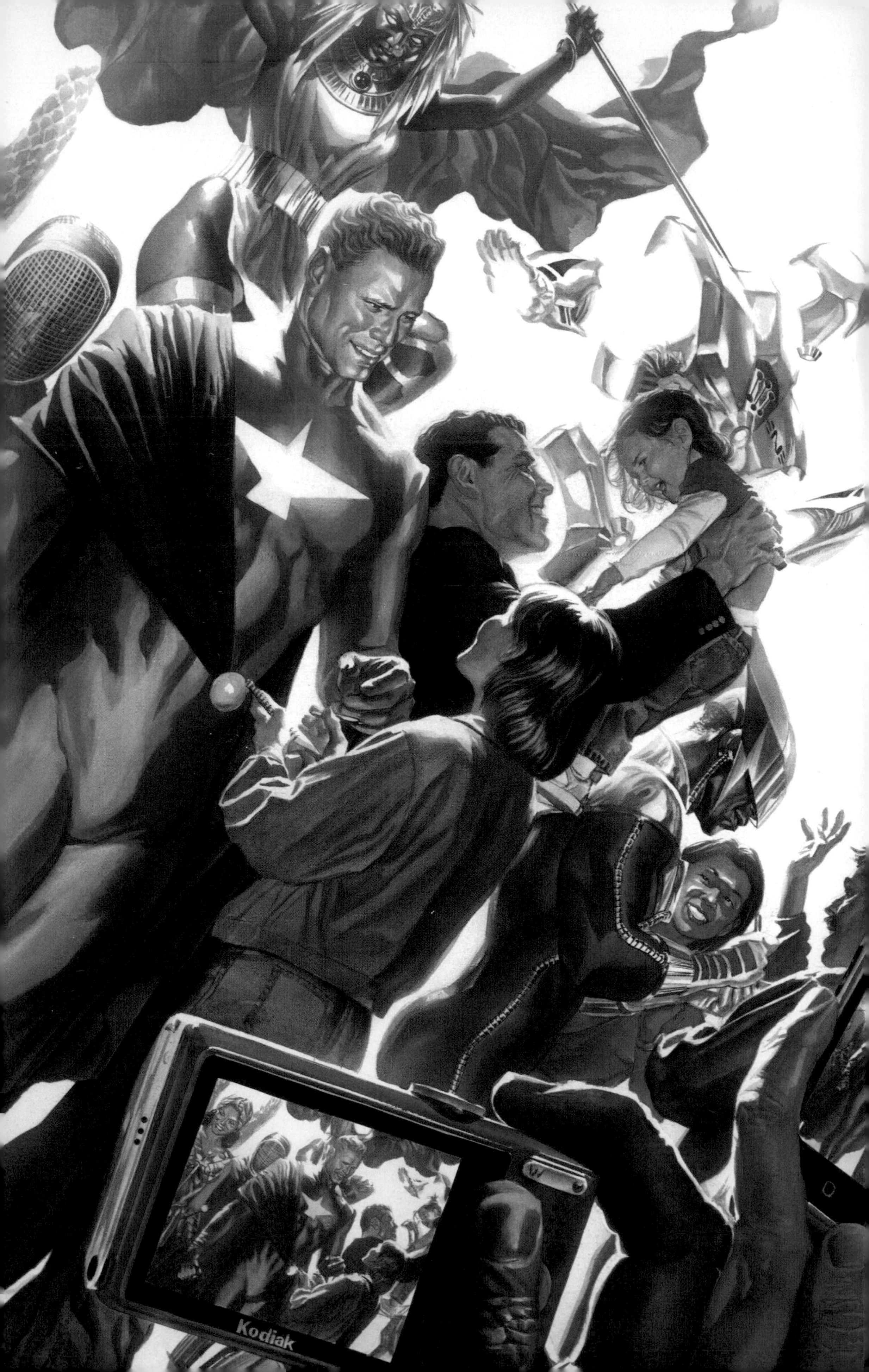
Kodiak

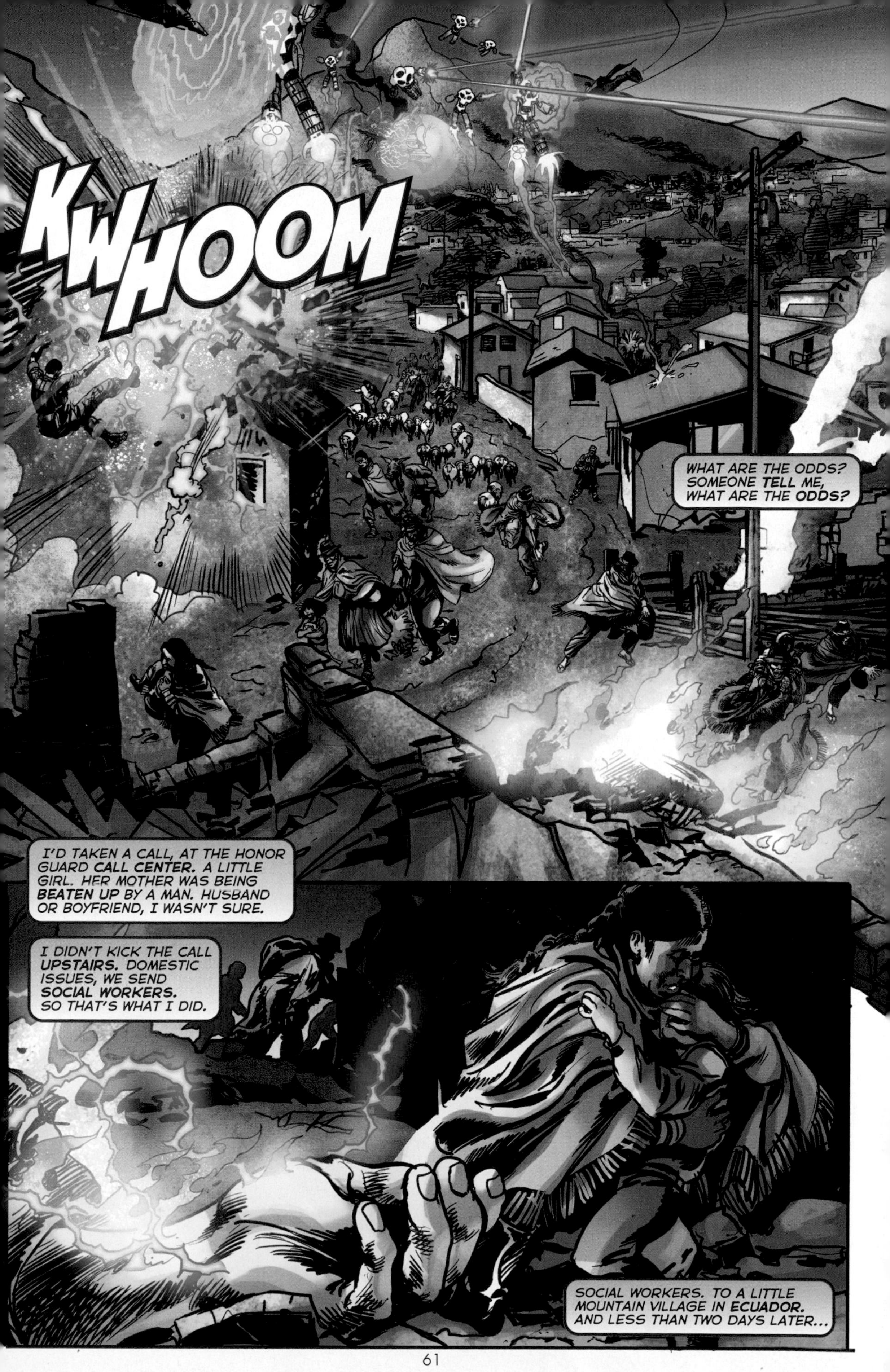
KWHOOM
WHAT ARE THE ODDS? SOMEONE TELL ME, WHAT ARE THE ODDS?
I'D TAKEN A CALL, AT THE HONOR GUARD CALL CENTER. A LITTLE GIRL. HER MOTHER WAS BEING BEATEN UP BY A MAN. HUSBAND OR BOYFRIEND, I WASN'T SURE.
I DIDN'T KICK THE CALL UPSTAIRS. DOMESTIC ISSUES, WE SEND SOCIAL WORKERS. SO THAT'S WHAT I DID.
SOCIAL WORKERS. TO A LITTLE MOUNTAIN VILLAGE IN ECUADOR. AND LESS THAN TWO DAYS LATER...

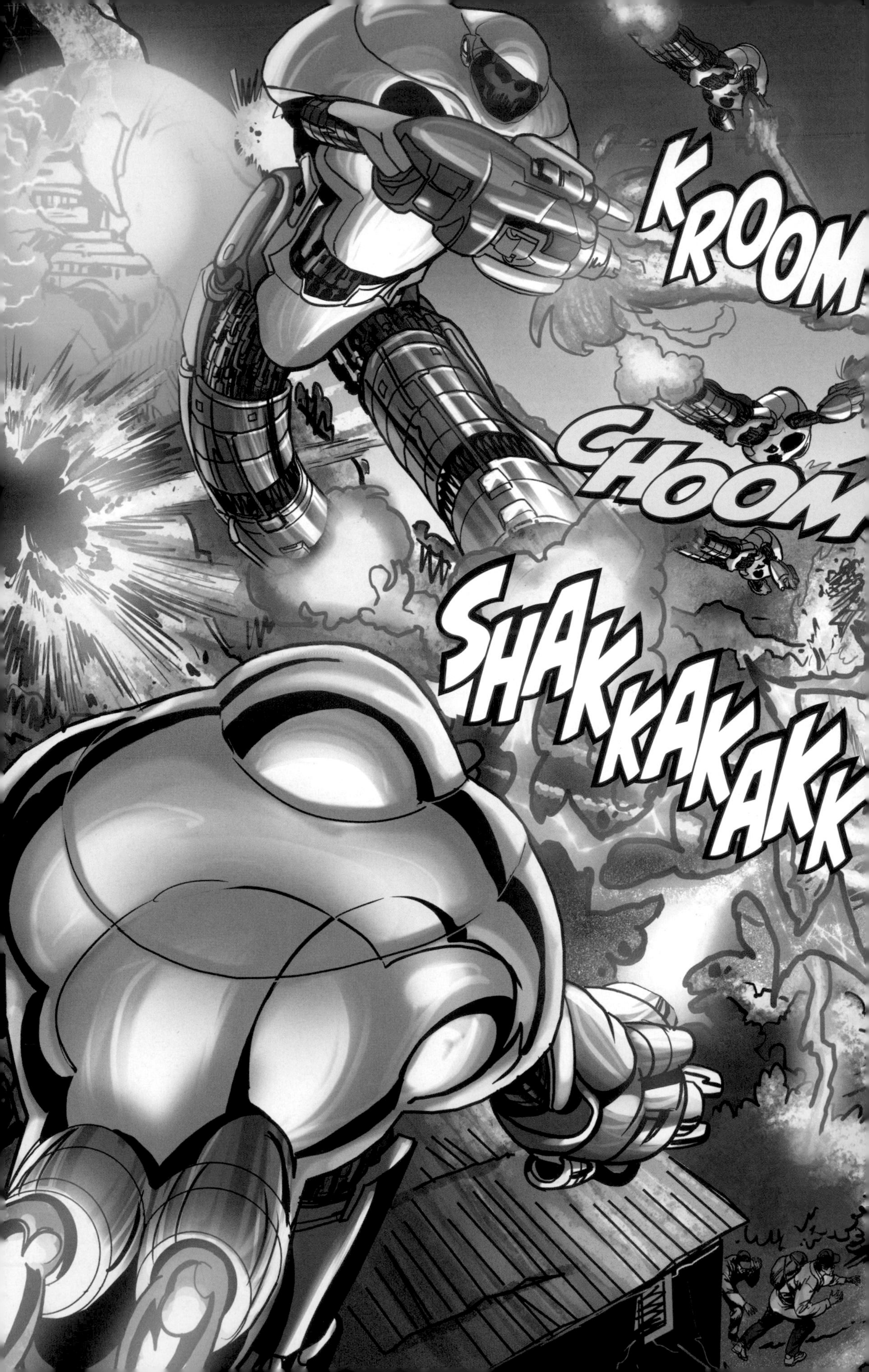
KROOM
CHOOM
SHAKKAKAKAKK

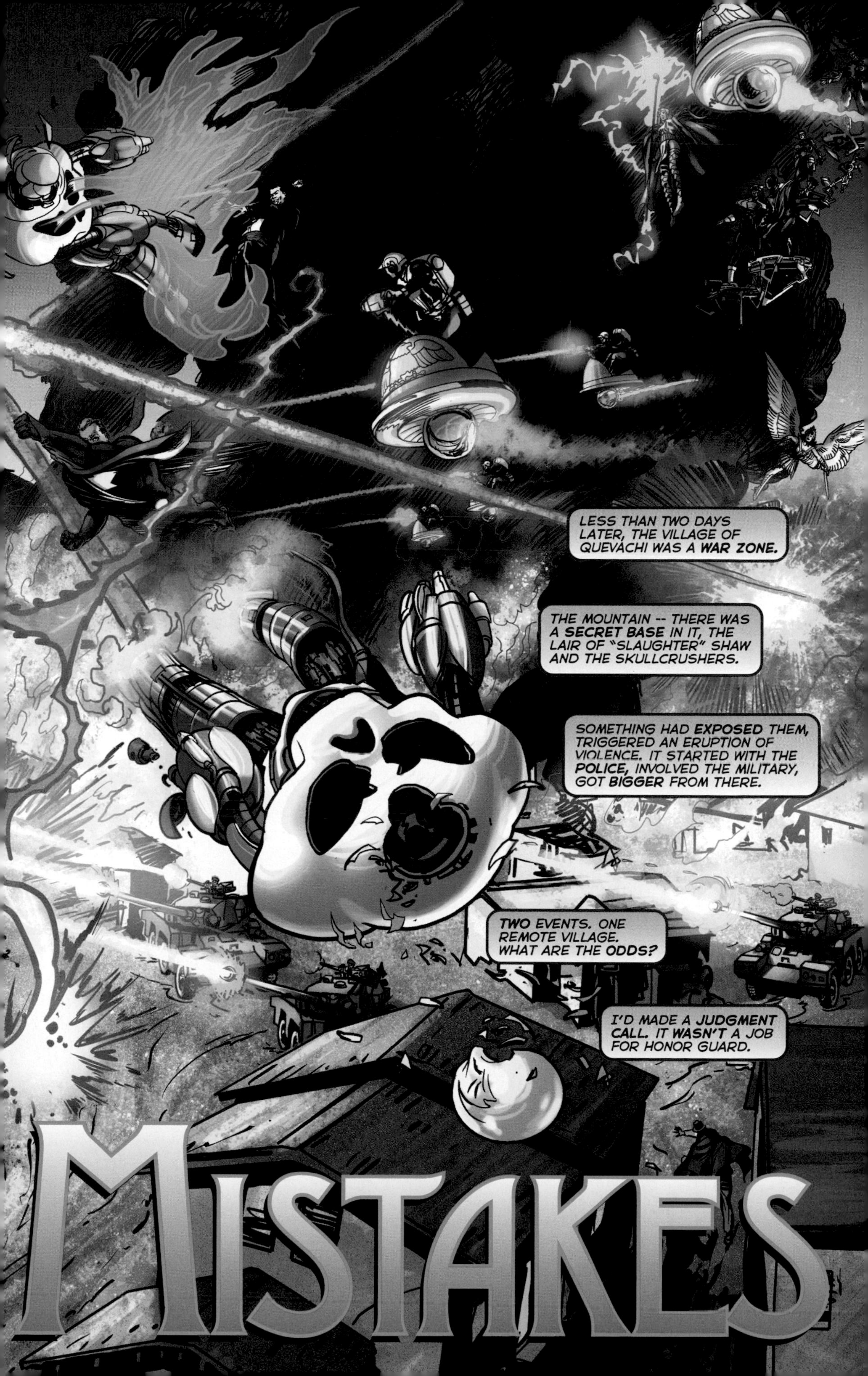
LESS THAN TWO DAYS LATER, THE VILLAGE OF QUEVACHI WAS A WAR ZONE.
THE MOUNTAIN -- THERE WAS A SECRET BASE IN IT, THE LAIR OF "SLAUGHTER" SHAW AND THE SKULLCRUSHERS.
SOMETHING HAD EXPOSED THEM, TRIGGERED AN ERUPTION OF VIOLENCE. IT STARTED WITH THE POLICE, INVOLVED THE MILITARY, GOT BIGGER FROM THERE.
TWO EVENTS. ONE REMOTE VILLAGE. WHAT ARE THE ODDS?
I'D MADE A JUDGMENT CALL. IT WASN'T A JOB FOR HONOR GUARD.
MISTAKES

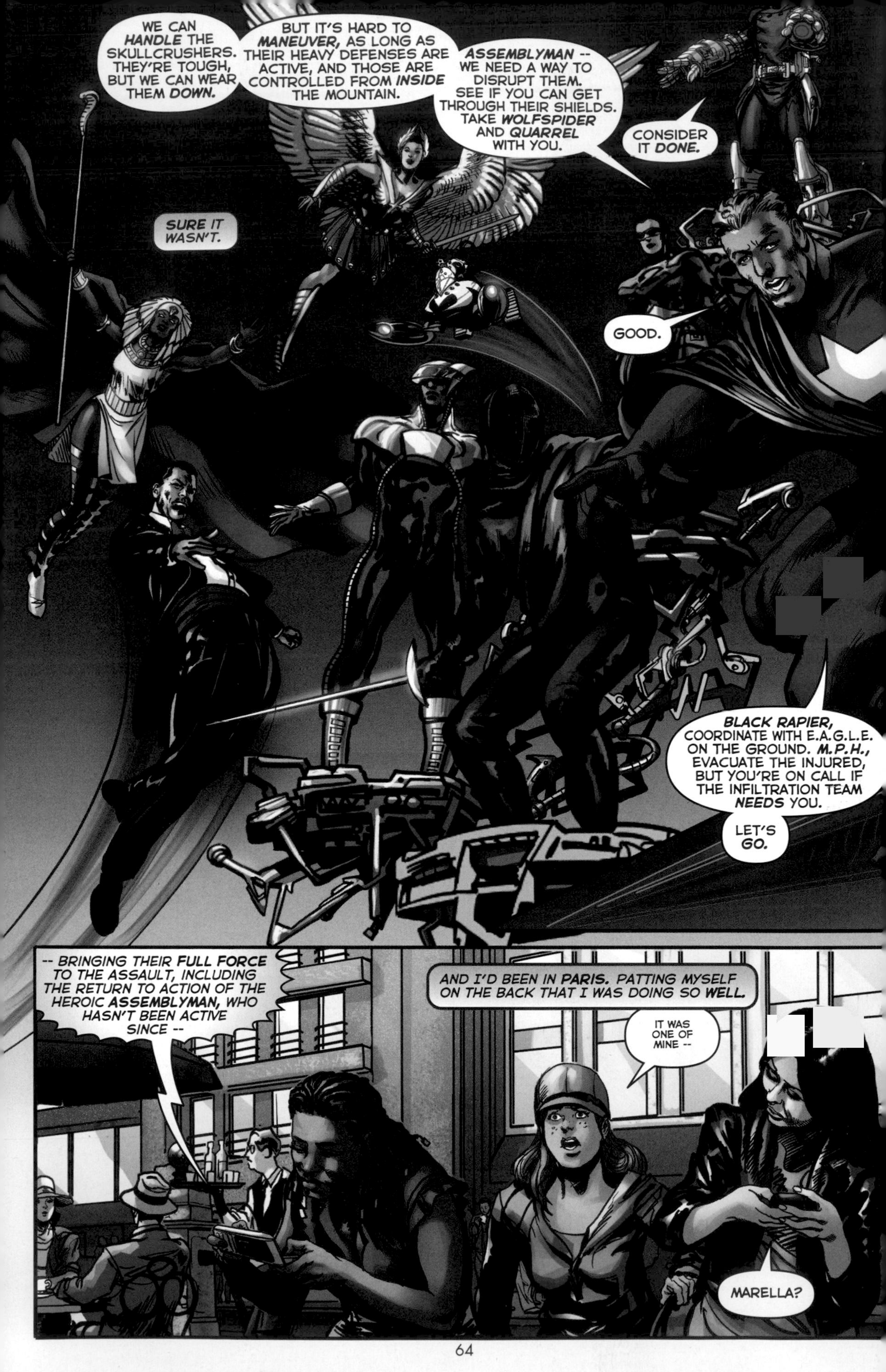
WE CAN HANDLE THE SKULLCRUSHERS. THEY'RE TOUGH, BUT WE CAN WEAR THEM DOWN.
BUT IT'S HARD TO MANEUVER, AS LONG AS THEIR HEAVY DEFENSES ARE ACTIVE, AND THOSE ARE CONTROLLED FROM INSIDE THE MOUNTAIN.
ASSEMBLYMAN -- WE NEED A WAY TO DISRUPT THEM. SEE IF YOU CAN GET THROUGH THEIR SHIELDS. TAKE WOLFSPIDER AND QUARREL WITH YOU.
CONSIDER IT DONE.
SURE IT WASN'T.
GOOD.
BLACK RAPIER, COORDINATE WITH E.A.G.L.E. ON THE GROUND. M.P.H., EVACUATE THE INJURED, BUT YOU'RE ON CALL IF THE INFILTRATION TEAM NEEDS YOU.
LET'S GO.
-- BRINGING THEIR FULL FORCE TO THE ASSAULT, INCLUDING THE RETURN TO ACTION OF THE HEROIC ASSEMBLYMAN, WHO HASN'T BEEN ACTIVE SINCE --
AND I'D BEEN IN PARIS. PATTING MYSELF ON THE BACK THAT I WAS DOING SO WELL.
IT WAS ONE OF MINE --
MARELLA?

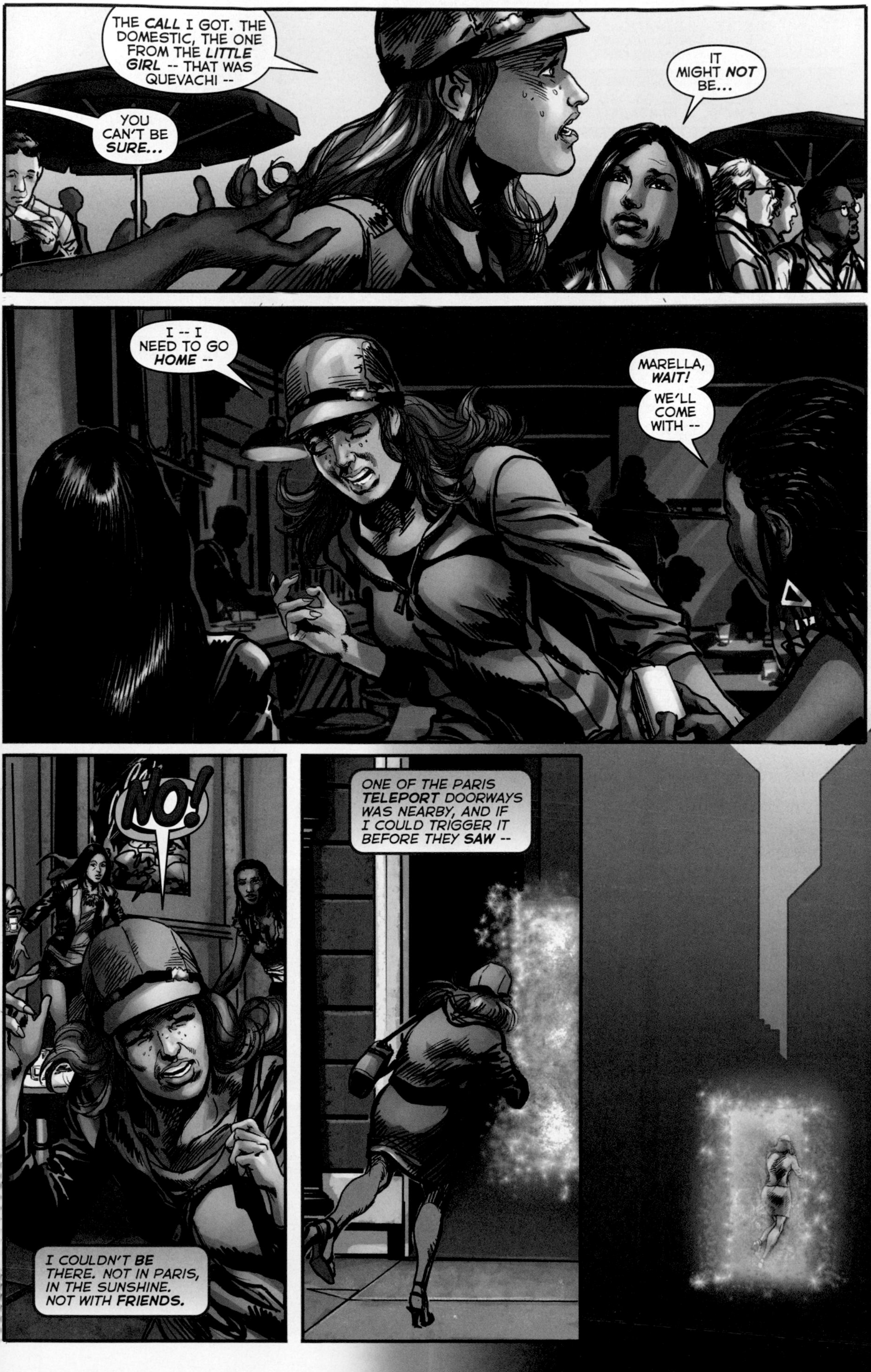
THE CALL I GOT. THE DOMESTIC, THE ONE FROM THE LITTLE GIRL -- THAT WAS QUEVACHI --
YOU CAN'T BE SURE...
IT MIGHT NOT BE...
I -- I NEED TO GO HOME --
MARELLA, WAIT!
WE'LL COME WITH --
NO!
I COULDN'T BE THERE. NOT IN PARIS, IN THE SUNSHINE. NOT WITH FRIENDS.
ONE OF THE PARIS TELEPORT DOORWAYS WAS NEARBY, AND IF I COULD TRIGGER IT BEFORE THEY SAW --

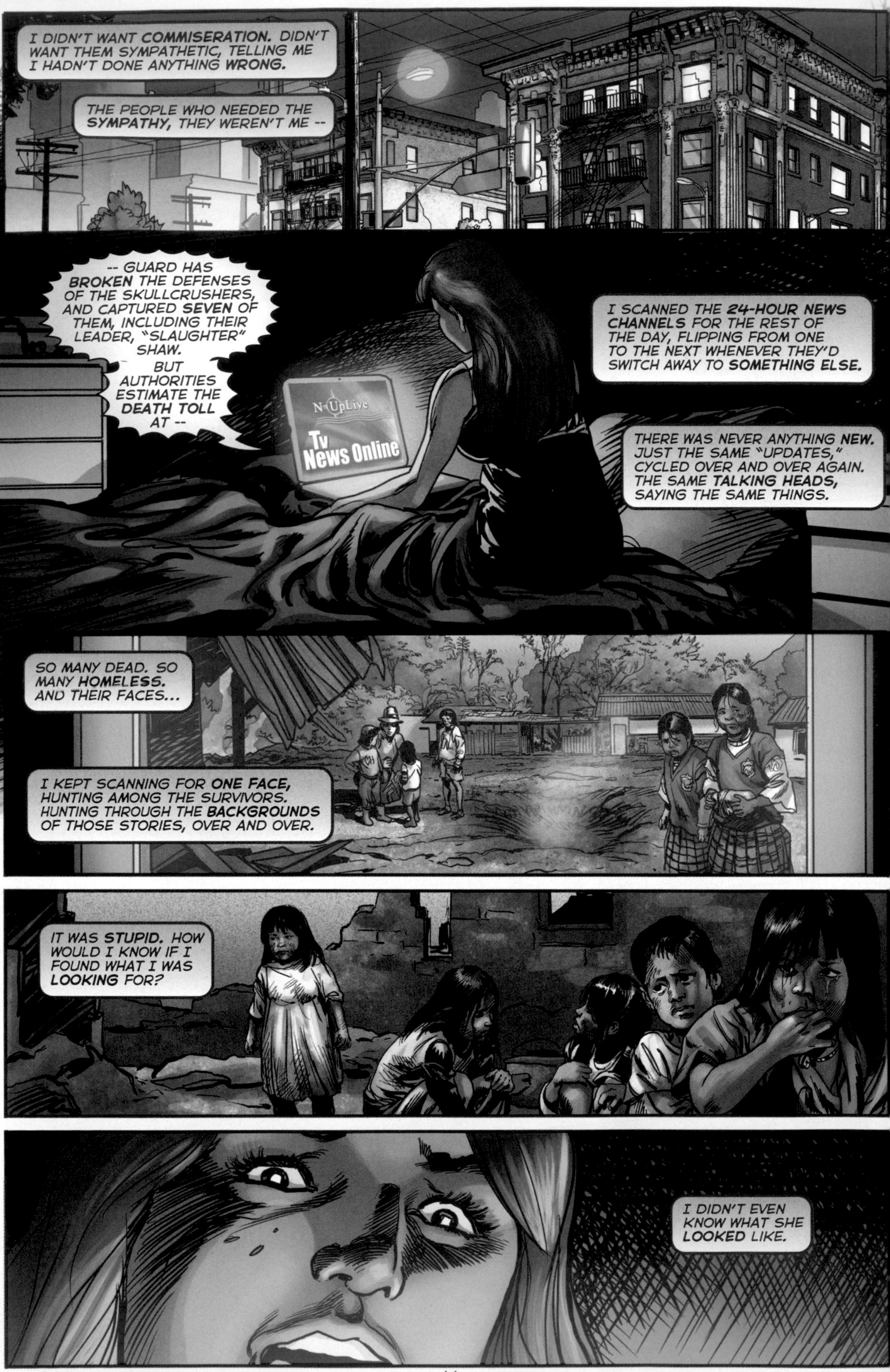

I DIDN'T WANT COMMISERATION. DIDN'T WANT THEM SYMPATHETIC, TELLING ME I HADN'T DONE ANYTHING WRONG.
THE PEOPLE WHO NEEDED THE SYMPATHY, THEY WEREN'T ME --
-- GUARD HAS BROKEN THE DEFENSES OF THE SKULLCRUSHERS, AND CAPTURED SEVEN OF THEM, INCLUDING THEIR LEADER, "SLAUGHTER" SHAW. BUT AUTHORITIES ESTIMATE THE DEATH TOLL AT --
N-UpLive
Tv News Online
I SCANNED THE 24-HOUR NEWS CHANNELS FOR THE REST OF THE DAY, FLIPPING FROM ONE TO THE NEXT WHENEVER THEY'D SWITCH AWAY TO SOMETHING ELSE.
THERE WAS NEVER ANYTHING NEW. JUST THE SAME "UPDATES," CYCLED OVER AND OVER AGAIN. THE SAME TALKING HEADS, SAYING THE SAME THINGS.
SO MANY DEAD. SO MANY HOMELESS. AND THEIR FACES...
I KEPT SCANNING FOR ONE FACE, HUNTING AMONG THE SURVIVORS. HUNTING THROUGH THE BACKGROUNDS OF THOSE STORIES, OVER AND OVER.
IT WAS STUPID. HOW WOULD I KNOW IF I FOUND WHAT I WAS LOOKING FOR?
I DIDN'T EVEN KNOW WHAT SHE LOOKED LIKE.

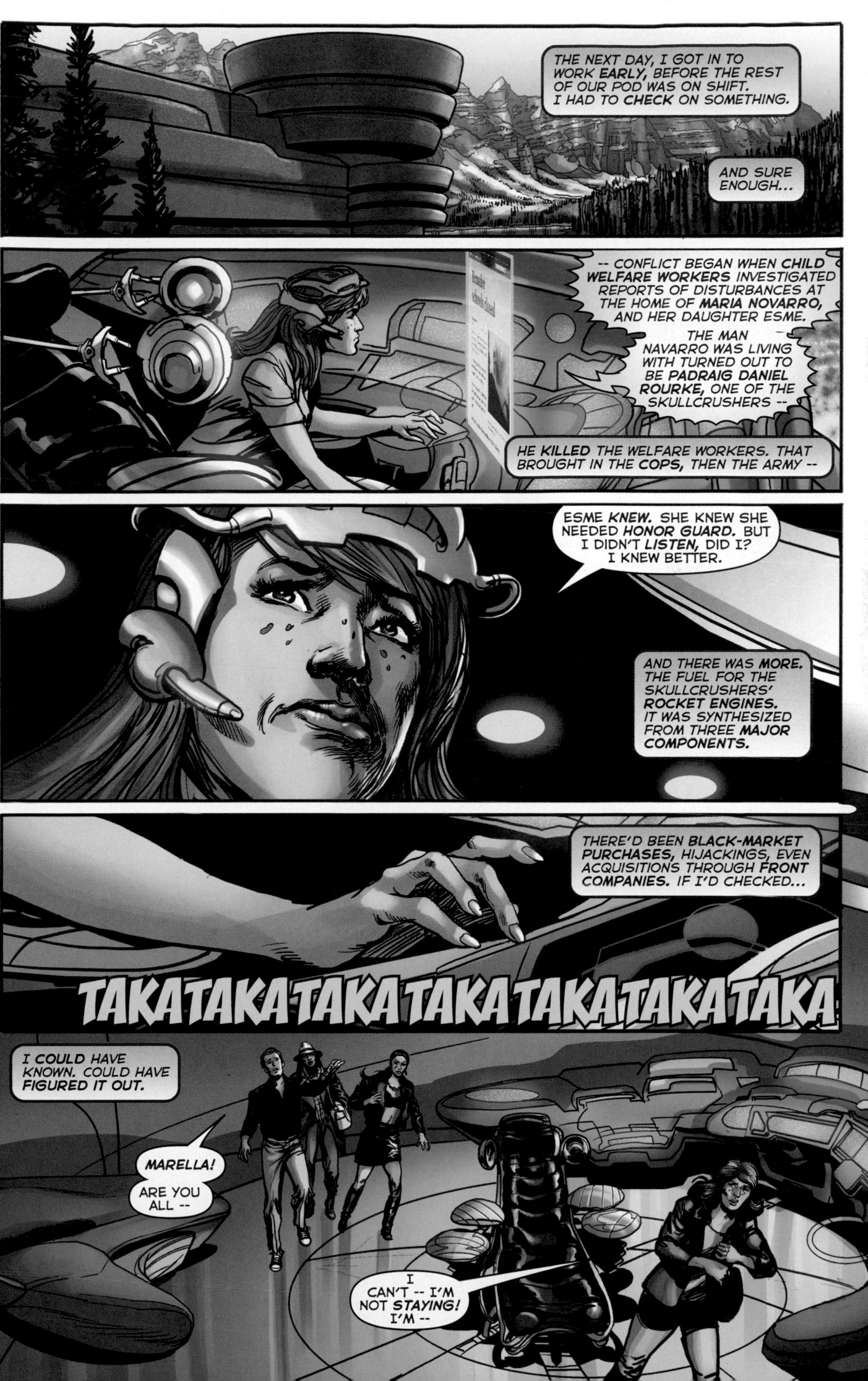
THE NEXT DAY, I GOT IN TO WORK EARLY, BEFORE THE REST OF OUR POD WAS ON SHIFT. I HAD TO CHECK ON SOMETHING.
AND SURE ENOUGH...
-- CONFLICT BEGAN WHEN CHILD WELFARE WORKERS INVESTIGATED REPORTS OF DISTURBANCES AT THE HOME OF MARIA NOVARRO, AND HER DAUGHTER ESME.
THE MAN NAVARRO WAS LIVING WITH TURNED OUT TO BE PADRAIG DANIEL ROURKE, ONE OF THE SKULLCRUSHERS --
HE KILLED THE WELFARE WORKERS. THAT BROUGHT IN THE COPS, THEN THE ARMY --
ESME KNEW. SHE KNEW SHE NEEDED HONOR GUARD. BUT I DIDN'T LISTEN, DID I? I KNEW BETTER.
AND THERE WAS MORE. THE FUEL FOR THE SKULLCRUSHERS' ROCKET ENGINES. IT WAS SYNTHESIZED FROM THREE MAJOR COMPONENTS.
THERE'D BEEN BLACK-MARKET PURCHASES, HIJACKINGS, EVEN ACQUISITIONS THROUGH FRONT COMPANIES. IF I'D CHECKED...
TAKA TAKA TAKA TAKA TAKA TAKA TAKA
I COULD HAVE KNOWN. COULD HAVE FIGURED IT OUT.
MARELLA!
ARE YOU ALL --
I CAN'T -- I'M NOT STAYING! I'M --

TELL MRS. BANNERJEE I'M NOT *FEELING* WELL! I HAVE TO TAKE A *SICK DAY!*

BUT --

NOK NOK

MARELLA?

MOM MADE YOU SOME *SOUP* AND STUFF...

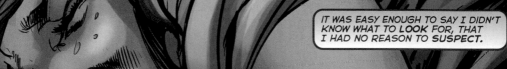

IT WAS EASY ENOUGH TO SAY I DIDN'T KNOW WHAT TO *LOOK* FOR, THAT I HAD NO REASON TO *SUSPECT.*

TELL THAT TO THOSE *CHILD WELFARE WORKERS.* TELL THAT TO THE REST OF THE DEAD. TO *ESME,* MAYBE.

I WAS GOING TO BE *FIRED.* OF COURSE I WAS.

I KNEW IT. I *DESERVED* IT. BUT --

IT WASN'T ENOUGH. IT COULDN'T BE ENOUGH. I COULDN'T JUST *LEAVE* IT LIKE THIS.

BEFORE THEY *FIRED* ME, I HAD TO DO SOMETHING.

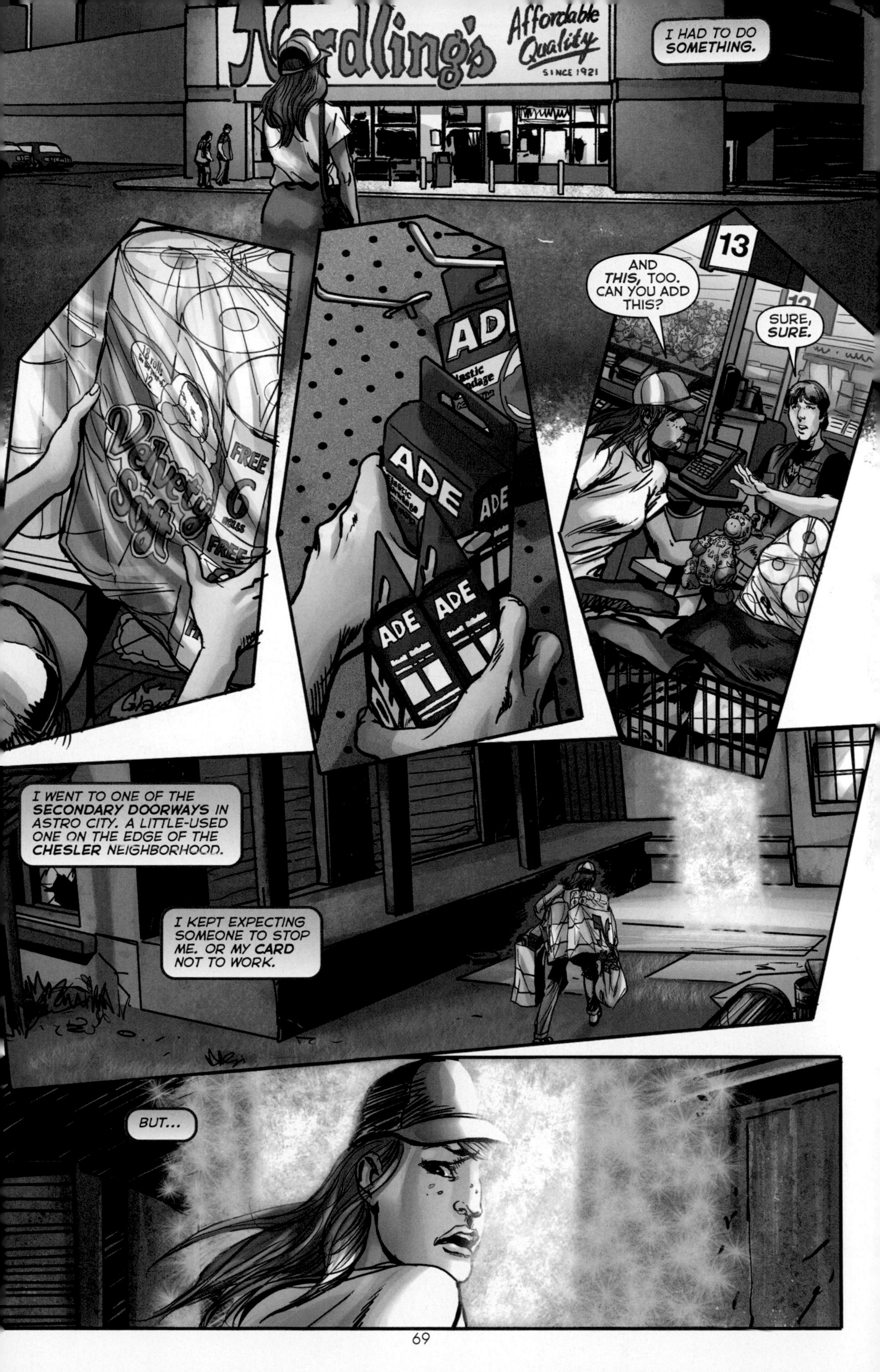
Nerdling's
Affordable Quality
SINCE 1921
I HAD TO DO SOMETHING.
AND THIS, TOO. CAN YOU ADD THIS?
SURE, SURE.
I WENT TO ONE OF THE SECONDARY DOORWAYS IN ASTRO CITY. A LITTLE-USED ONE ON THE EDGE OF THE CHESLER NEIGHBORHOOD.
I KEPT EXPECTING SOMEONE TO STOP ME. OR MY CARD NOT TO WORK.
BUT...

THE NEAREST DOORWAY IN ECUADOR WAS IN AZOGUES, ABOUT 40 MILES FROM QUEVACHI. I HAD A *WHOLE STORY* WORKED OUT --

I WAS ON A *STUDENT TRIP*, AND I HEARD ABOUT --

YOU BROUGHT TOILET PAPER. *TOILET PAPER.* OH, MY DEAR, YOU ARE A *GIFT* STRAIGHT FROM GOD.

TERESA! SHOW --

MARELLA.

SHOW MARELLA WHERE SHE CAN *BUNK IN*, AND GET HER ON A ROTATION.

FUNDACIÓN

EMERGENCÍA

AUG: 2011
COMIDA
PRECINCT JAP
AGUA POTABLE

AGUA POTABLE
CLÍNICA
0722654835

EMERGENCY RELIEF
COMIDA AGUA POTABLE CLÍNICA COMIDA

IT WAS THAT *SIMPLE.* THERE WERE SO MANY REFUGEES, THEY WERE *VERY* SHORT-HANDED.

BUT --

KHOOM KROOM

C41
C/41
C41

AHH! WHAT --

IT IS NOTHING -- DO NOT *WORRY* --

THE SKULLCRUSHERS HAD BEEN *BEATEN,* MOSTLY. BUT E.A.G.L.E. WAS STILL TRYING TO CRACK THEIR HEADQUARTERS.

AND THERE WERE *OTHERS,* AFTER THEIR EQUIPMENT --

THE PLUNDER SQUAD, OUT OF BELIZE. AGENTS OF THE BLACK MARKETEER AND THE CONTRABANDIT, WHO RE-SOLD HI-TECH ARMAMENTS WORLDWIDE.

AND I'D *STARTED* IT. BECAUSE A LITTLE GIRL WAS SCARED FOR HER *MOTHER,* AND I DIDN'T LISTEN WELL ENOUGH.

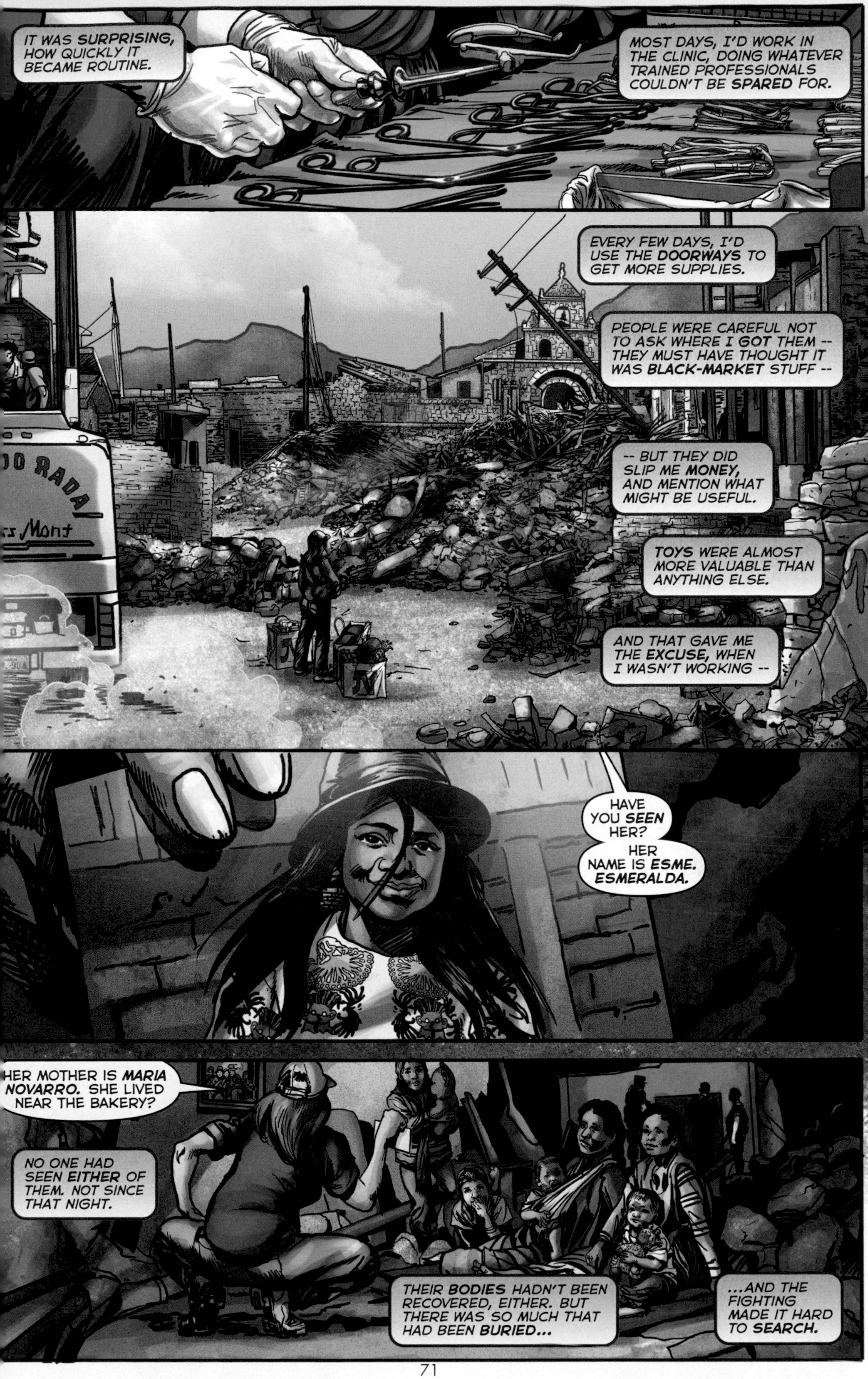
IT WAS SURPRISING, HOW QUICKLY IT BECAME ROUTINE.
MOST DAYS, I'D WORK IN THE CLINIC, DOING WHATEVER TRAINED PROFESSIONALS COULDN'T BE SPARED FOR.
EVERY FEW DAYS, I'D USE THE DOORWAYS TO GET MORE SUPPLIES.
PEOPLE WERE CAREFUL NOT TO ASK WHERE I GOT THEM -- THEY MUST HAVE THOUGHT IT WAS BLACK-MARKET STUFF --
-- BUT THEY DID SLIP ME MONEY, AND MENTION WHAT MIGHT BE USEFUL.
TOYS WERE ALMOST MORE VALUABLE THAN ANYTHING ELSE.
AND THAT GAVE ME THE EXCUSE, WHEN I WASN'T WORKING --
HAVE YOU SEEN HER?
HER NAME IS ESME. ESMERALDA.
HER MOTHER IS MARIA NOVARRO. SHE LIVED NEAR THE BAKERY?
NO ONE HAD SEEN EITHER OF THEM. NOT SINCE THAT NIGHT.
THEIR BODIES HADN'T BEEN RECOVERED, EITHER. BUT THERE WAS SO MUCH THAT HAD BEEN BURIED...
...AND THE FIGHTING MADE IT HARD TO SEARCH.

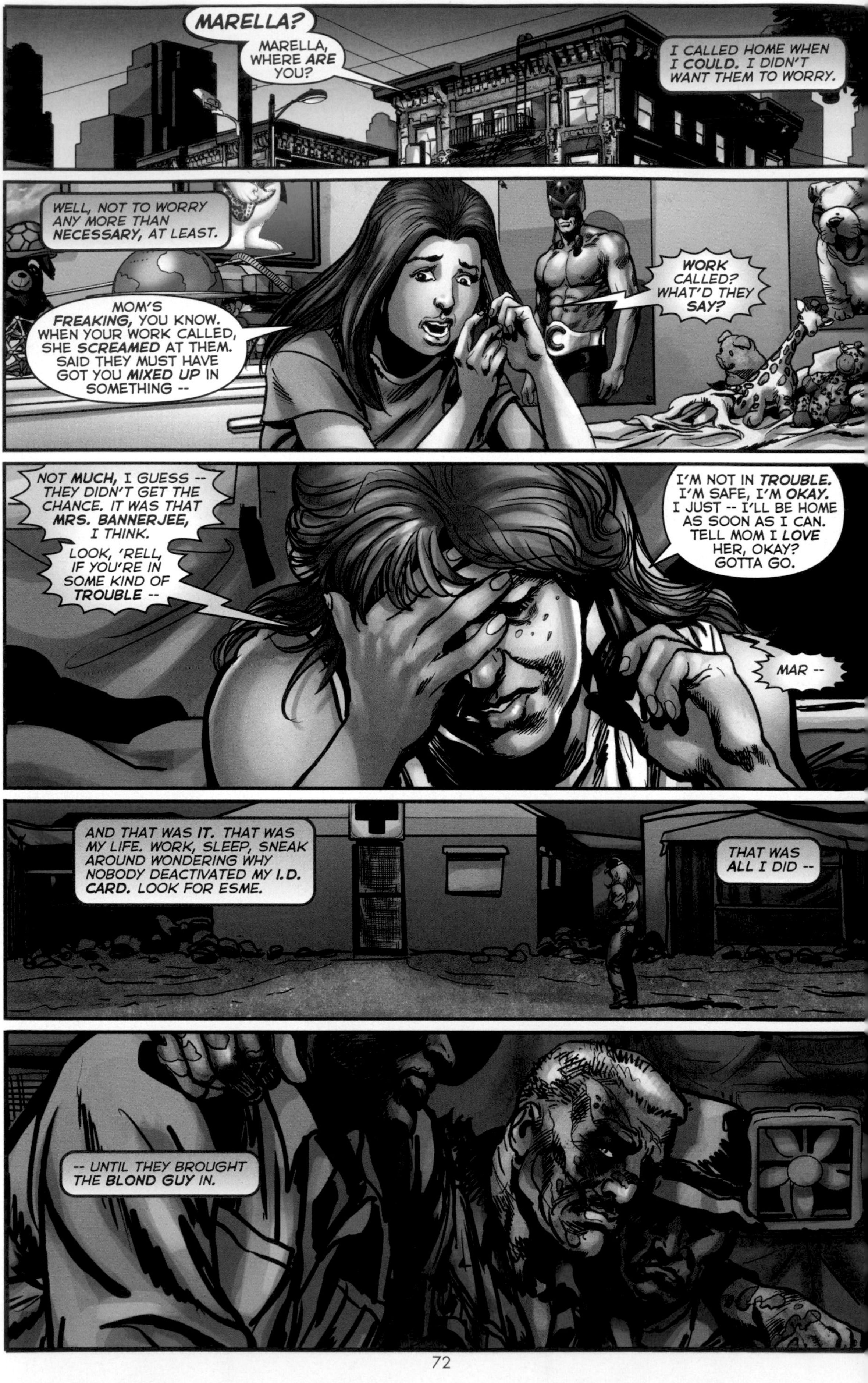
MARELLA?
MARELLA, WHERE ARE YOU?
I CALLED HOME WHEN I COULD. I DIDN'T WANT THEM TO WORRY.
WELL, NOT TO WORRY ANY MORE THAN NECESSARY, AT LEAST.
MOM'S FREAKING, YOU KNOW. WHEN YOUR WORK CALLED, SHE SCREAMED AT THEM. SAID THEY MUST HAVE GOT YOU MIXED UP IN SOMETHING --
WORK CALLED? WHAT'D THEY SAY?
NOT MUCH, I GUESS -- THEY DIDN'T GET THE CHANCE. IT WAS THAT MRS. BANNERJEE, I THINK.
LOOK, 'RELL, IF YOU'RE IN SOME KIND OF TROUBLE --
I'M NOT IN TROUBLE. I'M SAFE, I'M OKAY. I JUST -- I'LL BE HOME AS SOON AS I CAN. TELL MOM I LOVE HER, OKAY? GOTTA GO.
MAR --
AND THAT WAS IT. THAT WAS MY LIFE. WORK, SLEEP, SNEAK AROUND WONDERING WHY NOBODY DEACTIVATED MY I.D. CARD. LOOK FOR ESME.
THAT WAS ALL I DID --
-- UNTIL THEY BROUGHT THE BLOND GUY IN.

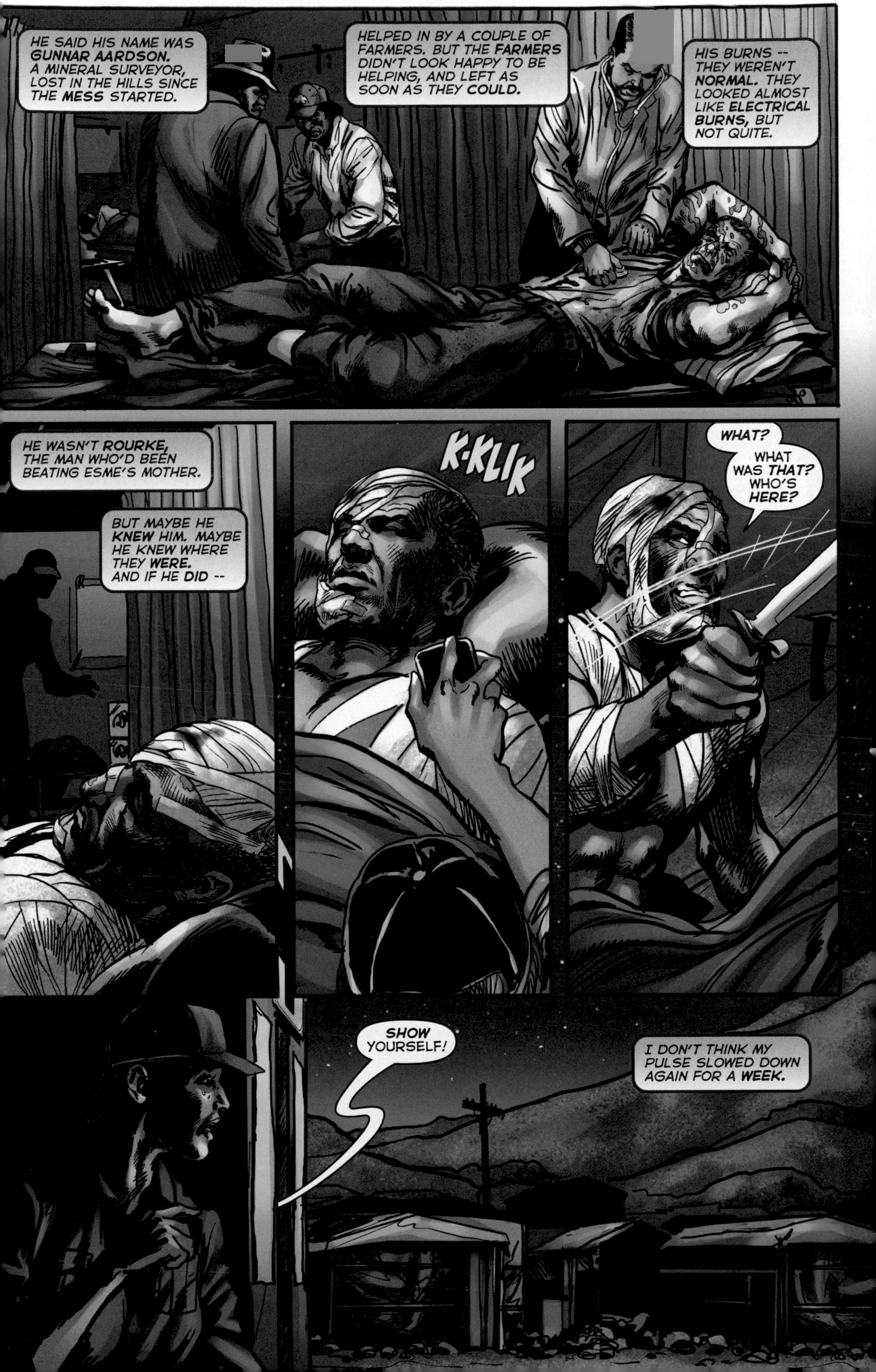
HE SAID HIS NAME WAS GUNNAR AARDSON. A MINERAL SURVEYOR, LOST IN THE HILLS SINCE THE MESS STARTED.
HELPED IN BY A COUPLE OF FARMERS. BUT THE FARMERS DIDN'T LOOK HAPPY TO BE HELPING, AND LEFT AS SOON AS THEY COULD.
HIS BURNS -- THEY WEREN'T NORMAL. THEY LOOKED ALMOST LIKE ELECTRICAL BURNS, BUT NOT QUITE.
HE WASN'T ROURKE, THE MAN WHO'D BEEN BEATING ESME'S MOTHER.
BUT MAYBE HE KNEW HIM. MAYBE HE KNEW WHERE THEY WERE. AND IF HE DID --
K-KLIK
WHAT?
WHAT WAS THAT? WHO'S HERE?
SHOW YOURSELF!
I DON'T THINK MY PULSE SLOWED DOWN AGAIN FOR A WEEK.

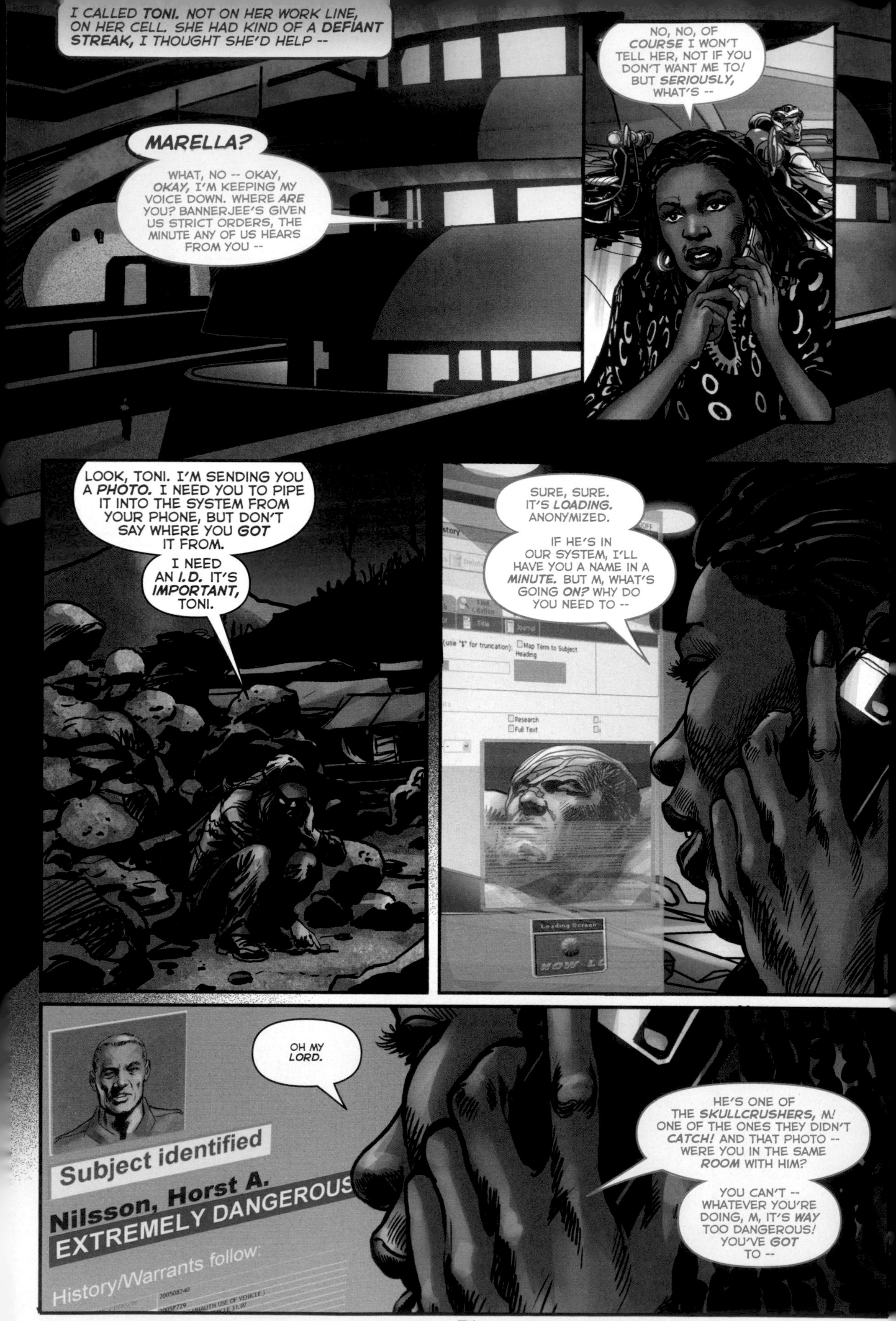

I CALLED **TONI.** NOT ON HER WORK LINE, ON HER CELL. SHE HAD KIND OF A **DEFIANT STREAK,** I THOUGHT SHE'D HELP --
MARELLA?
WHAT, NO -- OKAY, *OKAY,* I'M KEEPING MY VOICE DOWN. WHERE *ARE* YOU? BANNERJEE'S GIVEN US STRICT ORDERS, THE MINUTE ANY OF US HEARS FROM YOU --
NO, NO, OF *COURSE* I WON'T TELL HER, NOT IF YOU DON'T WANT ME TO! BUT *SERIOUSLY,* WHAT'S --
LOOK, TONI. I'M SENDING YOU A *PHOTO.* I NEED YOU TO PIPE IT INTO THE SYSTEM FROM YOUR PHONE, BUT DON'T SAY WHERE YOU *GOT* IT FROM.
I NEED AN *I.D.* IT'S *IMPORTANT,* TONI.
SURE, SURE. IT'S *LOADING.* ANONYMIZED.
IF HE'S IN OUR SYSTEM, I'LL HAVE YOU A NAME IN A *MINUTE.* BUT M, WHAT'S GOING *ON?* WHY DO YOU NEED TO --
(use "$" for truncation):
Map Term to Subject Heading
Research
Full Text
Loading Screen
Subject identified
Nilsson, Horst A.
EXTREMELY DANGEROUS
History/Warrants follow:
OH MY *LORD.*
HE'S ONE OF THE *SKULLCRUSHERS,* M! ONE OF THE ONES THEY DIDN'T *CATCH!* AND THAT PHOTO -- WERE YOU IN THE SAME *ROOM* WITH HIM?
YOU CAN'T -- WHATEVER YOU'RE DOING, M, IT'S *WAY* TOO DANGEROUS! YOU'VE *GOT* TO --

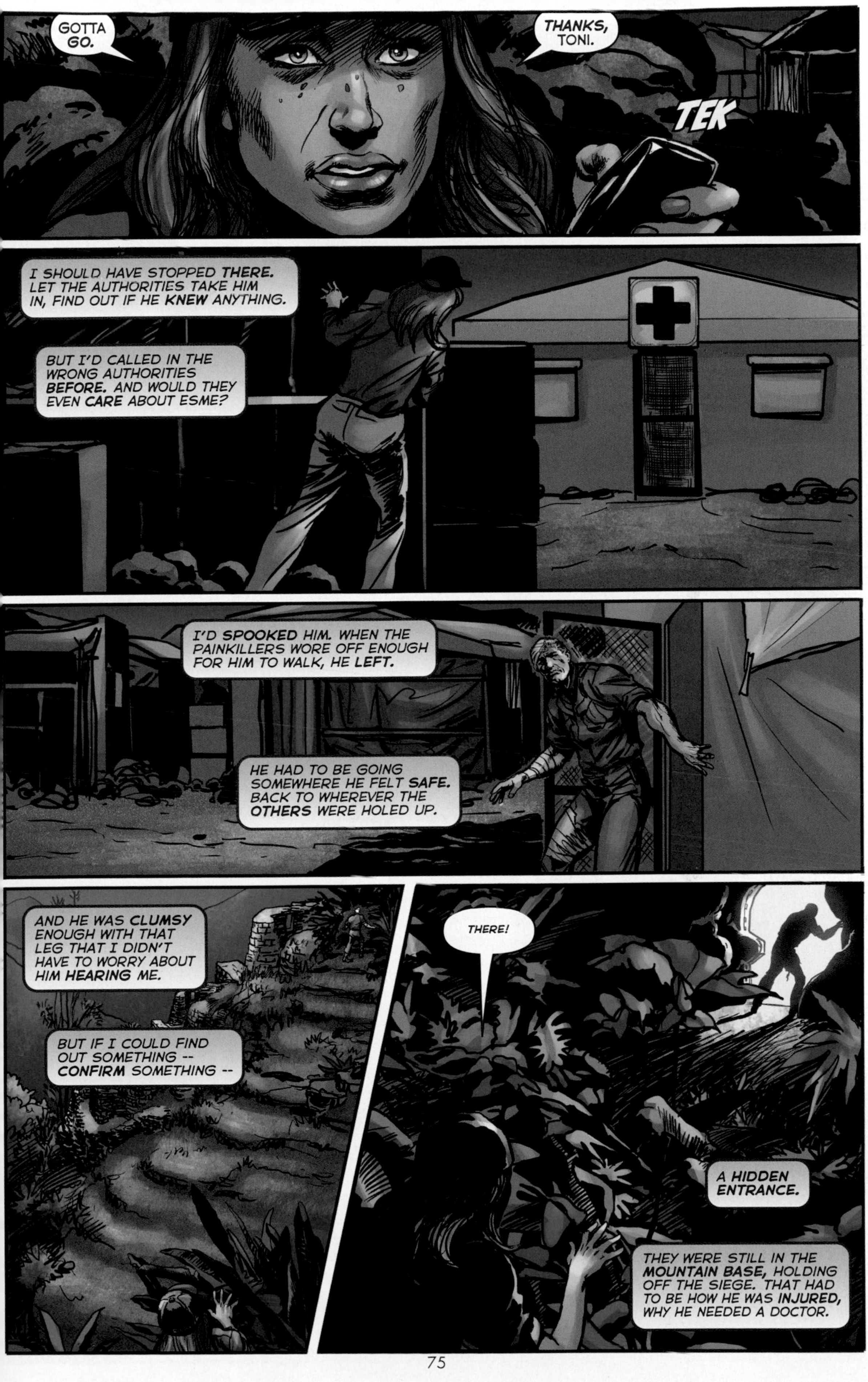
GOTTA GO.
THANKS, TONI.
TEK
I SHOULD HAVE STOPPED THERE. LET THE AUTHORITIES TAKE HIM IN, FIND OUT IF HE KNEW ANYTHING.
BUT I'D CALLED IN THE WRONG AUTHORITIES BEFORE. AND WOULD THEY EVEN CARE ABOUT ESME?
I'D SPOOKED HIM. WHEN THE PAINKILLERS WORE OFF ENOUGH FOR HIM TO WALK, HE LEFT.
HE HAD TO BE GOING SOMEWHERE HE FELT SAFE. BACK TO WHEREVER THE OTHERS WERE HOLED UP.
AND HE WAS CLUMSY ENOUGH WITH THAT LEG THAT I DIDN'T HAVE TO WORRY ABOUT HIM HEARING ME.
BUT IF I COULD FIND OUT SOMETHING -- CONFIRM SOMETHING --
THERE!
A HIDDEN ENTRANCE.
THEY WERE STILL IN THE MOUNTAIN BASE, HOLDING OFF THE SIEGE. THAT HAD TO BE HOW HE WAS INJURED, WHY HE NEEDED A DOCTOR.

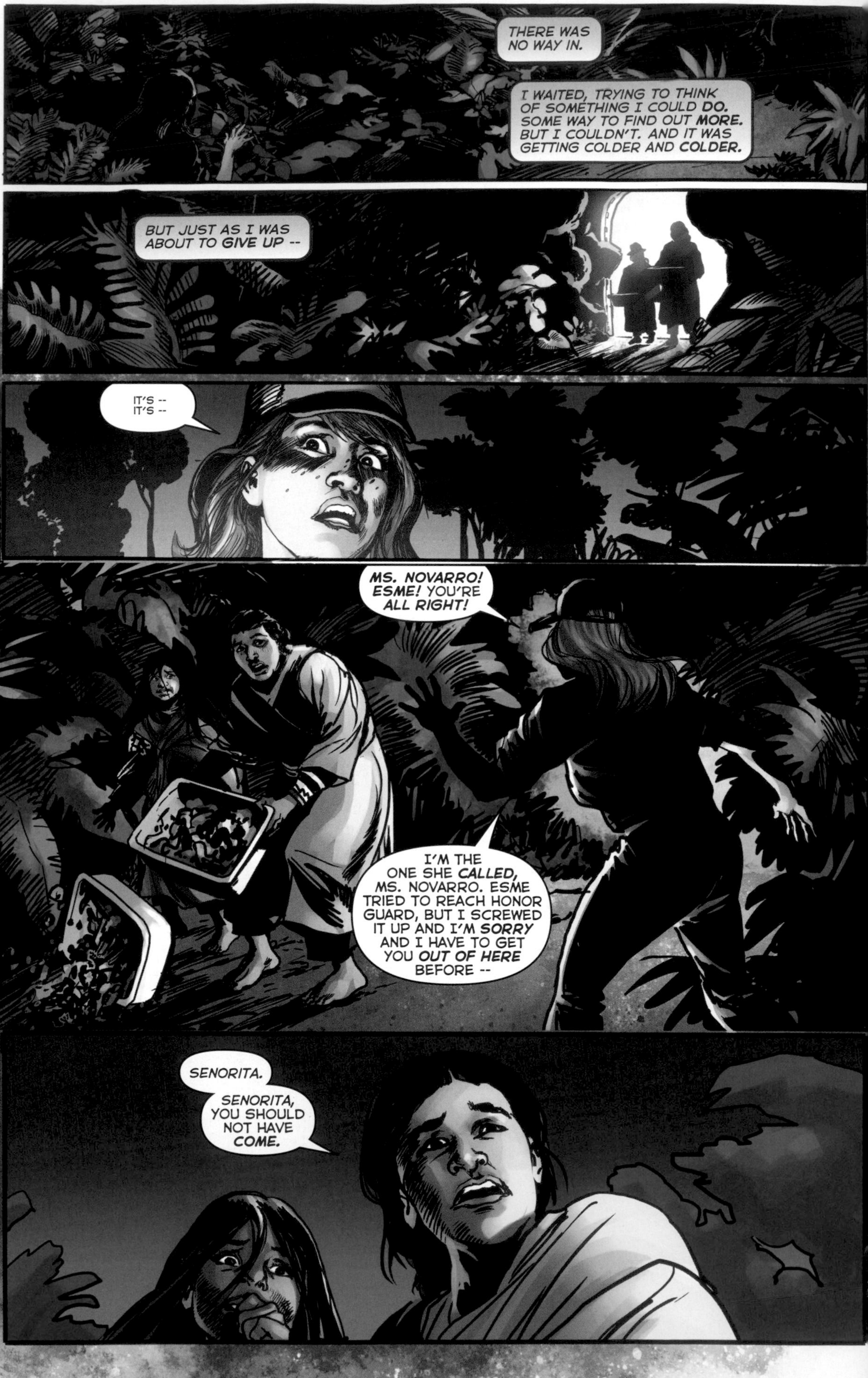
THERE WAS NO WAY IN.
I WAITED, TRYING TO THINK OF SOMETHING I COULD DO. SOME WAY TO FIND OUT MORE. BUT I COULDN'T. AND IT WAS GETTING COLDER AND COLDER.
BUT JUST AS I WAS ABOUT TO GIVE UP --
IT'S -- IT'S --
MS. NOVARRO! ESME! YOU'RE ALL RIGHT!
I'M THE ONE SHE CALLED, MS. NOVARRO. ESME TRIED TO REACH HONOR GUARD, BUT I SCREWED IT UP AND I'M SORRY AND I HAVE TO GET YOU OUT OF HERE BEFORE --
SENORITA.
SENORITA, YOU SHOULD NOT HAVE COME.

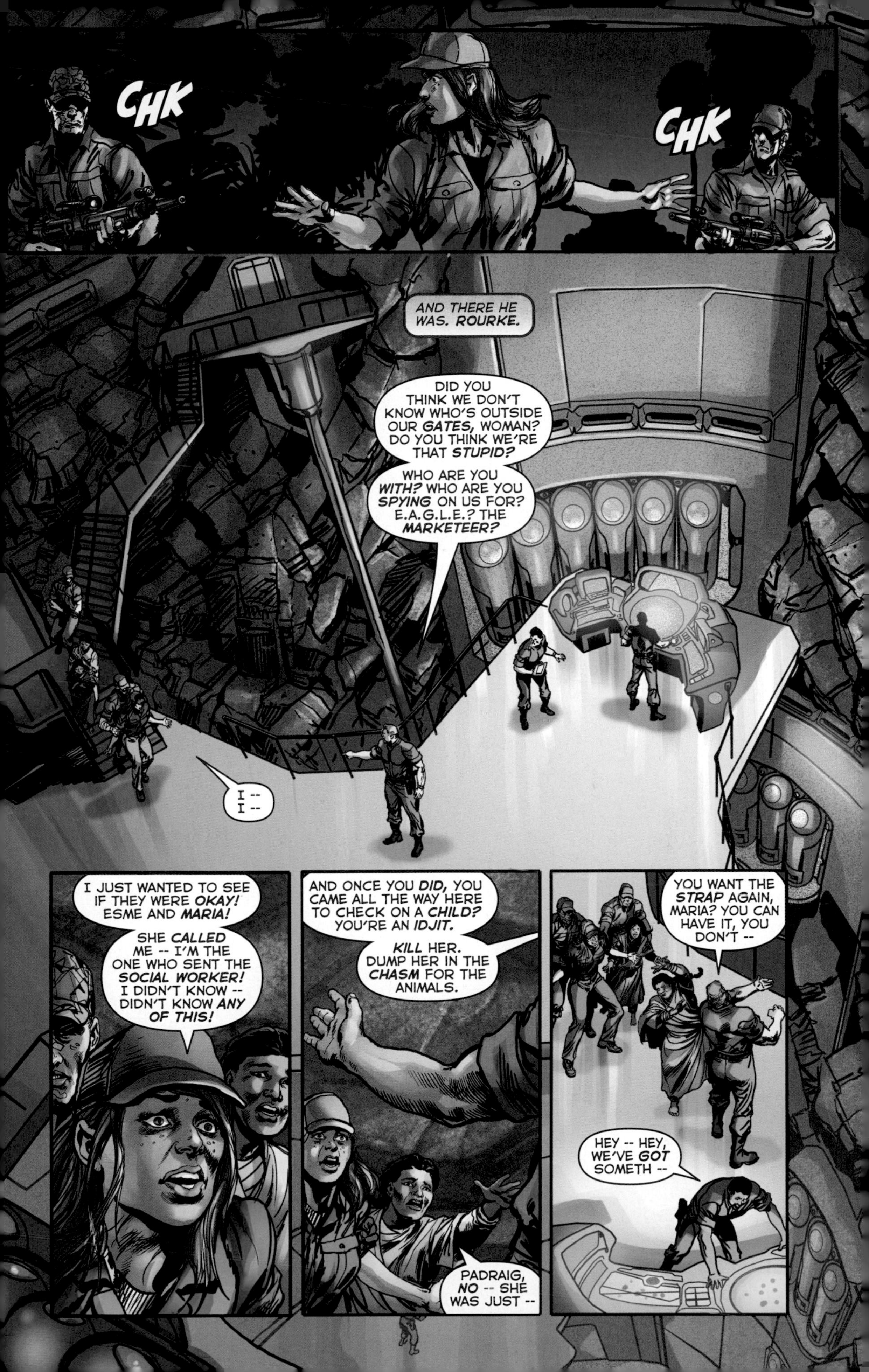
CHK
CHK
AND THERE HE WAS. ROURKE.
DID YOU THINK WE DON'T KNOW WHO'S OUTSIDE OUR GATES, WOMAN? DO YOU THINK WE'RE THAT STUPID?
WHO ARE YOU WITH? WHO ARE YOU SPYING ON US FOR? E.A.G.L.E.? THE MARKETEER?
I -- I --
I JUST WANTED TO SEE IF THEY WERE OKAY! ESME AND MARIA!
SHE CALLED ME -- I'M THE ONE WHO SENT THE SOCIAL WORKER! I DIDN'T KNOW -- DIDN'T KNOW ANY OF THIS!
AND ONCE YOU DID, YOU CAME ALL THE WAY HERE TO CHECK ON A CHILD? YOU'RE AN IDJIT.
KILL HER. DUMP HER IN THE CHASM FOR THE ANIMALS.
PADRAIG, NO -- SHE WAS JUST --
YOU WANT THE STRAP AGAIN, MARIA? YOU CAN HAVE IT, YOU DON'T --
HEY -- HEY, WE'VE GOT SOMETH --

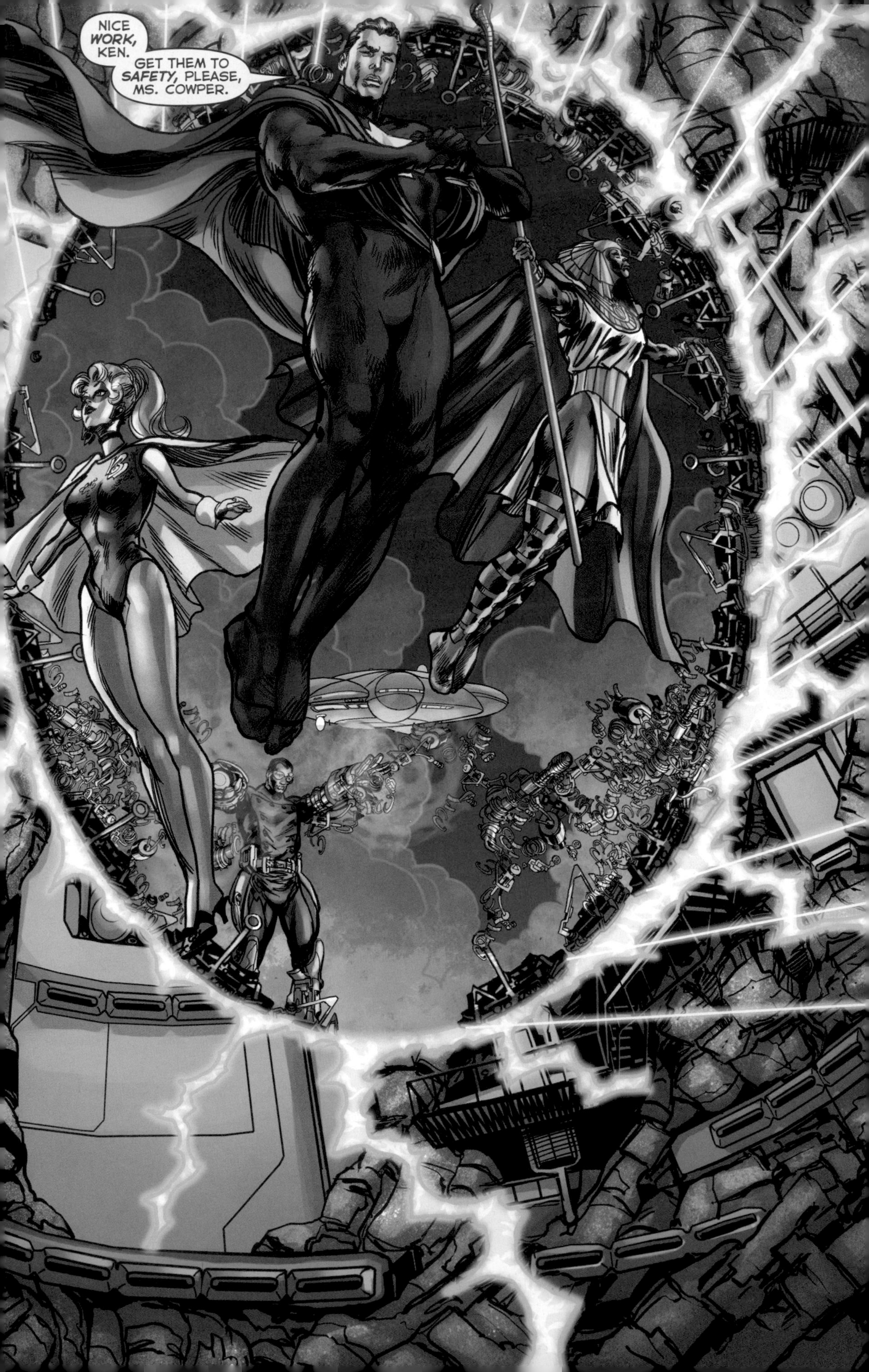
NICE WORK, KEN.
GET THEM TO SAFETY, PLEASE, MS. COWPER.

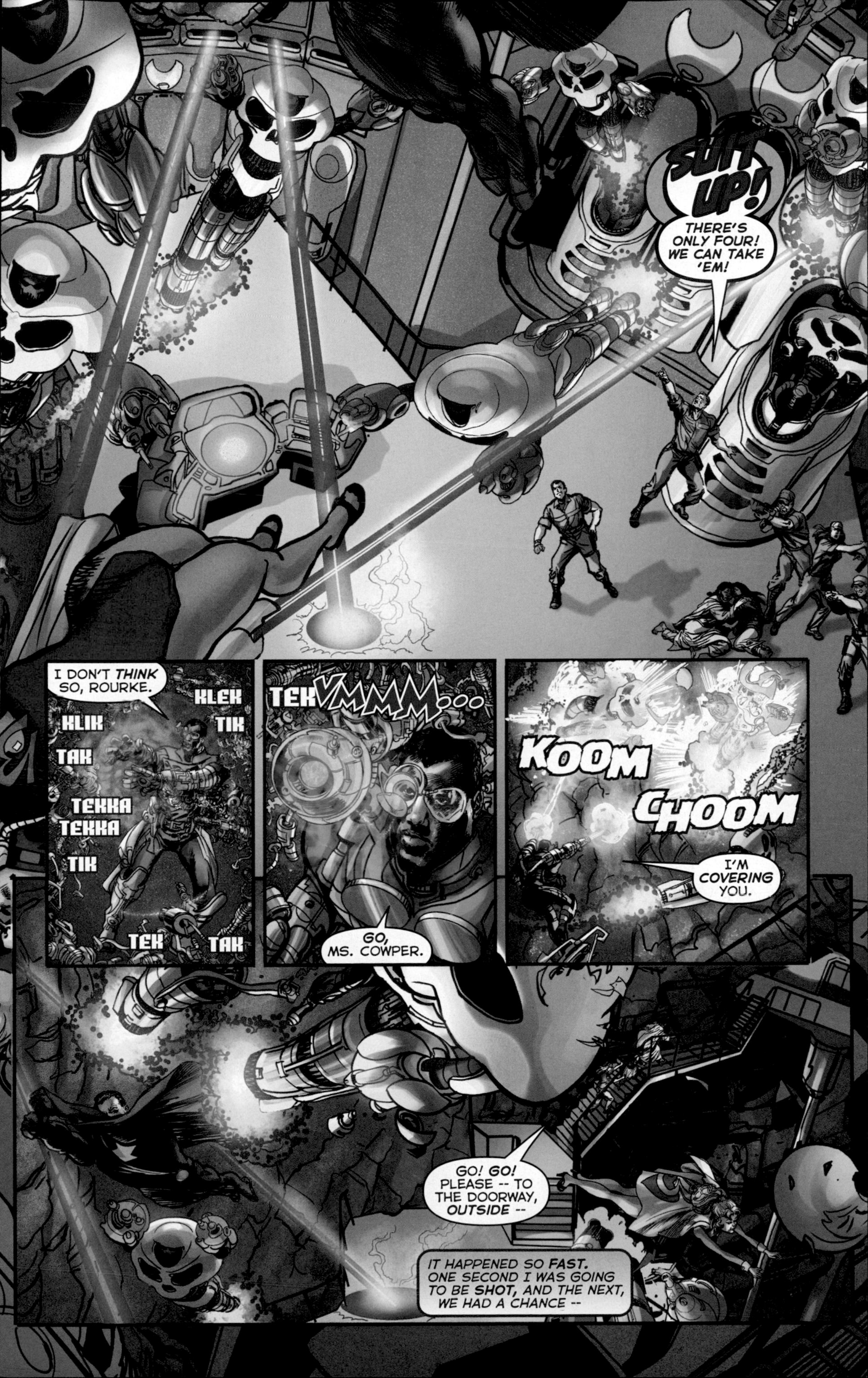
SUIT UP!
THERE'S ONLY FOUR! WE CAN TAKE 'EM!
I DON'T THINK SO, ROURKE.
KLEK
KLIK
TIK
TAK
TEKKA
TEKKA
TIK
TEK
TAK
TEKVMMM...
GO, MS. COWPER.
KOOM
CHOOM
I'M COVERING YOU.
GO! GO! PLEASE -- TO THE DOORWAY, OUTSIDE --
IT HAPPENED SO FAST. ONE SECOND I WAS GOING TO BE SHOT, AND THE NEXT, WE HAD A CHANCE --

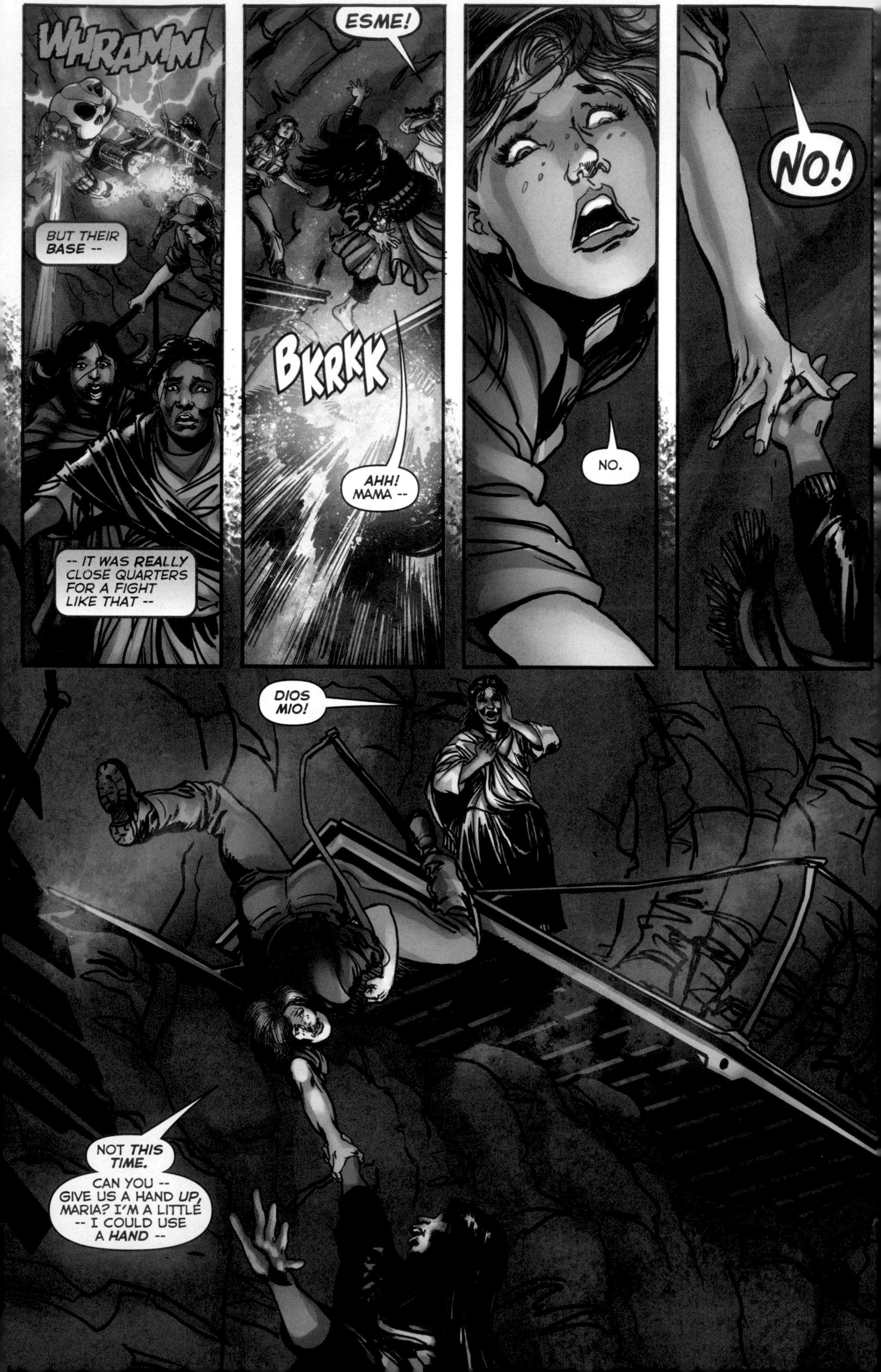
WHRAMM
BUT THEIR BASE --
-- IT WAS REALLY CLOSE QUARTERS FOR A FIGHT LIKE THAT --
ESME!
BKRKK
AHH! MAMA --
NO.
NO!
DIOS MIO!
NOT THIS TIME.
CAN YOU -- GIVE US A HAND UP, MARIA? I'M A LITTLE -- I COULD USE A HAND --

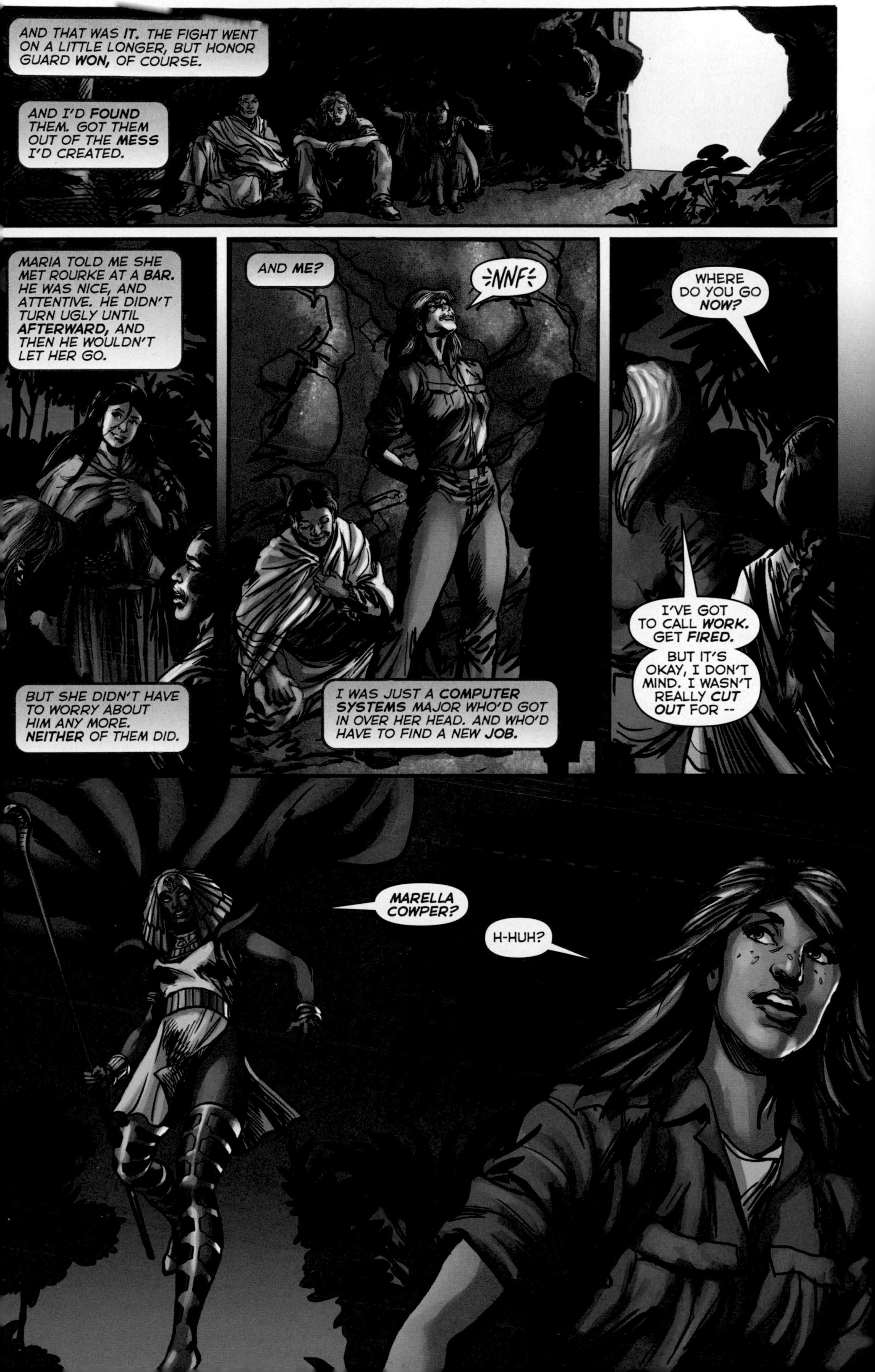
AND THAT WAS IT. THE FIGHT WENT ON A LITTLE LONGER, BUT HONOR GUARD WON, OF COURSE.
AND I'D FOUND THEM. GOT THEM OUT OF THE MESS I'D CREATED.
MARIA TOLD ME SHE MET ROURKE AT A BAR. HE WAS NICE, AND ATTENTIVE. HE DIDN'T TURN UGLY UNTIL AFTERWARD, AND THEN HE WOULDN'T LET HER GO.
BUT SHE DIDN'T HAVE TO WORRY ABOUT HIM ANY MORE. NEITHER OF THEM DID.
AND ME?
NNF
I WAS JUST A COMPUTER SYSTEMS MAJOR WHO'D GOT IN OVER HER HEAD. AND WHO'D HAVE TO FIND A NEW JOB.
WHERE DO YOU GO NOW?
I'VE GOT TO CALL WORK. GET FIRED.
BUT IT'S OKAY, I DON'T MIND. I WASN'T REALLY CUT OUT FOR --
MARELLA COWPER?
H-HUH?

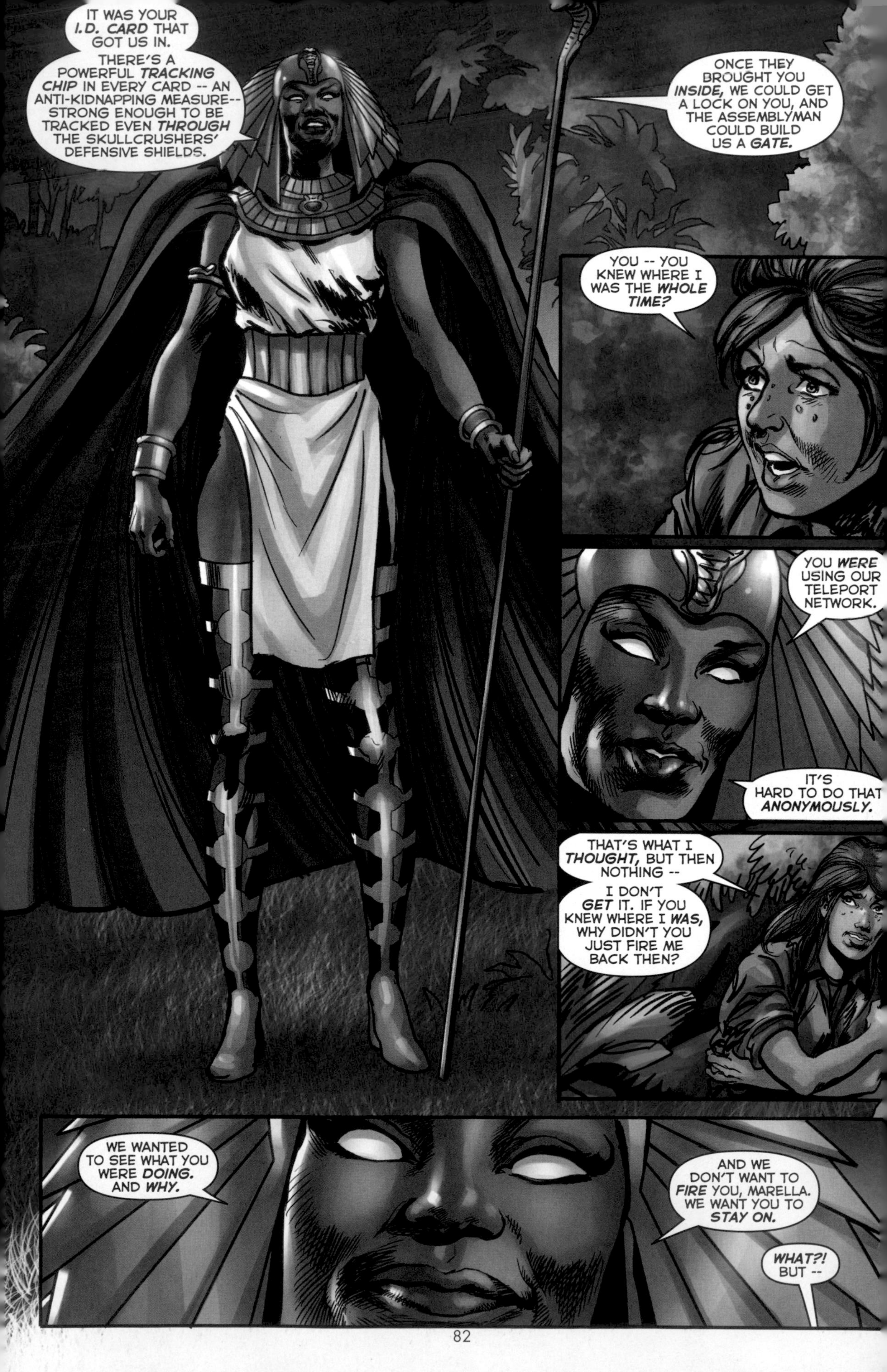
IT WAS YOUR I.D. CARD THAT GOT US IN.
THERE'S A POWERFUL TRACKING CHIP IN EVERY CARD -- AN ANTI-KIDNAPPING MEASURE-- STRONG ENOUGH TO BE TRACKED EVEN THROUGH THE SKULLCRUSHERS' DEFENSIVE SHIELDS.
ONCE THEY BROUGHT YOU INSIDE, WE COULD GET A LOCK ON YOU, AND THE ASSEMBLYMAN COULD BUILD US A GATE.
YOU -- YOU KNEW WHERE I WAS THE WHOLE TIME?
YOU WERE USING OUR TELEPORT NETWORK.
IT'S HARD TO DO THAT ANONYMOUSLY.
THAT'S WHAT I THOUGHT, BUT THEN NOTHING --
I DON'T GET IT. IF YOU KNEW WHERE I WAS, WHY DIDN'T YOU JUST FIRE ME BACK THEN?
WE WANTED TO SEE WHAT YOU WERE DOING. AND WHY.
AND WE DON'T WANT TO FIRE YOU, MARELLA. WE WANT YOU TO STAY ON.
WHAT?! BUT --

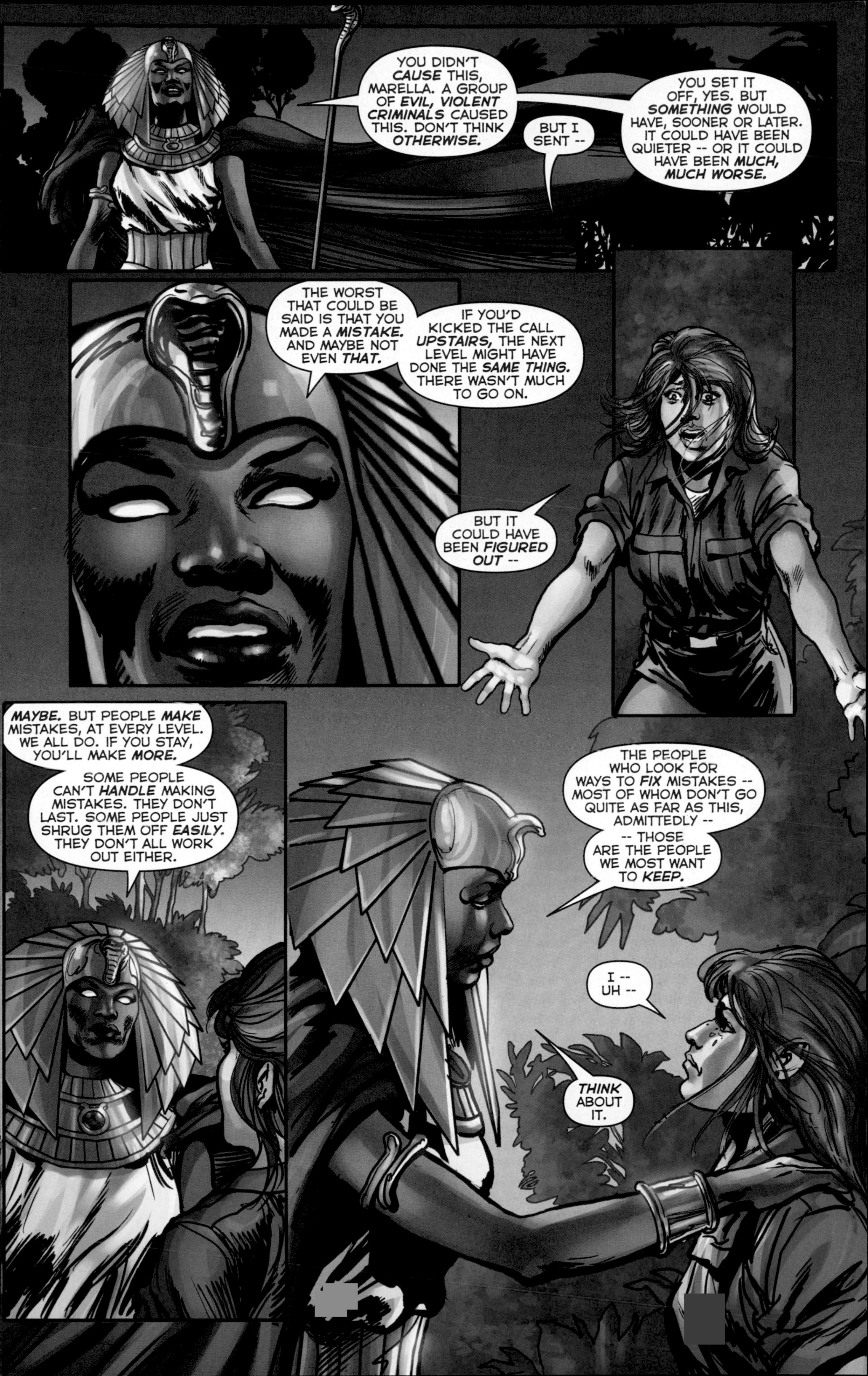
YOU DIDN'T CAUSE THIS, MARELLA. A GROUP OF EVIL, VIOLENT CRIMINALS CAUSED THIS. DON'T THINK OTHERWISE.
BUT I SENT --
YOU SET IT OFF, YES. BUT SOMETHING WOULD HAVE, SOONER OR LATER. IT COULD HAVE BEEN QUIETER -- OR IT COULD HAVE BEEN MUCH, MUCH WORSE.
THE WORST THAT COULD BE SAID IS THAT YOU MADE A MISTAKE. AND MAYBE NOT EVEN THAT.
IF YOU'D KICKED THE CALL UPSTAIRS, THE NEXT LEVEL MIGHT HAVE DONE THE SAME THING. THERE WASN'T MUCH TO GO ON.
BUT IT COULD HAVE BEEN FIGURED OUT --
MAYBE. BUT PEOPLE MAKE MISTAKES, AT EVERY LEVEL. WE ALL DO. IF YOU STAY, YOU'LL MAKE MORE.
SOME PEOPLE CAN'T HANDLE MAKING MISTAKES. THEY DON'T LAST. SOME PEOPLE JUST SHRUG THEM OFF EASILY. THEY DON'T ALL WORK OUT EITHER.
THE PEOPLE WHO LOOK FOR WAYS TO FIX MISTAKES -- MOST OF WHOM DON'T GO QUITE AS FAR AS THIS, ADMITTEDLY --
-- THOSE ARE THE PEOPLE WE MOST WANT TO KEEP.
I -- UH --
THINK ABOUT IT.

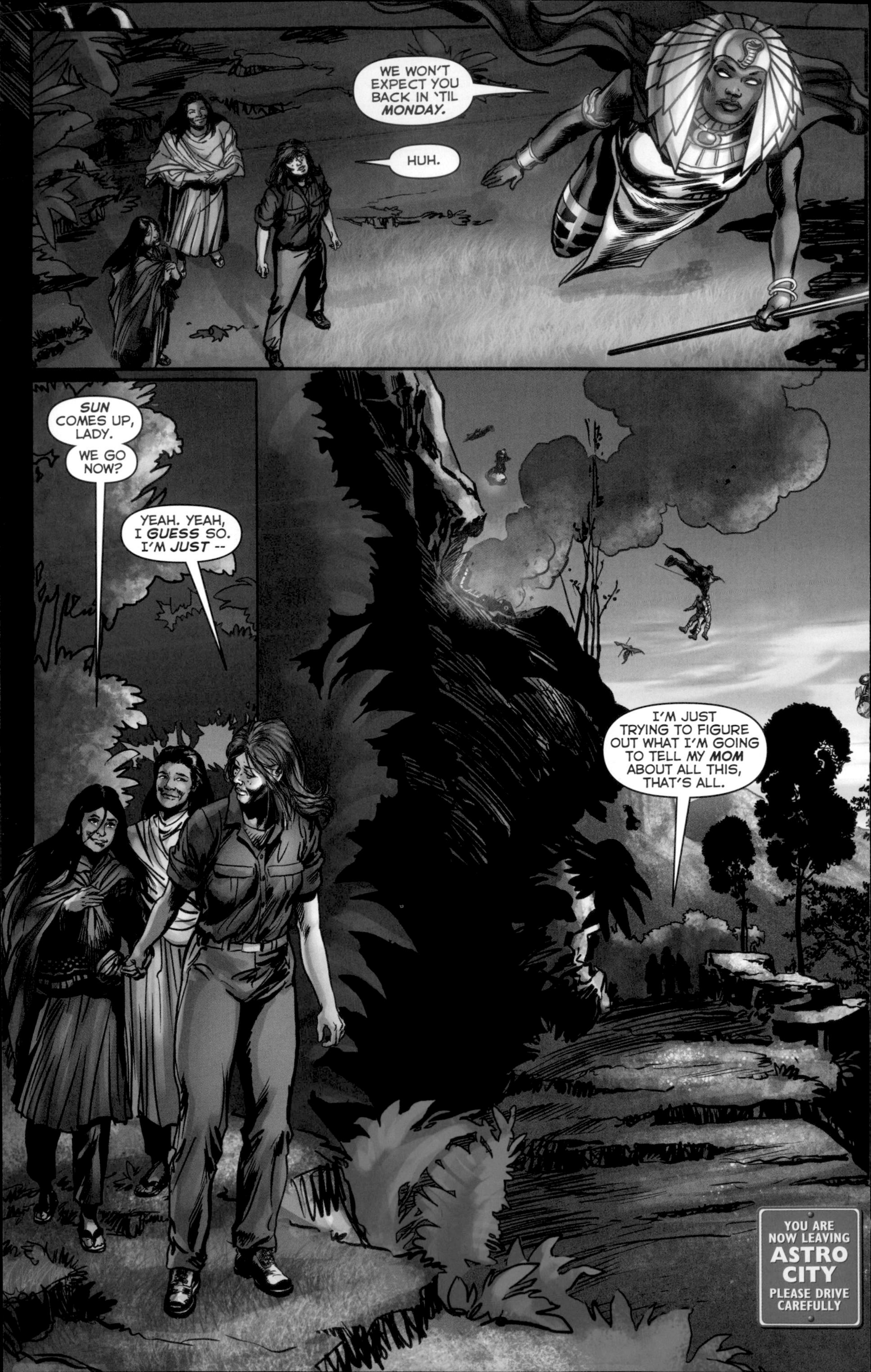
WE WON'T EXPECT YOU BACK IN 'TIL MONDAY.
HUH.
SUN COMES UP, LADY.
WE GO NOW?
YEAH. YEAH, I GUESS SO. I'M JUST --
I'M JUST TRYING TO FIGURE OUT WHAT I'M GOING TO TELL MY MOM ABOUT ALL THIS, THAT'S ALL.
YOU ARE NOW LEAVING ASTRO CITY PLEASE DRIVE CAREFULLY

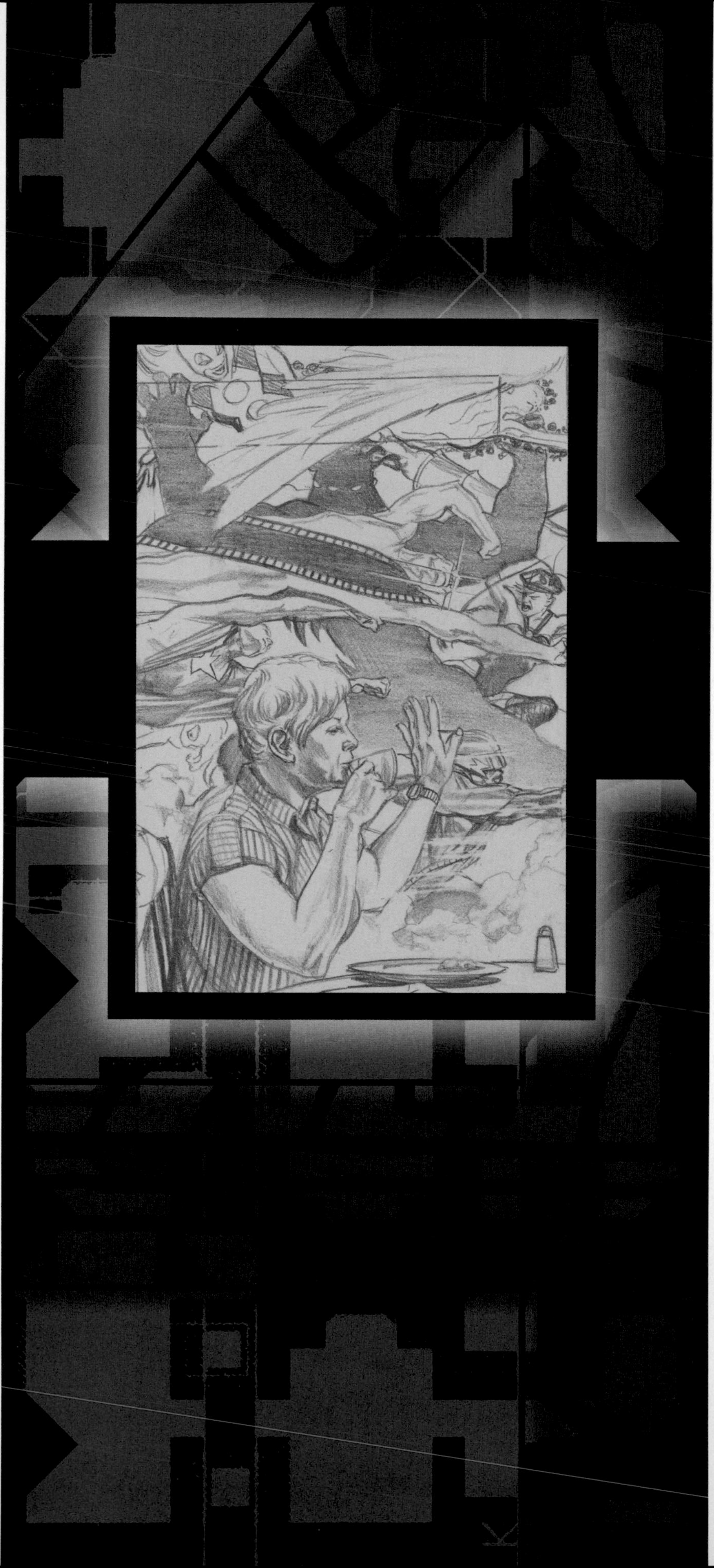

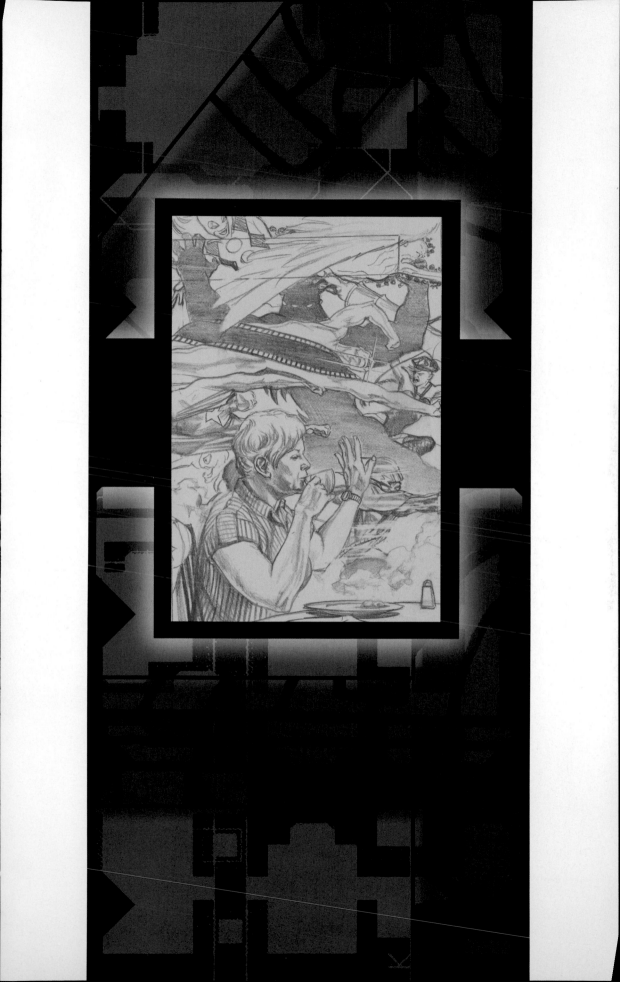

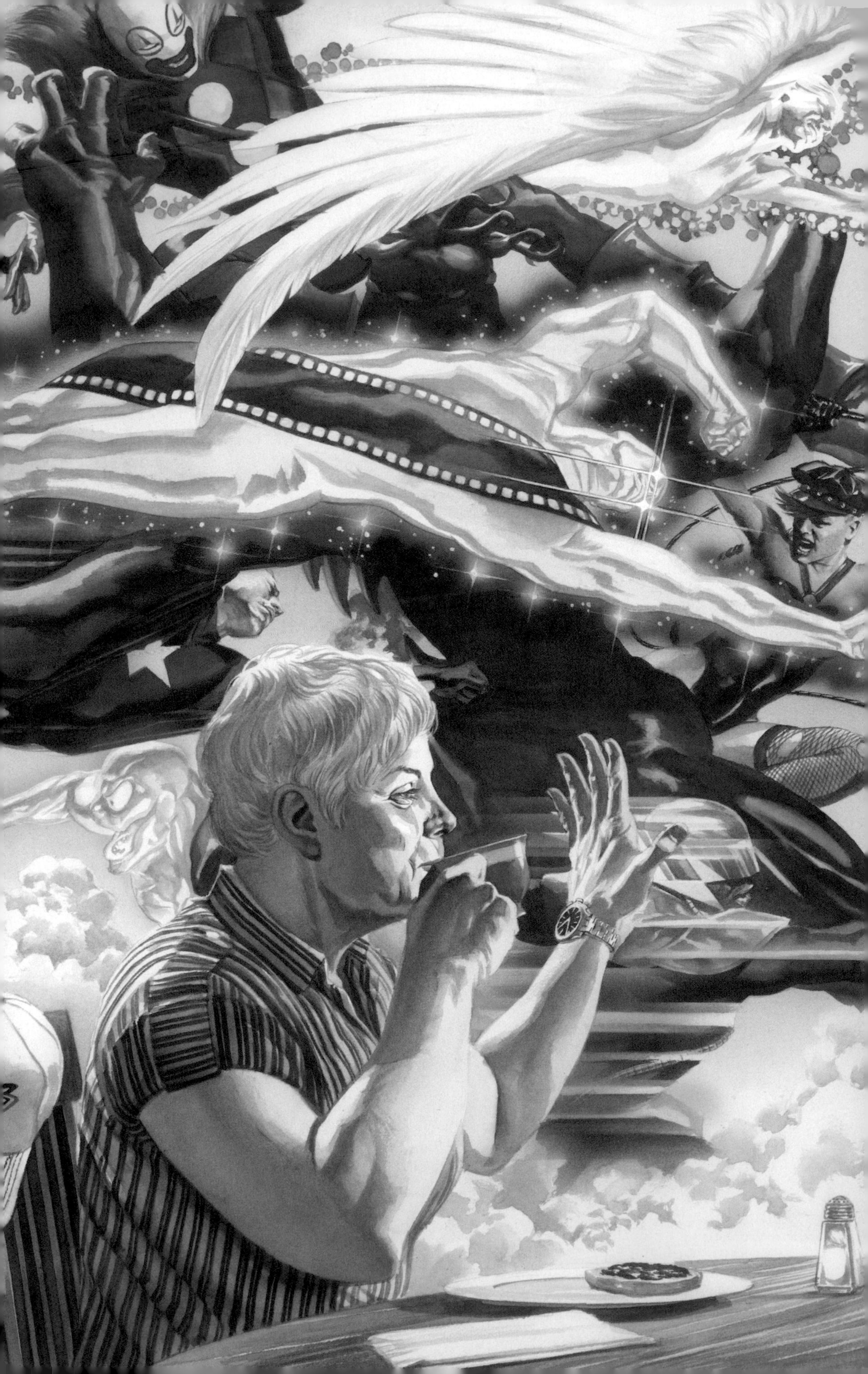

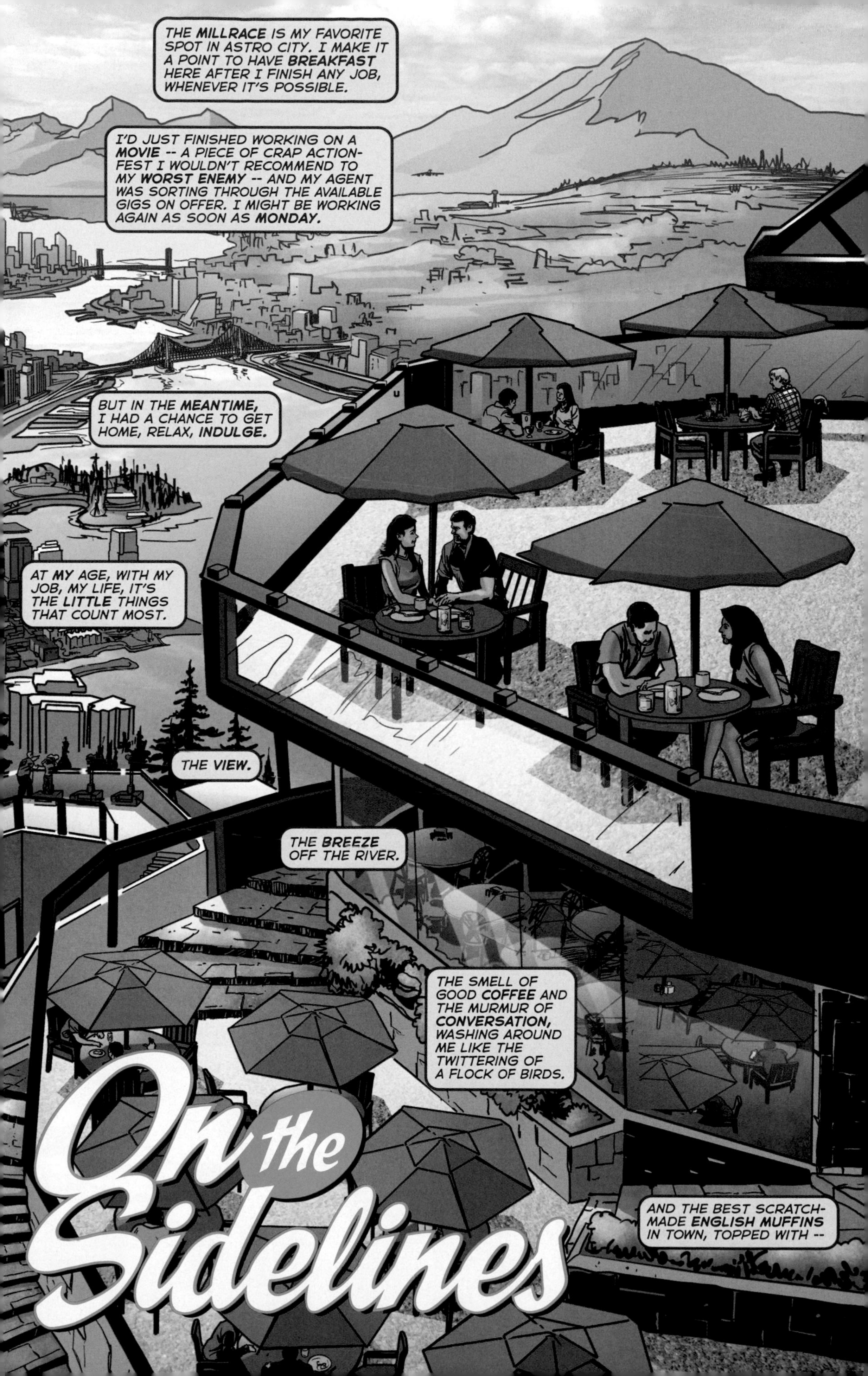
THE MILLRACE IS MY FAVORITE SPOT IN ASTRO CITY. I MAKE IT A POINT TO HAVE BREAKFAST HERE AFTER I FINISH ANY JOB, WHENEVER IT'S POSSIBLE.
I'D JUST FINISHED WORKING ON A MOVIE -- A PIECE OF CRAP ACTION-FEST I WOULDN'T RECOMMEND TO MY WORST ENEMY -- AND MY AGENT WAS SORTING THROUGH THE AVAILABLE GIGS ON OFFER. I MIGHT BE WORKING AGAIN AS SOON AS MONDAY.
BUT IN THE MEANTIME, I HAD A CHANCE TO GET HOME, RELAX, INDULGE.
AT MY AGE, WITH MY JOB, MY LIFE, IT'S THE LITTLE THINGS THAT COUNT MOST.
THE VIEW.
THE BREEZE OFF THE RIVER.
THE SMELL OF GOOD COFFEE AND THE MURMUR OF CONVERSATION, WASHING AROUND ME LIKE THE TWITTERING OF A FLOCK OF BIRDS.
On the Sidelines
AND THE BEST SCRATCH-MADE ENGLISH MUFFINS IN TOWN, TOPPED WITH --

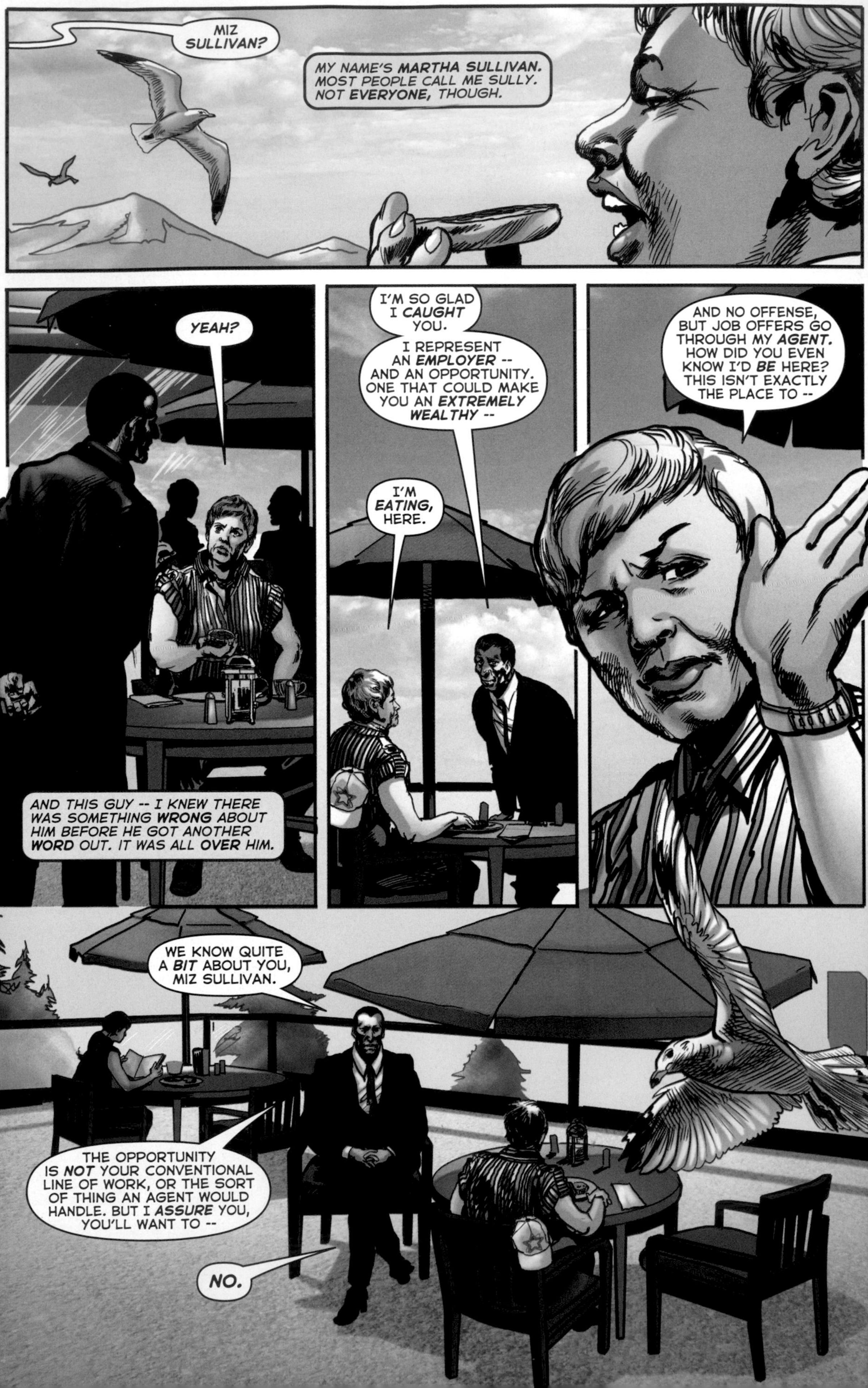
MIZ SULLIVAN?
MY NAME'S MARTHA SULLIVAN. MOST PEOPLE CALL ME SULLY. NOT EVERYONE, THOUGH.
YEAH?
AND THIS GUY -- I KNEW THERE WAS SOMETHING WRONG ABOUT HIM BEFORE HE GOT ANOTHER WORD OUT. IT WAS ALL OVER HIM.
I'M SO GLAD I CAUGHT YOU.
I REPRESENT AN EMPLOYER -- AND AN OPPORTUNITY. ONE THAT COULD MAKE YOU AN EXTREMELY WEALTHY --
I'M EATING, HERE.
AND NO OFFENSE, BUT JOB OFFERS GO THROUGH MY AGENT. HOW DID YOU EVEN KNOW I'D BE HERE? THIS ISN'T EXACTLY THE PLACE TO --
WE KNOW QUITE A BIT ABOUT YOU, MIZ SULLIVAN.
THE OPPORTUNITY IS NOT YOUR CONVENTIONAL LINE OF WORK, OR THE SORT OF THING AN AGENT WOULD HANDLE. BUT I ASSURE YOU, YOU'LL WANT TO --
NO.

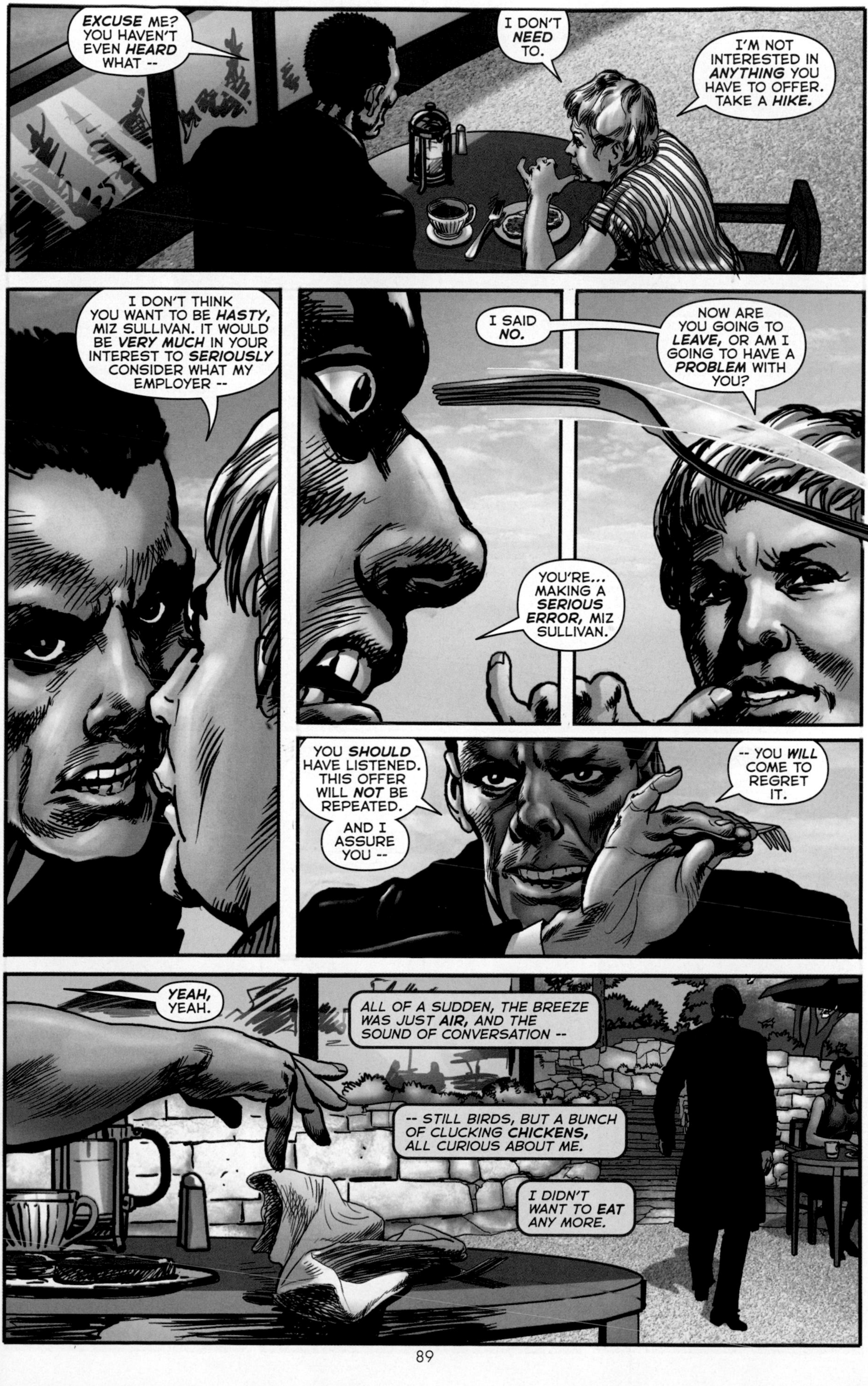
EXCUSE ME? YOU HAVEN'T EVEN HEARD WHAT --
I DON'T NEED TO.
I'M NOT INTERESTED IN ANYTHING YOU HAVE TO OFFER. TAKE A HIKE.
I DON'T THINK YOU WANT TO BE HASTY, MIZ SULLIVAN. IT WOULD BE VERY MUCH IN YOUR INTEREST TO SERIOUSLY CONSIDER WHAT MY EMPLOYER --
I SAID NO.
NOW ARE YOU GOING TO LEAVE, OR AM I GOING TO HAVE A PROBLEM WITH YOU?
YOU'RE... MAKING A SERIOUS ERROR, MIZ SULLIVAN.
YOU SHOULD HAVE LISTENED. THIS OFFER WILL NOT BE REPEATED.
AND I ASSURE YOU --
-- YOU WILL COME TO REGRET IT.
YEAH, YEAH.
ALL OF A SUDDEN, THE BREEZE WAS JUST AIR, AND THE SOUND OF CONVERSATION --
-- STILL BIRDS, BUT A BUNCH OF CLUCKING CHICKENS, ALL CURIOUS ABOUT ME.
I DIDN'T WANT TO EAT ANY MORE.

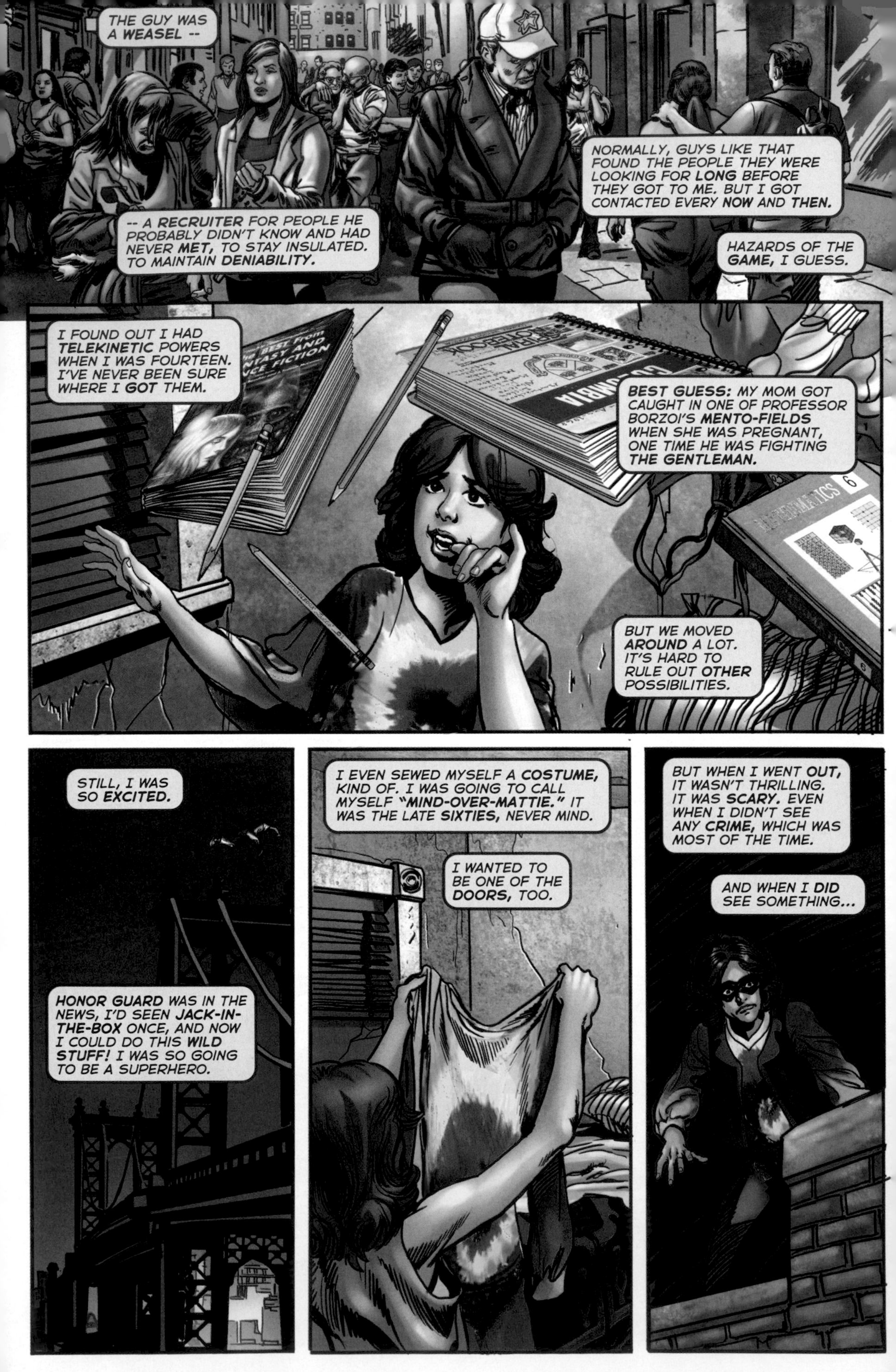
THE GUY WAS A WEASEL --
-- A RECRUITER FOR PEOPLE HE PROBABLY DIDN'T KNOW AND HAD NEVER MET, TO STAY INSULATED. TO MAINTAIN DENIABILITY.
NORMALLY, GUYS LIKE THAT FOUND THE PEOPLE THEY WERE LOOKING FOR LONG BEFORE THEY GOT TO ME. BUT I GOT CONTACTED EVERY NOW AND THEN.
HAZARDS OF THE GAME, I GUESS.
I FOUND OUT I HAD TELEKINETIC POWERS WHEN I WAS FOURTEEN. I'VE NEVER BEEN SURE WHERE I GOT THEM.
BEST GUESS: MY MOM GOT CAUGHT IN ONE OF PROFESSOR BORZOI'S MENTO-FIELDS WHEN SHE WAS PREGNANT, ONE TIME HE WAS FIGHTING THE GENTLEMAN.
BUT WE MOVED AROUND A LOT. IT'S HARD TO RULE OUT OTHER POSSIBILITIES.
STILL, I WAS SO EXCITED.
HONOR GUARD WAS IN THE NEWS, I'D SEEN JACK-IN-THE-BOX ONCE, AND NOW I COULD DO THIS WILD STUFF! I WAS SO GOING TO BE A SUPERHERO.
I EVEN SEWED MYSELF A COSTUME, KIND OF. I WAS GOING TO CALL MYSELF "MIND-OVER-MATTIE." IT WAS THE LATE SIXTIES, NEVER MIND.
I WANTED TO BE ONE OF THE DOORS, TOO.
BUT WHEN I WENT OUT, IT WASN'T THRILLING. IT WAS SCARY. EVEN WHEN I DIDN'T SEE ANY CRIME, WHICH WAS MOST OF THE TIME.
AND WHEN I DID SEE SOMETHING...

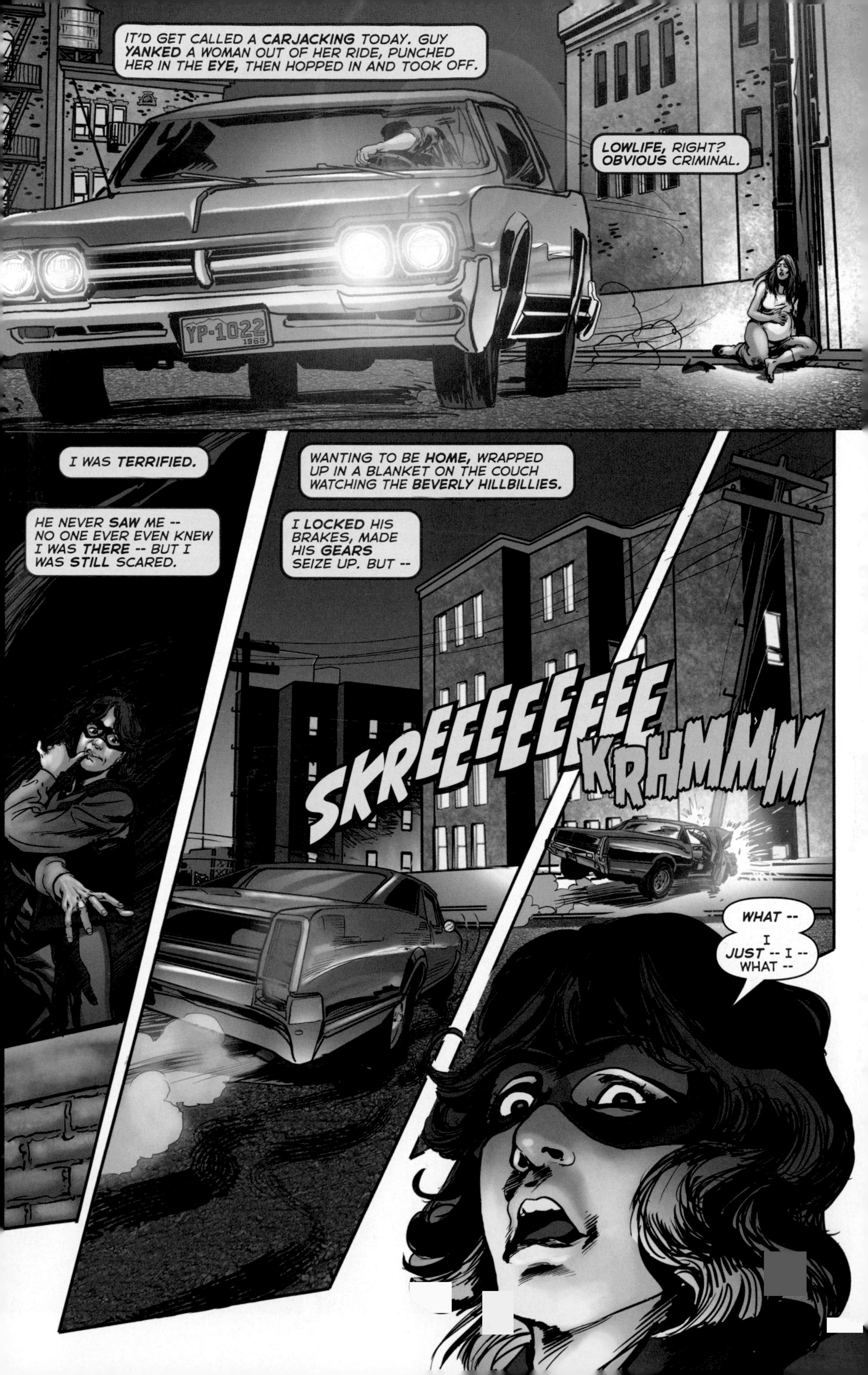
IT'D GET CALLED A CARJACKING TODAY. GUY YANKED A WOMAN OUT OF HER RIDE, PUNCHED HER IN THE EYE, THEN HOPPED IN AND TOOK OFF.
YP-1022
1968
LOWLIFE, RIGHT? OBVIOUS CRIMINAL.
I WAS TERRIFIED.
HE NEVER SAW ME -- NO ONE EVER EVEN KNEW I WAS THERE -- BUT I WAS STILL SCARED.
WANTING TO BE HOME, WRAPPED UP IN A BLANKET ON THE COUCH WATCHING THE BEVERLY HILLBILLIES.
I LOCKED HIS BRAKES, MADE HIS GEARS SEIZE UP. BUT --
SKREEEEEEEEEE
KRHMMMM
WHAT --
I JUST -- I -- WHAT --

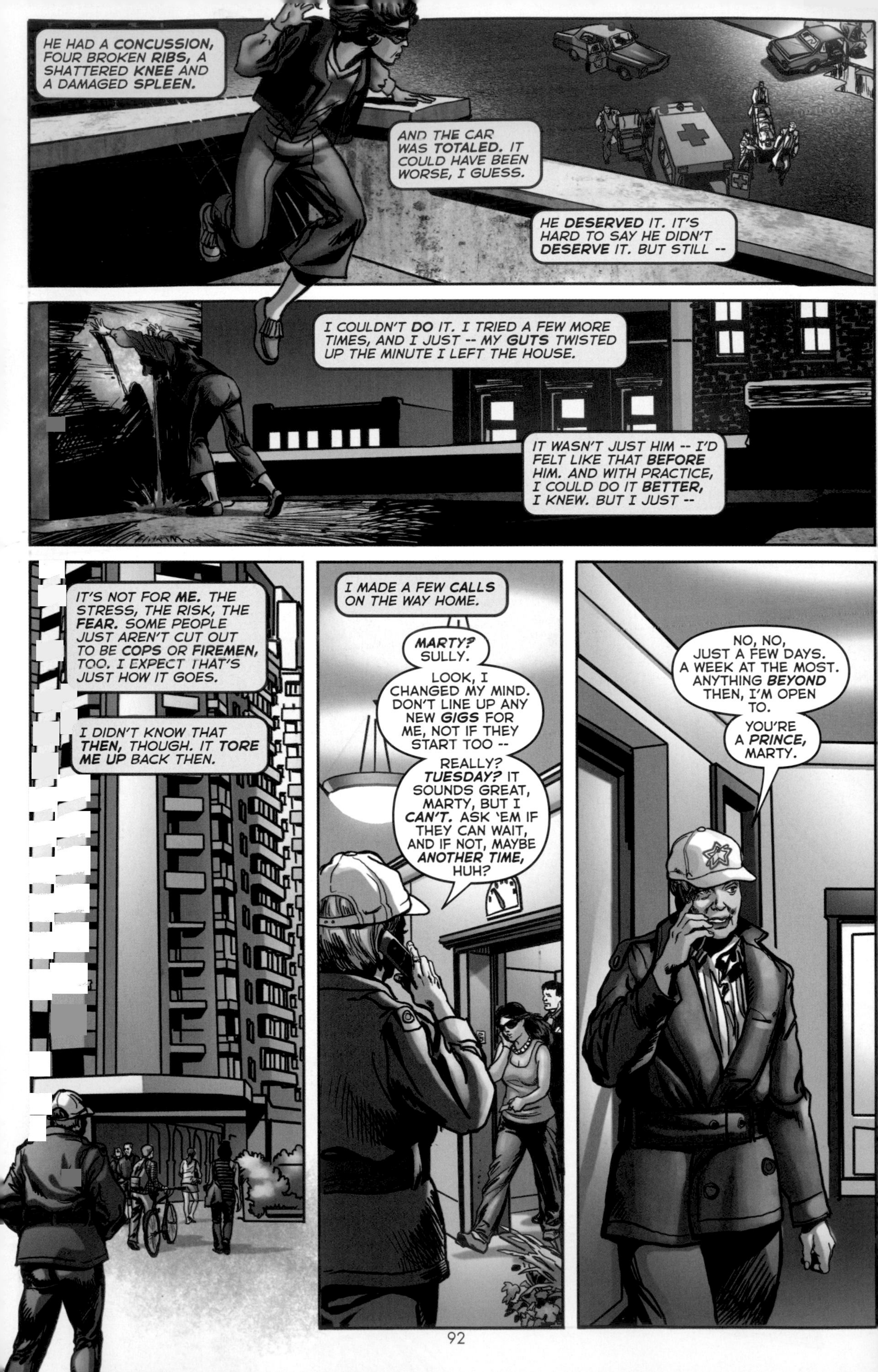
HE HAD A CONCUSSION, FOUR BROKEN RIBS, A SHATTERED KNEE AND A DAMAGED SPLEEN.
AND THE CAR WAS TOTALED. IT COULD HAVE BEEN WORSE, I GUESS.
HE DESERVED IT. IT'S HARD TO SAY HE DIDN'T DESERVE IT. BUT STILL --
I COULDN'T DO IT. I TRIED A FEW MORE TIMES, AND I JUST -- MY GUTS TWISTED UP THE MINUTE I LEFT THE HOUSE.
IT WASN'T JUST HIM -- I'D FELT LIKE THAT BEFORE HIM. AND WITH PRACTICE, I COULD DO IT BETTER, I KNEW. BUT I JUST --
IT'S NOT FOR ME. THE STRESS, THE RISK, THE FEAR. SOME PEOPLE JUST AREN'T CUT OUT TO BE COPS OR FIREMEN, TOO. I EXPECT THAT'S JUST HOW IT GOES.
I DIDN'T KNOW THAT THEN, THOUGH. IT TORE ME UP BACK THEN.
I MADE A FEW CALLS ON THE WAY HOME.
MARTY? SULLY.
LOOK, I CHANGED MY MIND. DON'T LINE UP ANY NEW GIGS FOR ME, NOT IF THEY START TOO --
REALLY? TUESDAY? IT SOUNDS GREAT, MARTY, BUT I CAN'T. ASK 'EM IF THEY CAN WAIT, AND IF NOT, MAYBE ANOTHER TIME, HUH?
NO, NO, JUST A FEW DAYS. A WEEK AT THE MOST. ANYTHING BEYOND THEN, I'M OPEN TO.
YOU'RE A PRINCE, MARTY.

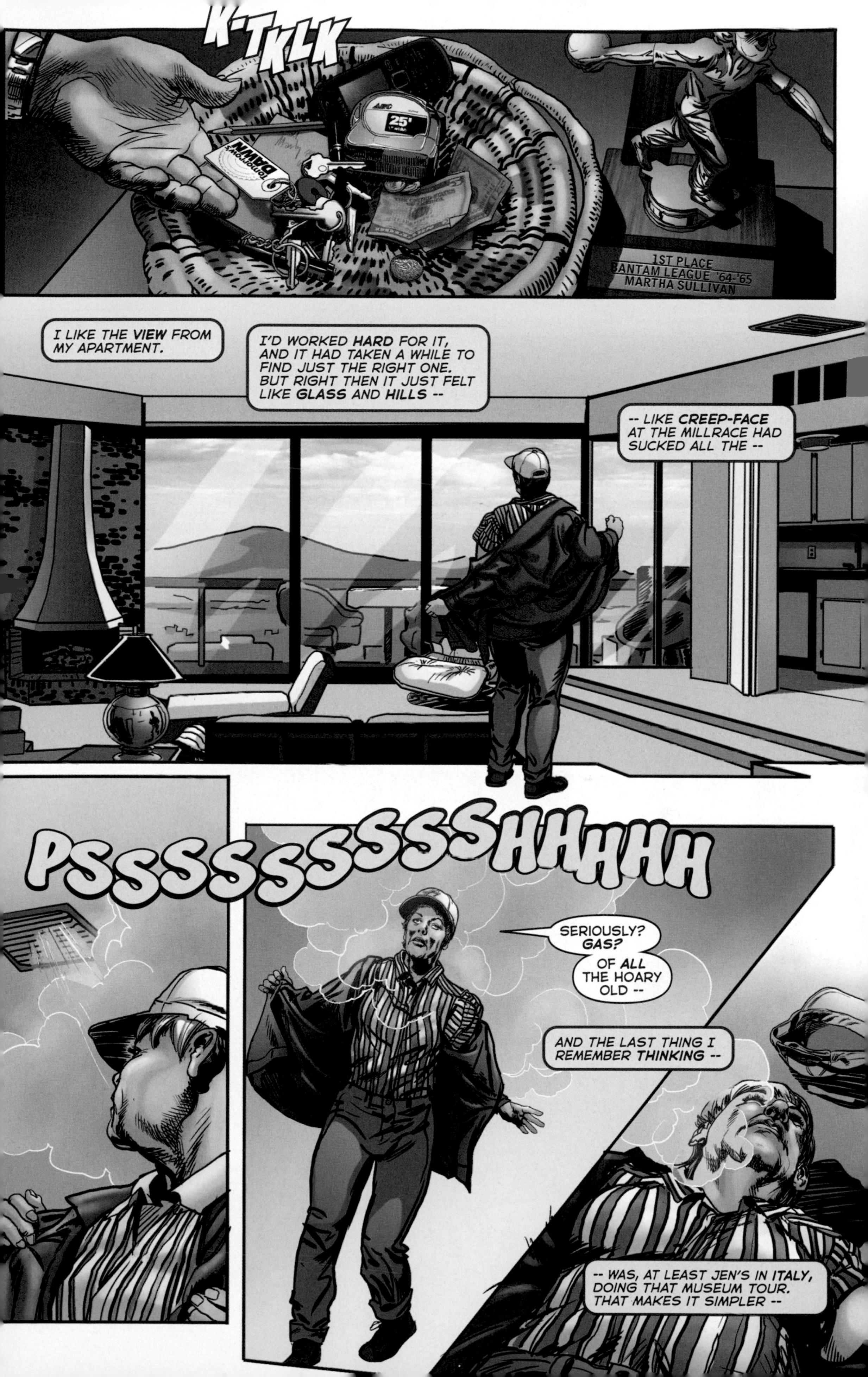
K-TKLK
TOMORROW'S DAWN
25'
1ST PLACE
BANTAM LEAGUE '64-'65
MARTHA SULLIVAN
I LIKE THE VIEW FROM MY APARTMENT.
I'D WORKED HARD FOR IT, AND IT HAD TAKEN A WHILE TO FIND JUST THE RIGHT ONE. BUT RIGHT THEN IT JUST FELT LIKE GLASS AND HILLS --
-- LIKE CREEP-FACE AT THE MILLRACE HAD SUCKED ALL THE --
PSSSSSSSSSSHHHHHH
SERIOUSLY? GAS?
OF ALL THE HOARY OLD --
AND THE LAST THING I REMEMBER THINKING --
-- WAS, AT LEAST JEN'S IN ITALY, DOING THAT MUSEUM TOUR. THAT MAKES IT SIMPLER --

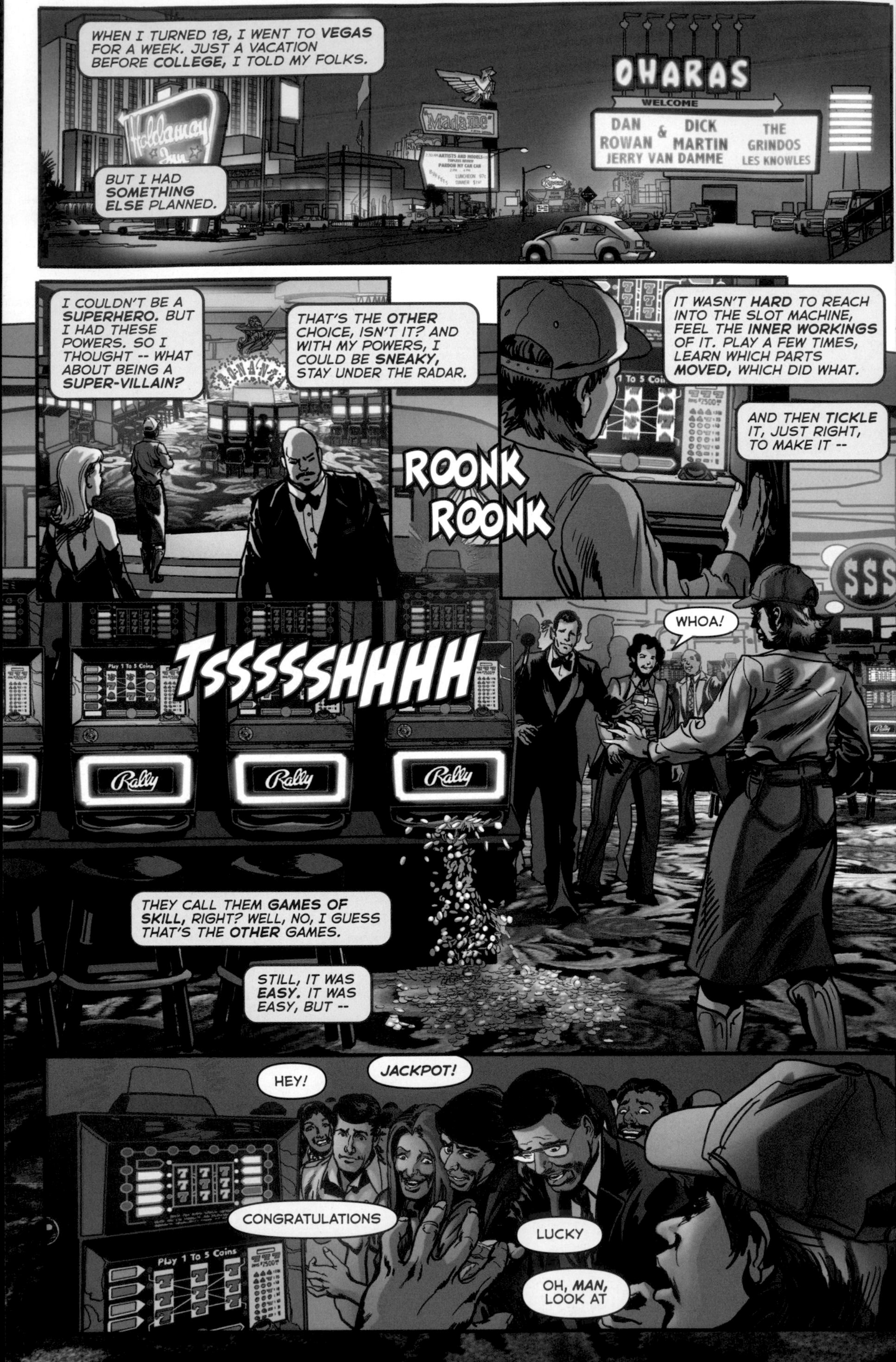
WHEN I TURNED 18, I WENT TO VEGAS FOR A WEEK. JUST A VACATION BEFORE COLLEGE, I TOLD MY FOLKS.
OHARAS
WELCOME
DAN ROWAN & DICK MARTIN
JERRY VAN DAMME
THE GRINDOS
LES KNOWLES
BUT I HAD SOMETHING ELSE PLANNED.
I COULDN'T BE A SUPERHERO. BUT I HAD THESE POWERS. SO I THOUGHT -- WHAT ABOUT BEING A SUPER-VILLAIN?
THAT'S THE OTHER CHOICE, ISN'T IT? AND WITH MY POWERS, I COULD BE SNEAKY, STAY UNDER THE RADAR.
IT WASN'T HARD TO REACH INTO THE SLOT MACHINE, FEEL THE INNER WORKINGS OF IT. PLAY A FEW TIMES, LEARN WHICH PARTS MOVED, WHICH DID WHAT.
AND THEN TICKLE IT, JUST RIGHT, TO MAKE IT --
ROONK ROONK
TSSSSSHHHH
Rally
Rally
Rally
WHOA!
THEY CALL THEM GAMES OF SKILL, RIGHT? WELL, NO, I GUESS THAT'S THE OTHER GAMES.
STILL, IT WAS EASY. IT WAS EASY, BUT --
HEY!
JACKPOT!
CONGRATULATIONS
LUCKY
OH, MAN, LOOK AT
Play 1 To 5 Coins

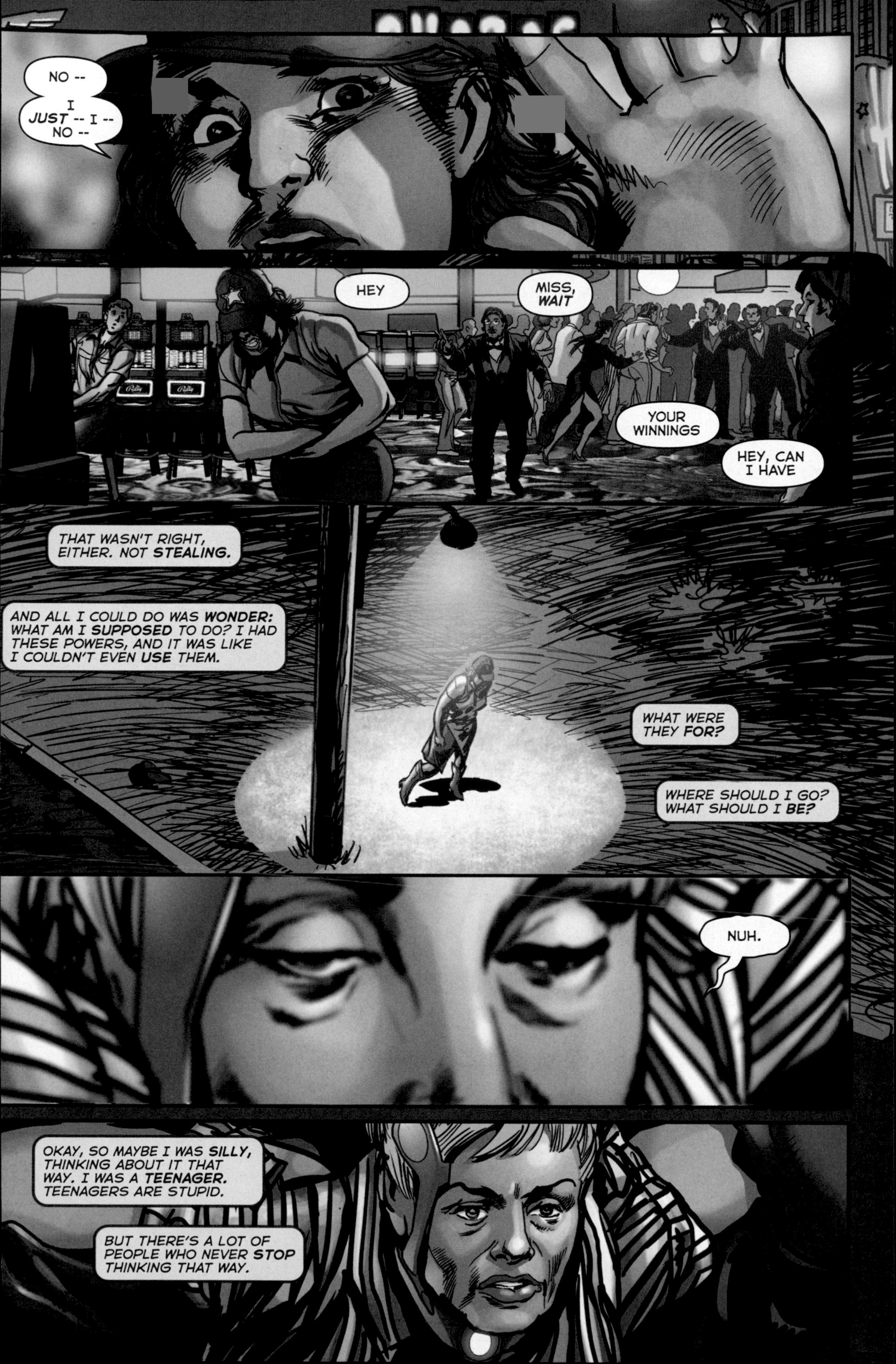
NO --
I JUST -- I -- NO --
HEY
MISS, WAIT
YOUR WINNINGS
HEY, CAN I HAVE
THAT WASN'T RIGHT, EITHER. NOT STEALING.
AND ALL I COULD DO WAS WONDER: WHAT AM I SUPPOSED TO DO? I HAD THESE POWERS, AND IT WAS LIKE I COULDN'T EVEN USE THEM.
WHAT WERE THEY FOR?
WHERE SHOULD I GO? WHAT SHOULD I BE?
NUH.
OKAY, SO MAYBE I WAS SILLY, THINKING ABOUT IT THAT WAY. I WAS A TEENAGER. TEENAGERS ARE STUPID.
BUT THERE'S A LOT OF PEOPLE WHO NEVER STOP THINKING THAT WAY.

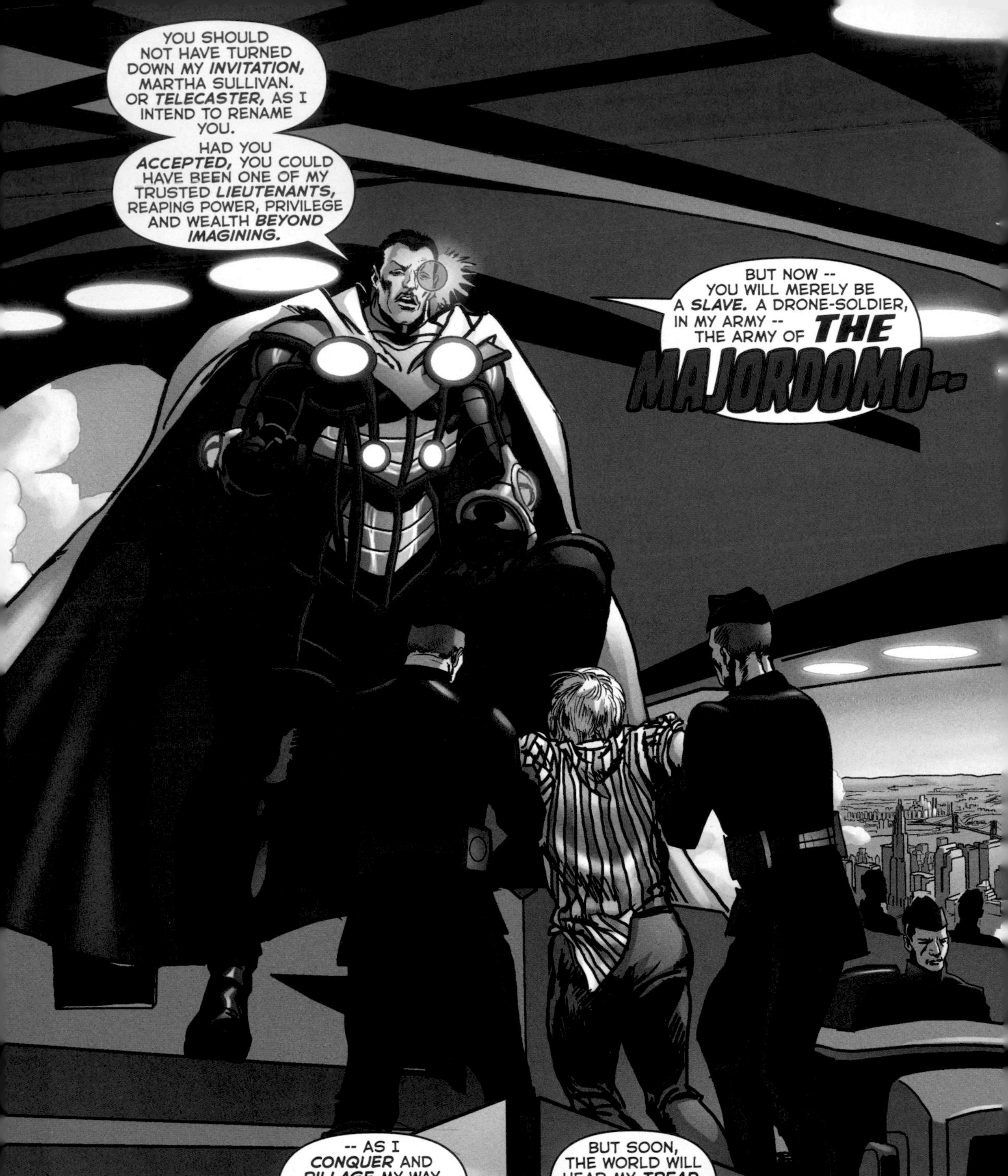
YOU SHOULD NOT HAVE TURNED DOWN MY INVITATION, MARTHA SULLIVAN. OR TELECASTER, AS I INTEND TO RENAME YOU.
HAD YOU ACCEPTED, YOU COULD HAVE BEEN ONE OF MY TRUSTED LIEUTENANTS, REAPING POWER, PRIVILEGE AND WEALTH BEYOND IMAGINING.
BUT NOW -- YOU WILL MERELY BE A SLAVE. A DRONE-SOLDIER, IN MY ARMY -- THE ARMY OF THE MAJORDOMO--

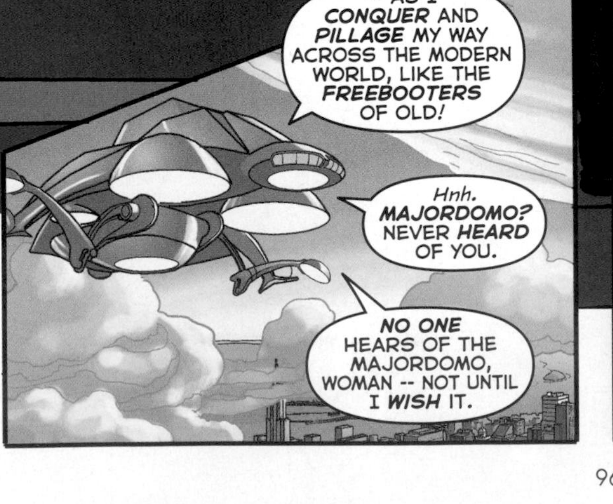
-- AS I CONQUER AND PILLAGE MY WAY ACROSS THE MODERN WORLD, LIKE THE FREEBOOTERS OF OLD!
Hnh. MAJORDOMO? NEVER HEARD OF YOU.
NO ONE HEARS OF THE MAJORDOMO, WOMAN -- NOT UNTIL I WISH IT.

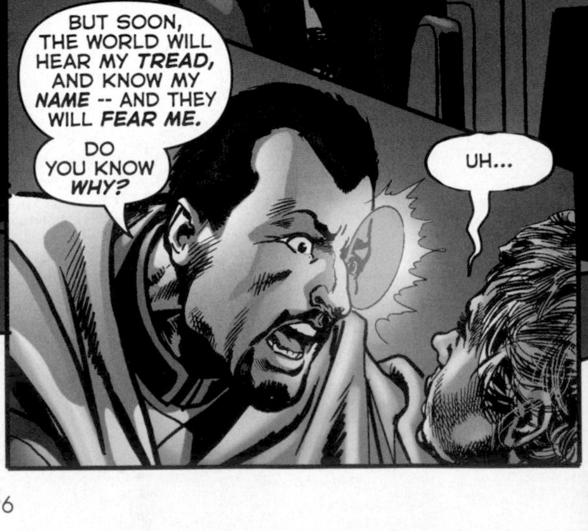
BUT SOON, THE WORLD WILL HEAR MY TREAD, AND KNOW MY NAME -- AND THEY WILL FEAR ME.
DO YOU KNOW WHY?
UH...

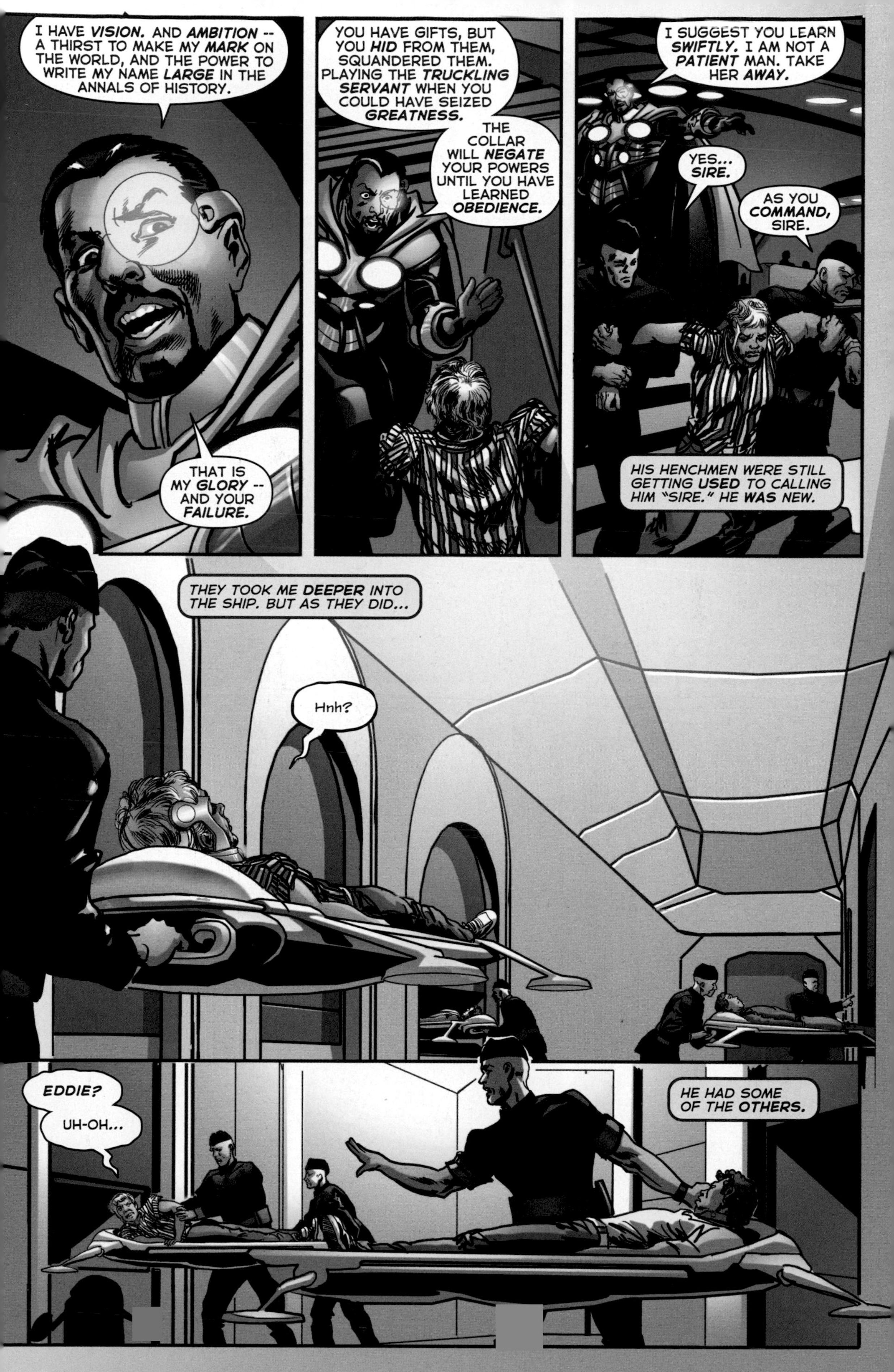
I HAVE VISION. AND AMBITION -- A THIRST TO MAKE MY MARK ON THE WORLD, AND THE POWER TO WRITE MY NAME LARGE IN THE ANNALS OF HISTORY.
THAT IS MY GLORY -- AND YOUR FAILURE.
YOU HAVE GIFTS, BUT YOU HID FROM THEM, SQUANDERED THEM. PLAYING THE TRUCKLING SERVANT WHEN YOU COULD HAVE SEIZED GREATNESS.
THE COLLAR WILL NEGATE YOUR POWERS UNTIL YOU HAVE LEARNED OBEDIENCE.
I SUGGEST YOU LEARN SWIFTLY. I AM NOT A PATIENT MAN. TAKE HER AWAY.
YES... SIRE.
AS YOU COMMAND, SIRE.
HIS HENCHMEN WERE STILL GETTING USED TO CALLING HIM "SIRE." HE WAS NEW.
THEY TOOK ME DEEPER INTO THE SHIP. BUT AS THEY DID...
Hnh?
EDDIE?
UH-OH...
HE HAD SOME OF THE OTHERS.

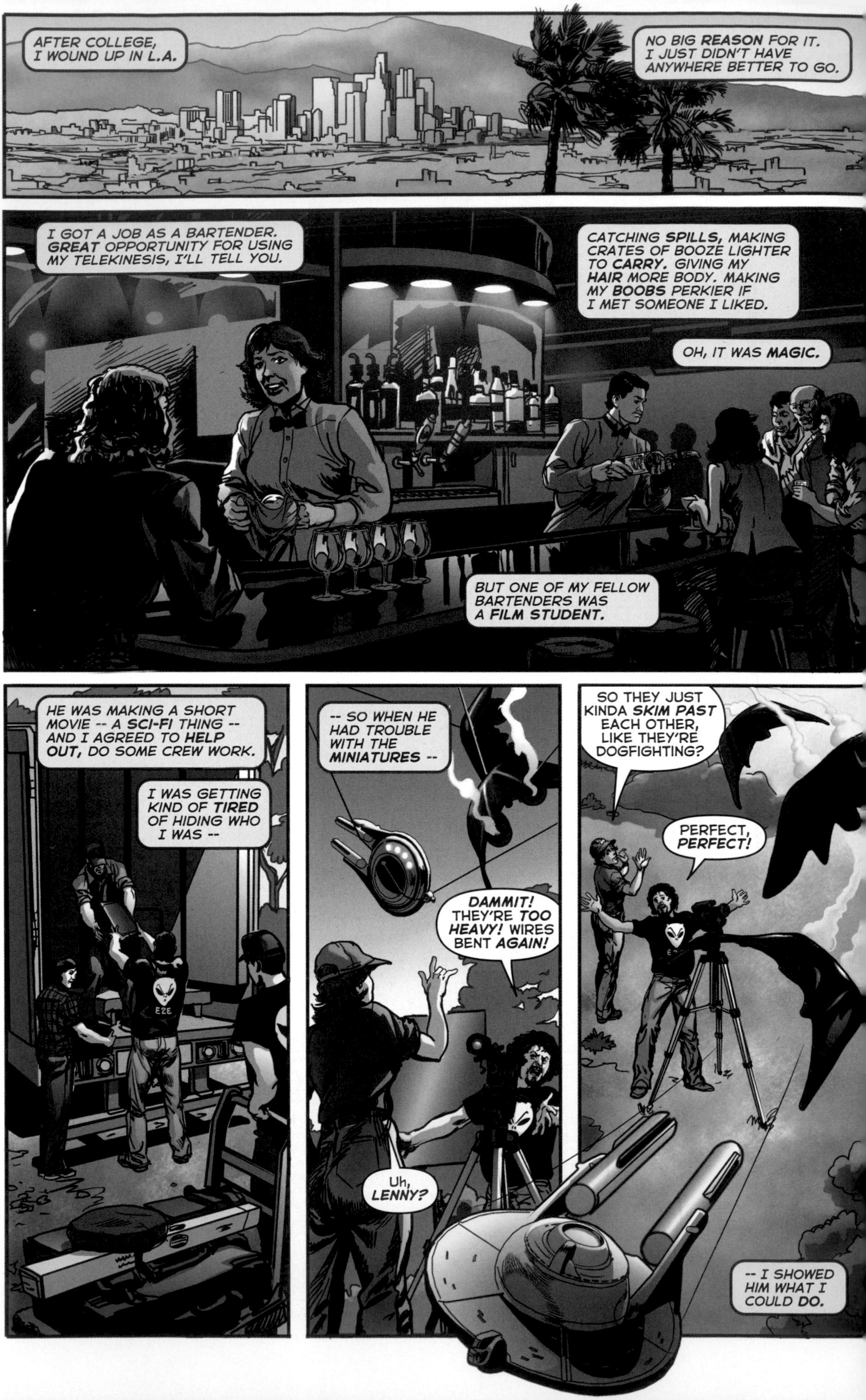

AFTER COLLEGE, I WOUND UP IN L.A.
NO BIG REASON FOR IT. I JUST DIDN'T HAVE ANYWHERE BETTER TO GO.
I GOT A JOB AS A BARTENDER. GREAT OPPORTUNITY FOR USING MY TELEKINESIS, I'LL TELL YOU.
CATCHING SPILLS, MAKING CRATES OF BOOZE LIGHTER TO CARRY. GIVING MY HAIR MORE BODY. MAKING MY BOOBS PERKIER IF I MET SOMEONE I LIKED.
OH, IT WAS MAGIC.
BUT ONE OF MY FELLOW BARTENDERS WAS A FILM STUDENT.
HE WAS MAKING A SHORT MOVIE -- A SCI-FI THING -- AND I AGREED TO HELP OUT, DO SOME CREW WORK.
I WAS GETTING KIND OF TIRED OF HIDING WHO I WAS --
E2E
-- SO WHEN HE HAD TROUBLE WITH THE MINIATURES --
DAMMIT! THEY'RE TOO HEAVY! WIRES BENT AGAIN!
Uh, LENNY?
SO THEY JUST KINDA SKIM PAST EACH OTHER, LIKE THEY'RE DOGFIGHTING?
PERFECT, PERFECT!
-- I SHOWED HIM WHAT I COULD DO.

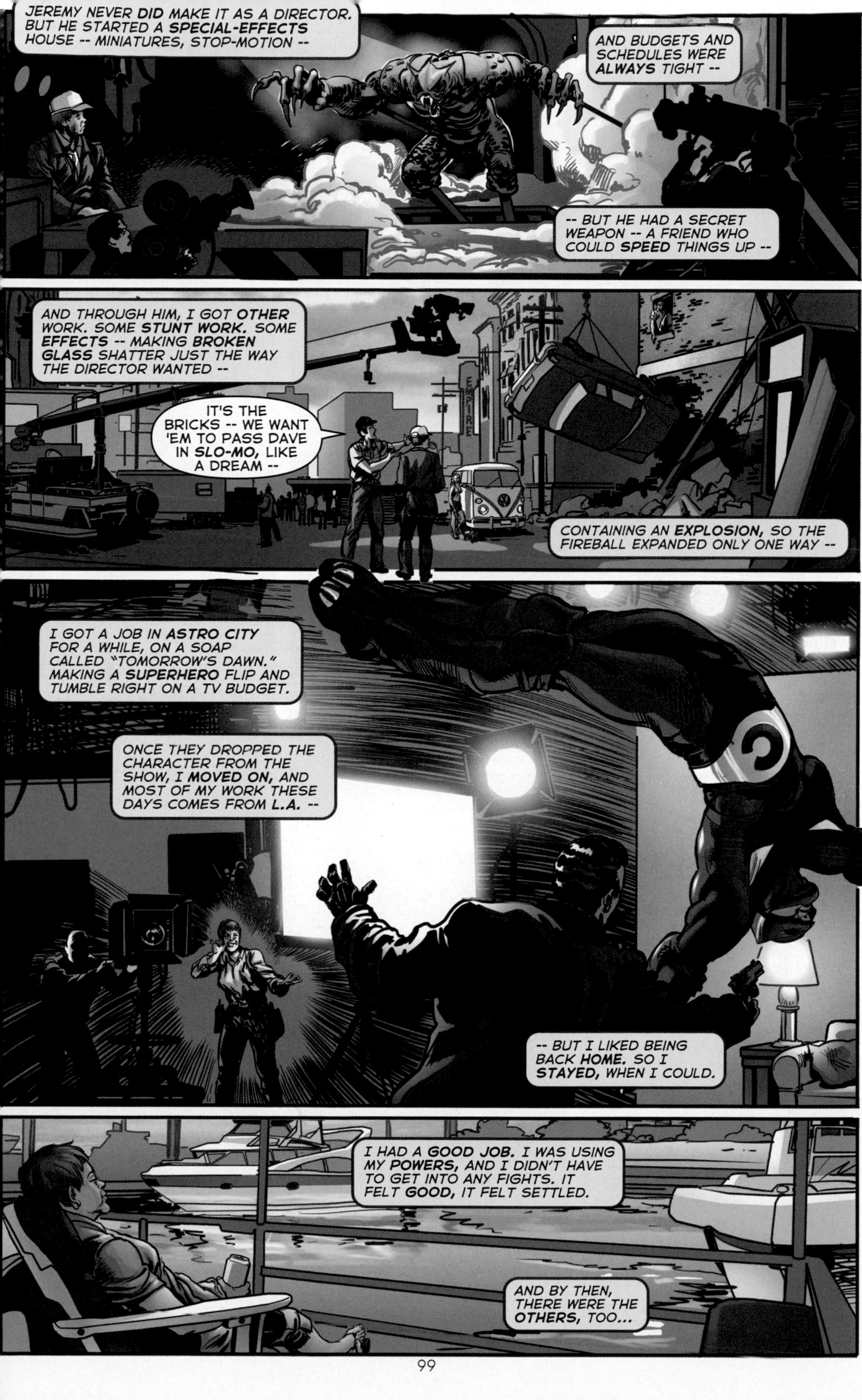
JEREMY NEVER DID MAKE IT AS A DIRECTOR. BUT HE STARTED A SPECIAL-EFFECTS HOUSE -- MINIATURES, STOP-MOTION --
AND BUDGETS AND SCHEDULES WERE ALWAYS TIGHT --
-- BUT HE HAD A SECRET WEAPON -- A FRIEND WHO COULD SPEED THINGS UP --
AND THROUGH HIM, I GOT OTHER WORK. SOME STUNT WORK. SOME EFFECTS -- MAKING BROKEN GLASS SHATTER JUST THE WAY THE DIRECTOR WANTED --
IT'S THE BRICKS -- WE WANT 'EM TO PASS DAVE IN SLO-MO, LIKE A DREAM --
EMPIRE
CONTAINING AN EXPLOSION, SO THE FIREBALL EXPANDED ONLY ONE WAY --
I GOT A JOB IN ASTRO CITY FOR A WHILE, ON A SOAP CALLED "TOMORROW'S DAWN." MAKING A SUPERHERO FLIP AND TUMBLE RIGHT ON A TV BUDGET.
ONCE THEY DROPPED THE CHARACTER FROM THE SHOW, I MOVED ON, AND MOST OF MY WORK THESE DAYS COMES FROM L.A. --
-- BUT I LIKED BEING BACK HOME. SO I STAYED, WHEN I COULD.
I HAD A GOOD JOB. I WAS USING MY POWERS, AND I DIDN'T HAVE TO GET INTO ANY FIGHTS. IT FELT GOOD, IT FELT SETTLED.
AND BY THEN, THERE WERE THE OTHERS, TOO...

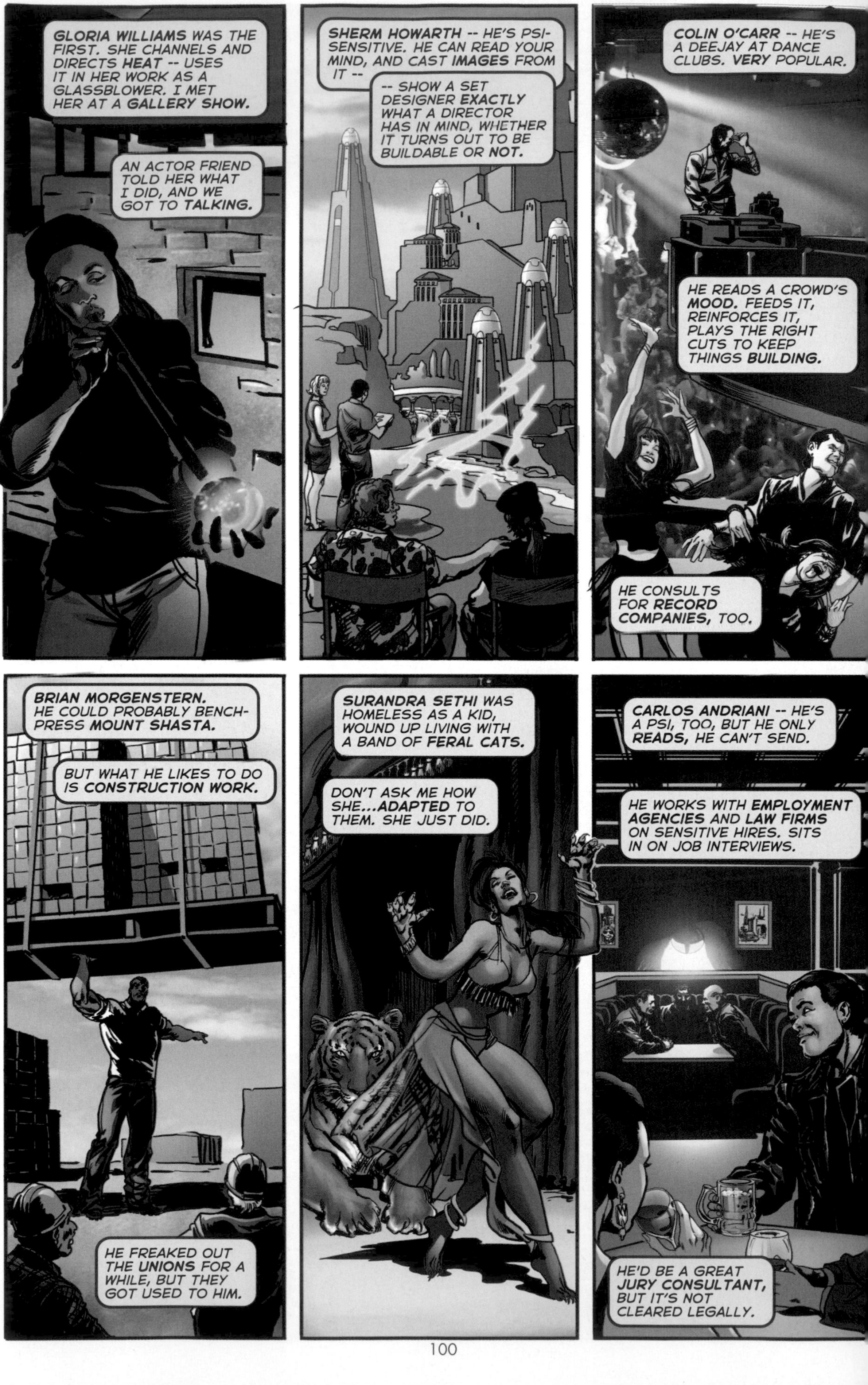
GLORIA WILLIAMS WAS THE FIRST. SHE CHANNELS AND DIRECTS HEAT -- USES IT IN HER WORK AS A GLASSBLOWER. I MET HER AT A GALLERY SHOW.
AN ACTOR FRIEND TOLD HER WHAT I DID, AND WE GOT TO TALKING.
SHERM HOWARTH -- HE'S PSI-SENSITIVE. HE CAN READ YOUR MIND, AND CAST IMAGES FROM IT --
-- SHOW A SET DESIGNER EXACTLY WHAT A DIRECTOR HAS IN MIND, WHETHER IT TURNS OUT TO BE BUILDABLE OR NOT.
COLIN O'CARR -- HE'S A DEEJAY AT DANCE CLUBS. VERY POPULAR.
HE READS A CROWD'S MOOD. FEEDS IT, REINFORCES IT, PLAYS THE RIGHT CUTS TO KEEP THINGS BUILDING.
HE CONSULTS FOR RECORD COMPANIES, TOO.
BRIAN MORGENSTERN. HE COULD PROBABLY BENCH-PRESS MOUNT SHASTA.
BUT WHAT HE LIKES TO DO IS CONSTRUCTION WORK.
HE FREAKED OUT THE UNIONS FOR A WHILE, BUT THEY GOT USED TO HIM.
SURANDRA SETHI WAS HOMELESS AS A KID, WOUND UP LIVING WITH A BAND OF FERAL CATS.
DON'T ASK ME HOW SHE...ADAPTED TO THEM. SHE JUST DID.
CARLOS ANDRIANI -- HE'S A PSI, TOO, BUT HE ONLY READS, HE CAN'T SEND.
HE WORKS WITH EMPLOYMENT AGENCIES AND LAW FIRMS ON SENSITIVE HIRES. SITS IN ON JOB INTERVIEWS.
HE'D BE A GREAT JURY CONSULTANT, BUT IT'S NOT CLEARED LEGALLY.

WE CALL OURSELVES *SIDELINERS.* WE'RE ALL AROUND THE WORLD. YOU MEET ONE, THEY KNOW A FEW OTHERS, IT GOES ON FROM *THERE.*

WE KEEP IN TOUCH. THROUGH PRIVATE COMPUTER *BULLETIN BOARDS...*

...GET-TOGETHERS WHEN ENOUGH OF US ARE *FREE...*

-- AND HE WANTS ME TO FIT IT OUT WITH *GPS* AND AN *MP3* SOUND SYSTEM! A *MODEL T,* CAN YOU BELIEVE IT?

HA!

THE *T* CAN'T EITHER, BUT SHE'S EAGER TO *TRY* IT!

AND SOMETIMES, I FEEL *GUILTY,* LIKE I SHOULD BE DOING MORE.

SOMETIMES WE *ALL* DO, I THINK.

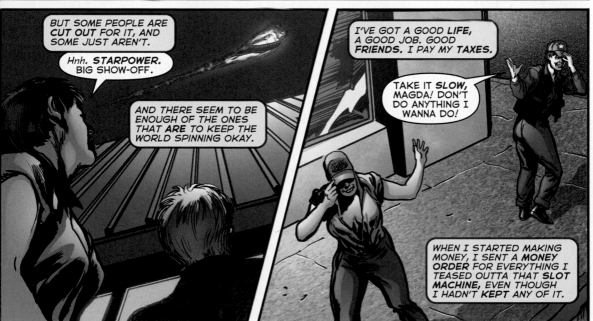

BUT SOME PEOPLE ARE *CUT OUT* FOR IT, AND SOME JUST *AREN'T.*

Hnh. *STARPOWER.* BIG SHOW-OFF.

AND THERE SEEM TO BE ENOUGH OF THE ONES THAT *ARE* TO KEEP THE WORLD SPINNING OKAY.

I'VE GOT A GOOD *LIFE,* A GOOD *JOB.* GOOD *FRIENDS.* I PAY MY *TAXES.*

TAKE IT *SLOW,* MAGDA! DON'T DO ANYTHING I WANNA DO!

WHEN I STARTED MAKING MONEY, I SENT A *MONEY ORDER* FOR EVERYTHING I TEASED OUTTA THAT *SLOT MACHINE,* EVEN THOUGH I HADN'T *KEPT* ANY OF IT.

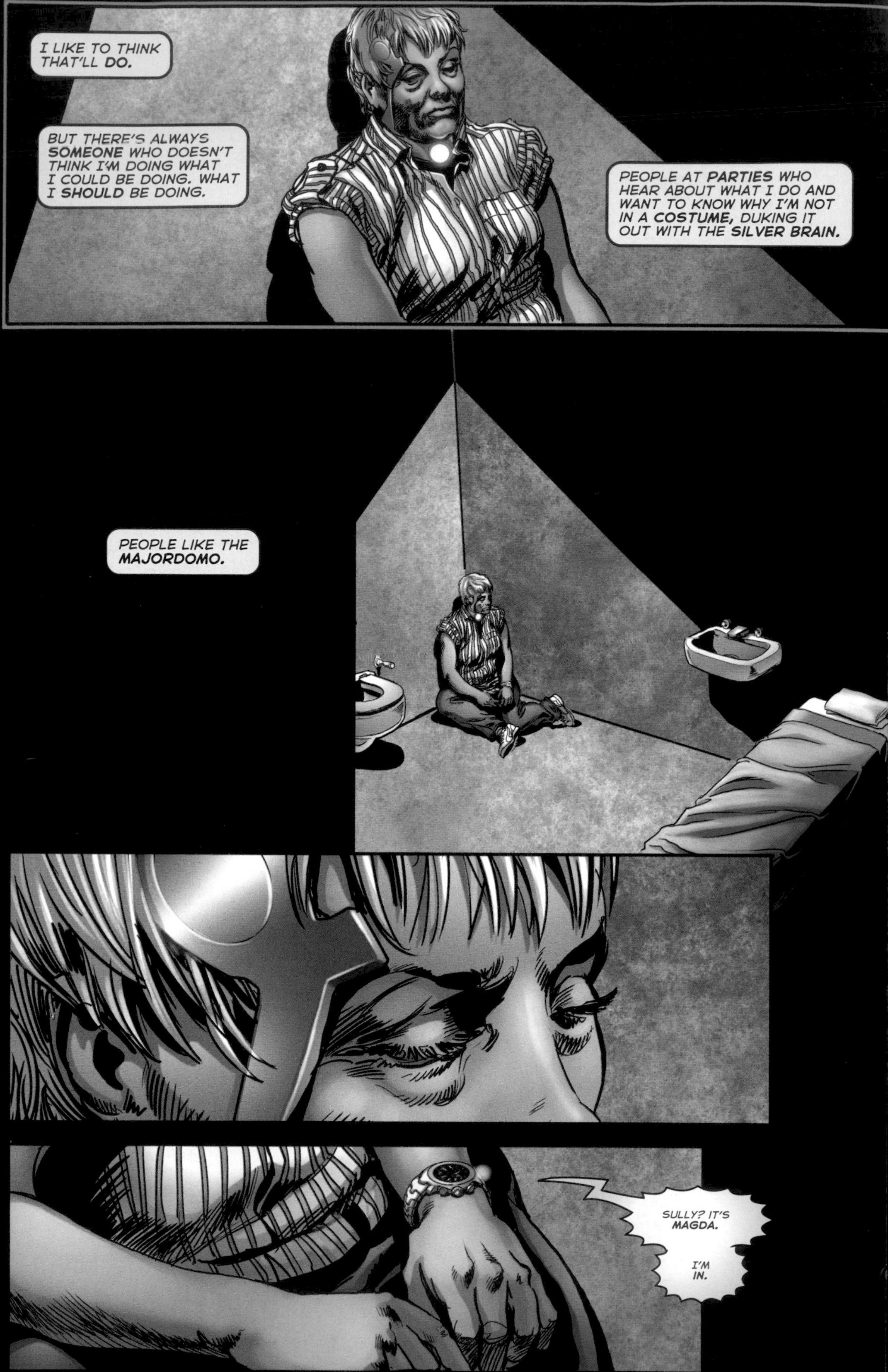
I LIKE TO THINK THAT'LL DO.
BUT THERE'S ALWAYS SOMEONE WHO DOESN'T THINK I'M DOING WHAT I COULD BE DOING. WHAT I SHOULD BE DOING.
PEOPLE AT PARTIES WHO HEAR ABOUT WHAT I DO AND WANT TO KNOW WHY I'M NOT IN A COSTUME, DUKING IT OUT WITH THE SILVER BRAIN.
PEOPLE LIKE THE MAJORDOMO.
SULLY? IT'S MAGDA.
I'M IN.

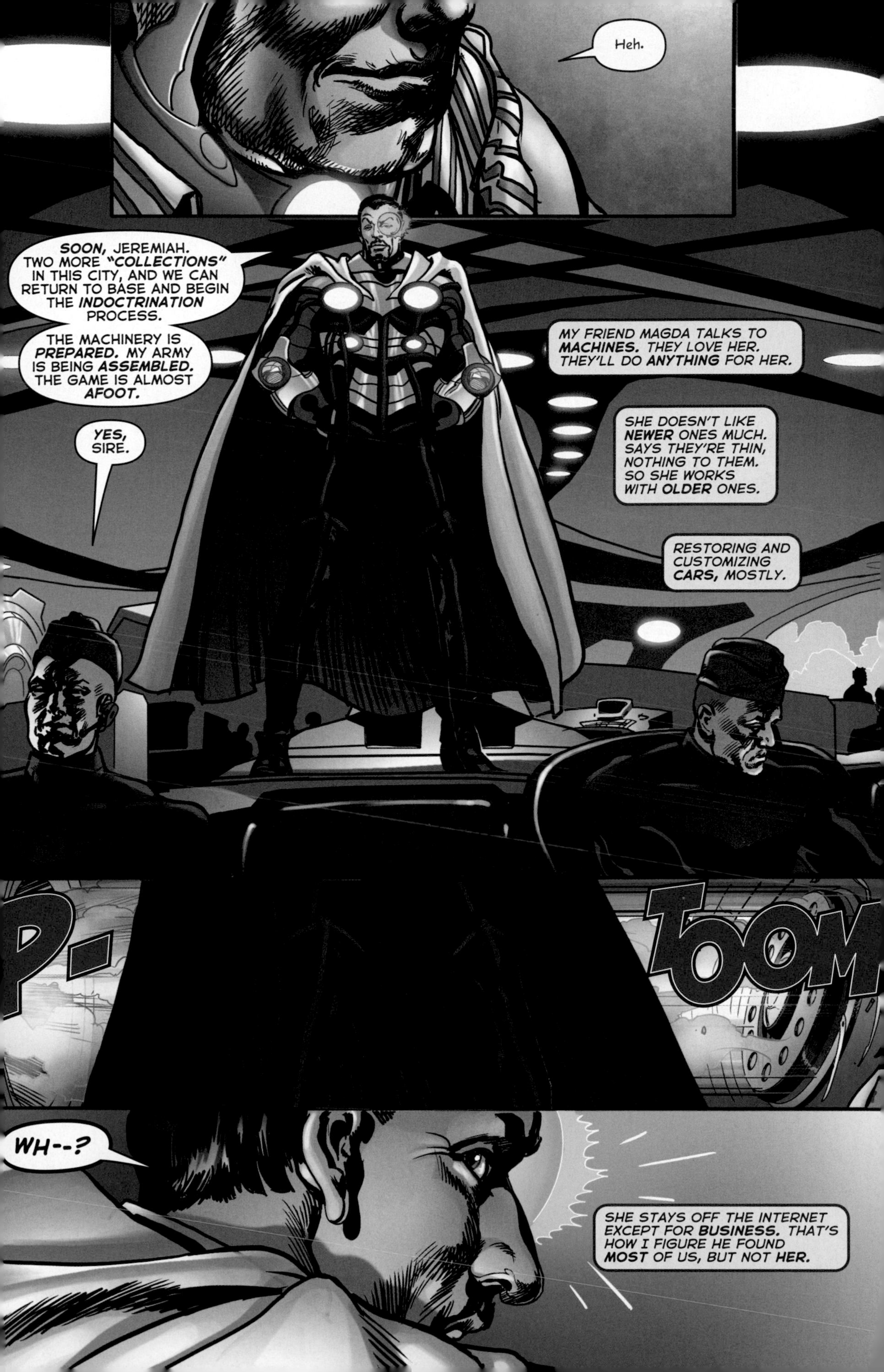
Heh.
SOON, JEREMIAH. TWO MORE "COLLECTIONS" IN THIS CITY, AND WE CAN RETURN TO BASE AND BEGIN THE INDOCTRINATION PROCESS.
THE MACHINERY IS PREPARED. MY ARMY IS BEING ASSEMBLED. THE GAME IS ALMOST AFOOT.
YES, SIRE.
MY FRIEND MAGDA TALKS TO MACHINES. THEY LOVE HER. THEY'LL DO ANYTHING FOR HER.
SHE DOESN'T LIKE NEWER ONES MUCH. SAYS THEY'RE THIN, NOTHING TO THEM. SO SHE WORKS WITH OLDER ONES.
RESTORING AND CUSTOMIZING CARS, MOSTLY.
P-
TOOM
WH--?
SHE STAYS OFF THE INTERNET EXCEPT FOR BUSINESS. THAT'S HOW I FIGURE HE FOUND MOST OF US, BUT NOT HER.

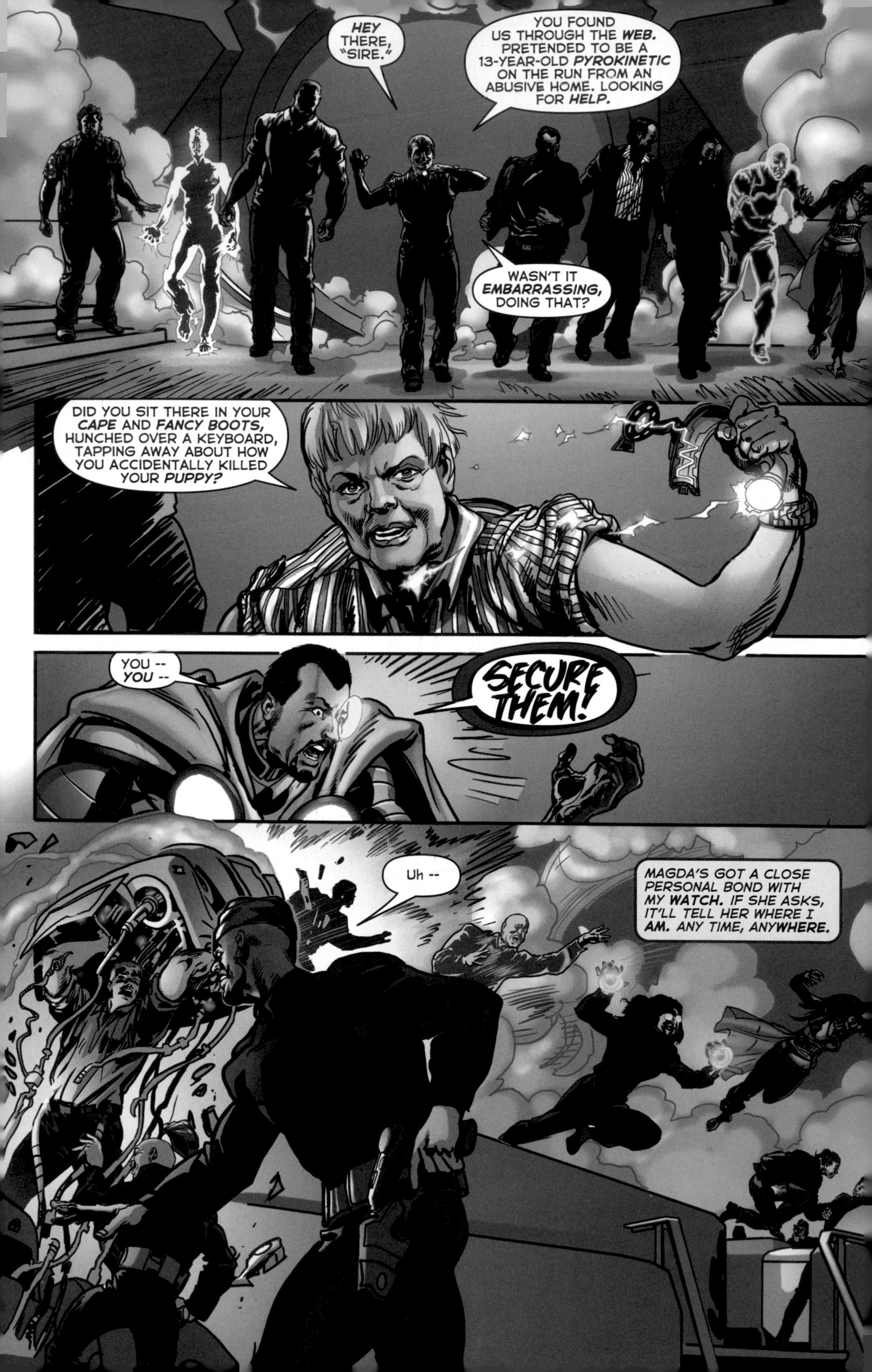
HEY THERE, "SIRE."
YOU FOUND US THROUGH THE WEB. PRETENDED TO BE A 13-YEAR-OLD PYROKINETIC ON THE RUN FROM AN ABUSIVE HOME. LOOKING FOR HELP.
WASN'T IT EMBARRASSING, DOING THAT?
DID YOU SIT THERE IN YOUR CAPE AND FANCY BOOTS, HUNCHED OVER A KEYBOARD, TAPPING AWAY ABOUT HOW YOU ACCIDENTALLY KILLED YOUR PUPPY?
YOU -- YOU --
SECURE THEM!
Uh --
MAGDA'S GOT A CLOSE PERSONAL BOND WITH MY WATCH. IF SHE ASKS, IT'LL TELL HER WHERE I AM. ANY TIME, ANYWHERE.

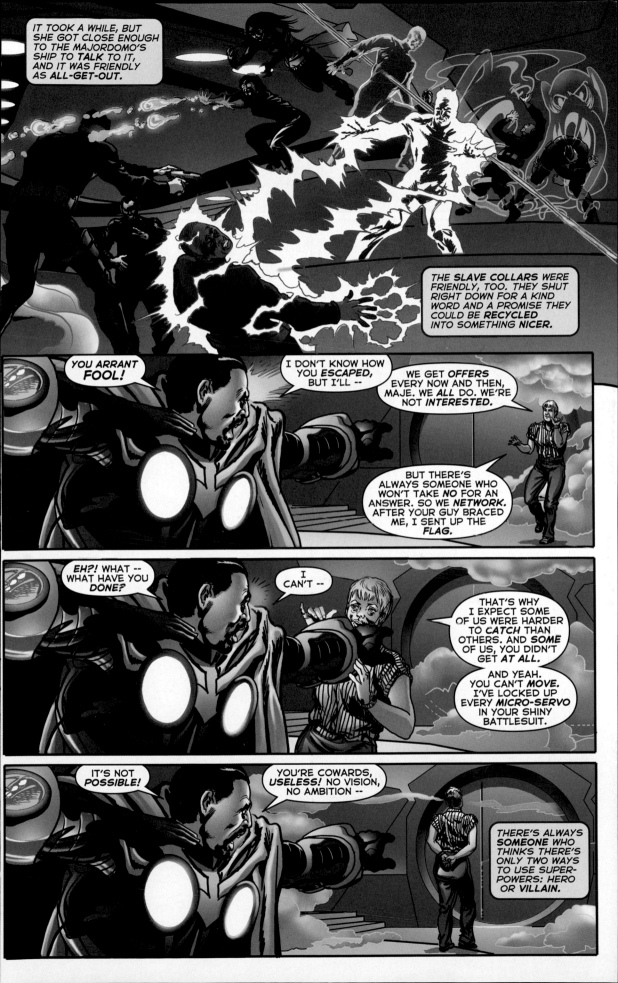

IT TOOK A WHILE, BUT SHE GOT CLOSE ENOUGH TO THE MAJORDOMO'S SHIP TO *TALK* TO IT, AND IT WAS FRIENDLY AS *ALL-GET-OUT.*

THE *SLAVE COLLARS* WERE FRIENDLY, TOO. THEY SHUT RIGHT DOWN FOR A KIND WORD AND A PROMISE THEY COULD BE *RECYCLED* INTO SOMETHING *NICER.*

YOU ARRANT *FOOL!*

I DON'T KNOW HOW YOU *ESCAPED,* BUT I'LL --

WE GET *OFFERS* EVERY NOW AND THEN, MAJE. WE *ALL* DO. WE'RE NOT *INTERESTED.*

BUT THERE'S ALWAYS SOMEONE WHO WON'T TAKE *NO* FOR AN ANSWER. SO WE *NETWORK.* AFTER YOUR GUY BRACED ME, I SENT UP THE *FLAG.*

EH?! WHAT -- WHAT HAVE YOU *DONE?*

I *CAN'T* --

THAT'S WHY I EXPECT SOME OF US WERE HARDER TO *CATCH* THAN OTHERS. AND *SOME* OF US, YOU DIDN'T GET *AT ALL.*

AND YEAH. YOU CAN'T *MOVE.* I'VE LOCKED UP EVERY *MICRO-SERVO* IN YOUR *SHINY BATTLESUIT.*

IT'S NOT *POSSIBLE!*

YOU'RE COWARDS, *USELESS!* NO VISION, NO AMBITION --

THERE'S ALWAYS SOMEONE WHO THINKS THERE'S ONLY TWO WAYS TO USE SUPER-POWERS: HERO OR VILLAIN.

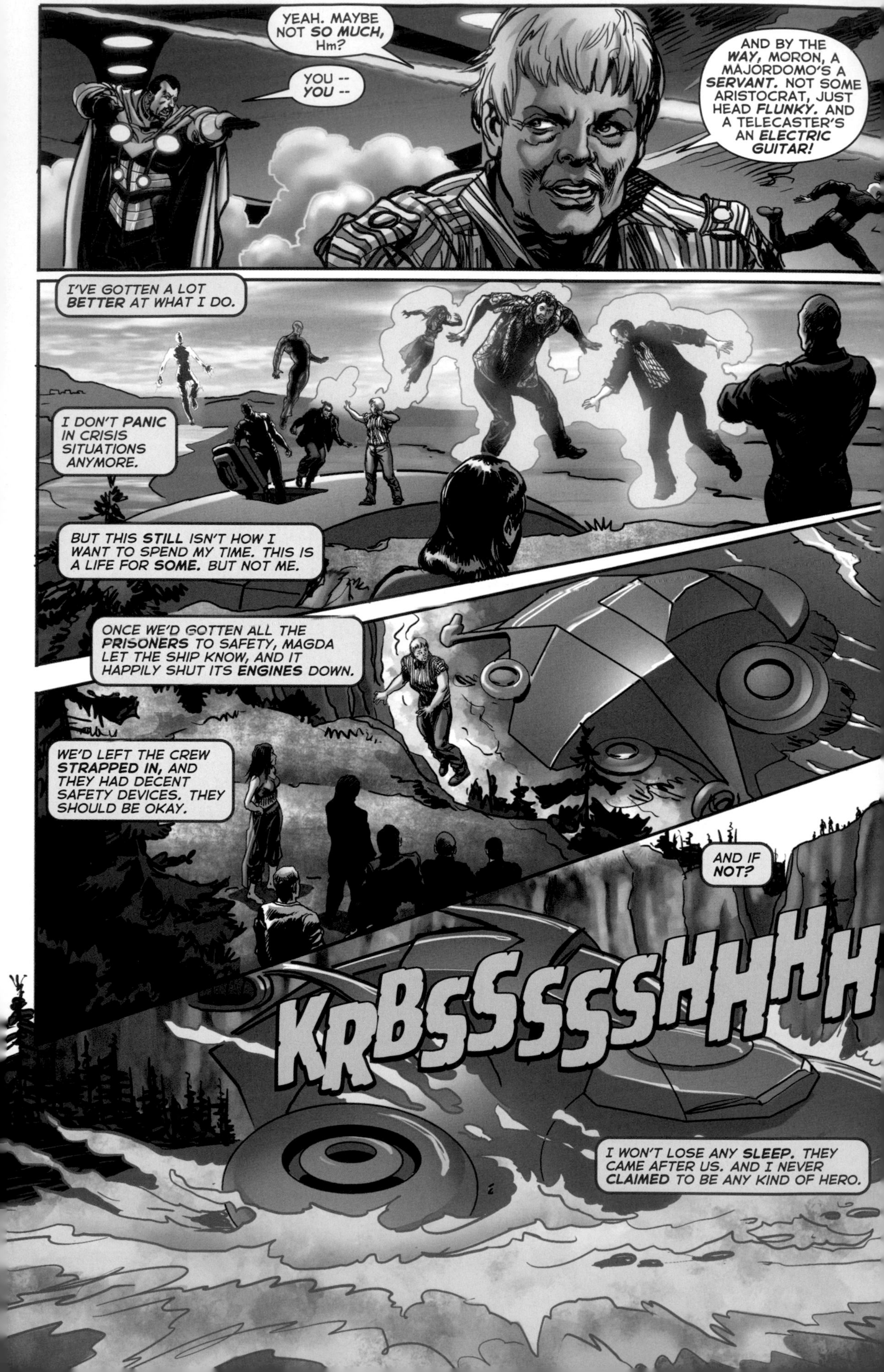
YEAH. MAYBE NOT SO MUCH, Hm?
YOU -- YOU --
AND BY THE WAY, MORON, A MAJORDOMO'S A SERVANT. NOT SOME ARISTOCRAT, JUST HEAD FLUNKY. AND A TELECASTER'S AN ELECTRIC GUITAR!
I'VE GOTTEN A LOT BETTER AT WHAT I DO.
I DON'T PANIC IN CRISIS SITUATIONS ANYMORE.
BUT THIS STILL ISN'T HOW I WANT TO SPEND MY TIME. THIS IS A LIFE FOR SOME. BUT NOT ME.
ONCE WE'D GOTTEN ALL THE PRISONERS TO SAFETY, MAGDA LET THE SHIP KNOW, AND IT HAPPILY SHUT ITS ENGINES DOWN.
WE'D LEFT THE CREW STRAPPED IN, AND THEY HAD DECENT SAFETY DEVICES. THEY SHOULD BE OKAY.
AND IF NOT?
KRBSSSSSSHHHH
I WON'T LOSE ANY SLEEP. THEY CAME AFTER US. AND I NEVER CLAIMED TO BE ANY KIND OF HERO.

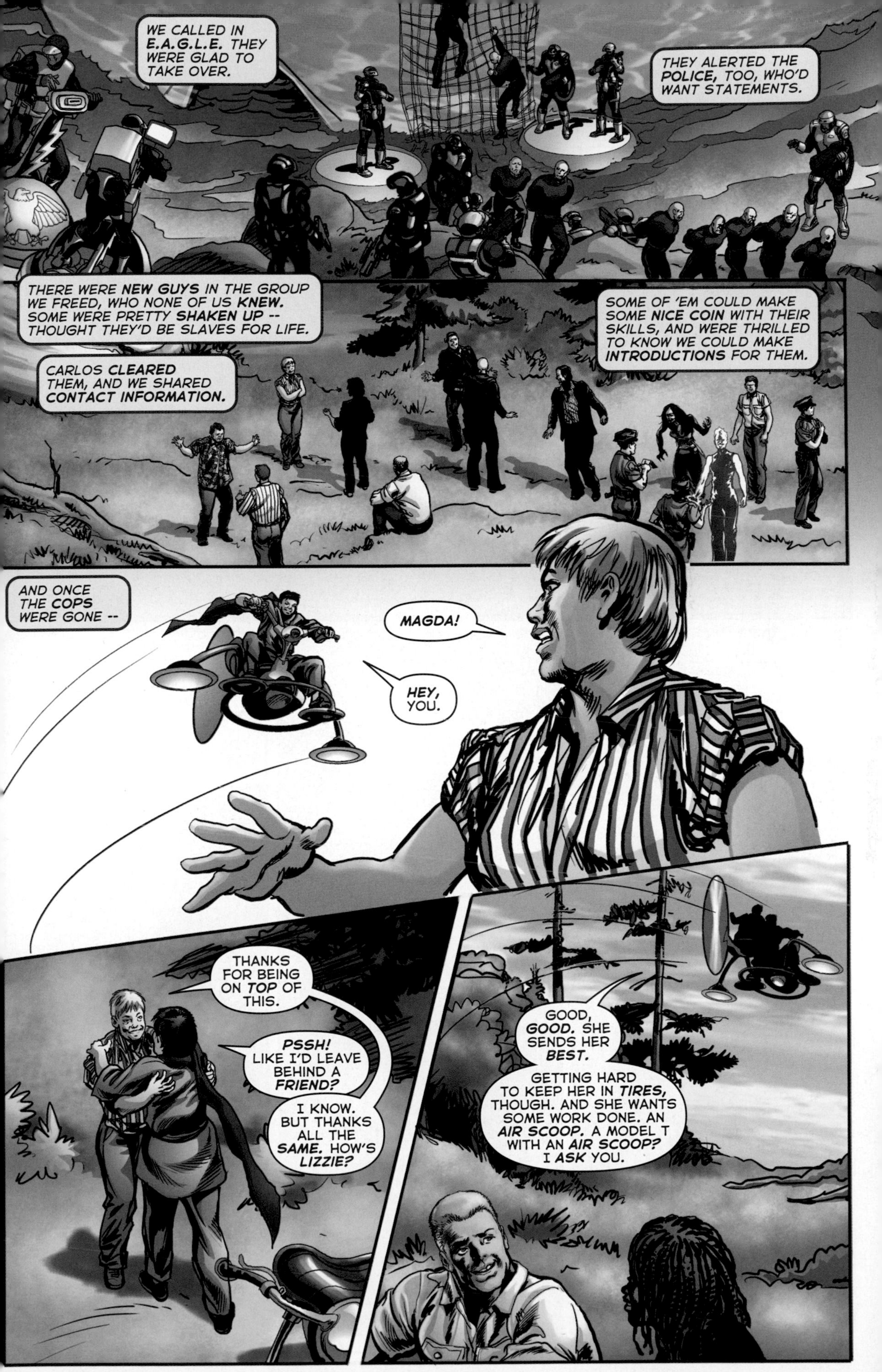

WE CALLED IN E.A.G.L.E. THEY WERE GLAD TO TAKE OVER.
THEY ALERTED THE POLICE, TOO, WHO'D WANT STATEMENTS.
THERE WERE NEW GUYS IN THE GROUP WE FREED, WHO NONE OF US KNEW. SOME WERE PRETTY SHAKEN UP -- THOUGHT THEY'D BE SLAVES FOR LIFE.
CARLOS CLEARED THEM, AND WE SHARED CONTACT INFORMATION.
SOME OF 'EM COULD MAKE SOME NICE COIN WITH THEIR SKILLS, AND WERE THRILLED TO KNOW WE COULD MAKE INTRODUCTIONS FOR THEM.
AND ONCE THE COPS WERE GONE --
MAGDA!
HEY, YOU.
THANKS FOR BEING ON TOP OF THIS.
PSSH! LIKE I'D LEAVE BEHIND A FRIEND?
I KNOW. BUT THANKS ALL THE SAME. HOW'S LIZZIE?
GOOD, GOOD. SHE SENDS HER BEST.
GETTING HARD TO KEEP HER IN TIRES, THOUGH. AND SHE WANTS SOME WORK DONE. AN AIR SCOOP. A MODEL T WITH AN AIR SCOOP? I ASK YOU.

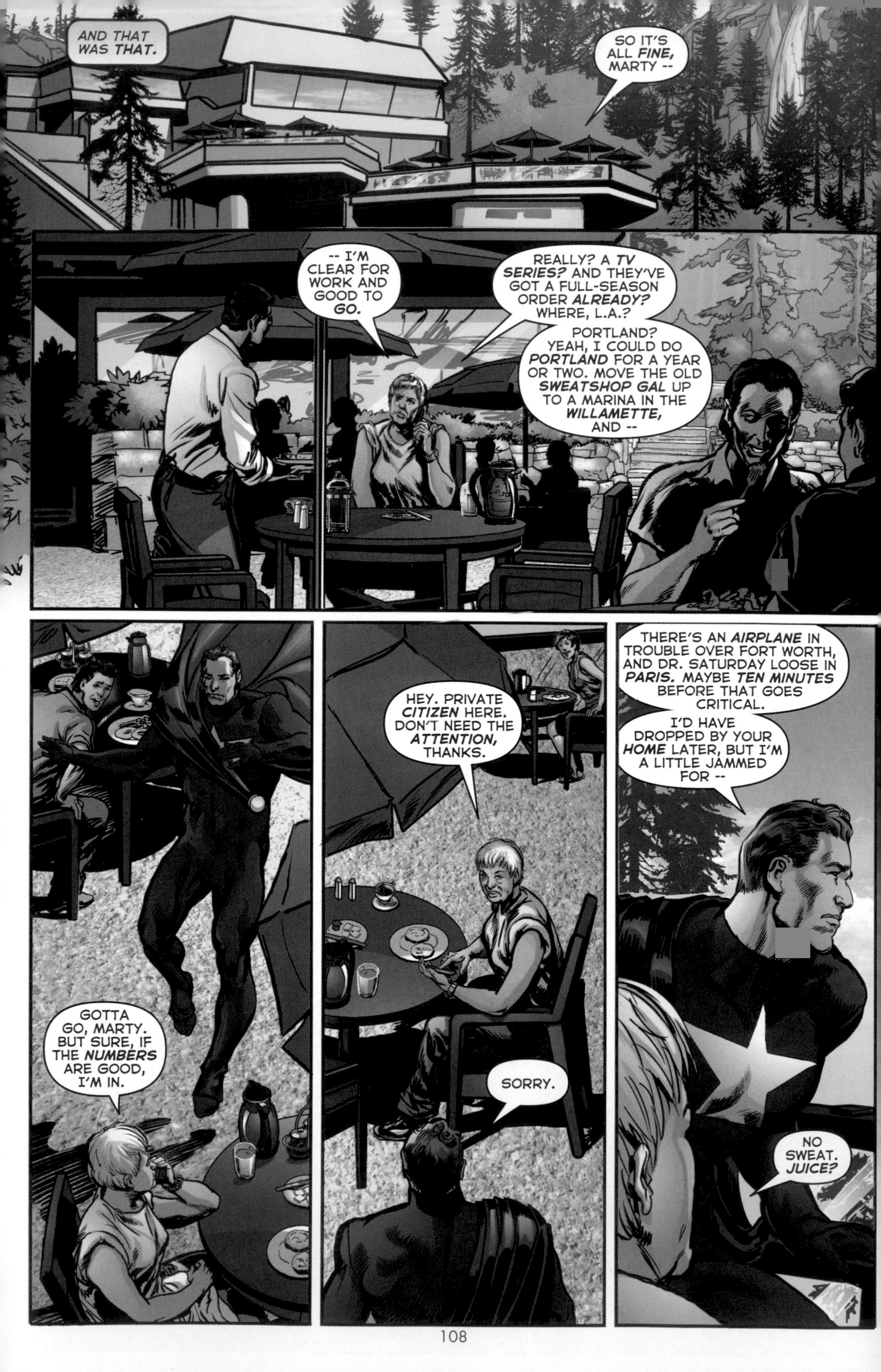
AND THAT WAS THAT.
SO IT'S ALL FINE, MARTY --
-- I'M CLEAR FOR WORK AND GOOD TO GO.
REALLY? A TV SERIES? AND THEY'VE GOT A FULL-SEASON ORDER ALREADY? WHERE, L.A.?
PORTLAND? YEAH, I COULD DO PORTLAND FOR A YEAR OR TWO. MOVE THE OLD SWEATSHOP GAL UP TO A MARINA IN THE WILLAMETTE, AND --
GOTTA GO, MARTY. BUT SURE, IF THE NUMBERS ARE GOOD, I'M IN.
HEY. PRIVATE CITIZEN HERE. DON'T NEED THE ATTENTION, THANKS.
SORRY.
THERE'S AN AIRPLANE IN TROUBLE OVER FORT WORTH, AND DR. SATURDAY LOOSE IN PARIS. MAYBE TEN MINUTES BEFORE THAT GOES CRITICAL.
I'D HAVE DROPPED BY YOUR HOME LATER, BUT I'M A LITTLE JAMMED FOR --
NO SWEAT. JUICE?

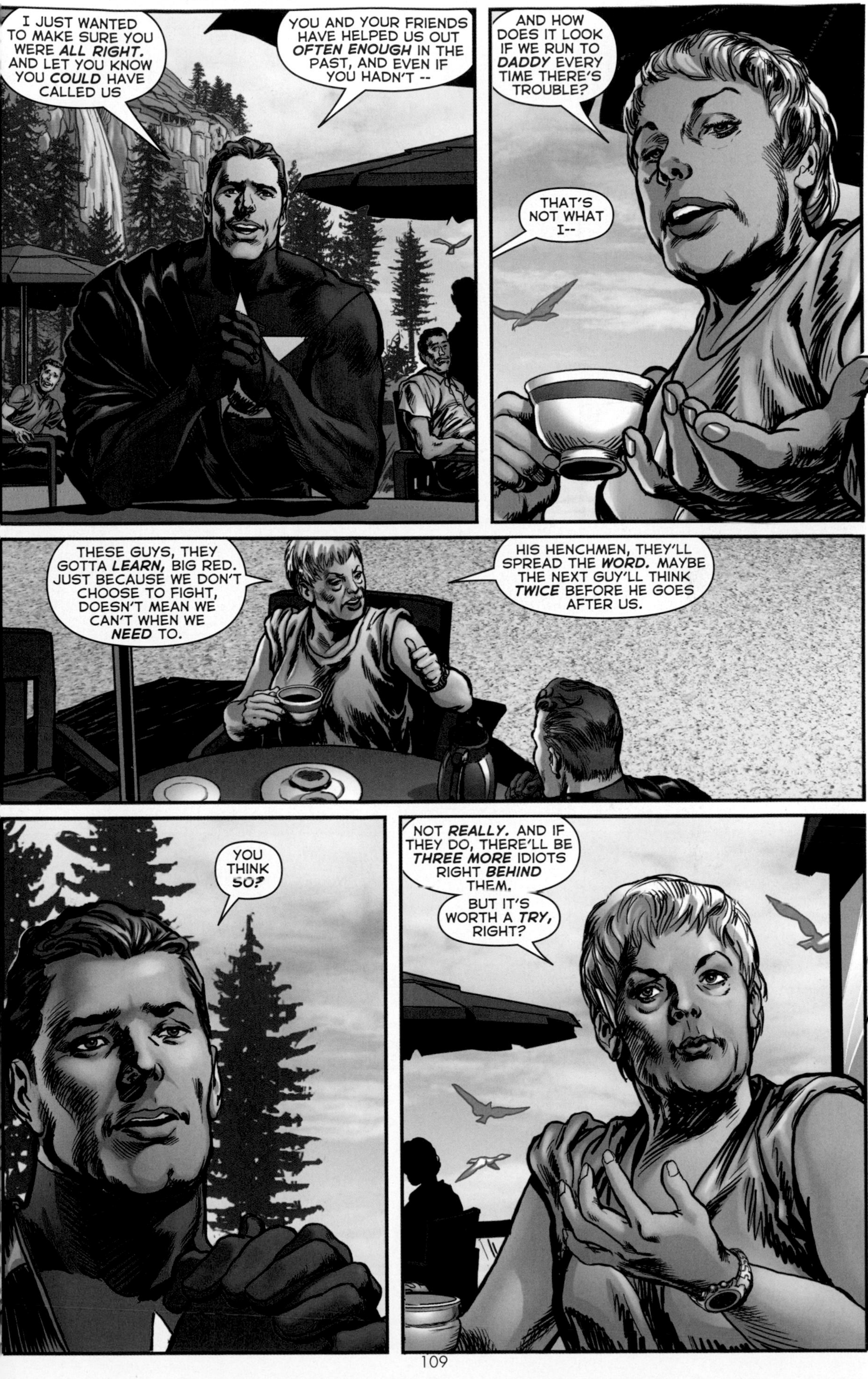
I JUST WANTED TO MAKE SURE YOU WERE ALL RIGHT. AND LET YOU KNOW YOU COULD HAVE CALLED US
YOU AND YOUR FRIENDS HAVE HELPED US OUT OFTEN ENOUGH IN THE PAST, AND EVEN IF YOU HADN'T --
AND HOW DOES IT LOOK IF WE RUN TO DADDY EVERY TIME THERE'S TROUBLE?
THAT'S NOT WHAT I--
THESE GUYS, THEY GOTTA LEARN, BIG RED. JUST BECAUSE WE DON'T CHOOSE TO FIGHT, DOESN'T MEAN WE CAN'T WHEN WE NEED TO.
HIS HENCHMEN, THEY'LL SPREAD THE WORD. MAYBE THE NEXT GUY'LL THINK TWICE BEFORE HE GOES AFTER US.
YOU THINK SO?
NOT REALLY. AND IF THEY DO, THERE'LL BE THREE MORE IDIOTS RIGHT BEHIND THEM.
BUT IT'S WORTH A TRY, RIGHT?

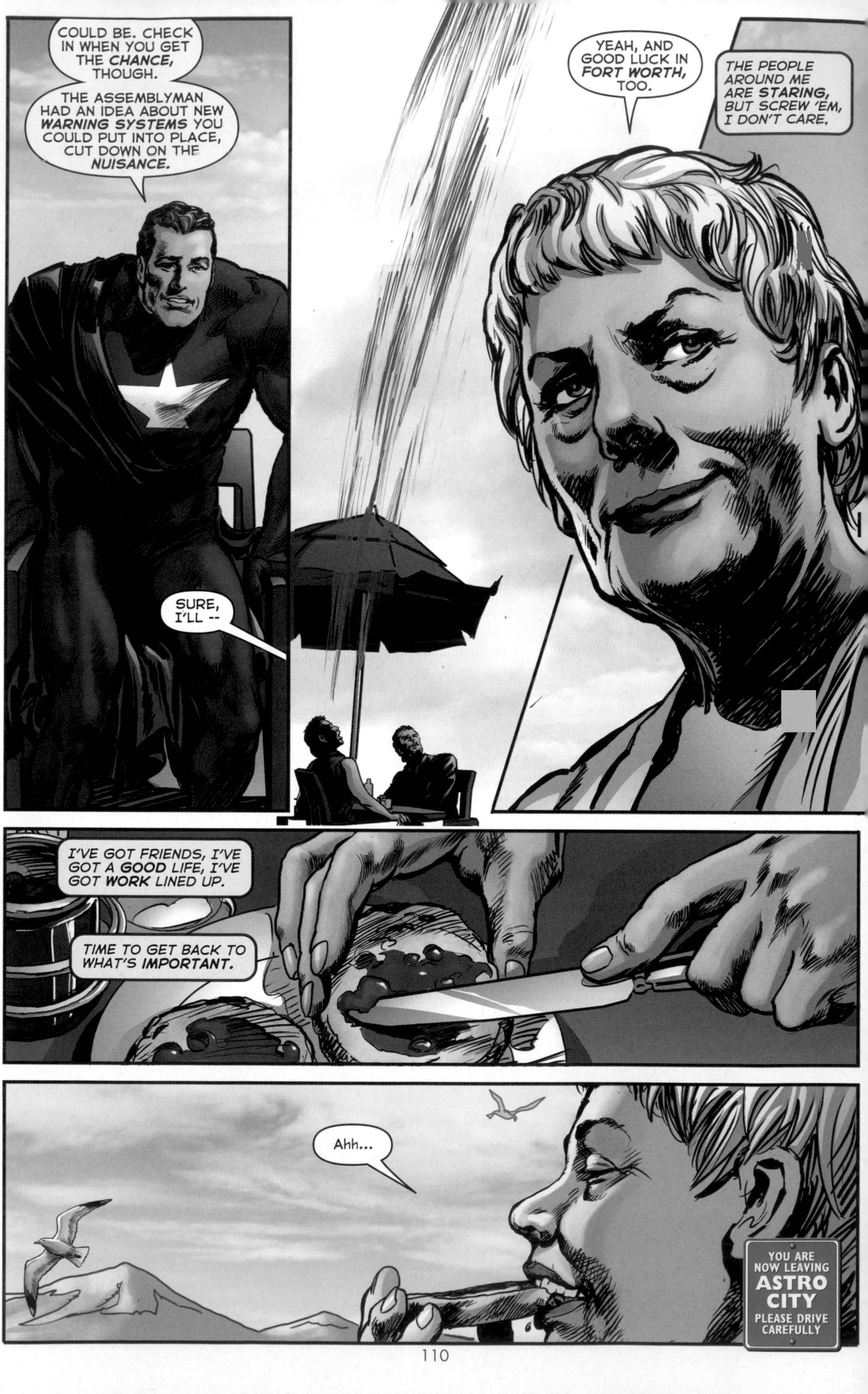
COULD BE. CHECK IN WHEN YOU GET THE CHANCE, THOUGH.
THE ASSEMBLYMAN HAD AN IDEA ABOUT NEW WARNING SYSTEMS YOU COULD PUT INTO PLACE, CUT DOWN ON THE NUISANCE.
SURE, I'LL --
YEAH, AND GOOD LUCK IN FORT WORTH, TOO.
THE PEOPLE AROUND ME ARE STARING, BUT SCREW 'EM, I DON'T CARE.
I'VE GOT FRIENDS, I'VE GOT A GOOD LIFE, I'VE GOT WORK LINED UP.
TIME TO GET BACK TO WHAT'S IMPORTANT.
Ahh...
YOU ARE NOW LEAVING ASTRO CITY PLEASE DRIVE CAREFULLY

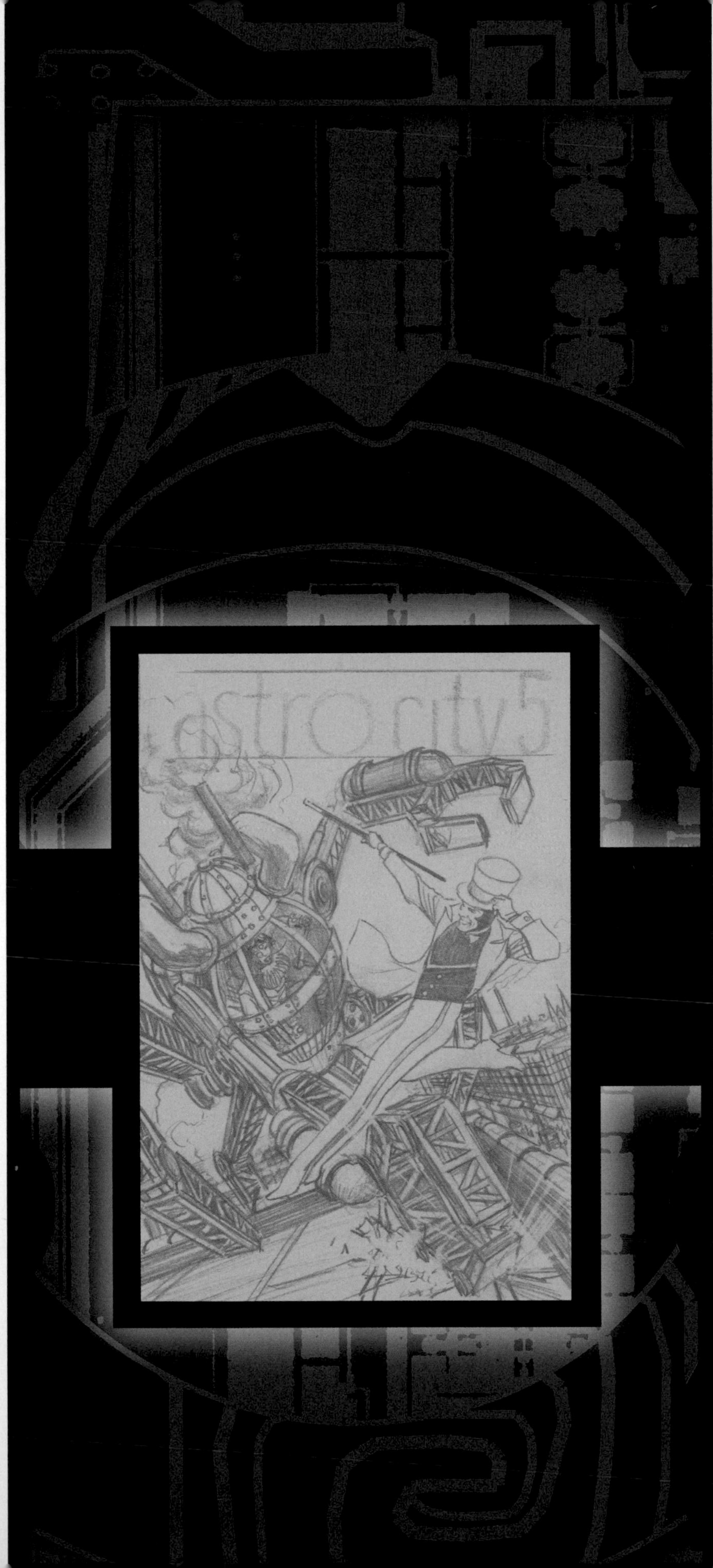
astro city5

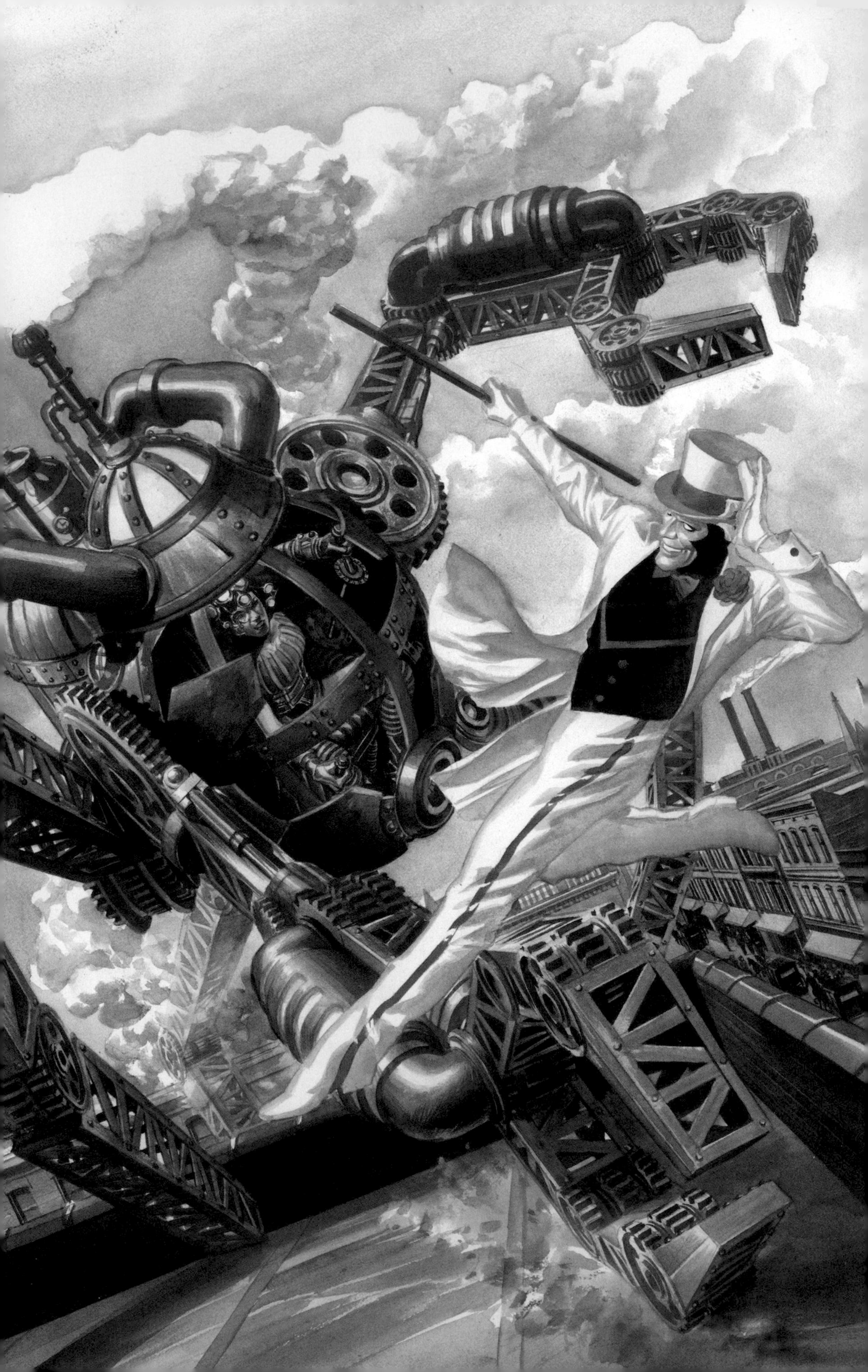

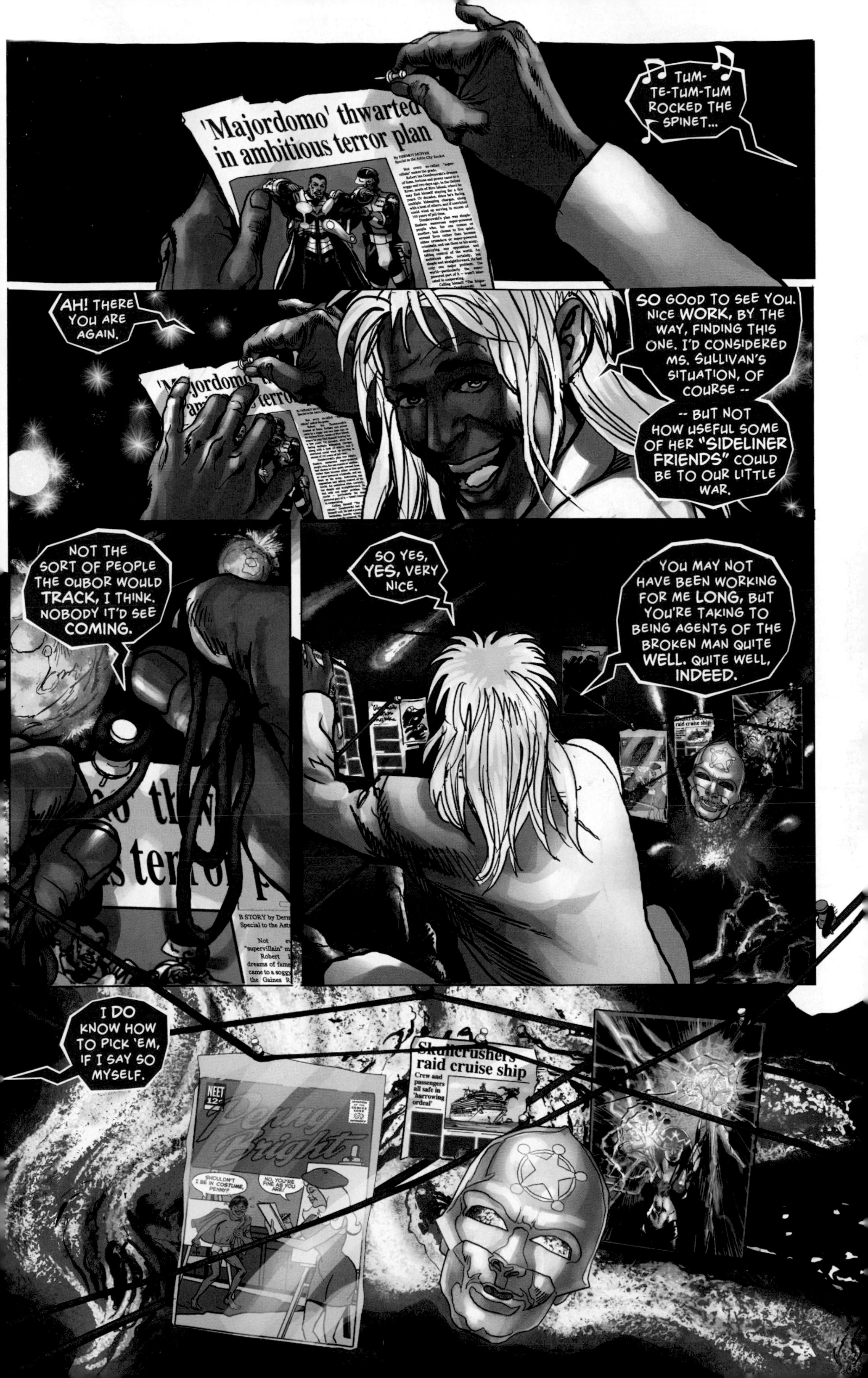

TUM-TE-TUM-TUM ROCKED THE SPINET...
'Majordomo' thwarted in ambitious terror plan
AH! THERE YOU ARE AGAIN.
SO GOOD TO SEE YOU. NICE WORK, BY THE WAY, FINDING THIS ONE. I'D CONSIDERED MS. SULLIVAN'S SITUATION, OF COURSE --
-- BUT NOT HOW USEFUL SOME OF HER "SIDELINER FRIENDS" COULD BE TO OUR LITTLE WAR.
NOT THE SORT OF PEOPLE THE OUBOR WOULD TRACK, I THINK. NOBODY IT'D SEE COMING.
SO YES, YES, VERY NICE.
YOU MAY NOT HAVE BEEN WORKING FOR ME LONG, BUT YOU'RE TAKING TO BEING AGENTS OF THE BROKEN MAN QUITE WELL. QUITE WELL, INDEED.
I DO KNOW HOW TO PICK 'EM, IF I SAY SO MYSELF.
Skullcrushers raid cruise ship
Crew and passengers all safe in 'harrowing ordeal'
NEET
Penny Bright
SHOULDN'T I BE IN COSTUME, PENNY?
NO, YOU'RE FINE AS YOU ARE!

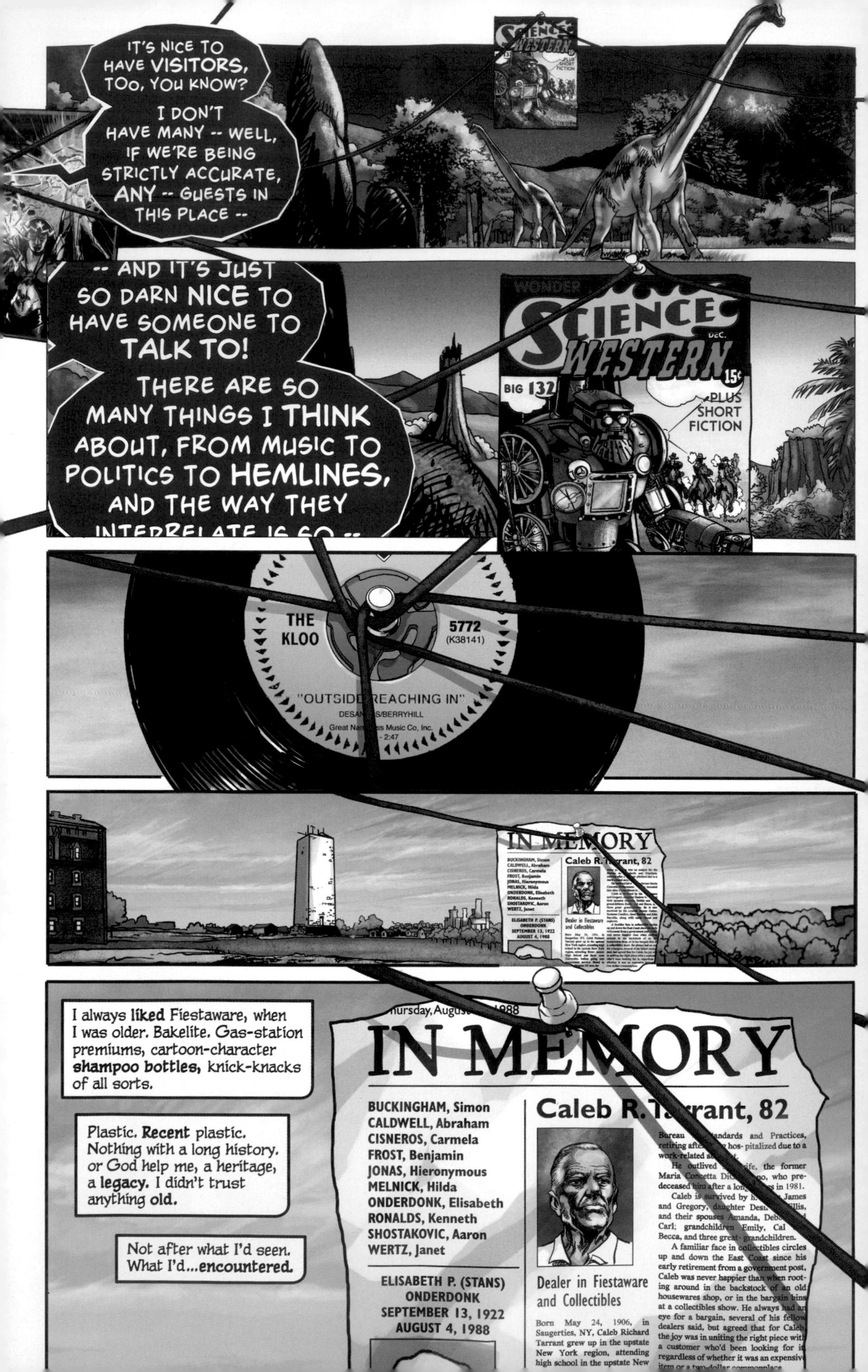

IT'S NICE TO HAVE VISITORS, TOO, YOU KNOW?
I DON'T HAVE MANY -- WELL, IF WE'RE BEING STRICTLY ACCURATE, ANY -- GUESTS IN THIS PLACE --
SCIENCE WESTERN
PLUS SHORT FICTION
-- AND IT'S JUST SO DARN NICE TO HAVE SOMEONE TO TALK TO!
THERE ARE SO MANY THINGS I THINK ABOUT, FROM MUSIC TO POLITICS TO HEMLINES, AND THE WAY THEY INTERRELATE IS SO --
WONDER SCIENCE WESTERN
DEC.
15¢
BIG 132
PLUS SHORT FICTION
THE KLOO
5772
(K38141)
"OUTSIDE REACHING IN"
DESAN S/BERRYHILL
Great Nam ss Music Co, Inc.
- 2:47
IN MEMORY
I always liked Fiestaware, when I was older. Bakelite. Gas-station premiums, cartoon-character shampoo bottles, knick-knacks of all sorts.
Plastic. Recent plastic. Nothing with a long history. or God help me, a heritage, a legacy. I didn't trust anything old.
Not after what I'd seen. What I'd...encountered.
hursday, August 1988
IN MEMORY
BUCKINGHAM, Simon
CALDWELL, Abraham
CISNEROS, Carmela
FROST, Benjamin
JONAS, Hieronymous
MELNICK, Hilda
ONDERDONK, Elisabeth
RONALDS, Kenneth
SHOSTAKOVIC, Aaron
WERTZ, Janet
ELISABETH P. (STANS) ONDERDONK SEPTEMBER 13, 1922 AUGUST 4, 1988
Caleb R. T rrant, 82
Dealer in Fiestaware and Collectibles
Born May 24, 1906, in Saugerties, NY, Caleb Richard Tarrant grew up in the upstate New York region, attending high school in the upstate New
Bureau andards and Practices, retiring afte hos- pitalized due to a work-related a
He outlived ife, the former Maria Concetta Di o, who pre- deceased him after a lon s in 1981.
Caleb is survived by h James and Gregory, daughter Des illis, and their spouses Amanda, Deb Carl; grandchildren Emily, Cal Becca, and three great- grandchildren.
A familiar face in collectibles circles up and down the East Coast since his early retirement from a government post, Caleb was never happier than when root- ing around in the backstock of an old housewares shop, or in the bargain bins at a collectibles show. He always had a eye for a bargain, several of his fellow dealers said, but agreed that for Caleb the joy was in uniting the right piece wit a customer who'd been looking for i regardless of whether it was an expensiv

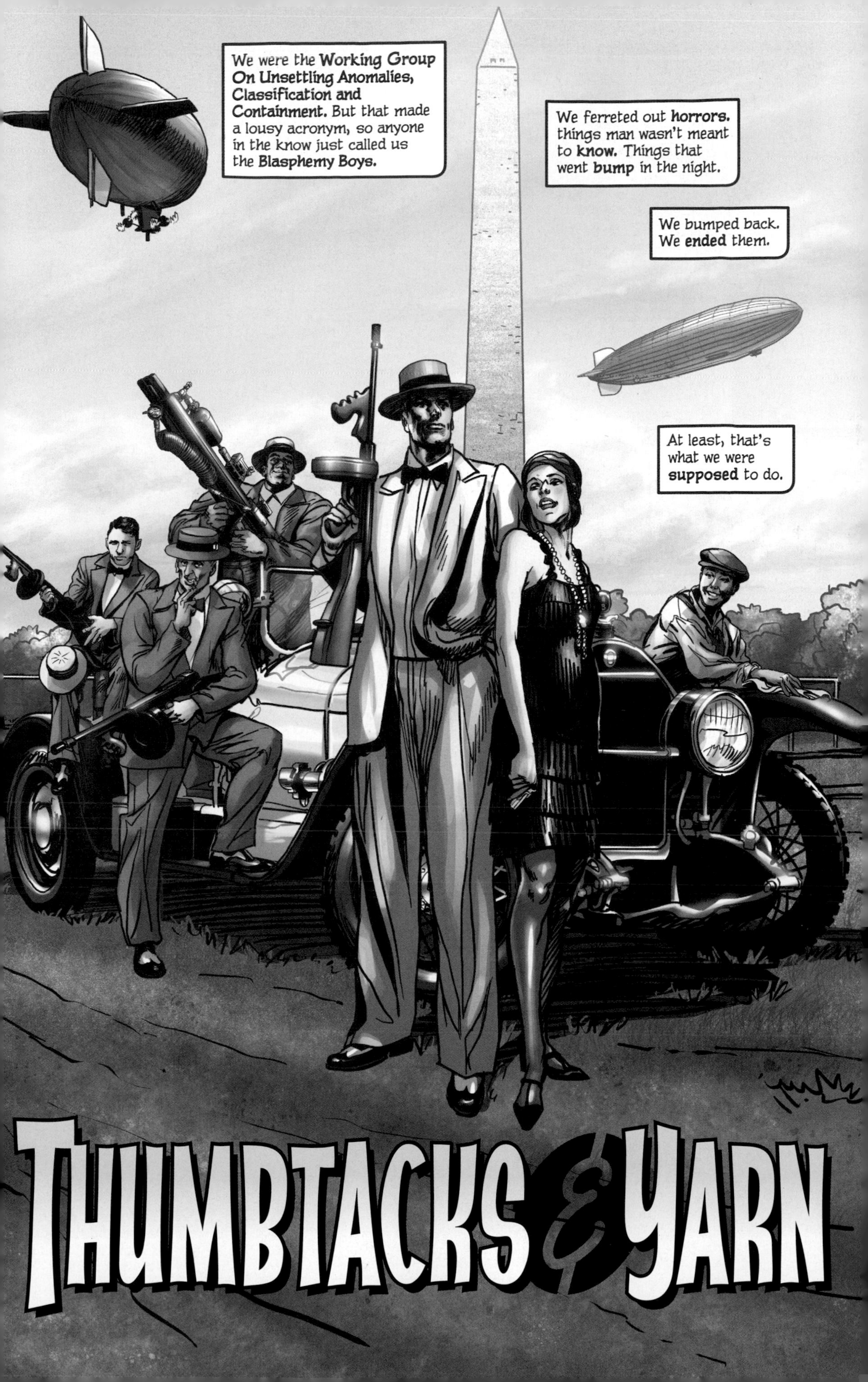
We were the Working Group On Unsettling Anomalies, Classification and Containment. But that made a lousy acronym, so anyone in the know just called us the Blasphemy Boys.
We ferreted out horrors. things man wasn't meant to know. Things that went bump in the night.
We bumped back. We ended them.
At least, that's what we were supposed to do.
THUMBTACKS & YARN

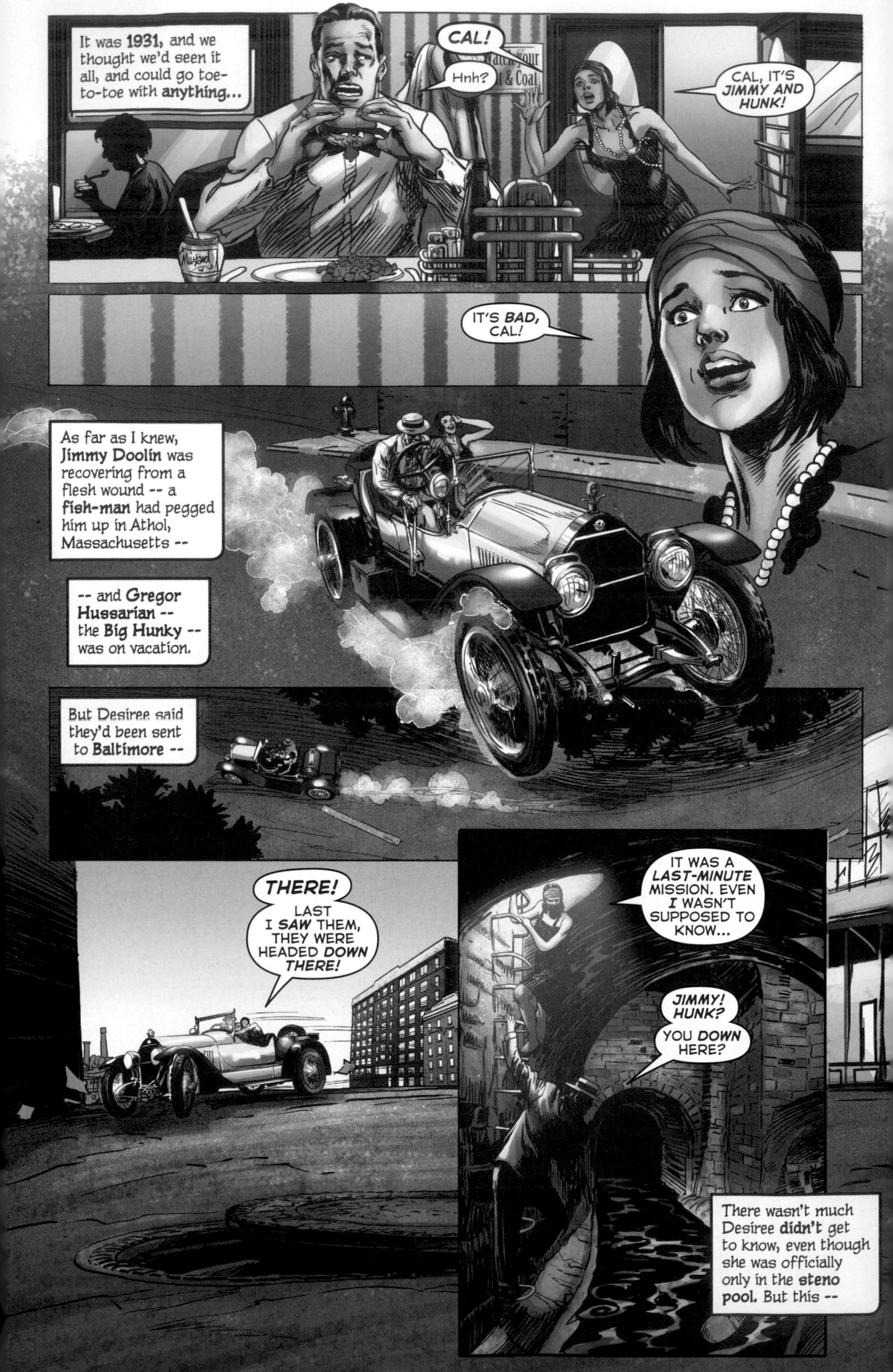
It was **1931,** and we thought we'd seen it all, and could go toe-to-toe with **anything...**
CAL!
Hnh?
Watch your Hat & Coat
CAL, IT'S JIMMY AND HUNK!
Mustard
IT'S *BAD,* CAL!
As far as I knew, **Jimmy Doolin** was recovering from a flesh wound -- a **fish-man** had pegged him up in Athol, Massachusetts --
-- and **Gregor Hussarian** -- the **Big Hunky** -- was on vacation.
But Desiree said they'd been sent to **Baltimore** --
THERE!
LAST I *SAW* THEM, THEY WERE HEADED *DOWN THERE!*
IT WAS A *LAST-MINUTE* MISSION. EVEN *I* WASN'T SUPPOSED TO KNOW...
JIMMY! HUNK?
YOU *DOWN* HERE?
There wasn't much Desiree **didn't** get to know, even though she was officially only in the **steno pool.** But this --

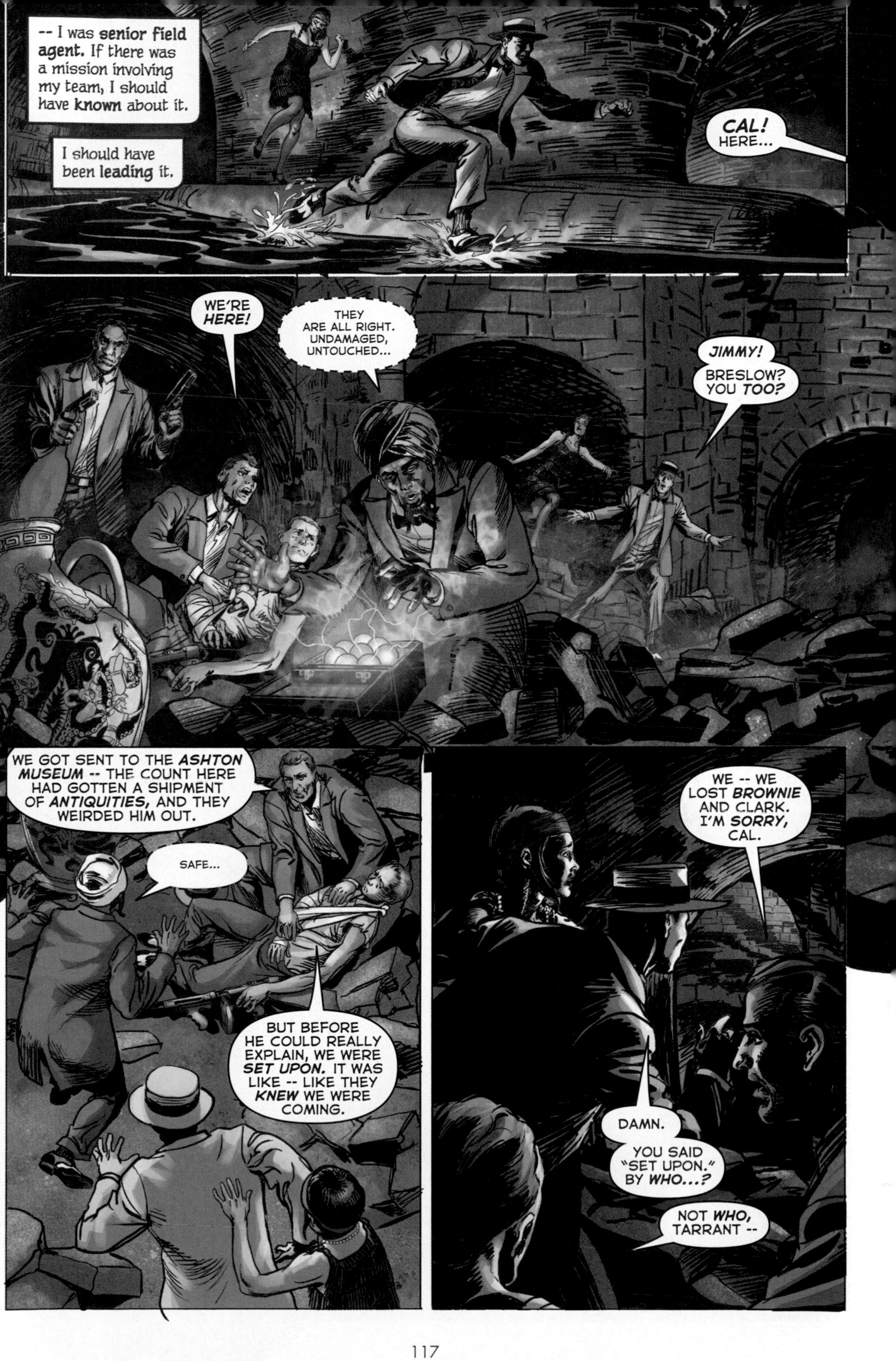
-- I was senior field agent. If there was a mission involving my team, I should have known about it.
I should have been leading it.
CAL! HERE...
WE'RE HERE!
THEY ARE ALL RIGHT. UNDAMAGED, UNTOUCHED...
JIMMY!
BRESLOW? YOU TOO?
WE GOT SENT TO THE ASHTON MUSEUM -- THE COUNT HERE HAD GOTTEN A SHIPMENT OF ANTIQUITIES, AND THEY WEIRDED HIM OUT.
SAFE...
BUT BEFORE HE COULD REALLY EXPLAIN, WE WERE SET UPON. IT WAS LIKE -- LIKE THEY KNEW WE WERE COMING.
WE -- WE LOST BROWNIE AND CLARK. I'M SORRY, CAL.
DAMN.
YOU SAID "SET UPON." BY WHO...?
NOT WHO, TARRANT --

AL!! ALIA-YA!

KECHH'ECHH ECCH!

GHKHIAHHH!

GHIYAAA! GHIYAAA!

-- WHAT!

BATRACHI! GUN 'EM DOWN!

BLAMBLAMBLAMBLAMBLI

It didn't make **sense**. It didn't make any sense **at all**.

There'd been occasional reports of them **down South**, but so far, nothing that had **panned out**.

No, they --

CAL...?

What were Batrachi doing this far from **Ipswich?** The sewers were a perfect base for them, but how'd they **get** here?

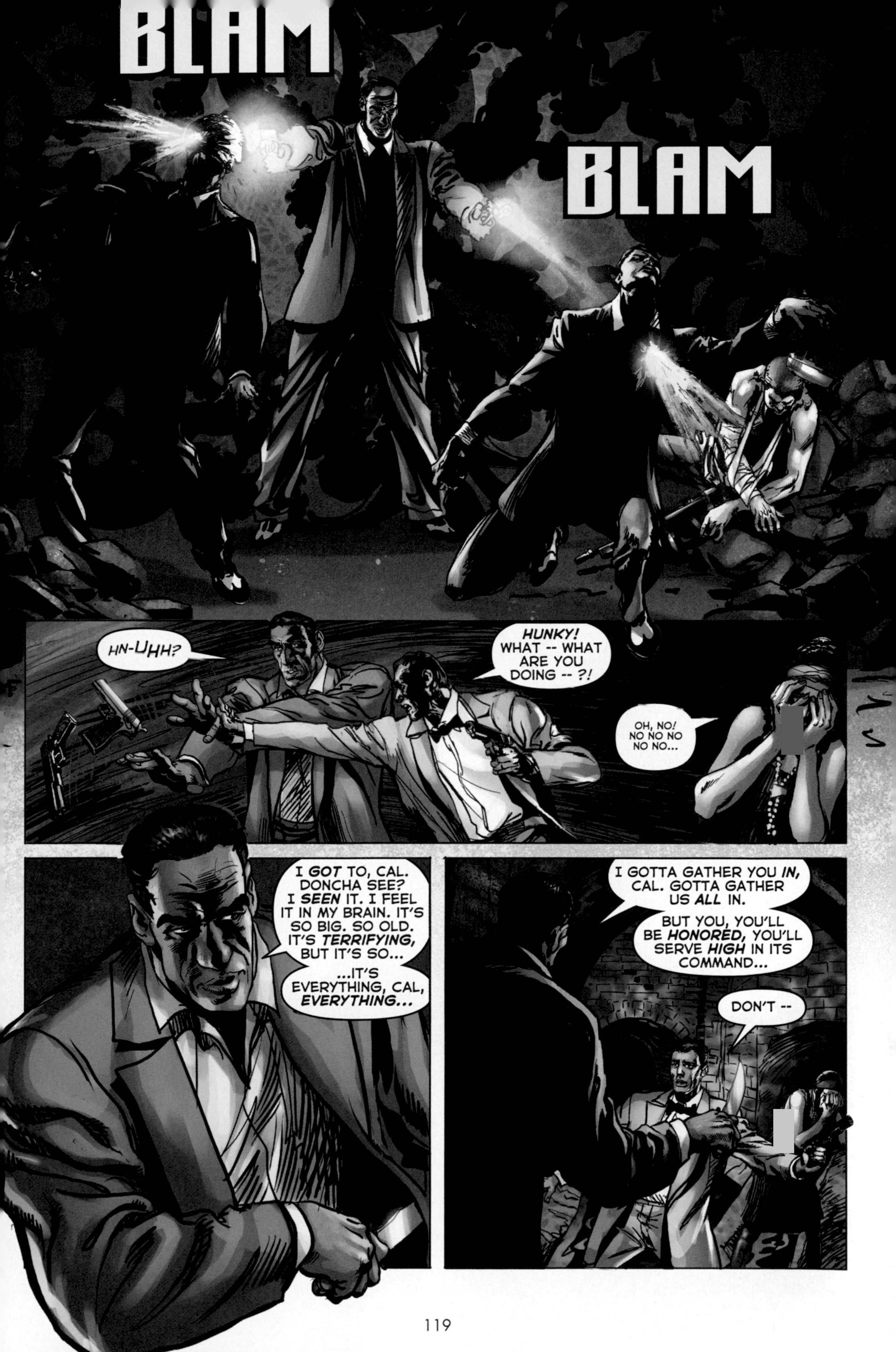
BLAM
BLAM
HN-UHH?
HUNKY! WHAT -- WHAT ARE YOU DOING -- ?!
OH, NO! NO NO NO NO NO...
I GOT TO, CAL. DONCHA SEE? I SEEN IT. I FEEL IT IN MY BRAIN. IT'S SO BIG. SO OLD. IT'S TERRIFYING, BUT IT'S SO...
...IT'S EVERYTHING, CAL, EVERYTHING...
I GOTTA GATHER YOU IN, CAL. GOTTA GATHER US ALL IN.
BUT YOU, YOU'LL BE HONORED, YOU'LL SERVE HIGH IN ITS COMMAND...
DON'T --

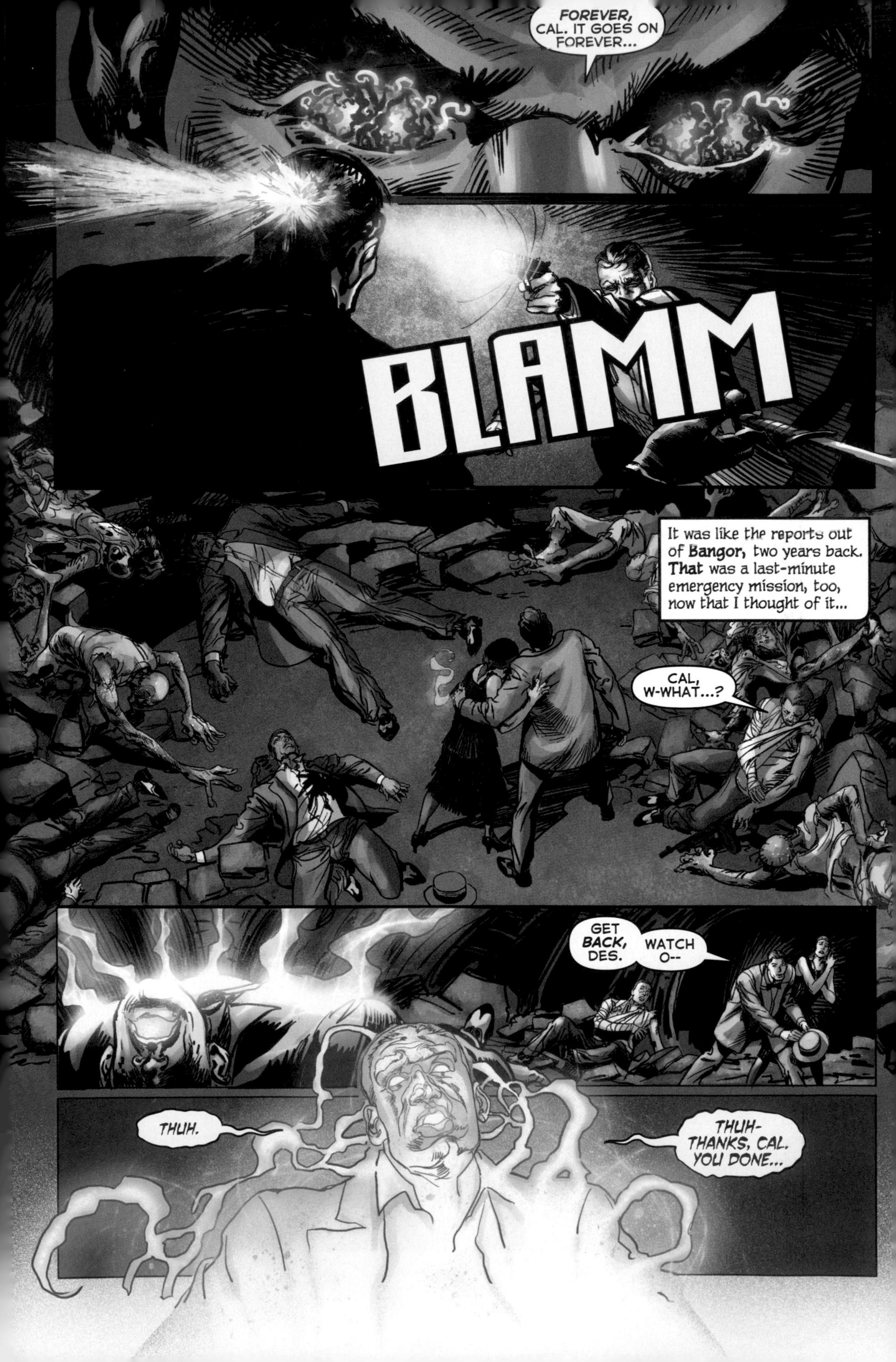
FOREVER, CAL. IT GOES ON FOREVER...
BLAMM
It was like the reports out of Bangor, two years back. That was a last-minute emergency mission, too, now that I thought of it...
CAL, W-WHAT...?
GET BACK, DES.
WATCH O--
THUH.
THUH- THANKS, CAL. YOU DONE...

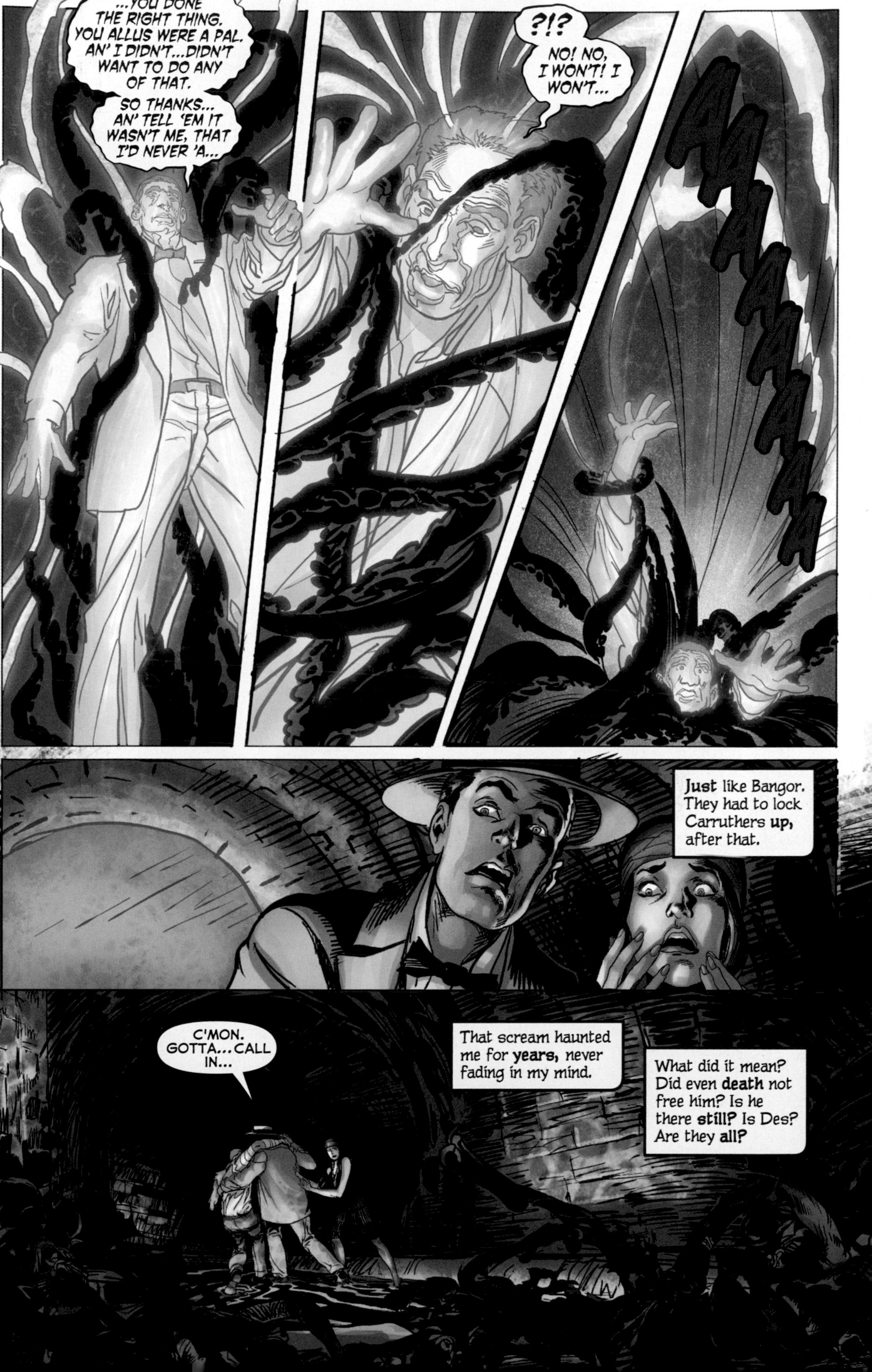
...YOU DONE THE RIGHT THING. YOU ALLUS WERE A PAL. AN' I DIDN'T...DIDN'T WANT TO DO ANY OF THAT.
SO THANKS... AN' TELL 'EM IT WASN'T ME, THAT I'D NEVER 'A...
?!?
NO! NO, I WON'T! I WON'T...
AAAAAAAAAAAA
Just like Bangor. They had to lock Carruthers up, after that.
C'MON. GOTTA...CALL IN...
That scream haunted me for years, never fading in my mind.
What did it mean? Did even death not free him? Is he there still? Is Des? Are they all?

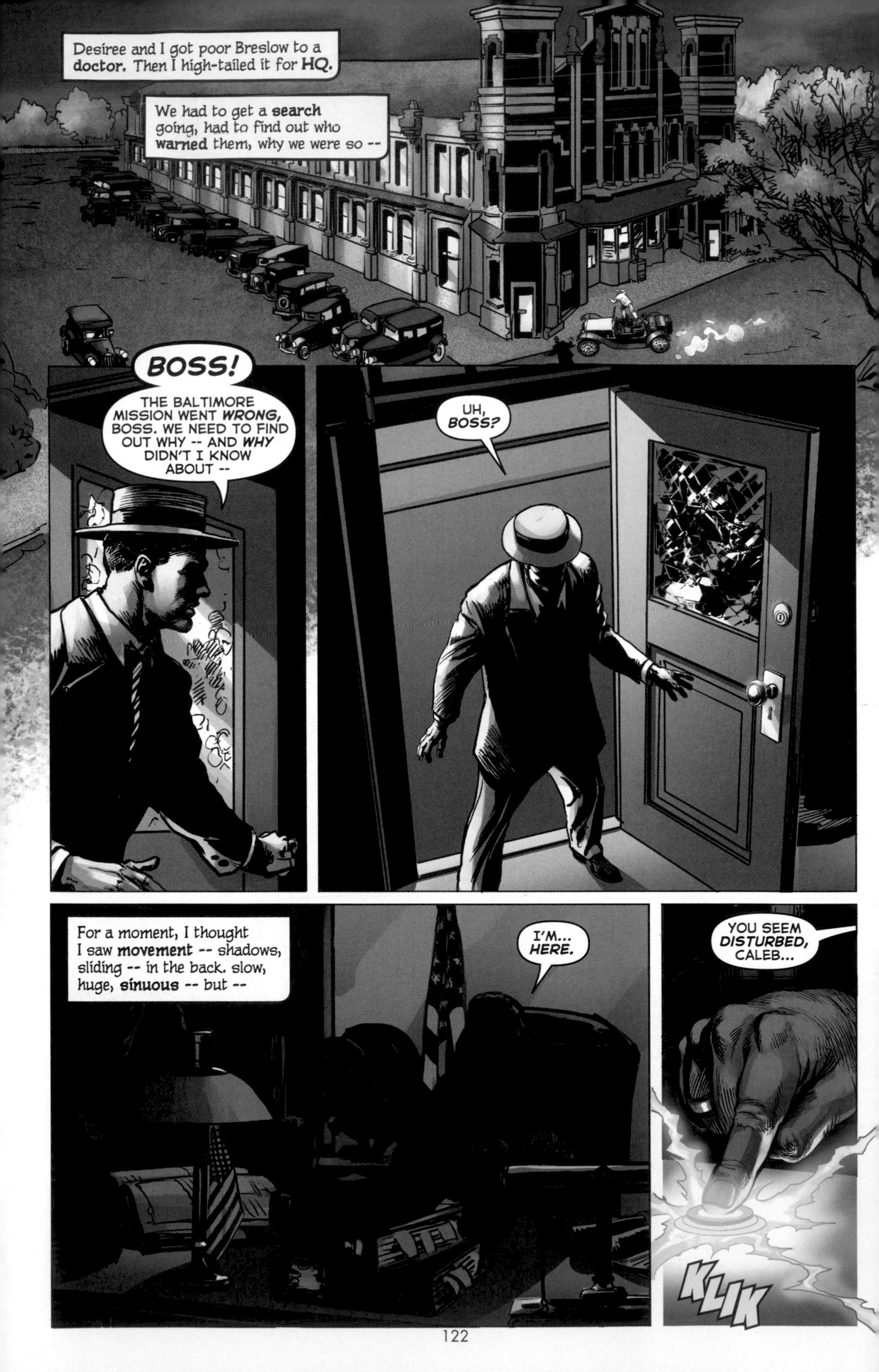
Desiree and I got poor Breslow to a **doctor.** Then I high-tailed it for **HQ.**
We had to get a **search** going, had to find out who **warned** them, why we were so --
BOSS!
THE BALTIMORE MISSION WENT *WRONG,* BOSS. WE NEED TO FIND OUT WHY -- AND *WHY* DIDN'T I KNOW ABOUT --
UH, *BOSS?*
For a moment, I thought I saw **movement** -- shadows, sliding -- in the back. slow, huge, **sinuous** -- but --
I'M... *HERE.*
YOU SEEM *DISTURBED,* CALEB...
KLIK

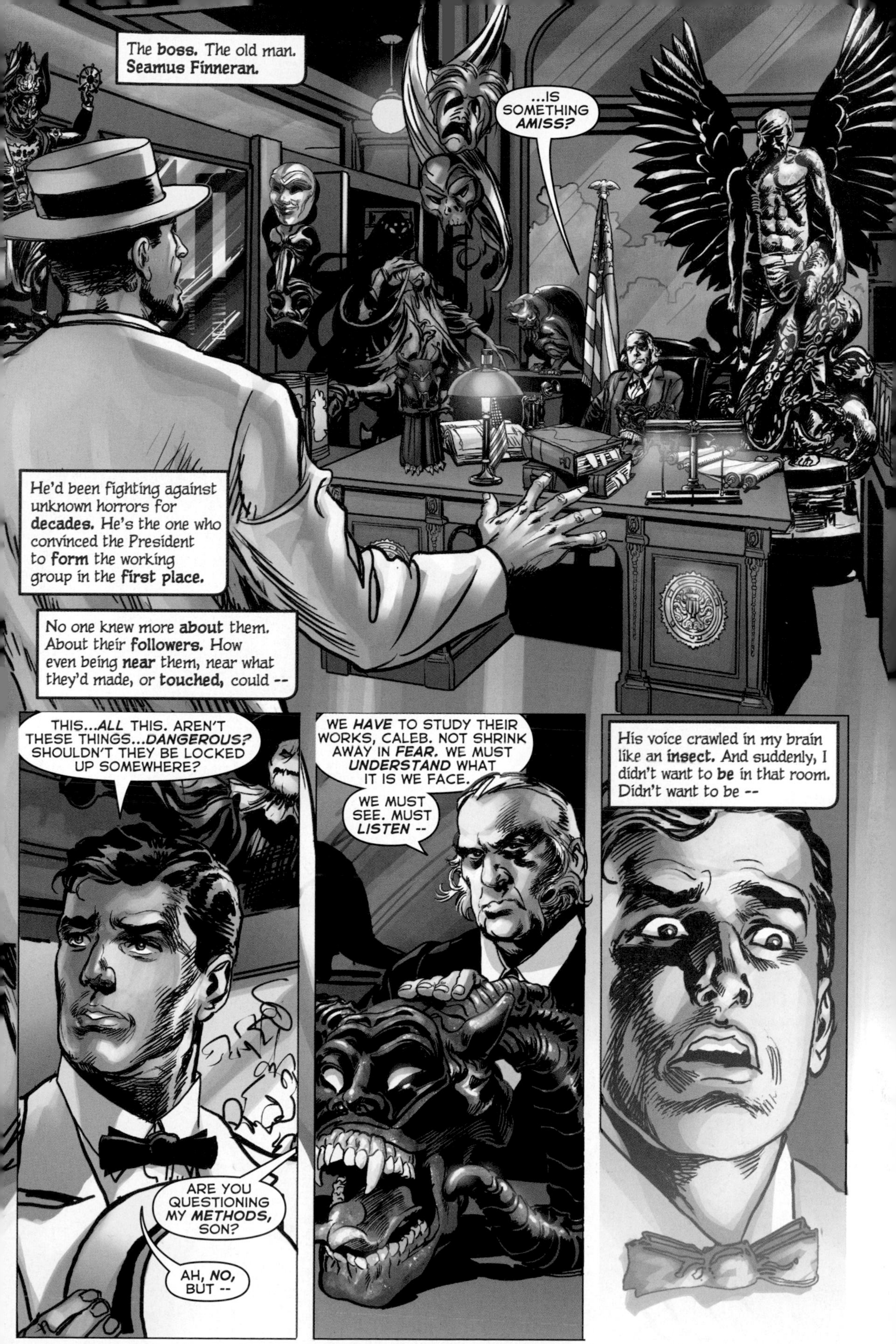
The boss. The old man. Seamus Finneran.
...IS SOMETHING AMISS?
He'd been fighting against unknown horrors for decades. He's the one who convinced the President to form the working group in the first place.
No one knew more about them. About their followers. How even being near them, near what they'd made, or touched, could --
THIS...ALL THIS. AREN'T THESE THINGS...DANGEROUS? SHOULDN'T THEY BE LOCKED UP SOMEWHERE?
ARE YOU QUESTIONING MY METHODS, SON?
AH, NO, BUT --
WE HAVE TO STUDY THEIR WORKS, CALEB. NOT SHRINK AWAY IN FEAR. WE MUST UNDERSTAND WHAT IT IS WE FACE.
WE MUST SEE. MUST LISTEN --
His voice crawled in my brain like an insect. And suddenly, I didn't want to be in that room. Didn't want to be --

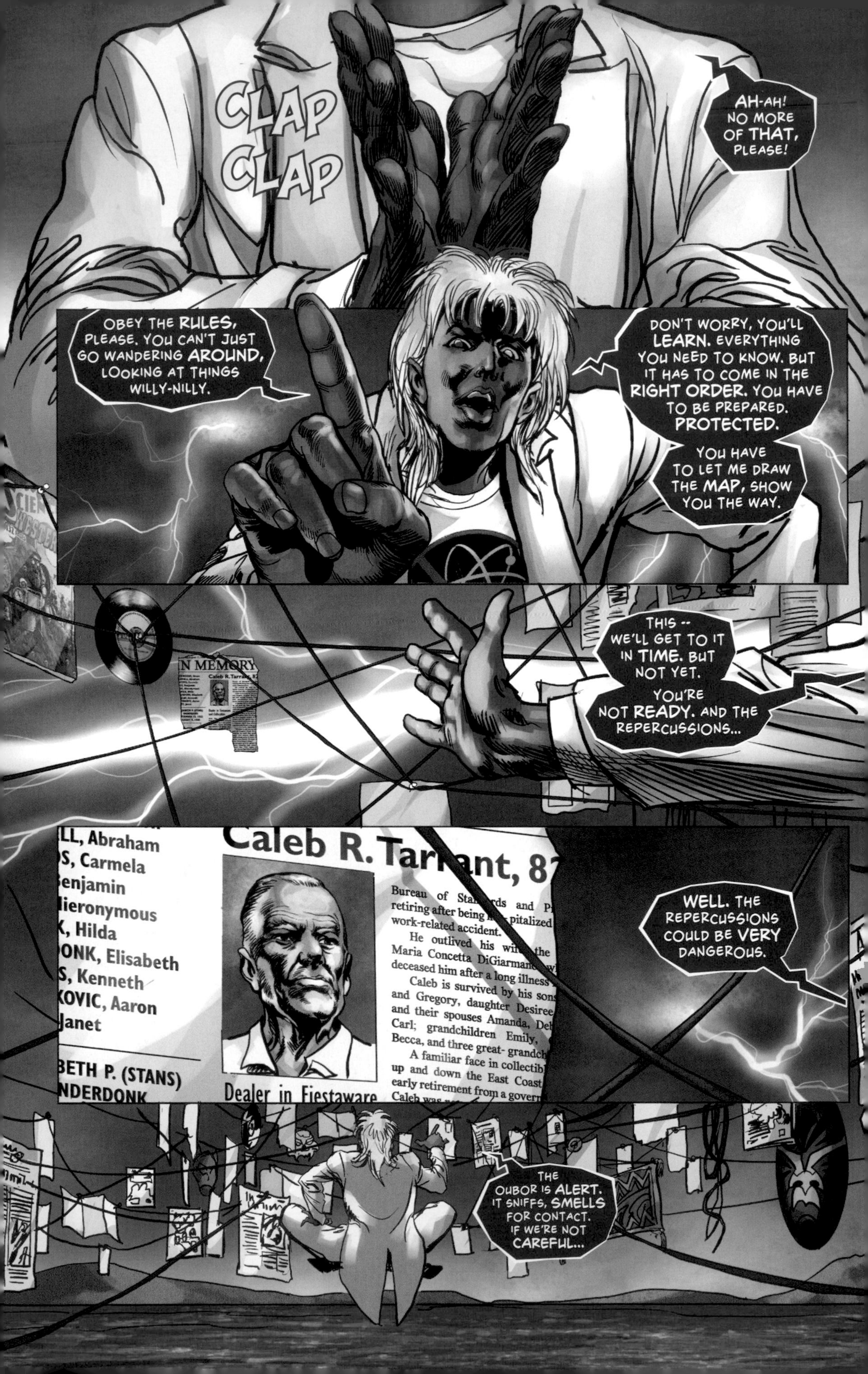

CLAP CLAP
AH-AH! NO MORE OF THAT, PLEASE!
OBEY THE RULES, PLEASE. YOU CAN'T JUST GO WANDERING AROUND, LOOKING AT THINGS WILLY-NILLY.
DON'T WORRY, YOU'LL LEARN. EVERYTHING YOU NEED TO KNOW. BUT IT HAS TO COME IN THE RIGHT ORDER. YOU HAVE TO BE PREPARED. PROTECTED.
YOU HAVE TO LET ME DRAW THE MAP, SHOW YOU THE WAY.
N MEMORY
THIS -- WE'LL GET TO IT IN TIME. BUT NOT YET.
YOU'RE NOT READY. AND THE REPERCUSSIONS...
LL, Abraham
S, Carmela
Benjamin
Hieronymous
K, Hilda
DONK, Elisabeth
S, Kenneth
KOVIC, Aaron
Janet
BETH P. (STANS)
NDERDONK
Caleb R. Tarrant, 8
Dealer in Fiestaware
Bureau of Sta rds and P
retiring after being h pitalized
work-related accident.
He outlived his wif the
Maria Concetta DiGiarman
deceased him after a long illness
Caleb is survived by his sons
and Gregory, daughter Desiree
and their spouses Amanda, Deb
Carl; grandchildren Emily,
Becca, and three great- grandch
A familiar face in collectib
up and down the East Coast
early retirement from a govern
WELL. THE REPERCUSSIONS COULD BE VERY DANGEROUS.
THE OUBOR IS ALERT. IT SNIFFS, SMELLS FOR CONTACT. IF WE'RE NOT CAREFUL...

If we're not careful, it could be the end of everything that matters, not only for my world...

Silver Agent scheduled for execution

By ELLIOT MILLS
Special to the Astro City Rocket

The controversial career of the Silver Agent will finally reach an end this Thursday, in February of premeditated murder, Alan Jay Craig was sentenced to death, and yesterday, a three-judge panel scheduled his execution. Craig's lawyers said he would make no appeal, and there is little expectation that President Nixon will pardon Craig, or commute his sentence. Indeed, the White House, behind the scenes, is reported to have urged swift action in order to remove stumbling block from Southeast Asian peace talks.

SUCCESSION IN MAGA-DHOR MURKY

Nation Laments the Loss of Much-Loved 'Dancing Maharajah,' Grieving 'Rhumba Mobs' Abound

WOULD-BE ASSASSIN KILLED

British Forces May Have to Step In to Restore Order in Tiny State

ALIEN TEMPLES
by ASHTON COLT

Are Demons From Space Still Among Us?

mba Mobs' Abound

ULD-BE ASSASSIN KILLED

Forces May Have tep In to Restore der in Tiny State

INDIA - He was famous for his lance, and for his reputed claim ou can take my rubies, you can pearls, take my camels and all my umba lessons are wanted for the arajah of Maga-Dhor." One of the bcontinent's wealthiest rulers, his ved in peace and harmony even turbulent upheavals in the world nd their borders, due in great is skill in forging alliances and his n defusing disputes among his s. But his death after a sudden s left his tiny nation grieving, and ring, potentially-dangerous brew claimants to the throne argue

NAPARSKI BENJAMIN 461 - 88 - 4001 RH POSITIVE SERGEANT US ARMY

1947. INDIA, I THINK.

THE VALLEY OF THE NAJI, SOMEWHERE NEAR LAHKIMPUR. THOUGH I'LL ADMIT, I'VE NEVER BEEN COMPLETELY SURE JUST HOW NEAR.

NOT THE KIND OF PLACE THAT HAS A LOT OF **CONTACT** WITH THE INDIAN GOVERNMENT, MOST OF THE TIME.

MAYBE EVEN ALL OF THE TIME.

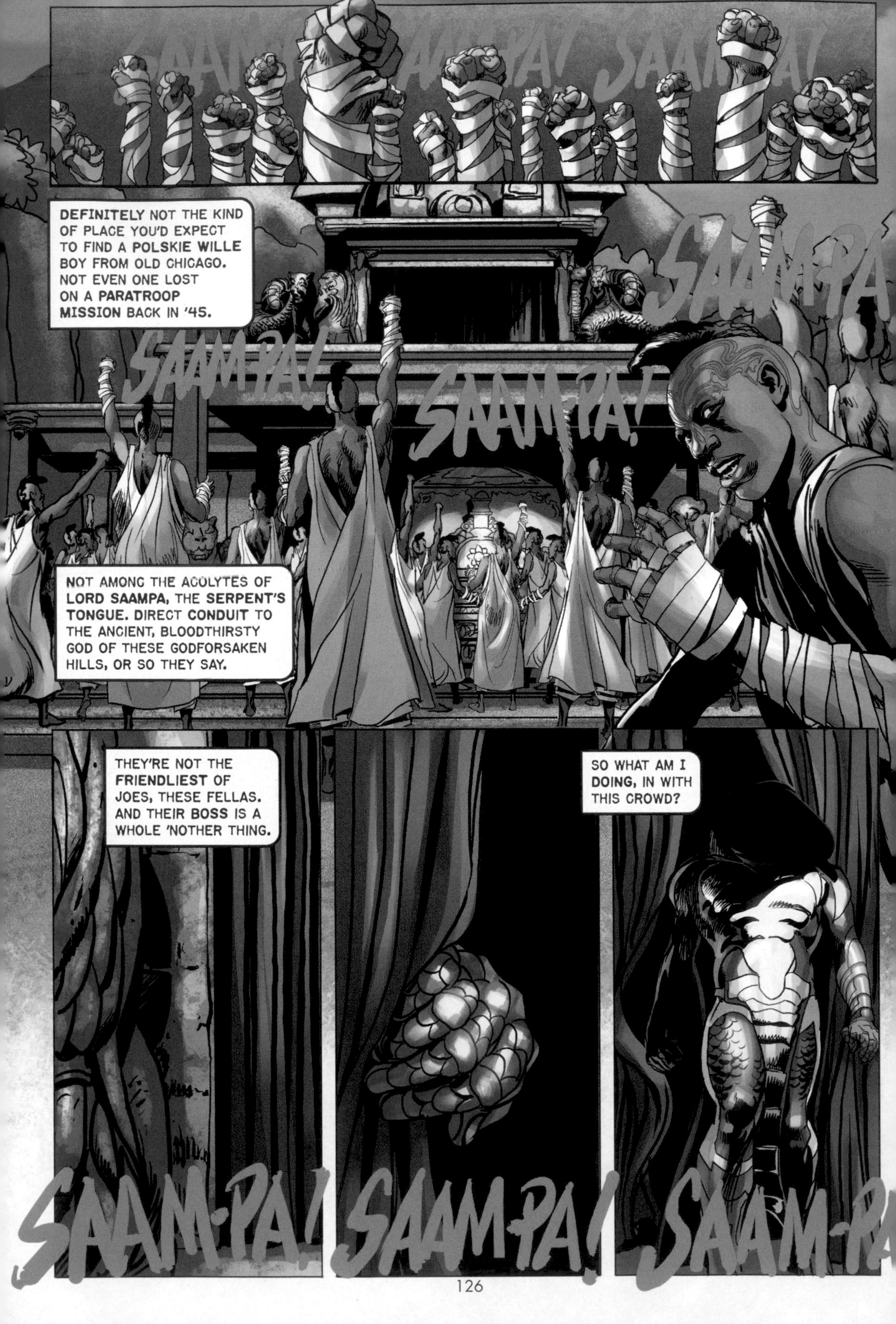
SAAMPA! SAAMPA! SAAMPA!
DEFINITELY NOT THE KIND OF PLACE YOU'D EXPECT TO FIND A POLSKIE WILLE BOY FROM OLD CHICAGO. NOT EVEN ONE LOST ON A PARATROOP MISSION BACK IN '45.
SAAMPA!
SAAMPA!
SAAM-PA!
NOT AMONG THE ACOLYTES OF LORD SAAMPA, THE SERPENT'S TONGUE. DIRECT CONDUIT TO THE ANCIENT, BLOODTHIRSTY GOD OF THESE GODFORSAKEN HILLS, OR SO THEY SAY.
THEY'RE NOT THE FRIENDLIEST OF JOES, THESE FELLAS. AND THEIR BOSS IS A WHOLE 'NOTHER THING.
SO WHAT AM I DOING, IN WITH THIS CROWD?
SAAM-PA! SAAM-PA! SAAM-PA

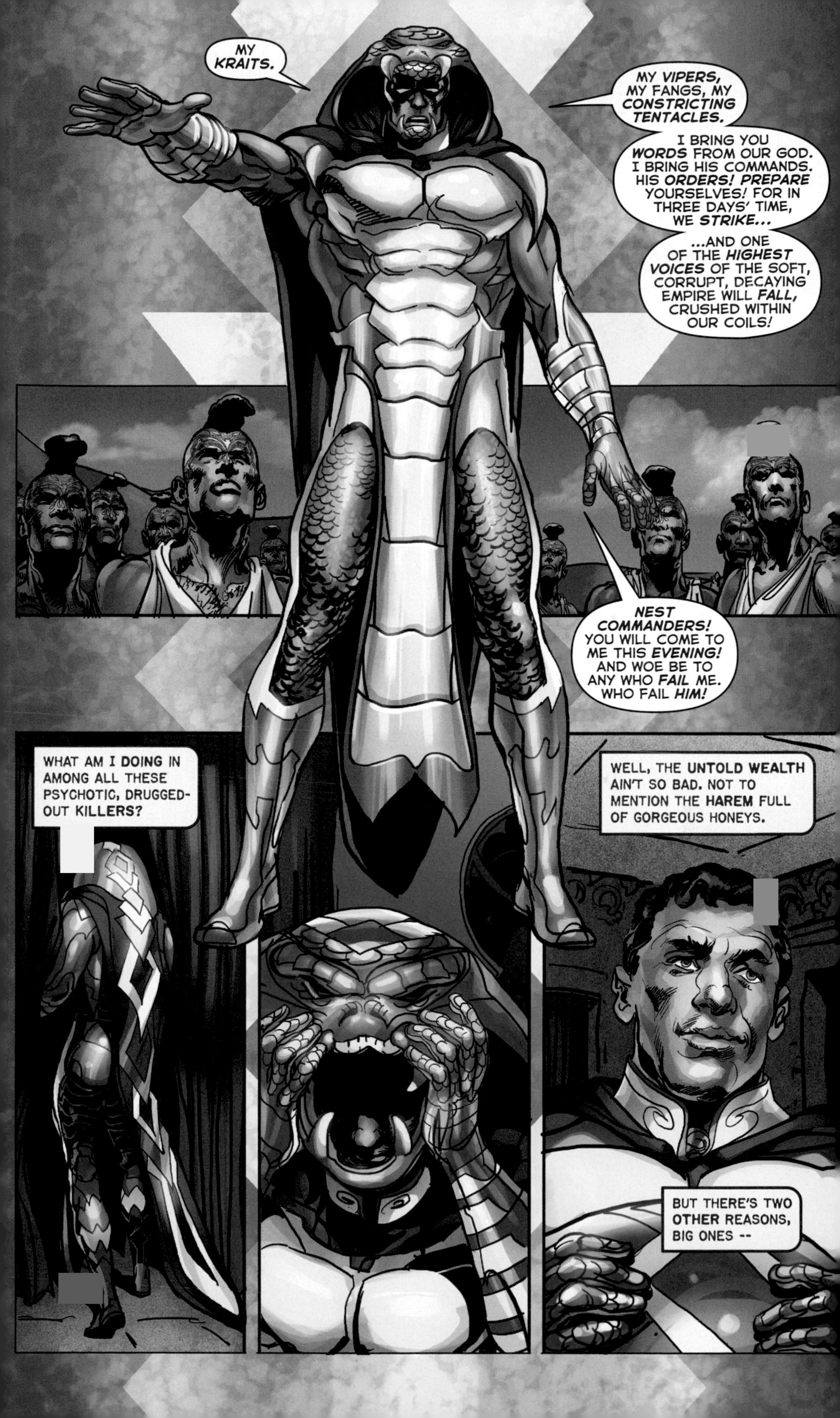
MY KRAITS.
MY VIPERS, MY FANGS, MY CONSTRICTING TENTACLES.
I BRING YOU WORDS FROM OUR GOD. I BRING HIS COMMANDS. HIS ORDERS! PREPARE YOURSELVES! FOR IN THREE DAYS' TIME, WE STRIKE...
...AND ONE OF THE HIGHEST VOICES OF THE SOFT, CORRUPT, DECAYING EMPIRE WILL FALL, CRUSHED WITHIN OUR COILS!
NEST COMMANDERS! YOU WILL COME TO ME THIS EVENING! AND WOE BE TO ANY WHO FAIL ME. WHO FAIL HIM!
WHAT AM I DOING IN AMONG ALL THESE PSYCHOTIC, DRUGGED-OUT KILLERS?
WELL, THE UNTOLD WEALTH AIN'T SO BAD. NOT TO MENTION THE HAREM FULL OF GORGEOUS HONEYS.
BUT THERE'S TWO OTHER REASONS, BIG ONES --

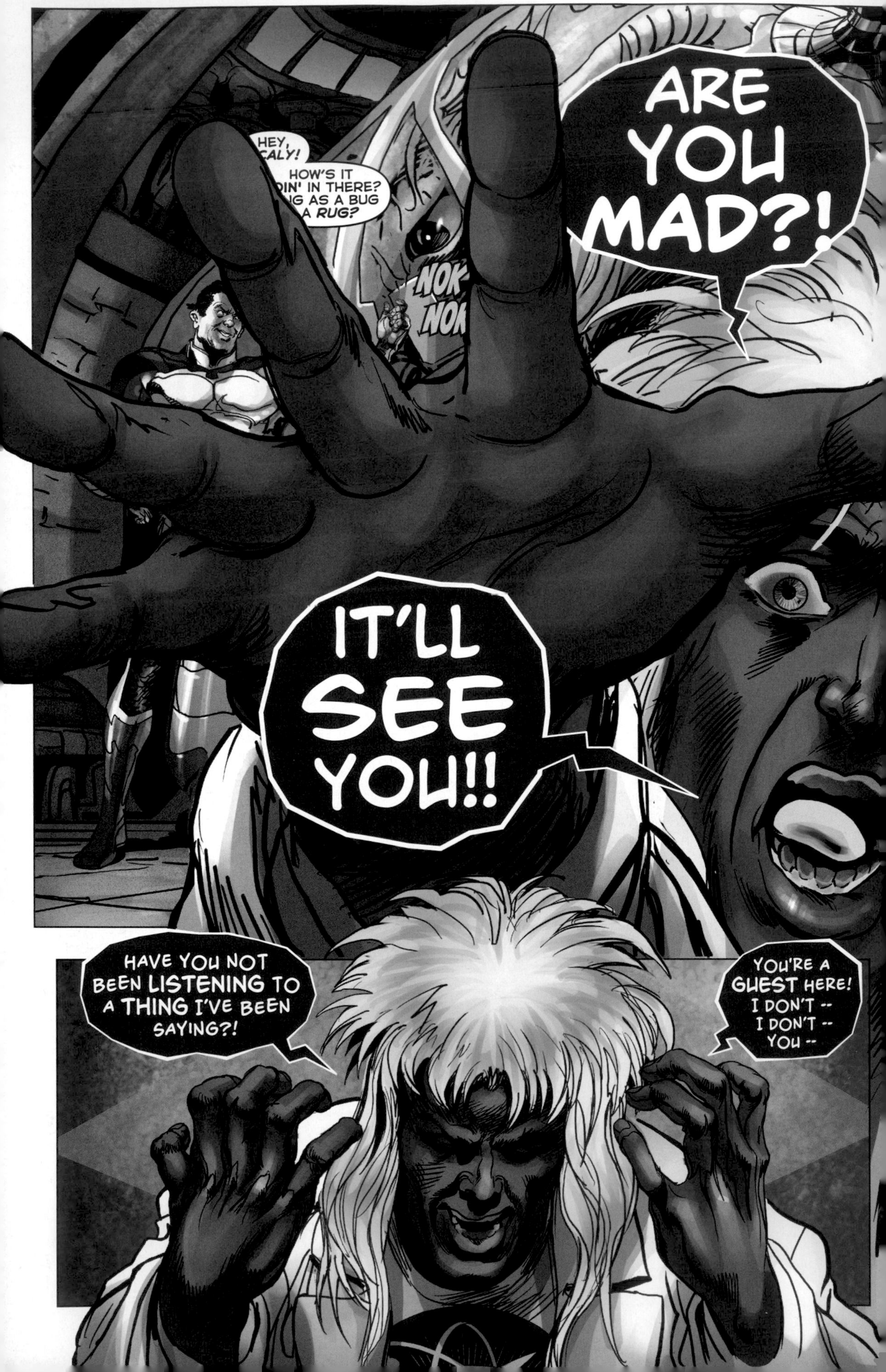
HEY, CALY!
HOW'S IT DIN' IN THERE? IG AS A BUG A RUG?
NOK NOK
ARE YOU MAD?!
IT'LL SEE YOU!!
HAVE YOU NOT BEEN LISTENING TO A THING I'VE BEEN SAYING?!
YOU'RE A GUEST HERE! I DON'T -- I DON'T -- YOU --

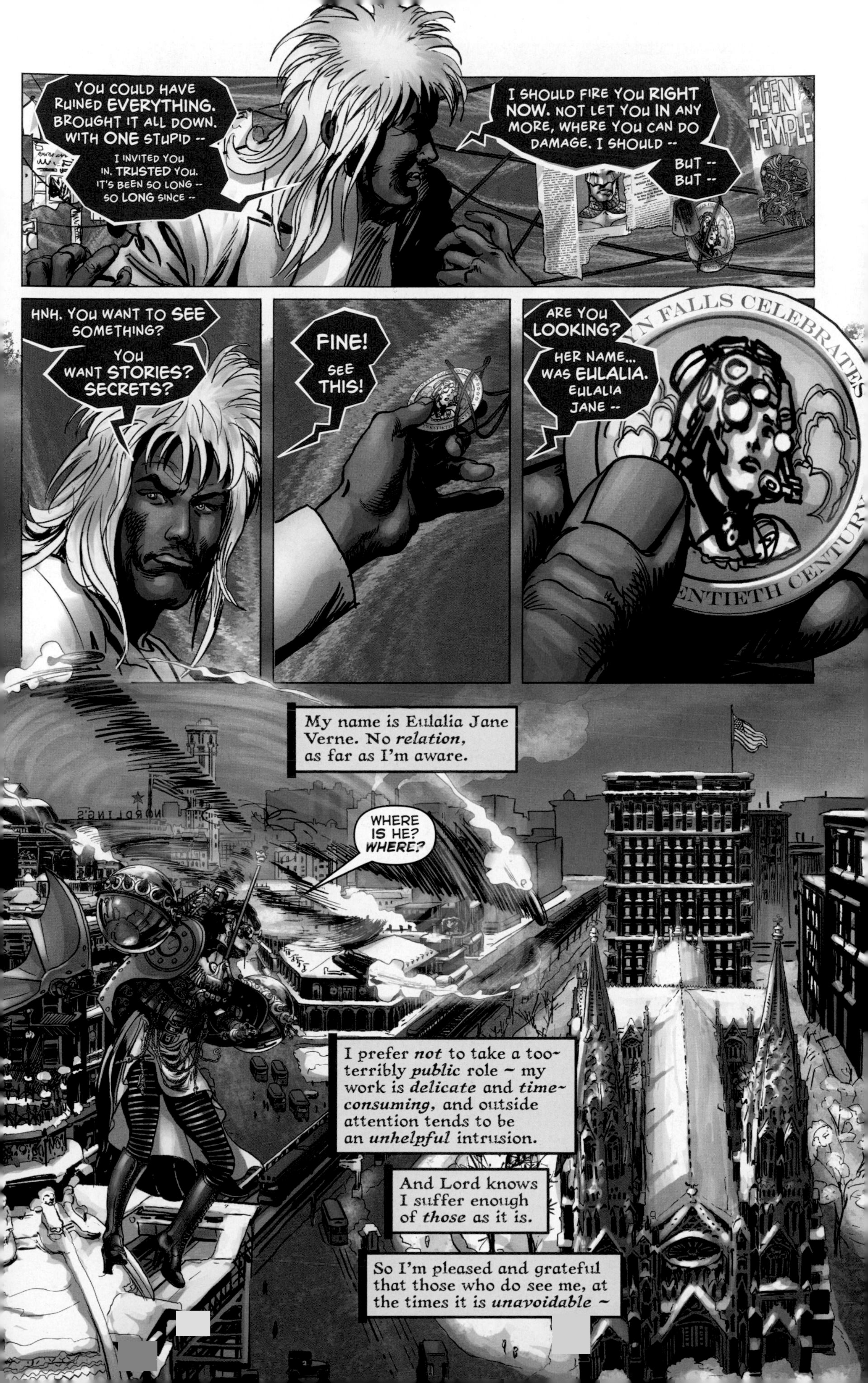
YOU COULD HAVE RUINED EVERYTHING. BROUGHT IT ALL DOWN. WITH ONE STUPID --
I INVITED YOU IN. TRUSTED YOU. IT'S BEEN SO LONG -- SO LONG SINCE --
I SHOULD FIRE YOU RIGHT NOW. NOT LET YOU IN ANY MORE, WHERE YOU CAN DO DAMAGE. I SHOULD --
BUT -- BUT --
ALIEN TEMPLE!
HNH. YOU WANT TO SEE SOMETHING?
YOU WANT STORIES? SECRETS?
FINE!
SEE THIS!
ARE YOU LOOKING?
HER NAME... WAS EULALIA. EULALIA JANE --
YN FALLS CELEBRATES
ENTIETH CENTURY
My name is Eulalia Jane Verne. No *relation*, as far as I'm aware.
WHERE IS HE? *WHERE?*
NORDLING'S
I prefer *not* to take a too-terribly *public* role ~ my work is *delicate* and *time-consuming*, and outside attention tends to be an *unhelpful* intrusion.
And Lord knows I suffer enough of *those* as it is.
So I'm pleased and grateful that those who do see me, at the times it is *unavoidable* ~

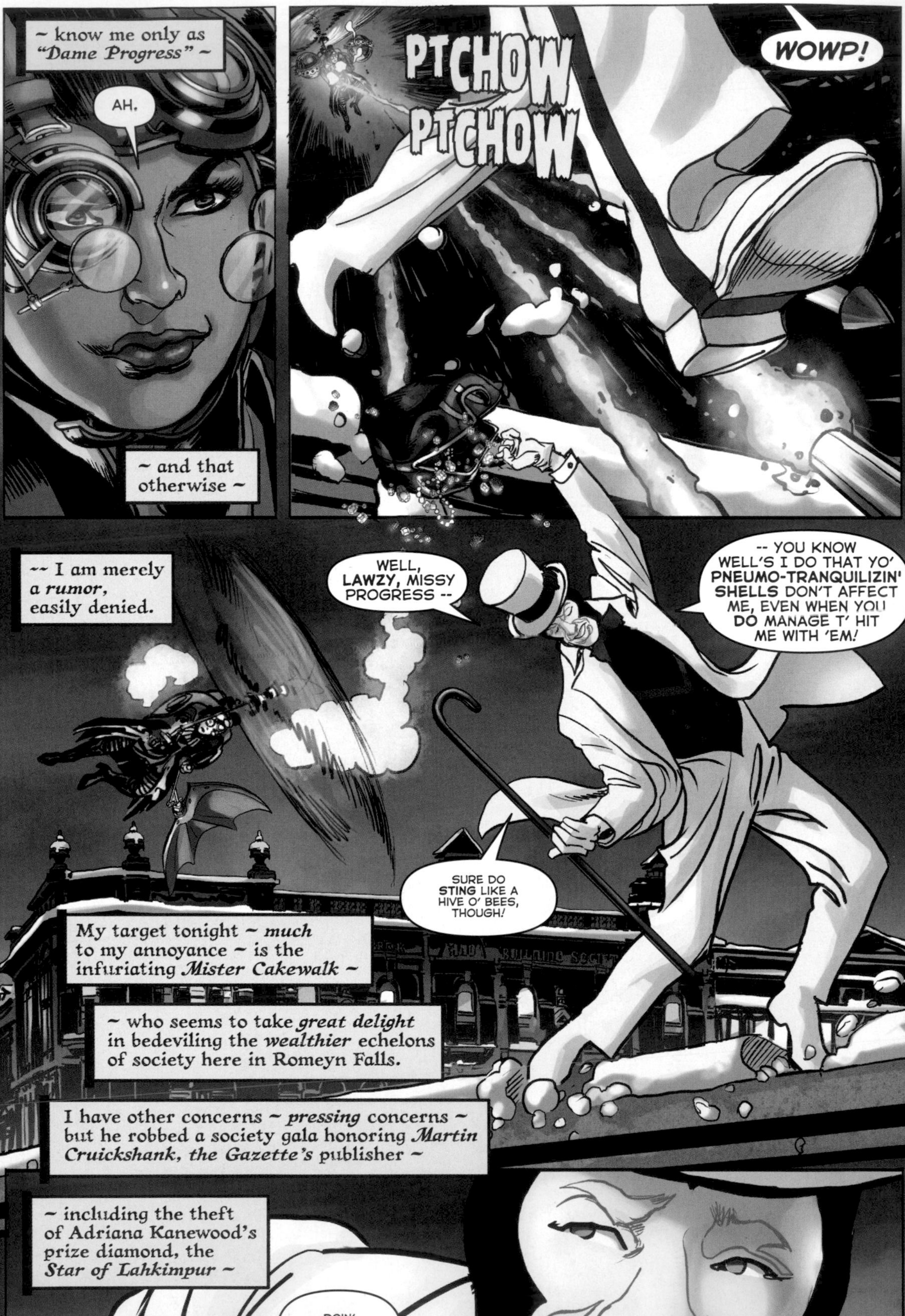
~ know me only as "Dame Progress" ~
AH.
~ and that otherwise ~
PTCHOW PTCHOW
WOWP!
~~ I am merely a *rumor*, easily denied.
WELL, **LAWZY,** MISSY PROGRESS --
-- YOU KNOW WELL'S I DO THAT YO' **PNEUMO-TRANQUILIZIN' SHELLS** DON'T AFFECT ME, EVEN WHEN YOU **DO** MANAGE T' HIT ME WITH 'EM!
SURE DO **STING** LIKE A HIVE O' BEES, THOUGH!
My target tonight ~ *much* to my annoyance ~ is the infuriating *Mister Cakewalk* ~
~ who seems to take *great delight* in bedeviling the *wealthier* echelons of society here in Romeyn Falls.
I have other concerns ~ *pressing* concerns ~ but he robbed a society gala honoring *Martin Cruickshank, the Gazette's* publisher ~
~ including the theft of Adriana Kanewood's prize diamond, the *Star of Lahkimpur* ~
DOIN' *FINE*, GIRL. DOIN' *JES'* FINE --

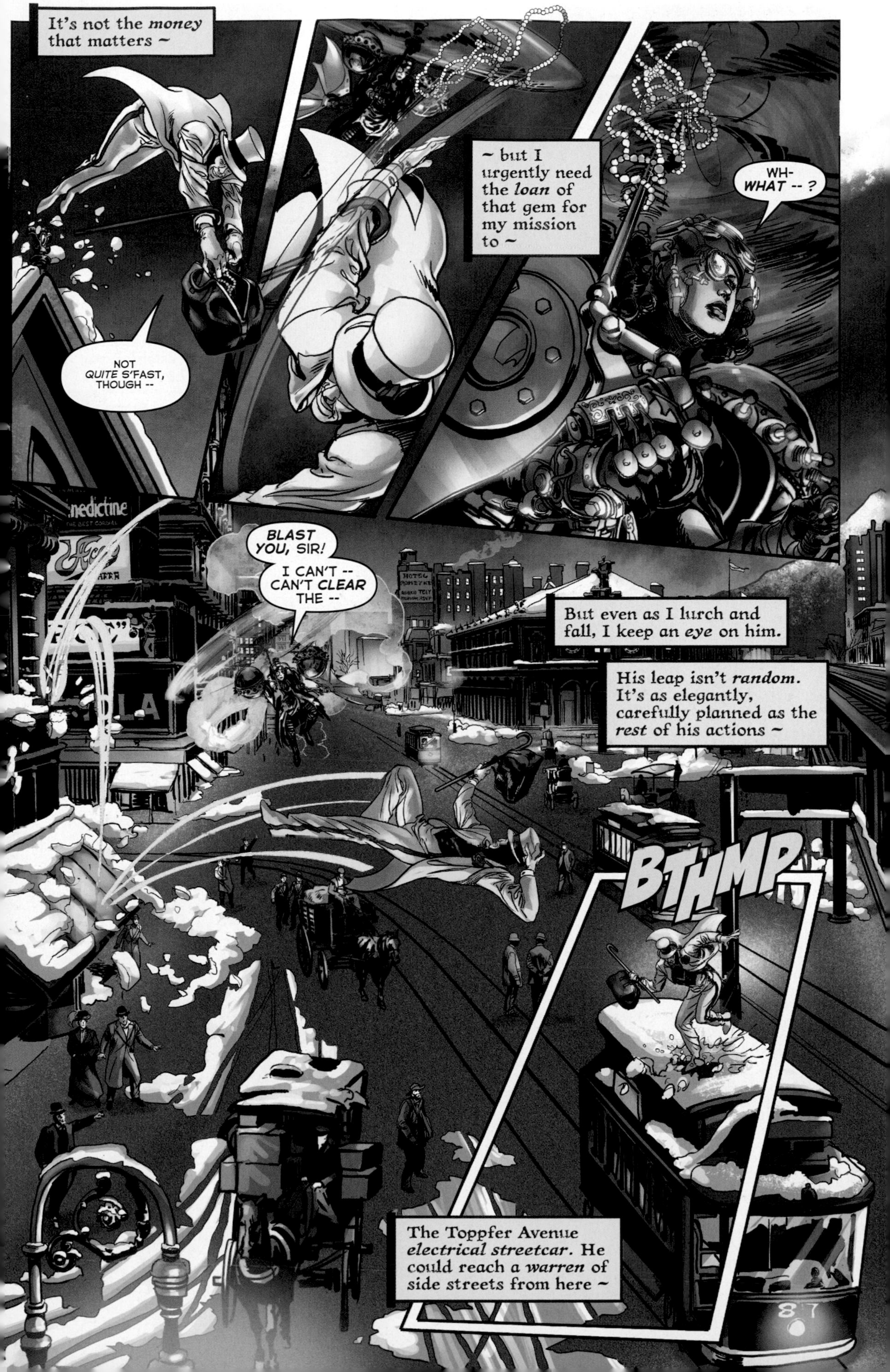
It's not the *money* that matters ~
NOT *QUITE* S'FAST, THOUGH --
~ but I urgently need the *loan* of that gem for my mission to ~
WH- *WHAT* -- ?
BLAST YOU, SIR!
I CAN'T -- CAN'T *CLEAR* THE --
But even as I lurch and fall, I keep an *eye* on him.
His leap isn't *random*. It's as elegantly, carefully planned as the *rest* of his actions ~
BTHMP
The Toppfer Avenue *electrical streetcar*. He could reach a *warren* of side streets from here ~

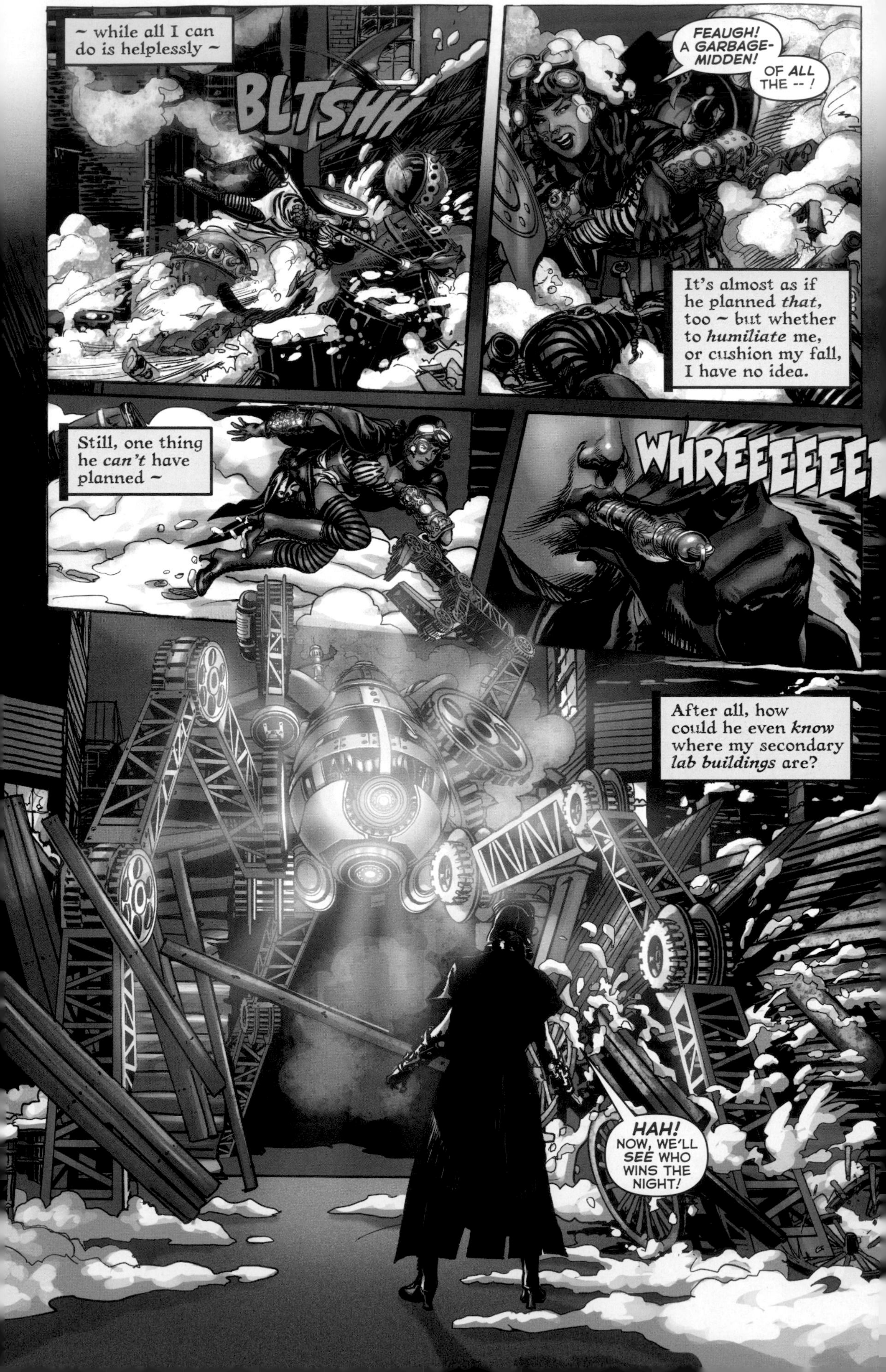
~ while all I can do is helplessly ~
BLTSHH
FEAUGH! A GARBAGE-MIDDEN!
OF ALL THE -- !
It's almost as if he planned that, too ~ but whether to humiliate me, or cushion my fall, I have no idea.
Still, one thing he can't have planned ~
WHREEEEEET
After all, how could he even know where my secondary lab buildings are?
HAH! NOW, WE'LL SEE WHO WINS THE NIGHT!

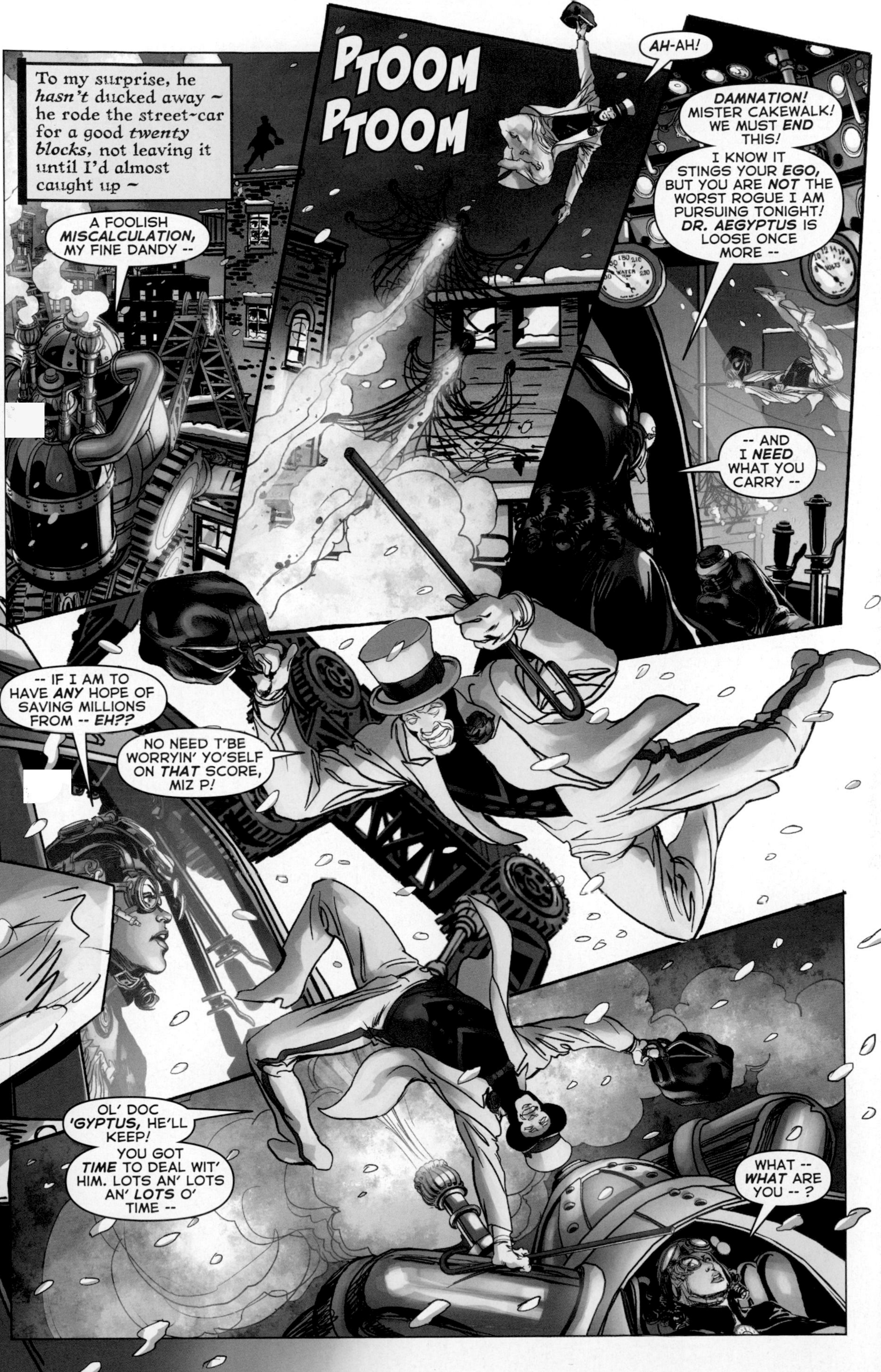
To my surprise, he *hasn't* ducked away ~ he rode the street~car for a good *twenty blocks*, not leaving it until I'd almost caught up ~
A FOOLISH **MISCALCULATION,** MY FINE DANDY --
PTOOM PTOOM
AH-AH!
DAMNATION! MISTER CAKEWALK! WE MUST **END** THIS!
I KNOW IT STINGS YOUR **EGO,** BUT YOU ARE **NOT** THE WORST ROGUE I AM PURSUING TONIGHT! **DR. AEGYPTUS** IS LOOSE ONCE MORE --
-- AND I **NEED** WHAT YOU CARRY --
-- IF I AM TO HAVE **ANY** HOPE OF SAVING MILLIONS FROM -- **EH??**
NO NEED T'BE WORRYIN' YO'SELF ON **THAT** SCORE, MIZ P!
OL' DOC **'GYPTUS,** HE'LL KEEP!
YOU GOT **TIME** TO DEAL WIT' HIM. LOTS AN' LOTS AN' **LOTS** O' TIME --
WHAT -- **WHAT** ARE YOU -- ?

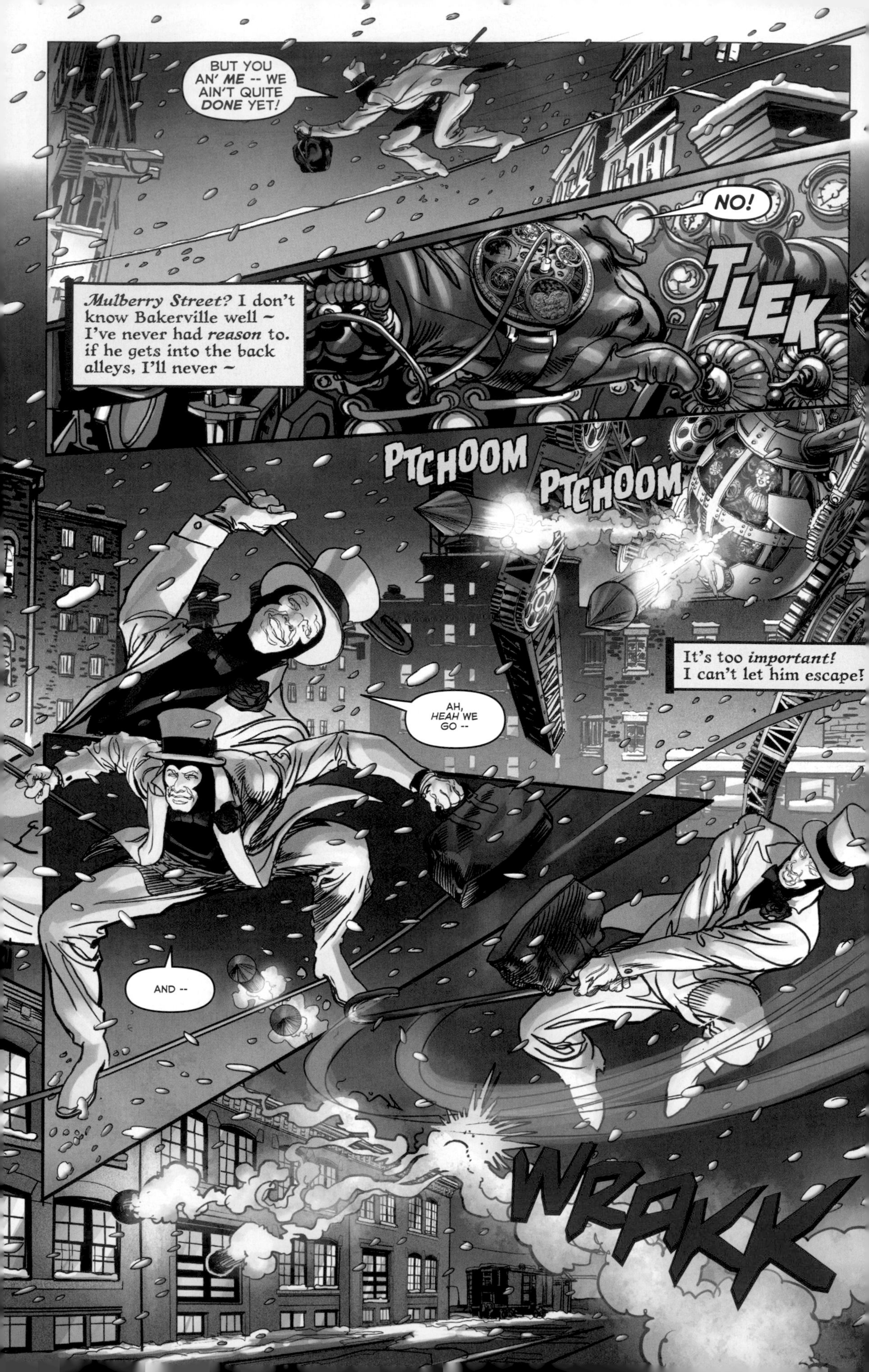
BUT YOU AN' *ME* -- WE AIN'T QUITE *DONE* YET!
NO!
TLEK
Mulberry Street? I don't know Bakerville well ~ I've never had *reason* to. if he gets into the back alleys, I'll never ~
PTCHOOM
PTCHOOM
It's too *important!* I can't let him escape!
AH, *HEAH* WE GO --
AND --
WRAKK

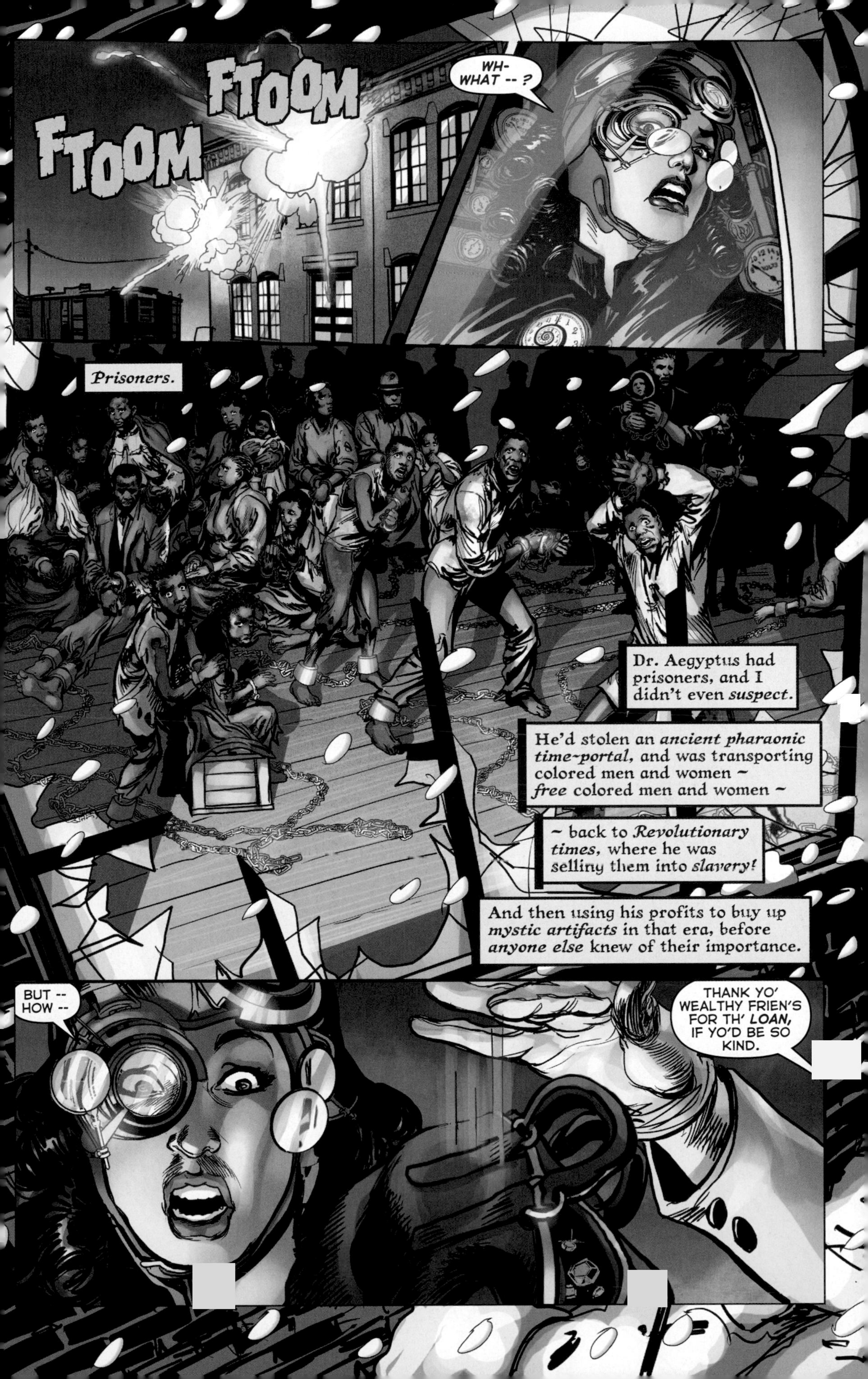
FTOOM
FTOOM
WH- WHAT -- ?
Prisoners.
Dr. Aegyptus had prisoners, and I didn't even suspect.
He'd stolen an ancient pharaonic time-portal, and was transporting colored men and women ~ free colored men and women ~
~ back to Revolutionary times, where he was selling them into slavery!
And then using his profits to buy up mystic artifacts in that era, before anyone else knew of their importance.
BUT -- HOW --
THANK YO' WEALTHY FRIEN'S FOR TH' LOAN, IF YO'D BE SO KIND.

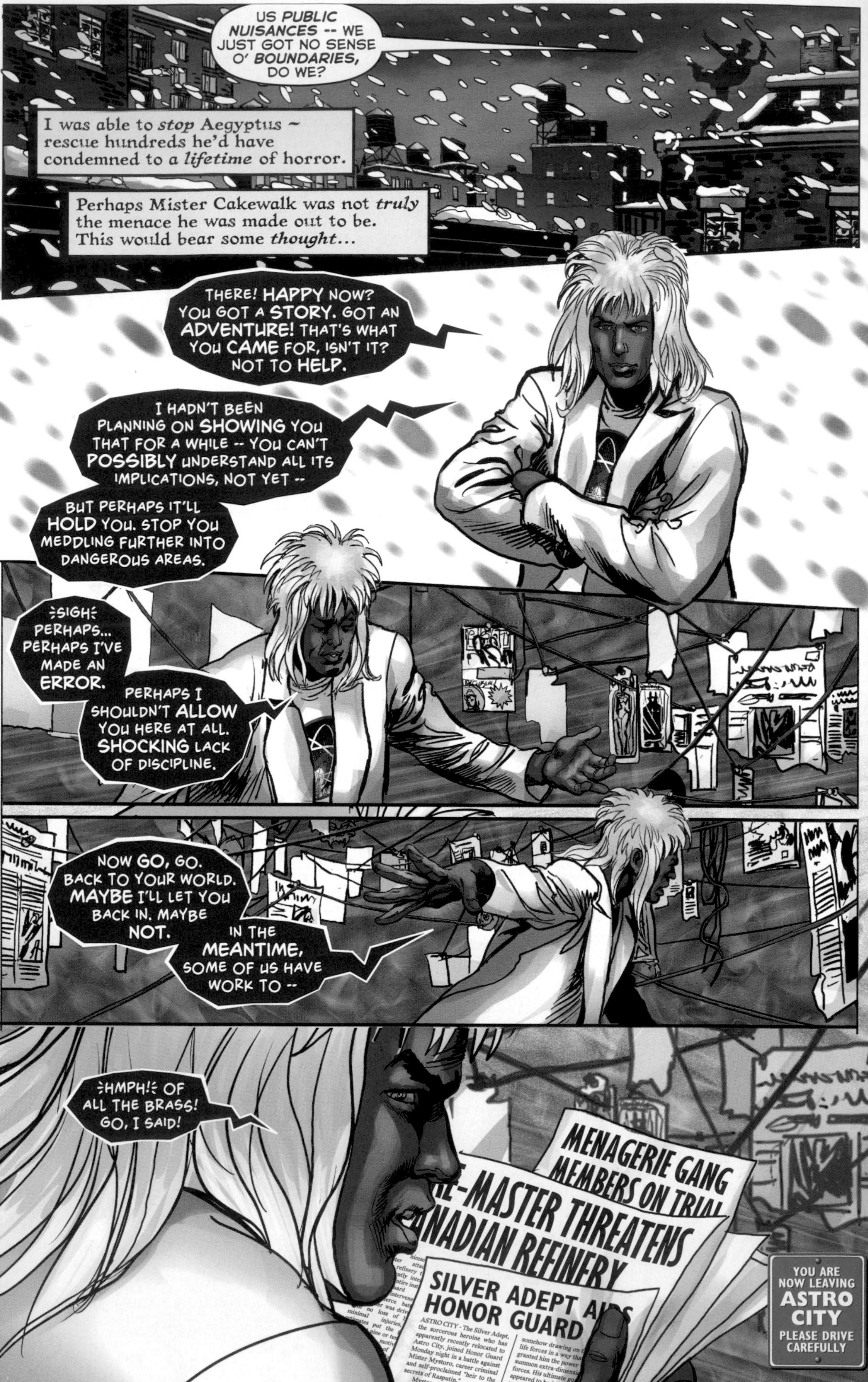
US PUBLIC NUISANCES -- WE JUST GOT NO SENSE O' BOUNDARIES, DO WE?
I was able to stop Aegyptus ~ rescue hundreds he'd have condemned to a lifetime of horror.
Perhaps Mister Cakewalk was not truly the menace he was made out to be. This would bear some thought...
THERE! HAPPY NOW? YOU GOT A STORY. GOT AN ADVENTURE! THAT'S WHAT YOU CAME FOR, ISN'T IT? NOT TO HELP.
I HADN'T BEEN PLANNING ON SHOWING YOU THAT FOR A WHILE -- YOU CAN'T POSSIBLY UNDERSTAND ALL ITS IMPLICATIONS, NOT YET --
BUT PERHAPS IT'LL HOLD YOU. STOP YOU MEDDLING FURTHER INTO DANGEROUS AREAS.
SIGH PERHAPS... PERHAPS I'VE MADE AN ERROR.
PERHAPS I SHOULDN'T ALLOW YOU HERE AT ALL. SHOCKING LACK OF DISCIPLINE.
NOW GO, GO. BACK TO YOUR WORLD. MAYBE I'LL LET YOU BACK IN. MAYBE NOT.
IN THE MEANTIME, SOME OF US HAVE WORK TO --
HMPH! OF ALL THE BRASS! GO, I SAID!
MENAGERIE GANG MEMBERS ON TRIAL
-MASTER THREATENS
NADIAN REFINERY
SILVER ADEPT
HONOR GUARD
YOU ARE NOW LEAVING ASTRO CITY PLEASE DRIVE CAREFULLY

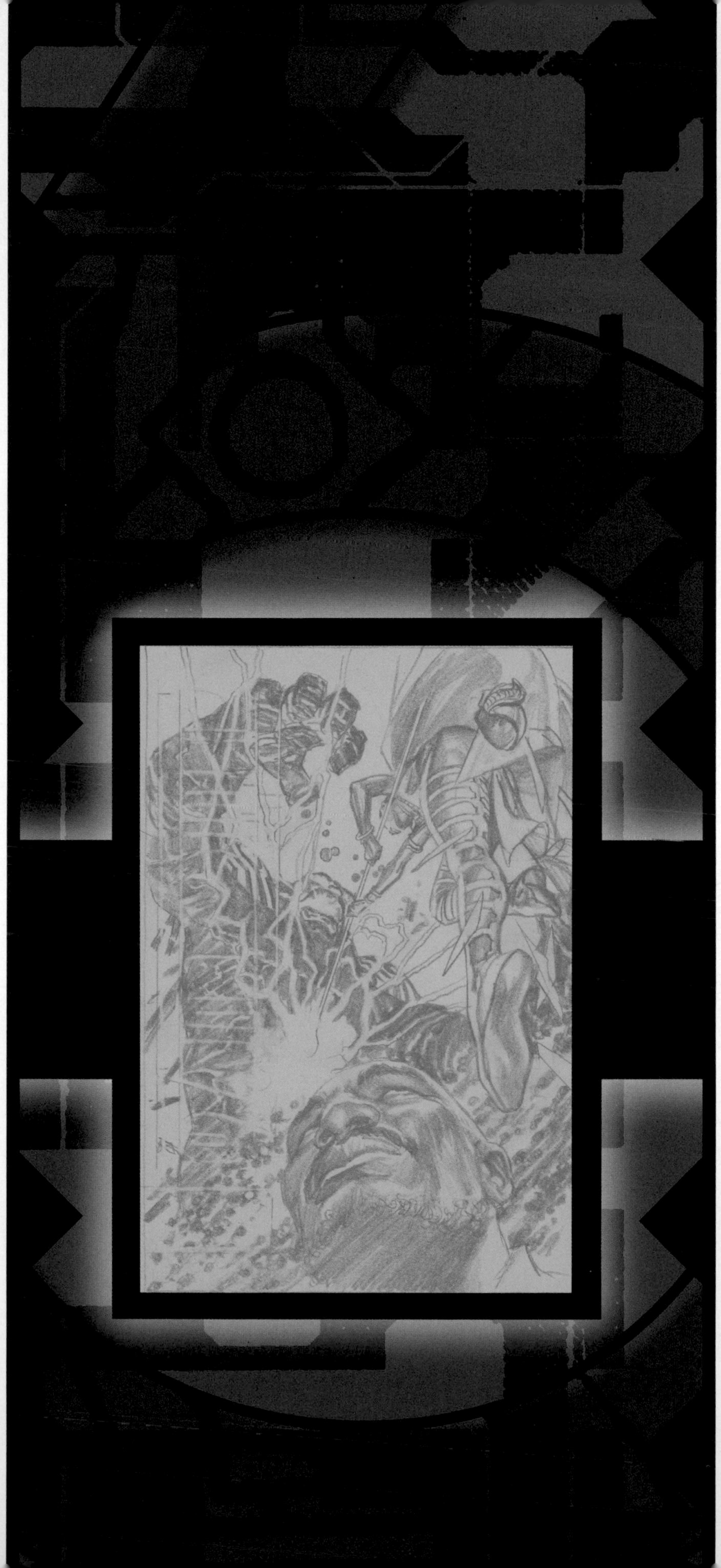

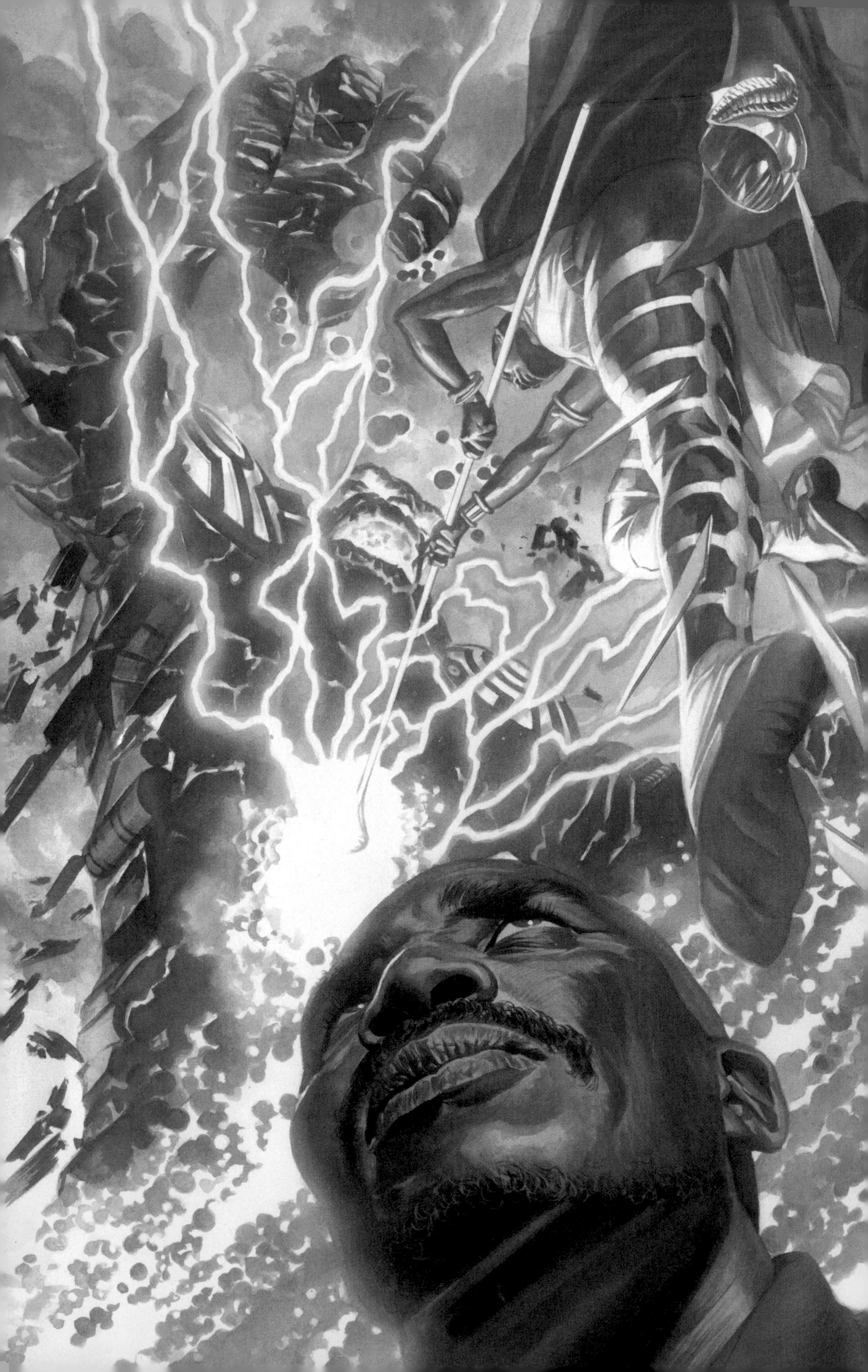

HNFF
VILLAIN! HALT THIS --
I AM THE ORE-MASTER!
through open doors
part two

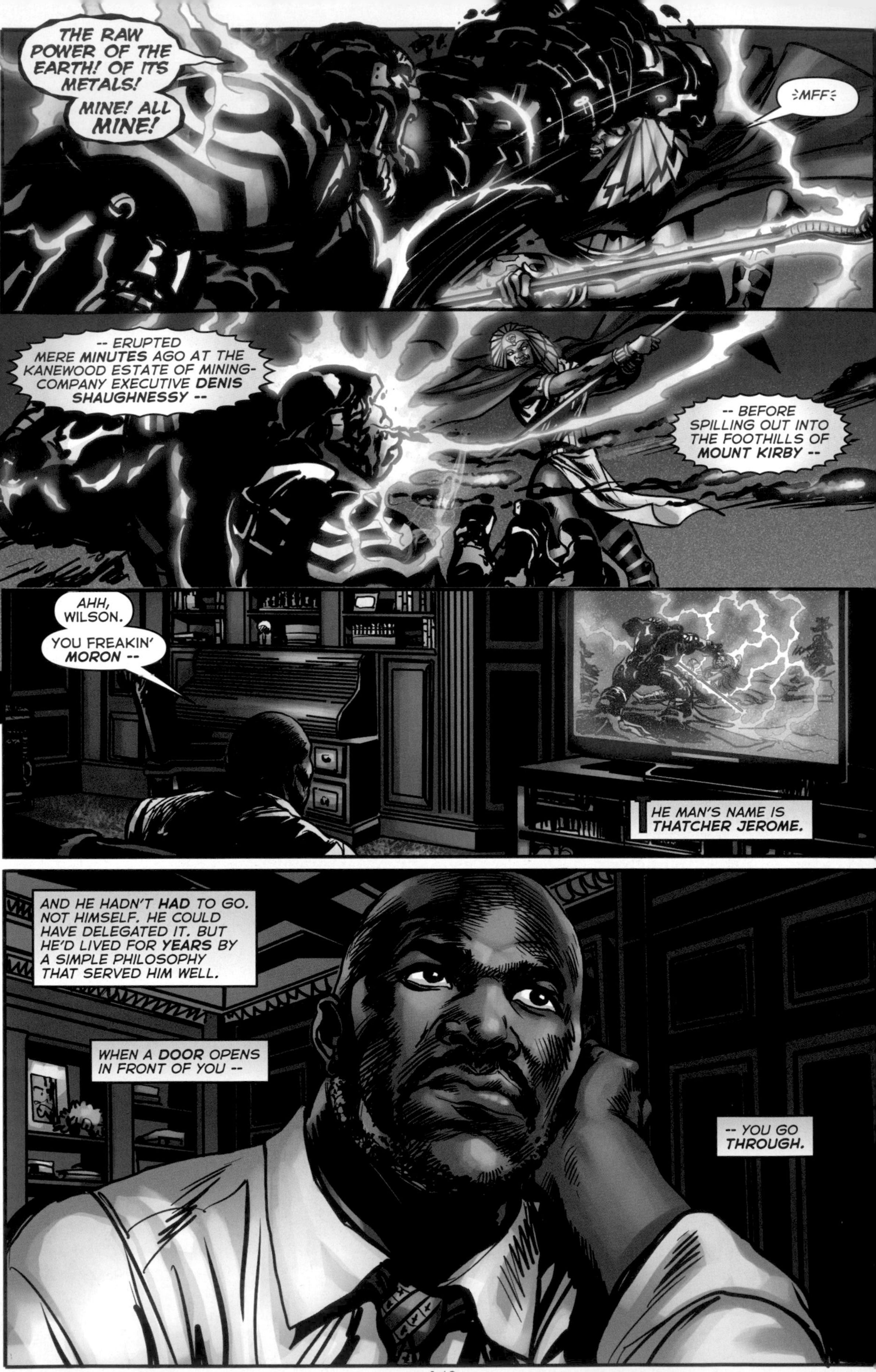
THE RAW POWER OF THE EARTH! OF ITS METALS!
MINE! ALL MINE!
MFF
-- ERUPTED MERE MINUTES AGO AT THE KANEWOOD ESTATE OF MINING-COMPANY EXECUTIVE DENIS SHAUGHNESSY --
-- BEFORE SPILLING OUT INTO THE FOOTHILLS OF MOUNT KIRBY --
AHH, WILSON.
YOU FREAKIN' MORON --
THE MAN'S NAME IS THATCHER JEROME.
AND HE HADN'T HAD TO GO. NOT HIMSELF. HE COULD HAVE DELEGATED IT. BUT HE'D LIVED FOR YEARS BY A SIMPLE PHILOSOPHY THAT SERVED HIM WELL.
WHEN A DOOR OPENS IN FRONT OF YOU --
-- YOU GO THROUGH.

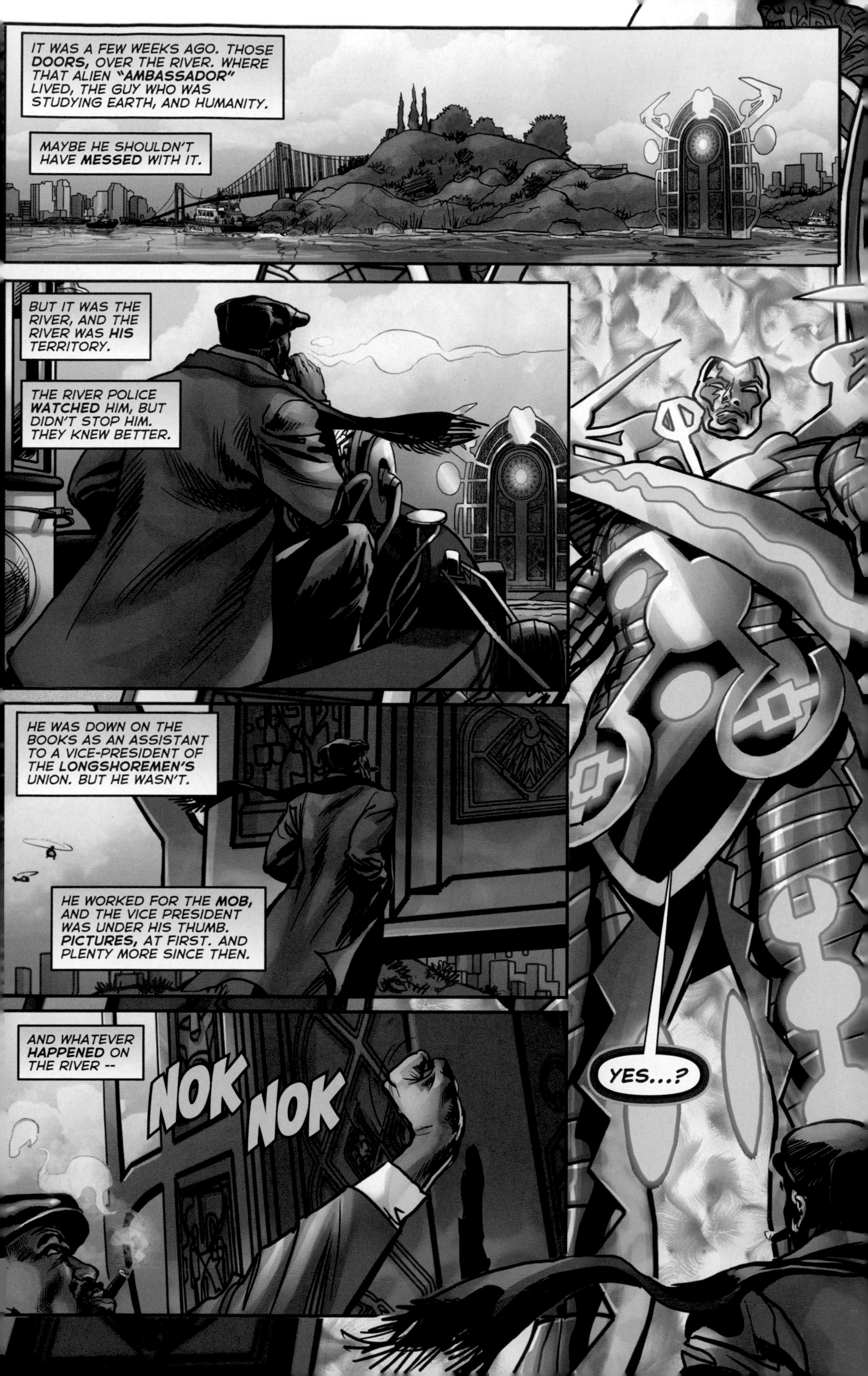
IT WAS A FEW WEEKS AGO. THOSE DOORS, OVER THE RIVER. WHERE THAT ALIEN "AMBASSADOR" LIVED, THE GUY WHO WAS STUDYING EARTH, AND HUMANITY.
MAYBE HE SHOULDN'T HAVE MESSED WITH IT.
BUT IT WAS THE RIVER, AND THE RIVER WAS HIS TERRITORY.
THE RIVER POLICE WATCHED HIM, BUT DIDN'T STOP HIM. THEY KNEW BETTER.
HE WAS DOWN ON THE BOOKS AS AN ASSISTANT TO A VICE-PRESIDENT OF THE LONGSHOREMEN'S UNION. BUT HE WASN'T.
HE WORKED FOR THE MOB, AND THE VICE PRESIDENT WAS UNDER HIS THUMB. PICTURES, AT FIRST. AND PLENTY MORE SINCE THEN.
AND WHATEVER HAPPENED ON THE RIVER --
NOK NOK
YES...?

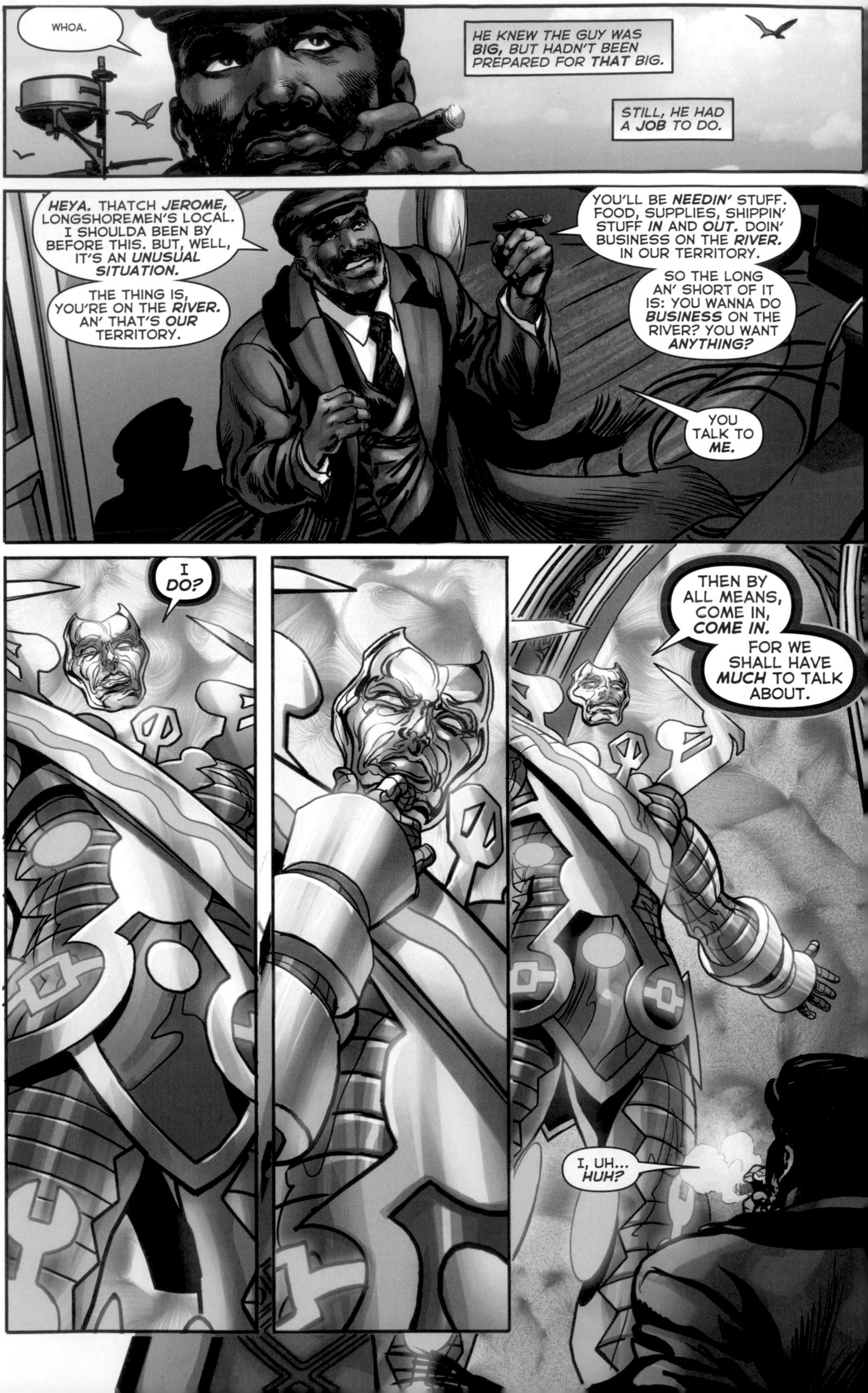
WHOA.
HE KNEW THE GUY WAS BIG, BUT HADN'T BEEN PREPARED FOR THAT BIG.
STILL, HE HAD A JOB TO DO.
HEYA. THATCH JEROME, LONGSHOREMEN'S LOCAL. I SHOULDA BEEN BY BEFORE THIS. BUT, WELL, IT'S AN UNUSUAL SITUATION.
THE THING IS, YOU'RE ON THE RIVER. AN' THAT'S OUR TERRITORY.
YOU'LL BE NEEDIN' STUFF. FOOD, SUPPLIES, SHIPPIN' STUFF IN AND OUT. DOIN' BUSINESS ON THE RIVER. IN OUR TERRITORY.
SO THE LONG AN' SHORT OF IT IS: YOU WANNA DO BUSINESS ON THE RIVER? YOU WANT ANYTHING?
YOU TALK TO ME.
I DO?
THEN BY ALL MEANS, COME IN, COME IN.
FOR WE SHALL HAVE MUCH TO TALK ABOUT.
I, UH... HUH?

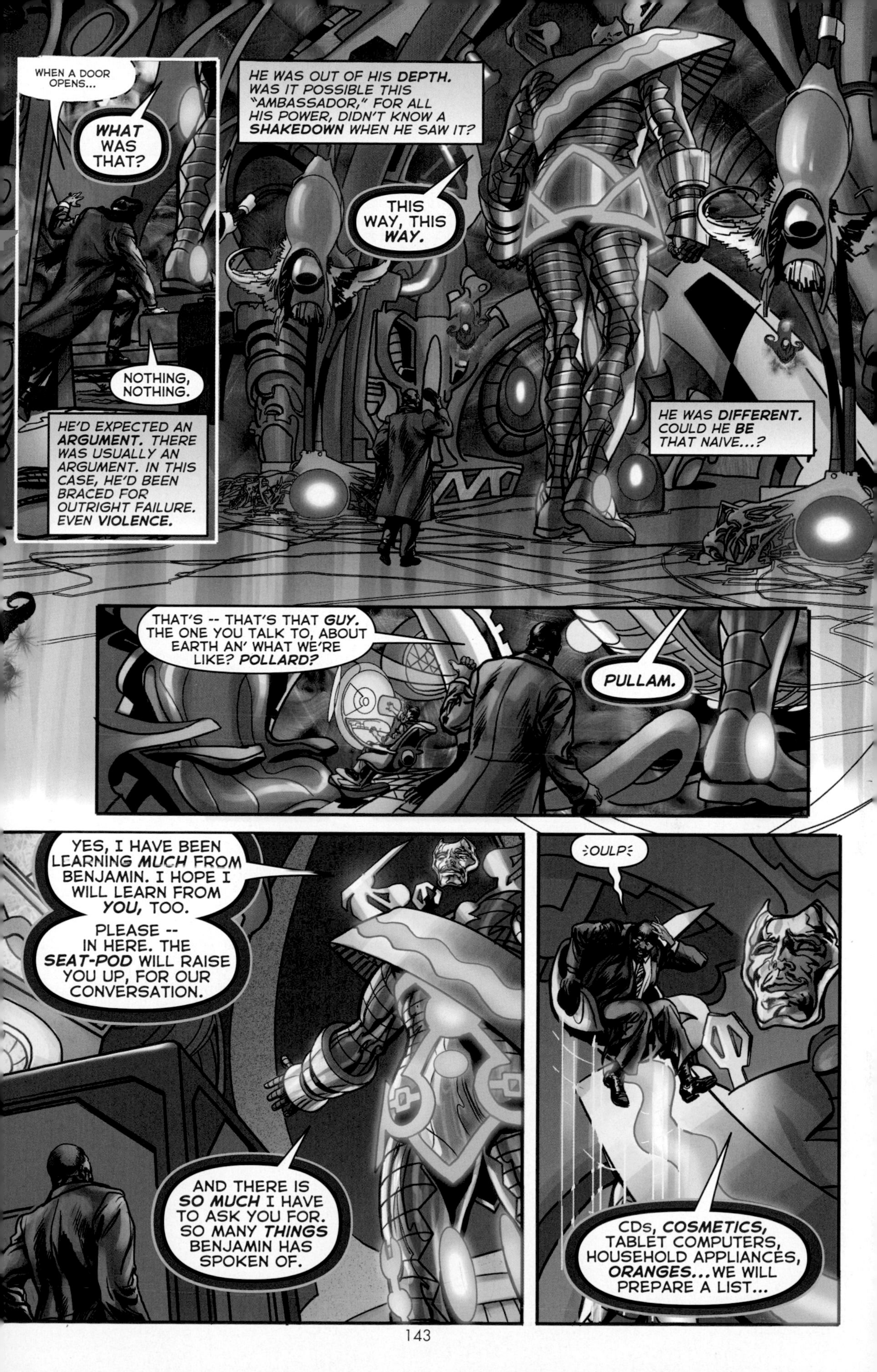
WHEN A DOOR OPENS...
WHAT WAS THAT?
NOTHING, NOTHING.
HE'D EXPECTED AN ARGUMENT. THERE WAS USUALLY AN ARGUMENT. IN THIS CASE, HE'D BEEN BRACED FOR OUTRIGHT FAILURE. EVEN VIOLENCE.
HE WAS OUT OF HIS DEPTH. WAS IT POSSIBLE THIS "AMBASSADOR," FOR ALL HIS POWER, DIDN'T KNOW A SHAKEDOWN WHEN HE SAW IT?
THIS WAY, THIS WAY.
HE WAS DIFFERENT. COULD HE BE THAT NAIVE...?
THAT'S -- THAT'S THAT GUY. THE ONE YOU TALK TO, ABOUT EARTH AN' WHAT WE'RE LIKE? POLLARD?
PULLAM.
YES, I HAVE BEEN LEARNING MUCH FROM BENJAMIN. I HOPE I WILL LEARN FROM YOU, TOO.
PLEASE -- IN HERE. THE SEAT-POD WILL RAISE YOU UP, FOR OUR CONVERSATION.
AND THERE IS SO MUCH I HAVE TO ASK YOU FOR. SO MANY THINGS BENJAMIN HAS SPOKEN OF.
GULP
CDs, COSMETICS, TABLET COMPUTERS, HOUSEHOLD APPLIANCES, ORANGES...WE WILL PREPARE A LIST...

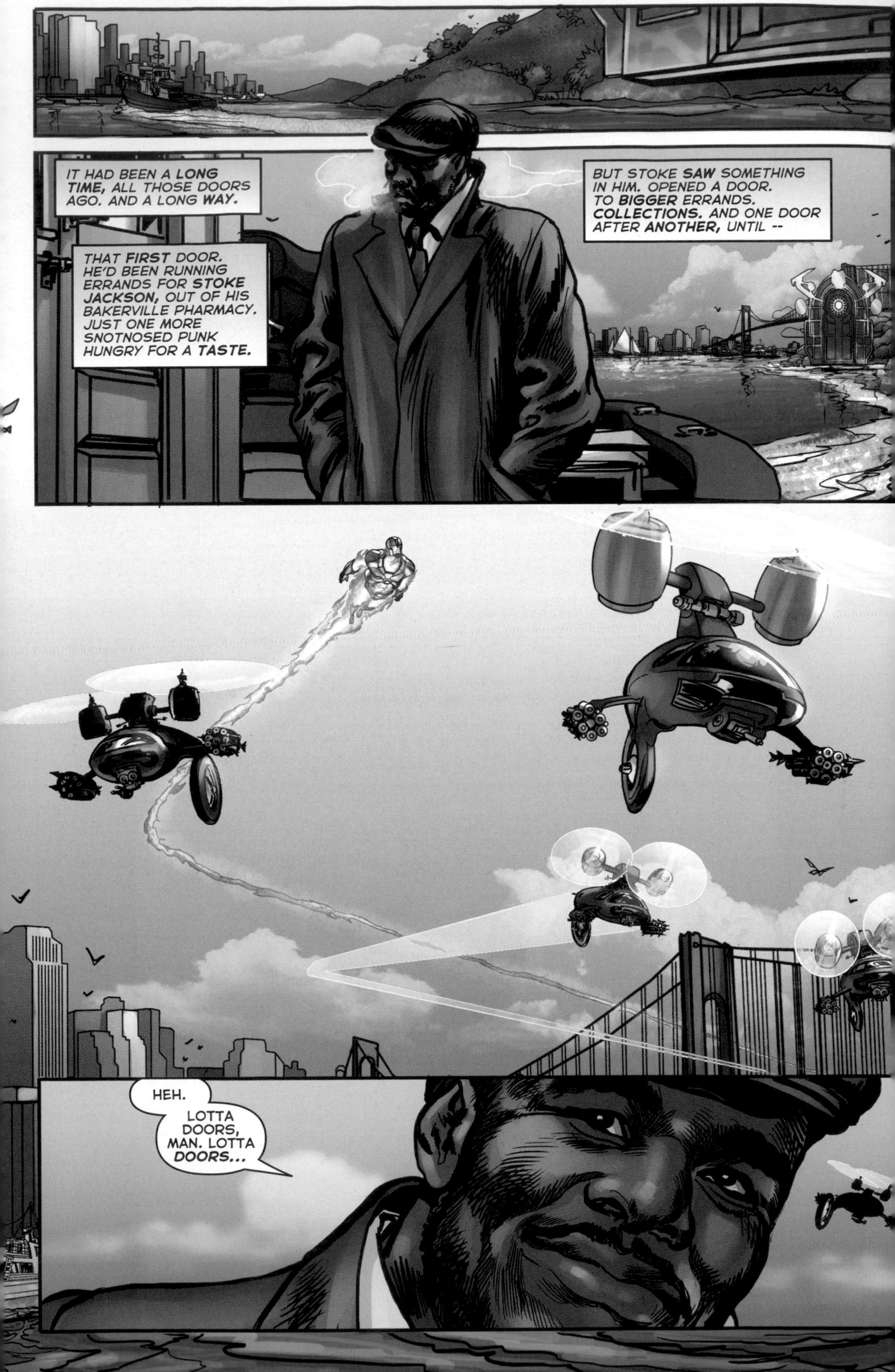
IT HAD BEEN A LONG TIME, ALL THOSE DOORS AGO. AND A LONG WAY.
THAT FIRST DOOR. HE'D BEEN RUNNING ERRANDS FOR STOKE JACKSON, OUT OF HIS BAKERVILLE PHARMACY. JUST ONE MORE SNOTNOSED PUNK HUNGRY FOR A TASTE.
BUT STOKE SAW SOMETHING IN HIM. OPENED A DOOR. TO BIGGER ERRANDS. COLLECTIONS. AND ONE DOOR AFTER ANOTHER, UNTIL --
HEH.
LOTTA DOORS, MAN. LOTTA DOORS...

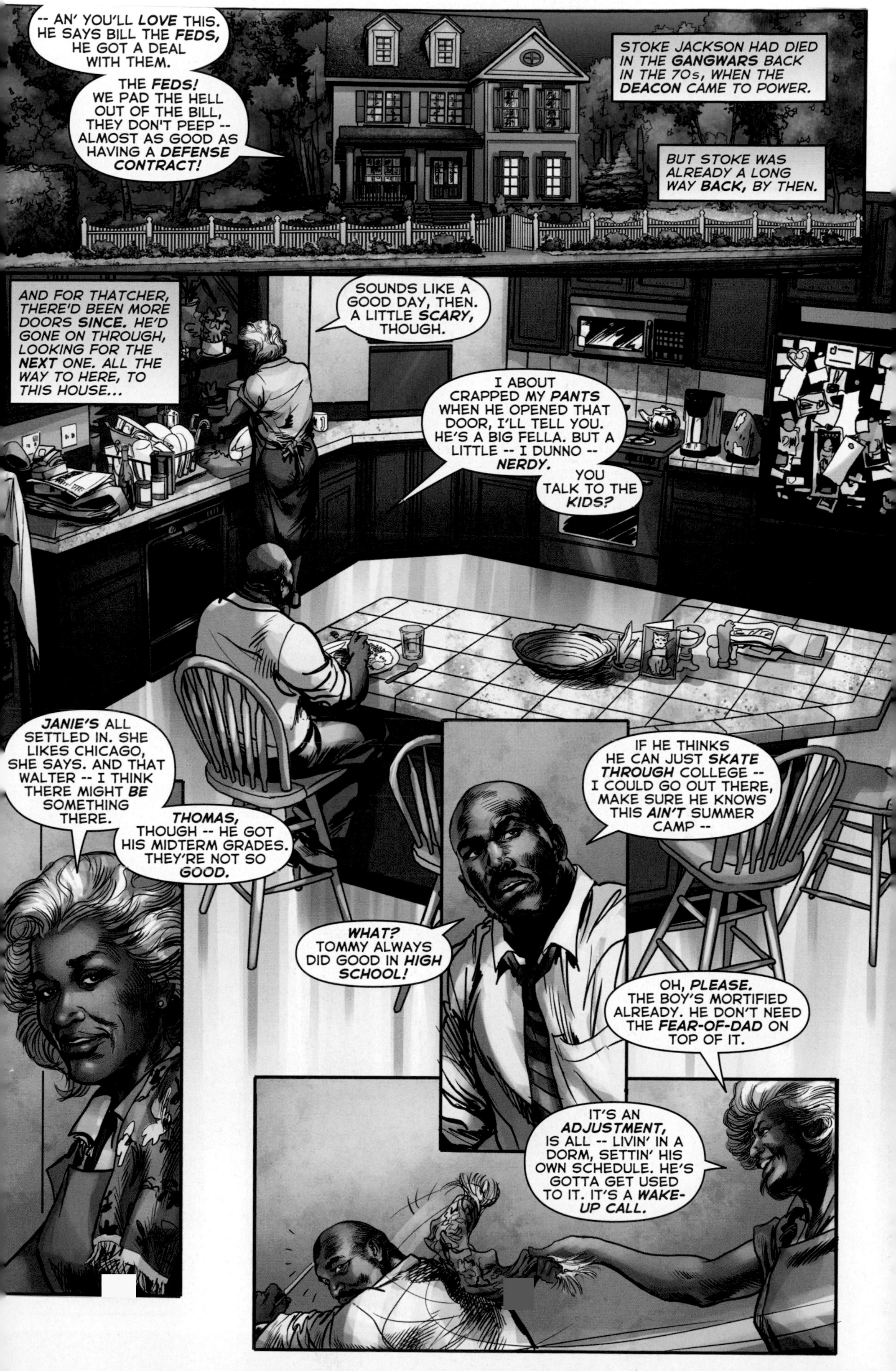

-- AN' YOU'LL LOVE THIS. HE SAYS BILL THE FEDS, HE GOT A DEAL WITH THEM.
THE FEDS! WE PAD THE HELL OUT OF THE BILL, THEY DON'T PEEP -- ALMOST AS GOOD AS HAVING A DEFENSE CONTRACT!
STOKE JACKSON HAD DIED IN THE GANGWARS BACK IN THE 70s, WHEN THE DEACON CAME TO POWER.
BUT STOKE WAS ALREADY A LONG WAY BACK, BY THEN.
AND FOR THATCHER, THERE'D BEEN MORE DOORS SINCE. HE'D GONE ON THROUGH, LOOKING FOR THE NEXT ONE. ALL THE WAY TO HERE, TO THIS HOUSE...
SOUNDS LIKE A GOOD DAY, THEN. A LITTLE SCARY, THOUGH.
I ABOUT CRAPPED MY PANTS WHEN HE OPENED THAT DOOR, I'LL TELL YOU. HE'S A BIG FELLA. BUT A LITTLE -- I DUNNO -- NERDY.
YOU TALK TO THE KIDS?
JANIE'S ALL SETTLED IN. SHE LIKES CHICAGO, SHE SAYS. AND THAT WALTER -- I THINK THERE MIGHT BE SOMETHING THERE.
THOMAS, THOUGH -- HE GOT HIS MIDTERM GRADES. THEY'RE NOT SO GOOD.
IF HE THINKS HE CAN JUST SKATE THROUGH COLLEGE -- I COULD GO OUT THERE, MAKE SURE HE KNOWS THIS AIN'T SUMMER CAMP --
WHAT? TOMMY ALWAYS DID GOOD IN HIGH SCHOOL!
OH, PLEASE. THE BOY'S MORTIFIED ALREADY. HE DON'T NEED THE FEAR-OF-DAD ON TOP OF IT.
IT'S AN ADJUSTMENT, IS ALL -- LIVIN' IN A DORM, SETTIN' HIS OWN SCHEDULE. HE'S GOTTA GET USED TO IT. IT'S A WAKE-UP CALL.

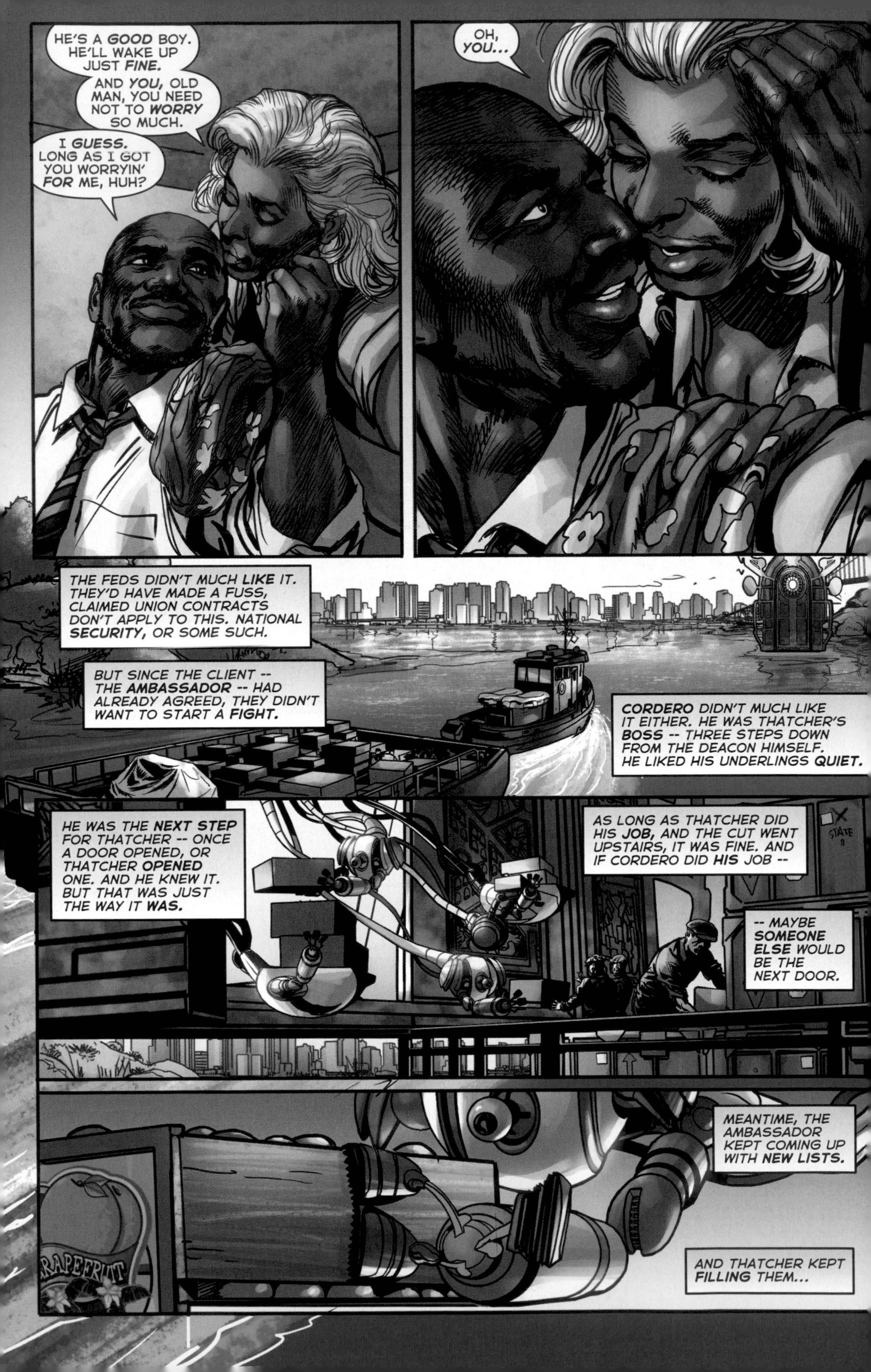
HE'S A GOOD BOY. HE'LL WAKE UP JUST FINE.
AND YOU, OLD MAN, YOU NEED NOT TO WORRY SO MUCH.
I GUESS. LONG AS I GOT YOU WORRYIN' FOR ME, HUH?
OH, YOU...
THE FEDS DIDN'T MUCH LIKE IT. THEY'D HAVE MADE A FUSS, CLAIMED UNION CONTRACTS DON'T APPLY TO THIS. NATIONAL SECURITY, OR SOME SUCH.
BUT SINCE THE CLIENT -- THE AMBASSADOR -- HAD ALREADY AGREED, THEY DIDN'T WANT TO START A FIGHT.
CORDERO DIDN'T MUCH LIKE IT EITHER. HE WAS THATCHER'S BOSS -- THREE STEPS DOWN FROM THE DEACON HIMSELF. HE LIKED HIS UNDERLINGS QUIET.
HE WAS THE NEXT STEP FOR THATCHER -- ONCE A DOOR OPENED, OR THATCHER OPENED ONE. AND HE KNEW IT. BUT THAT WAS JUST THE WAY IT WAS.
AS LONG AS THATCHER DID HIS JOB, AND THE CUT WENT UPSTAIRS, IT WAS FINE. AND IF CORDERO DID HIS JOB --
-- MAYBE SOMEONE ELSE WOULD BE THE NEXT DOOR.
MEANTIME, THE AMBASSADOR KEPT COMING UP WITH NEW LISTS.
AND THATCHER KEPT FILLING THEM...

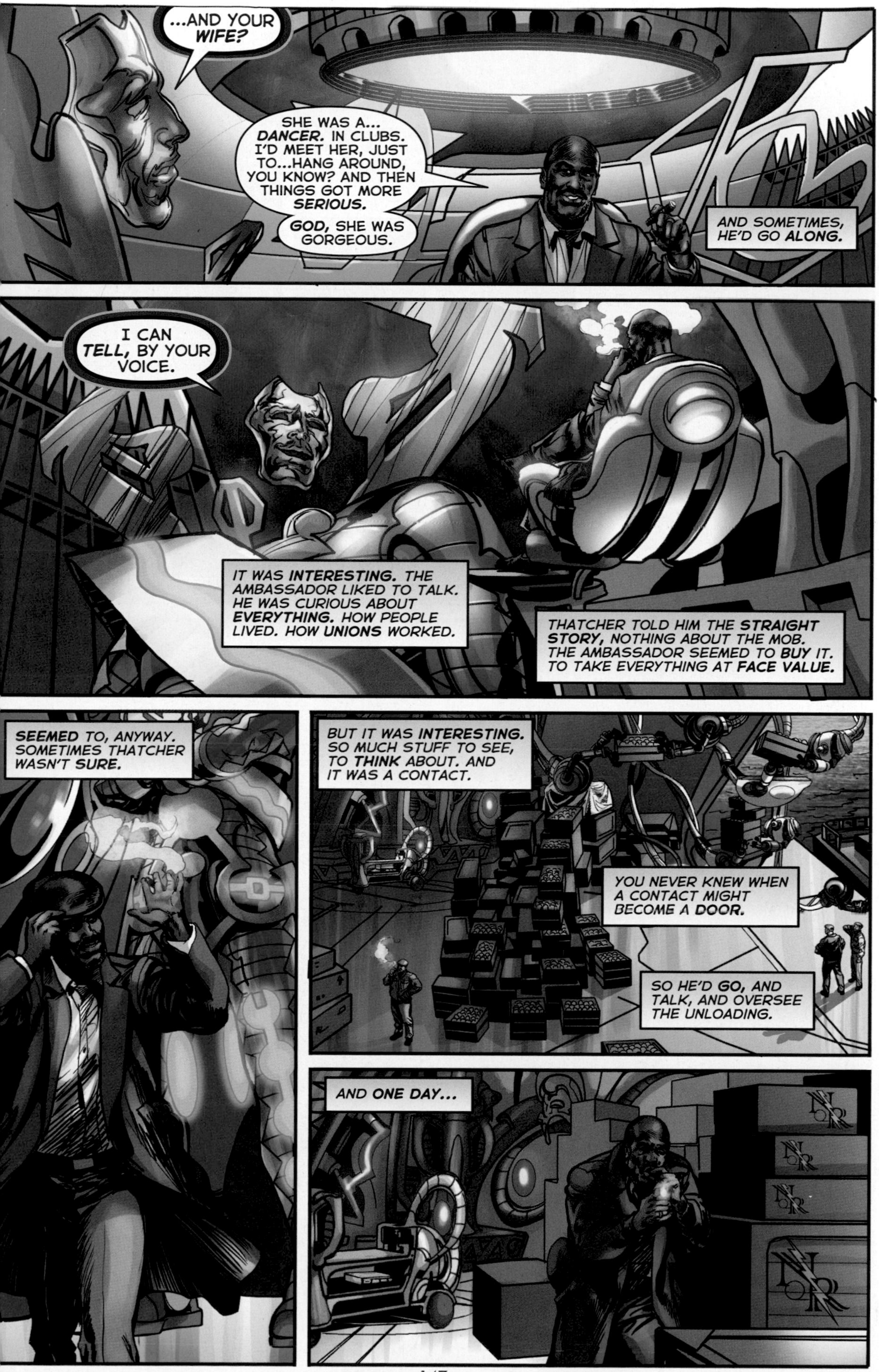
...AND YOUR WIFE?
SHE WAS A... DANCER. IN CLUBS. I'D MEET HER, JUST TO...HANG AROUND, YOU KNOW? AND THEN THINGS GOT MORE SERIOUS.
GOD, SHE WAS GORGEOUS.
AND SOMETIMES, HE'D GO ALONG.
I CAN TELL, BY YOUR VOICE.
IT WAS INTERESTING. THE AMBASSADOR LIKED TO TALK. HE WAS CURIOUS ABOUT EVERYTHING. HOW PEOPLE LIVED. HOW UNIONS WORKED.
THATCHER TOLD HIM THE STRAIGHT STORY, NOTHING ABOUT THE MOB. THE AMBASSADOR SEEMED TO BUY IT. TO TAKE EVERYTHING AT FACE VALUE.
SEEMED TO, ANYWAY. SOMETIMES THATCHER WASN'T SURE.
BUT IT WAS INTERESTING. SO MUCH STUFF TO SEE, TO THINK ABOUT. AND IT WAS A CONTACT.
YOU NEVER KNEW WHEN A CONTACT MIGHT BECOME A DOOR.
SO HE'D GO, AND TALK, AND OVERSEE THE UNLOADING.
AND ONE DAY...

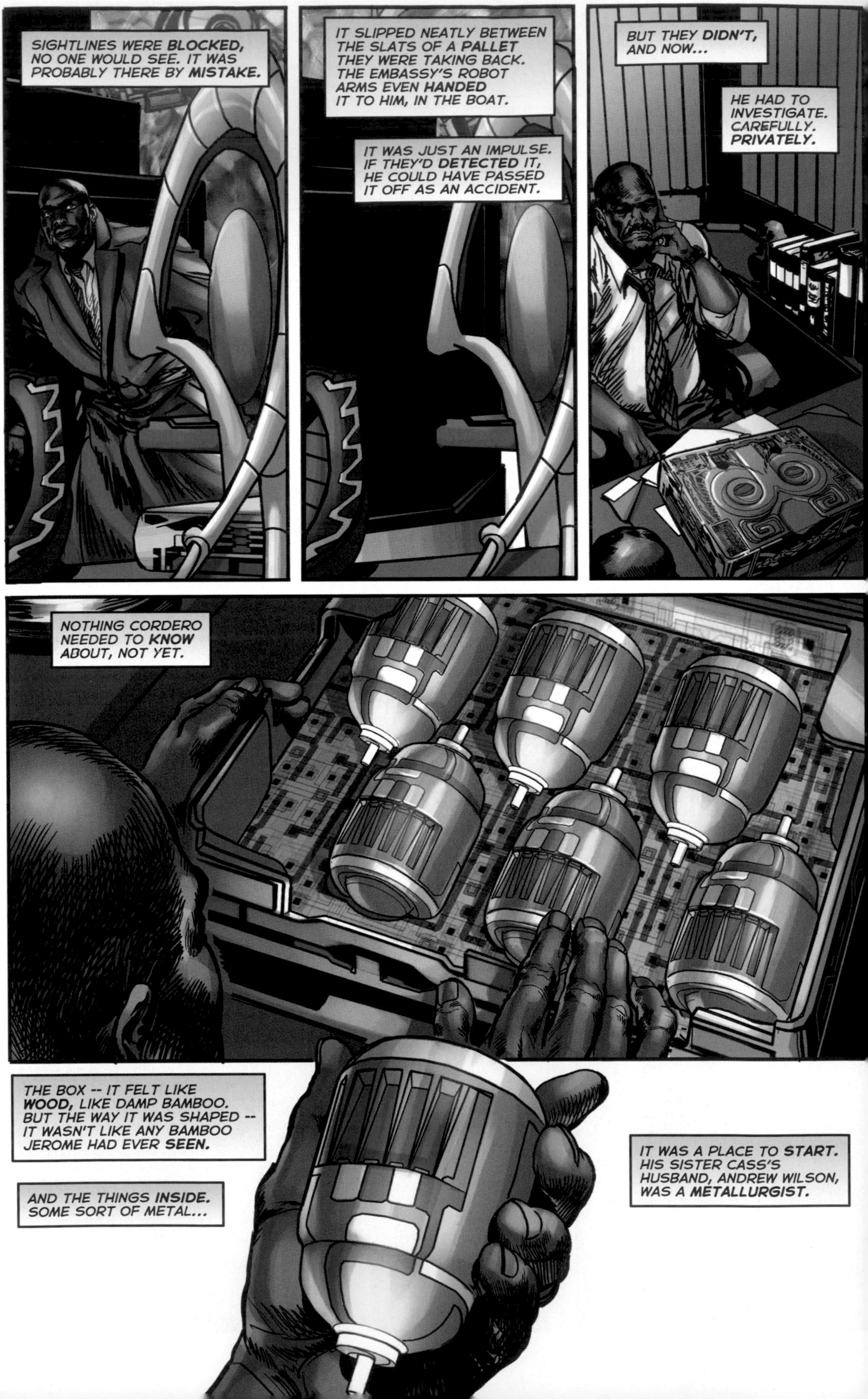
SIGHTLINES WERE BLOCKED, NO ONE WOULD SEE. IT WAS PROBABLY THERE BY MISTAKE.
IT SLIPPED NEATLY BETWEEN THE SLATS OF A PALLET THEY WERE TAKING BACK. THE EMBASSY'S ROBOT ARMS EVEN HANDED IT TO HIM, IN THE BOAT.
IT WAS JUST AN IMPULSE. IF THEY'D DETECTED IT, HE COULD HAVE PASSED IT OFF AS AN ACCIDENT.
BUT THEY DIDN'T, AND NOW...
HE HAD TO INVESTIGATE. CAREFULLY. PRIVATELY.
NOTHING CORDERO NEEDED TO KNOW ABOUT, NOT YET.
THE BOX -- IT FELT LIKE WOOD, LIKE DAMP BAMBOO. BUT THE WAY IT WAS SHAPED -- IT WASN'T LIKE ANY BAMBOO JEROME HAD EVER SEEN.
AND THE THINGS INSIDE. SOME SORT OF METAL...
IT WAS A PLACE TO START. HIS SISTER CASS'S HUSBAND, ANDREW WILSON, WAS A METALLURGIST.

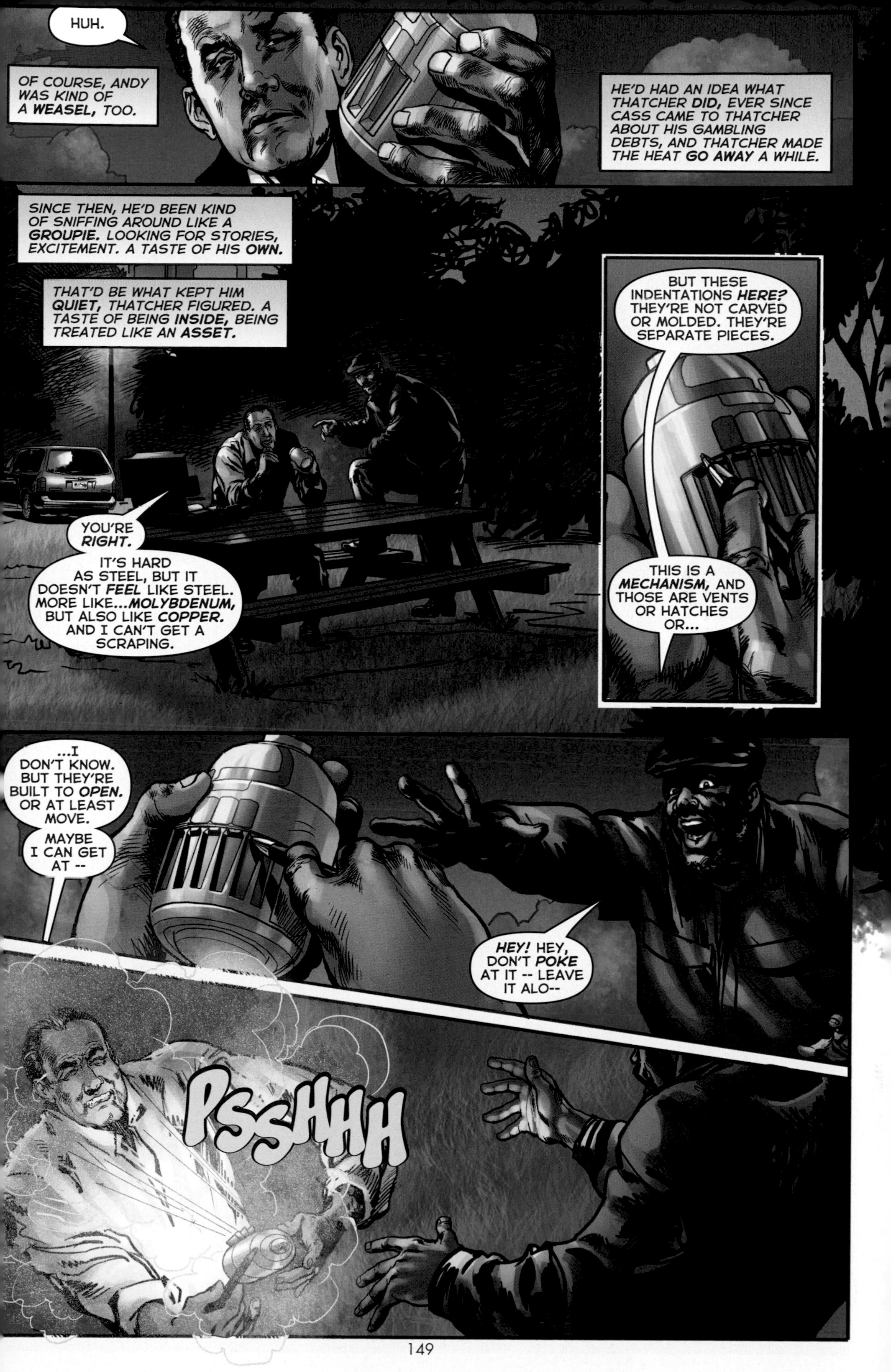
HUH.
OF COURSE, ANDY WAS KIND OF A WEASEL, TOO.
HE'D HAD AN IDEA WHAT THATCHER DID, EVER SINCE CASS CAME TO THATCHER ABOUT HIS GAMBLING DEBTS, AND THATCHER MADE THE HEAT GO AWAY A WHILE.
SINCE THEN, HE'D BEEN KIND OF SNIFFING AROUND LIKE A GROUPIE. LOOKING FOR STORIES, EXCITEMENT. A TASTE OF HIS OWN.
THAT'D BE WHAT KEPT HIM QUIET, THATCHER FIGURED. A TASTE OF BEING INSIDE, BEING TREATED LIKE AN ASSET.
YOU'RE RIGHT.
IT'S HARD AS STEEL, BUT IT DOESN'T FEEL LIKE STEEL. MORE LIKE...MOLYBDENUM, BUT ALSO LIKE COPPER. AND I CAN'T GET A SCRAPING.
BUT THESE INDENTATIONS HERE? THEY'RE NOT CARVED OR MOLDED. THEY'RE SEPARATE PIECES.
THIS IS A MECHANISM, AND THOSE ARE VENTS OR HATCHES OR...
...I DON'T KNOW. BUT THEY'RE BUILT TO OPEN. OR AT LEAST MOVE.
MAYBE I CAN GET AT --
HEY! HEY, DON'T POKE AT IT -- LEAVE IT ALO--
PSSHHH

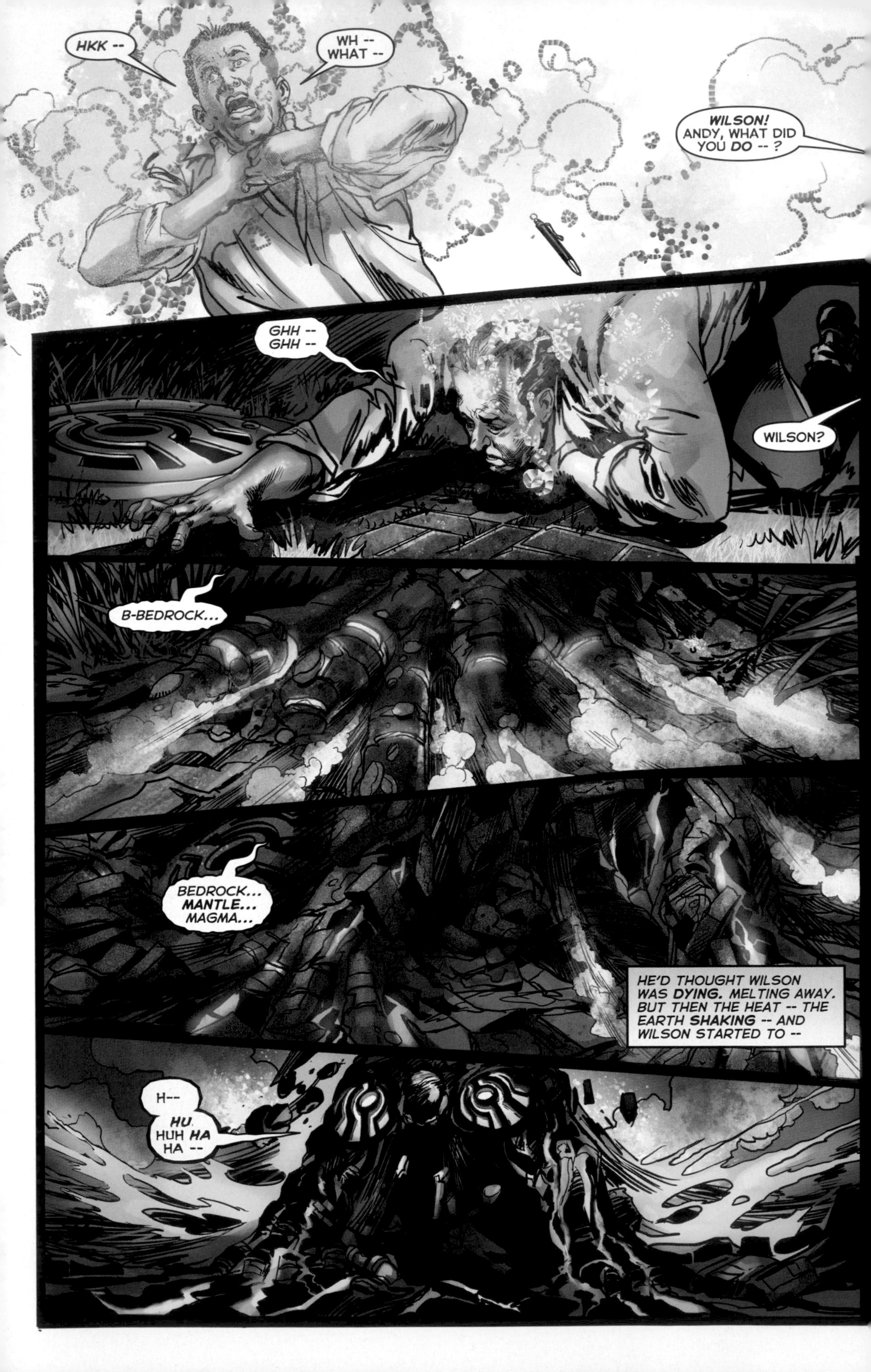
HKK --
WH -- WHAT --
WILSON! ANDY, WHAT DID YOU DO -- ?
GHH -- GHH --
WILSON?
B-BEDROCK...
BEDROCK... MANTLE... MAGMA...
HE'D THOUGHT WILSON WAS DYING. MELTING AWAY. BUT THEN THE HEAT -- THE EARTH SHAKING -- AND WILSON STARTED TO --
H--
HU. HUH HA HA --

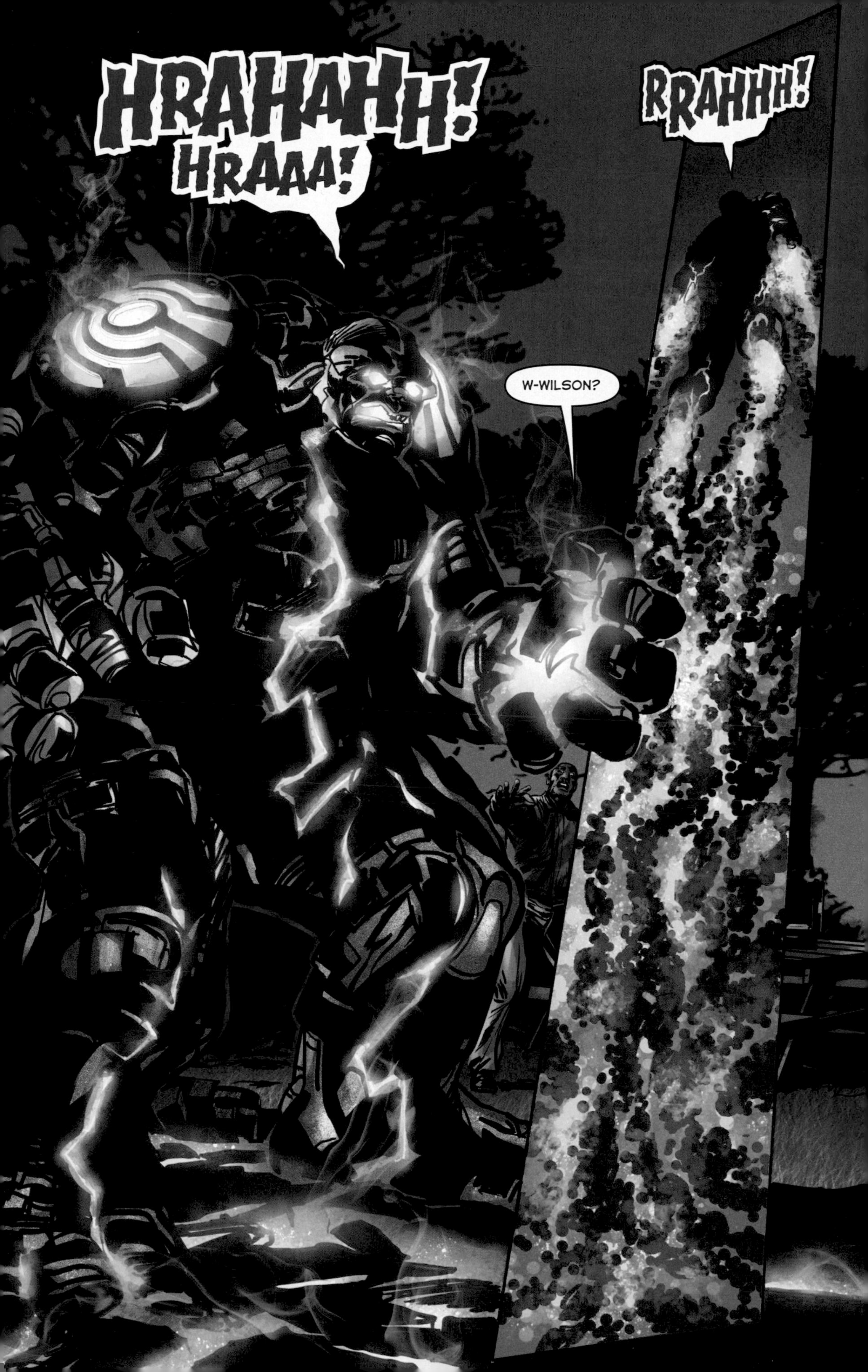
HRAHAHH! HRAAA!
W-WILSON?
RRAHHH!

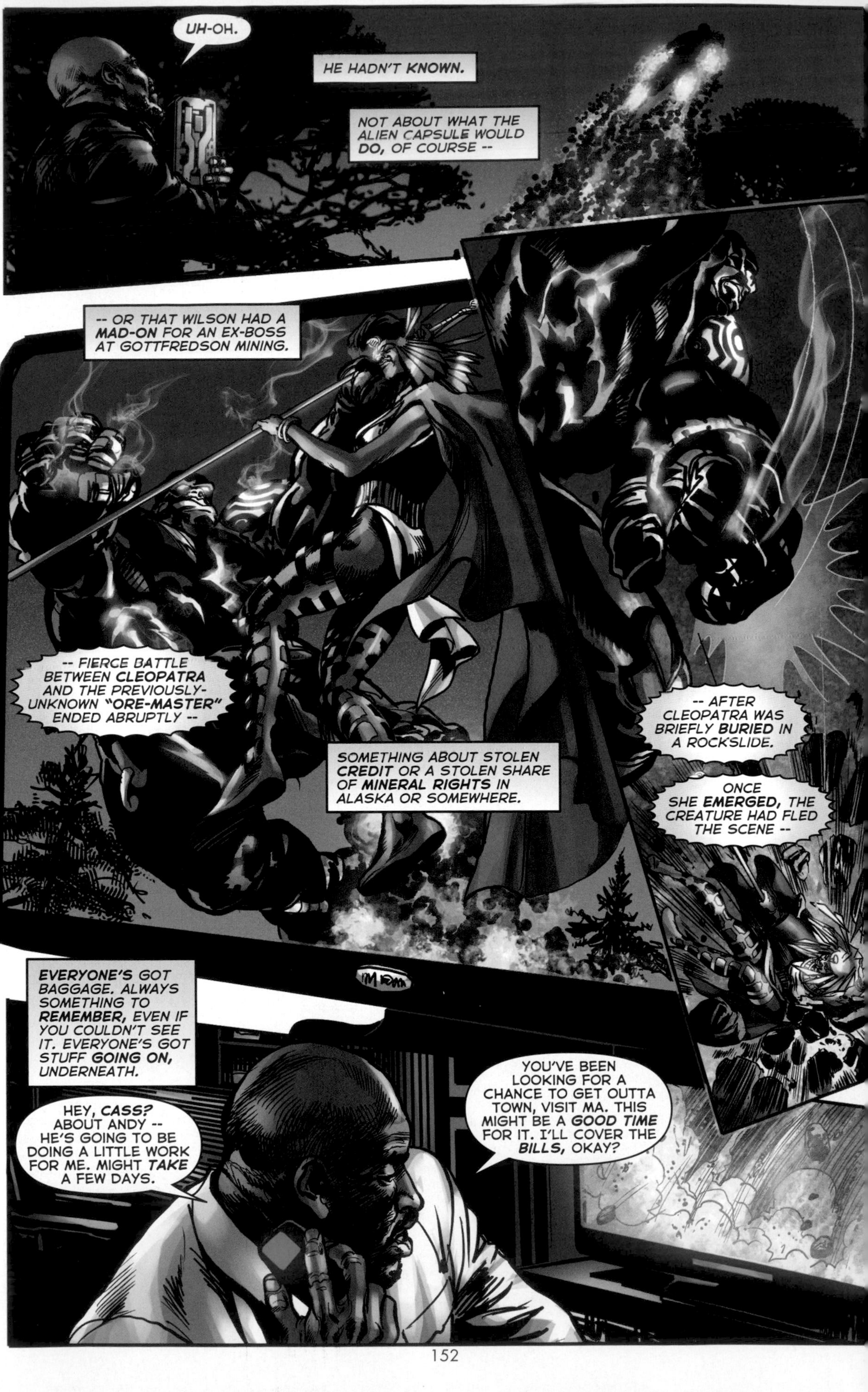
UH-OH.
HE HADN'T KNOWN.
NOT ABOUT WHAT THE ALIEN CAPSULE WOULD DO, OF COURSE --
-- OR THAT WILSON HAD A MAD-ON FOR AN EX-BOSS AT GOTTFREDSON MINING.
-- FIERCE BATTLE BETWEEN CLEOPATRA AND THE PREVIOUSLY-UNKNOWN "ORE-MASTER" ENDED ABRUPTLY --
SOMETHING ABOUT STOLEN CREDIT OR A STOLEN SHARE OF MINERAL RIGHTS IN ALASKA OR SOMEWHERE.
-- AFTER CLEOPATRA WAS BRIEFLY BURIED IN A ROCKSLIDE.
ONCE SHE EMERGED, THE CREATURE HAD FLED THE SCENE --
EVERYONE'S GOT BAGGAGE. ALWAYS SOMETHING TO REMEMBER, EVEN IF YOU COULDN'T SEE IT. EVERYONE'S GOT STUFF GOING ON, UNDERNEATH.
HEY, CASS? ABOUT ANDY -- HE'S GOING TO BE DOING A LITTLE WORK FOR ME. MIGHT TAKE A FEW DAYS.
YOU'VE BEEN LOOKING FOR A CHANCE TO GET OUTTA TOWN, VISIT MA. THIS MIGHT BE A GOOD TIME FOR IT. I'LL COVER THE BILLS, OKAY?

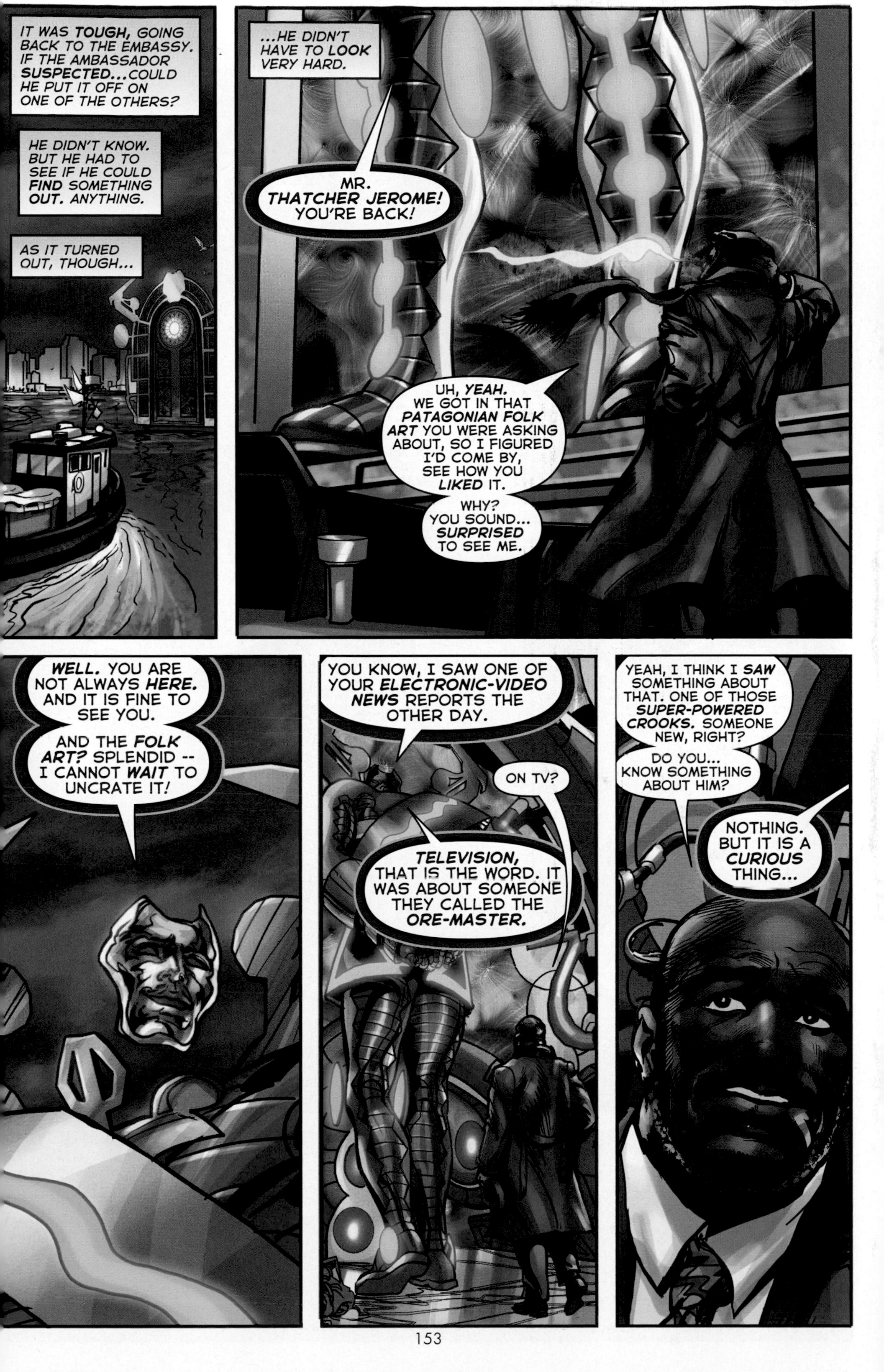
IT WAS TOUGH, GOING BACK TO THE EMBASSY. IF THE AMBASSADOR SUSPECTED...COULD HE PUT IT OFF ON ONE OF THE OTHERS?
HE DIDN'T KNOW. BUT HE HAD TO SEE IF HE COULD FIND SOMETHING OUT. ANYTHING.
AS IT TURNED OUT, THOUGH...
...HE DIDN'T HAVE TO LOOK VERY HARD.
MR. THATCHER JEROME! YOU'RE BACK!
UH, YEAH. WE GOT IN THAT PATAGONIAN FOLK ART YOU WERE ASKING ABOUT, SO I FIGURED I'D COME BY, SEE HOW YOU LIKED IT.
WHY? YOU SOUND... SURPRISED TO SEE ME.
WELL. YOU ARE NOT ALWAYS HERE. AND IT IS FINE TO SEE YOU.
AND THE FOLK ART? SPLENDID -- I CANNOT WAIT TO UNCRATE IT!
YOU KNOW, I SAW ONE OF YOUR ELECTRONIC-VIDEO NEWS REPORTS THE OTHER DAY.
ON TV?
TELEVISION, THAT IS THE WORD. IT WAS ABOUT SOMEONE THEY CALLED THE ORE-MASTER.
YEAH, I THINK I SAW SOMETHING ABOUT THAT. ONE OF THOSE SUPER-POWERED CROOKS. SOMEONE NEW, RIGHT?
DO YOU... KNOW SOMETHING ABOUT HIM?
NOTHING. BUT IT IS A CURIOUS THING...

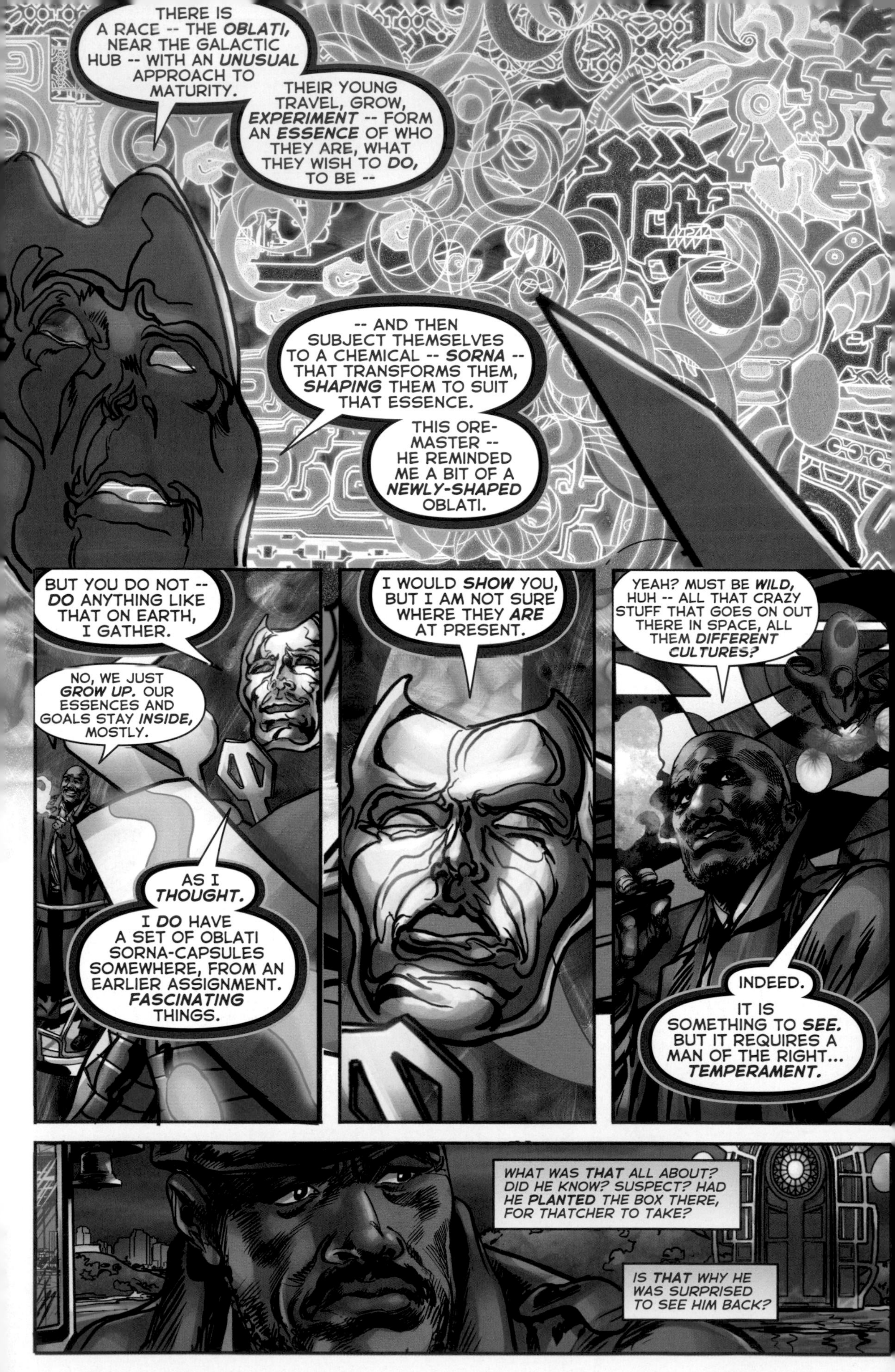
THERE IS A RACE -- THE OBLATI, NEAR THE GALACTIC HUB -- WITH AN UNUSUAL APPROACH TO MATURITY.
THEIR YOUNG TRAVEL, GROW, EXPERIMENT -- FORM AN ESSENCE OF WHO THEY ARE, WHAT THEY WISH TO DO, TO BE --
-- AND THEN SUBJECT THEMSELVES TO A CHEMICAL -- SORNA -- THAT TRANSFORMS THEM, SHAPING THEM TO SUIT THAT ESSENCE.
THIS ORE-MASTER -- HE REMINDED ME A BIT OF A NEWLY-SHAPED OBLATI.
BUT YOU DO NOT -- DO ANYTHING LIKE THAT ON EARTH, I GATHER.
NO, WE JUST GROW UP. OUR ESSENCES AND GOALS STAY INSIDE, MOSTLY.
AS I THOUGHT.
I DO HAVE A SET OF OBLATI SORNA-CAPSULES SOMEWHERE, FROM AN EARLIER ASSIGNMENT. FASCINATING THINGS.
I WOULD SHOW YOU, BUT I AM NOT SURE WHERE THEY ARE AT PRESENT.
YEAH? MUST BE WILD, HUH -- ALL THAT CRAZY STUFF THAT GOES ON OUT THERE IN SPACE, ALL THEM DIFFERENT CULTURES?
INDEED.
IT IS SOMETHING TO SEE. BUT IT REQUIRES A MAN OF THE RIGHT... TEMPERAMENT.
WHAT WAS THAT ALL ABOUT? DID HE KNOW? SUSPECT? HAD HE PLANTED THE BOX THERE, FOR THATCHER TO TAKE?
IS THAT WHY HE WAS SURPRISED TO SEE HIM BACK?

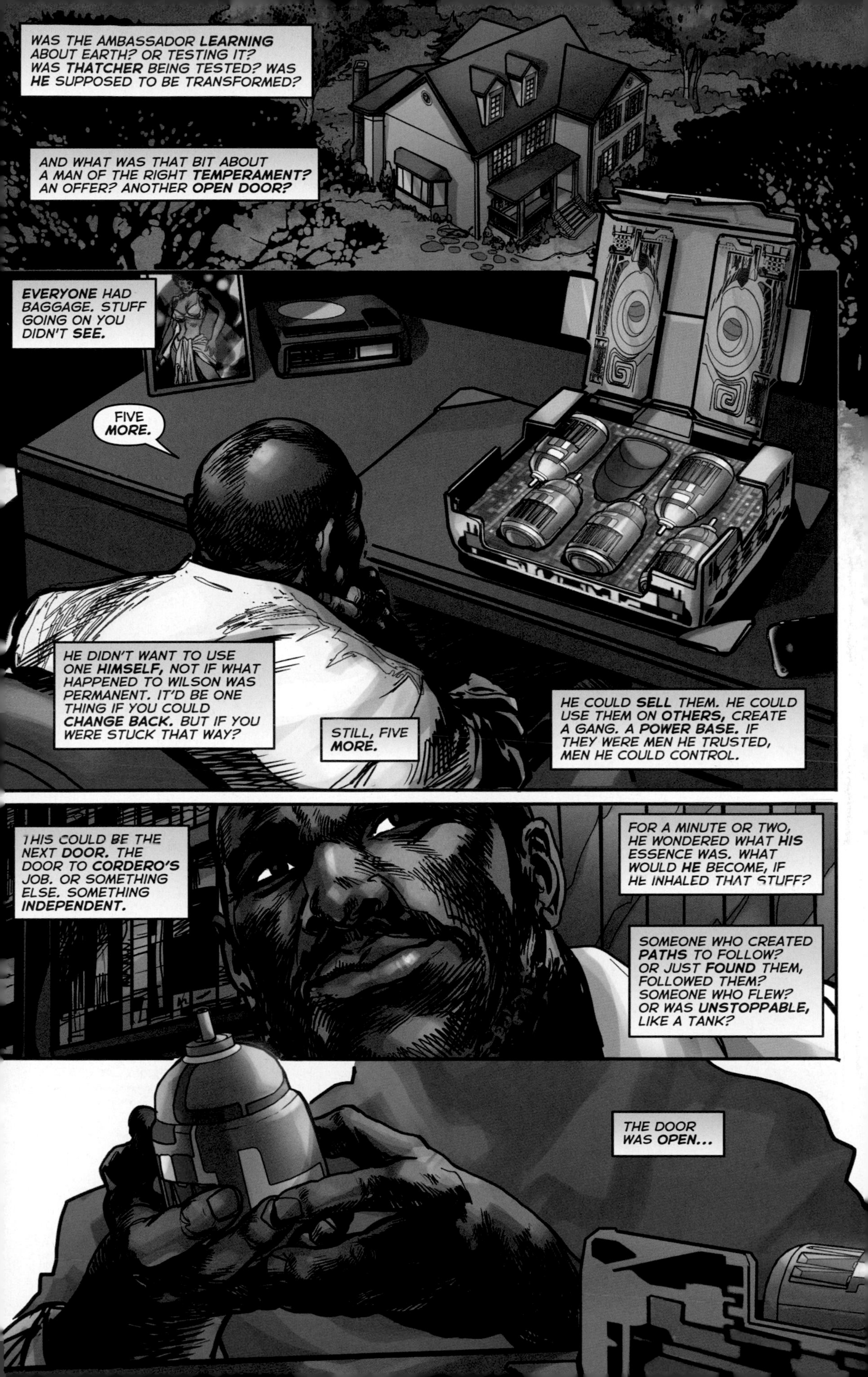
WAS THE AMBASSADOR LEARNING ABOUT EARTH? OR TESTING IT? WAS THATCHER BEING TESTED? WAS HE SUPPOSED TO BE TRANSFORMED?
AND WHAT WAS THAT BIT ABOUT A MAN OF THE RIGHT TEMPERAMENT? AN OFFER? ANOTHER OPEN DOOR?
EVERYONE HAD BAGGAGE. STUFF GOING ON YOU DIDN'T SEE.
FIVE MORE.
HE DIDN'T WANT TO USE ONE HIMSELF, NOT IF WHAT HAPPENED TO WILSON WAS PERMANENT. IT'D BE ONE THING IF YOU COULD CHANGE BACK. BUT IF YOU WERE STUCK THAT WAY?
STILL, FIVE MORE.
HE COULD SELL THEM. HE COULD USE THEM ON OTHERS, CREATE A GANG. A POWER BASE. IF THEY WERE MEN HE TRUSTED, MEN HE COULD CONTROL.
THIS COULD BE THE NEXT DOOR. THE DOOR TO CORDERO'S JOB. OR SOMETHING ELSE. SOMETHING INDEPENDENT.
FOR A MINUTE OR TWO, HE WONDERED WHAT HIS ESSENCE WAS. WHAT WOULD HE BECOME, IF HE INHALED THAT STUFF?
SOMEONE WHO CREATED PATHS TO FOLLOW? OR JUST FOUND THEM, FOLLOWED THEM? SOMEONE WHO FLEW? OR WAS UNSTOPPABLE, LIKE A TANK?
THE DOOR WAS OPEN...

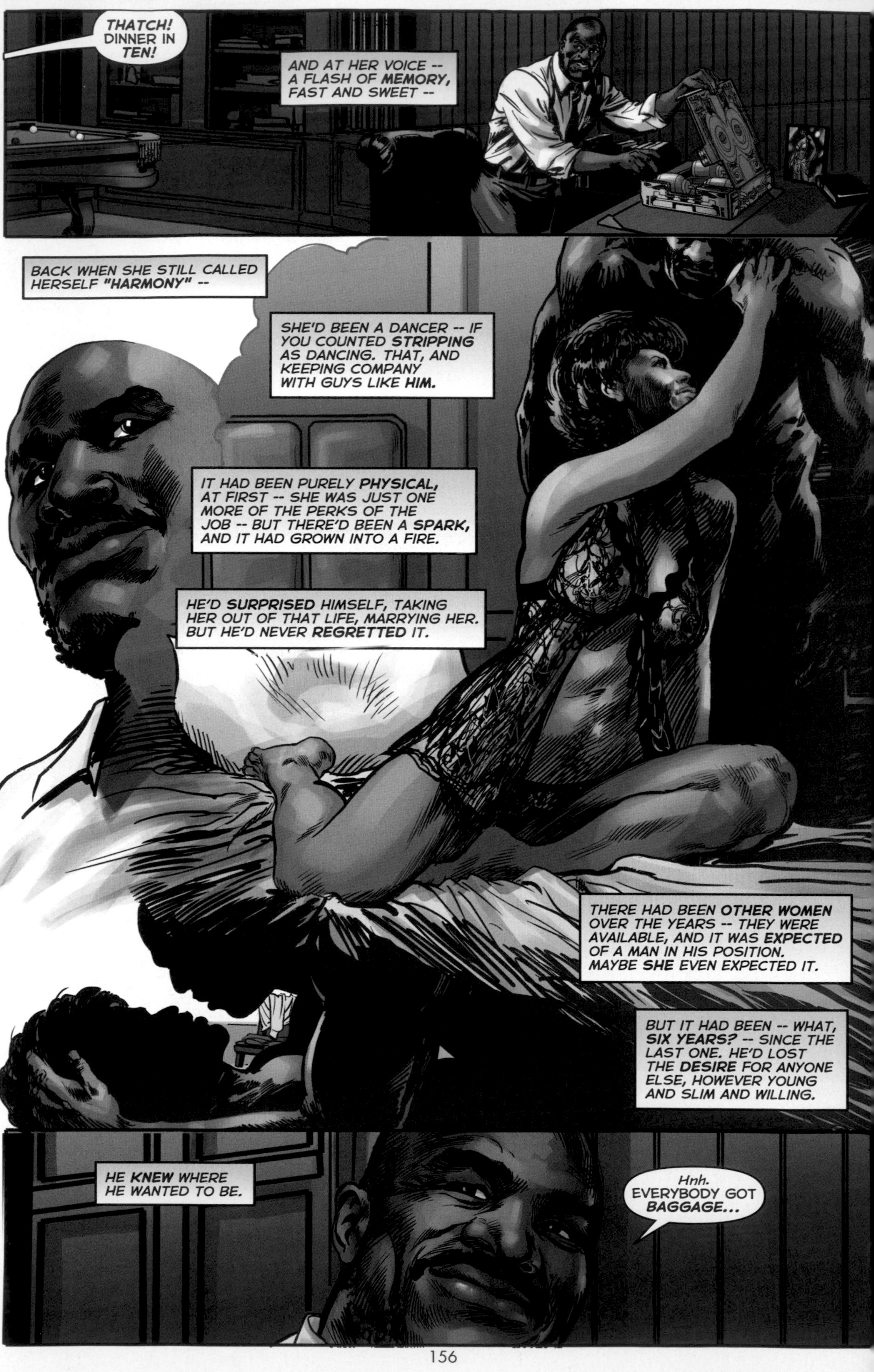
THATCH! DINNER IN TEN!
AND AT HER VOICE -- A FLASH OF MEMORY, FAST AND SWEET --
BACK WHEN SHE STILL CALLED HERSELF "HARMONY" --
SHE'D BEEN A DANCER -- IF YOU COUNTED STRIPPING AS DANCING. THAT, AND KEEPING COMPANY WITH GUYS LIKE HIM.
IT HAD BEEN PURELY PHYSICAL, AT FIRST -- SHE WAS JUST ONE MORE OF THE PERKS OF THE JOB -- BUT THERE'D BEEN A SPARK, AND IT HAD GROWN INTO A FIRE.
HE'D SURPRISED HIMSELF, TAKING HER OUT OF THAT LIFE, MARRYING HER. BUT HE'D NEVER REGRETTED IT.
THERE HAD BEEN OTHER WOMEN OVER THE YEARS -- THEY WERE AVAILABLE, AND IT WAS EXPECTED OF A MAN IN HIS POSITION. MAYBE SHE EVEN EXPECTED IT.
BUT IT HAD BEEN -- WHAT, SIX YEARS? -- SINCE THE LAST ONE. HE'D LOST THE DESIRE FOR ANYONE ELSE, HOWEVER YOUNG AND SLIM AND WILLING.
HE KNEW WHERE HE WANTED TO BE.
Hnh. EVERYBODY GOT BAGGAGE...

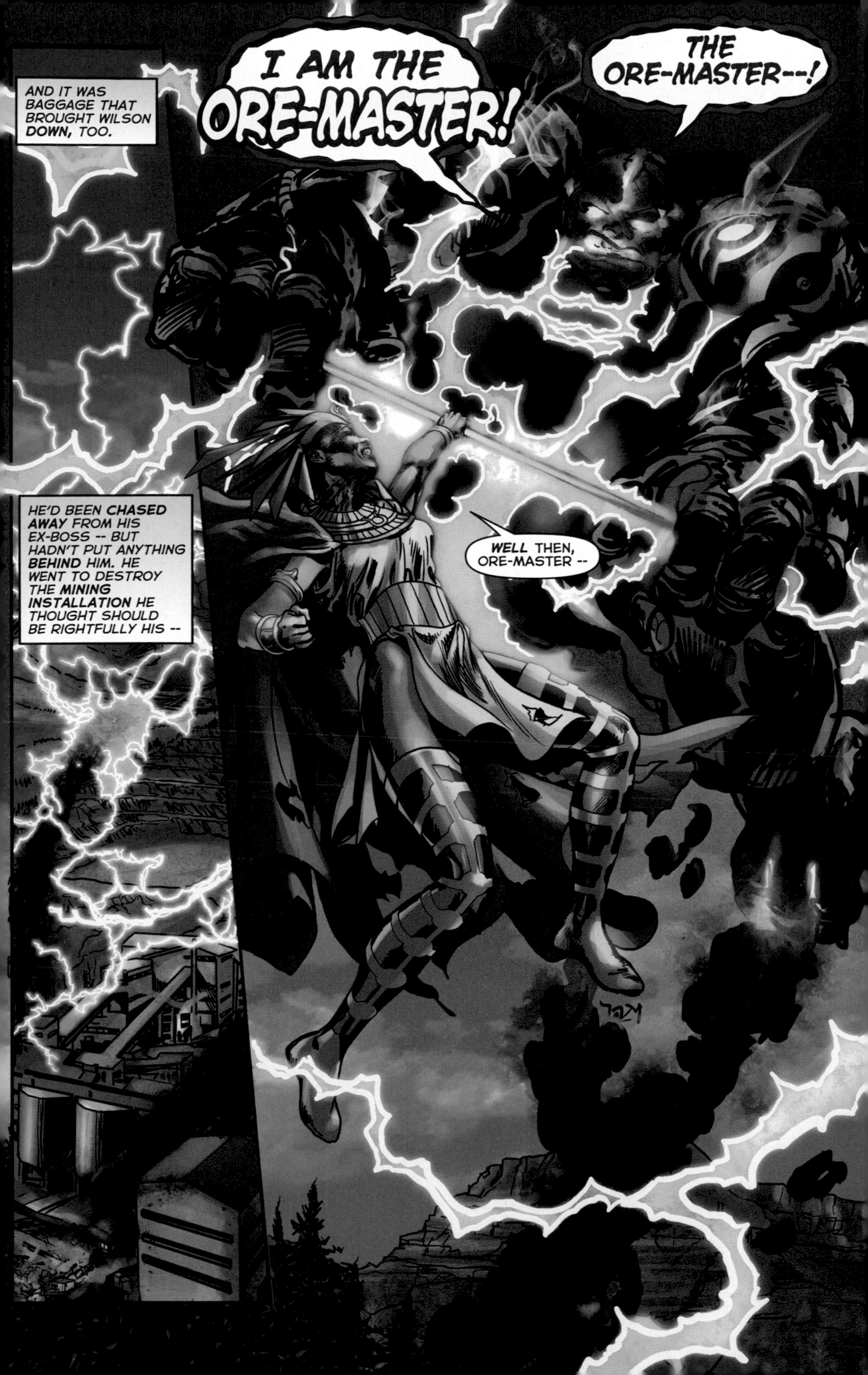
AND IT WAS BAGGAGE THAT BROUGHT WILSON DOWN, TOO.
I AM THE ORE-MASTER!
THE ORE-MASTER--!
HE'D BEEN CHASED AWAY FROM HIS EX-BOSS -- BUT HADN'T PUT ANYTHING BEHIND HIM. HE WENT TO DESTROY THE MINING INSTALLATION HE THOUGHT SHOULD BE RIGHTFULLY HIS --
WELL THEN, ORE-MASTER --

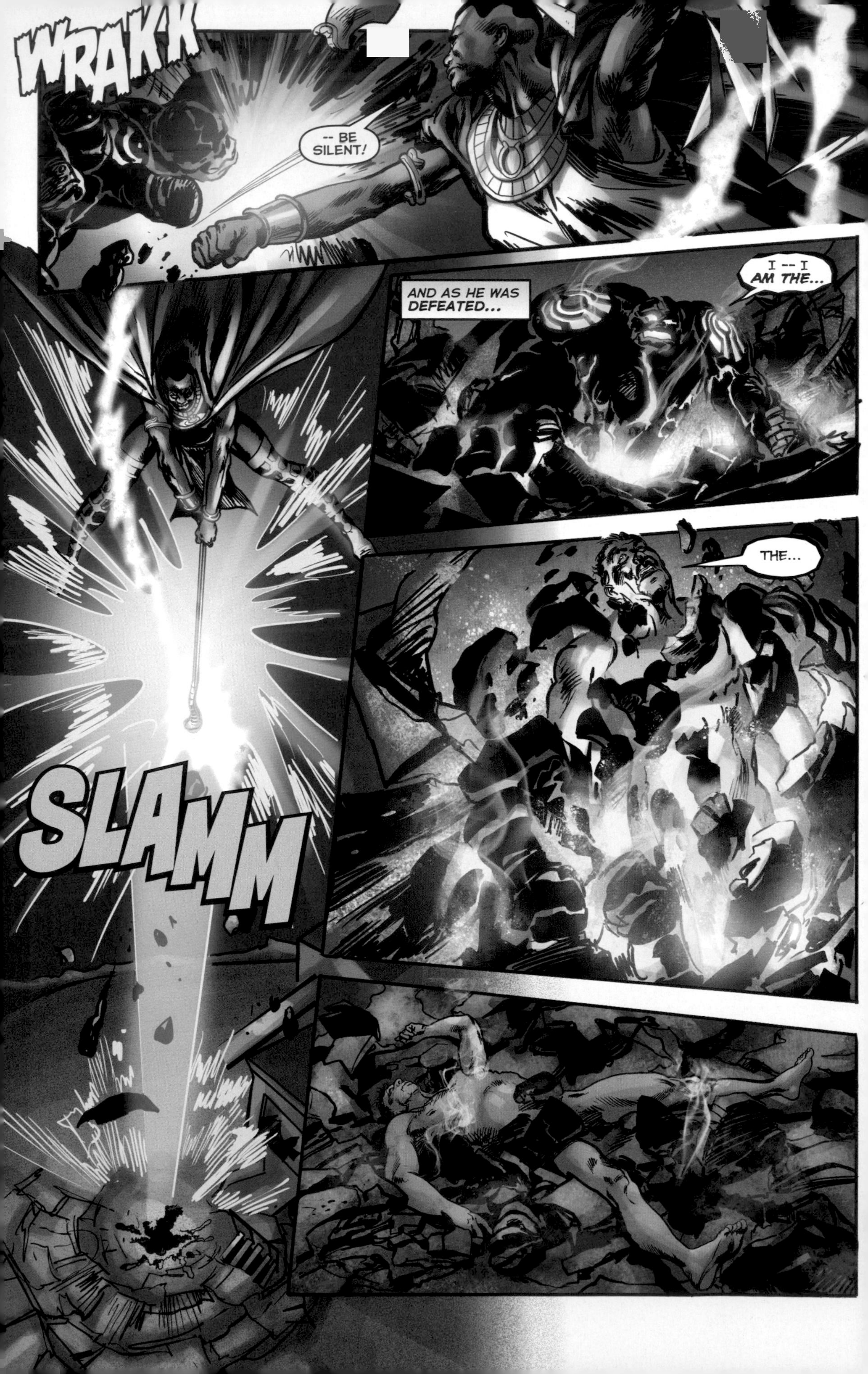
WRAKK
-- BE SILENT!
SLAMM
AND AS HE WAS DEFEATED...
I -- I AM THE...
THE...

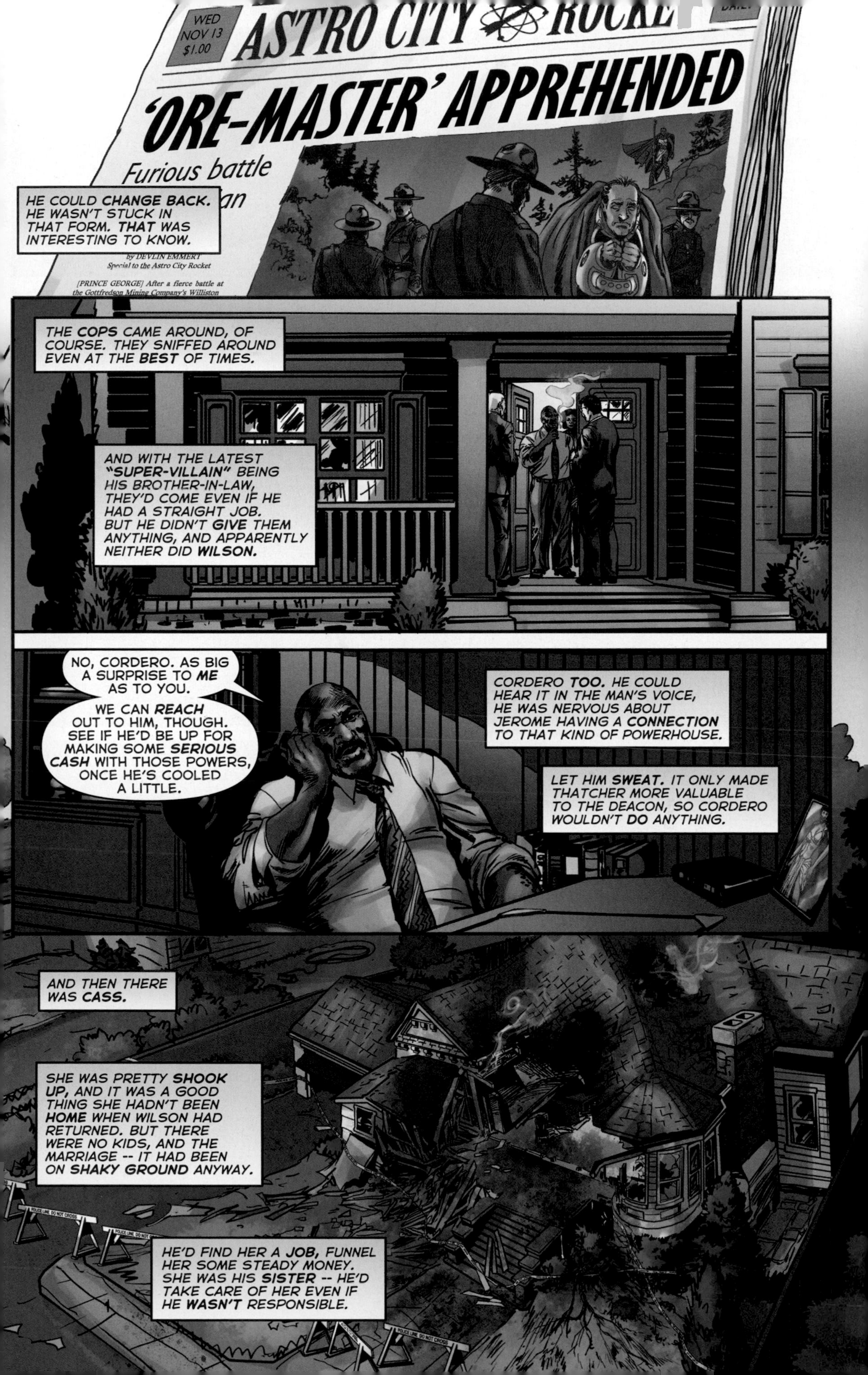
WED NOV 13 $1.00
ASTRO CITY ROCKE
'ORE-MASTER' APPREHENDED
Furious battle
an
HE COULD CHANGE BACK. HE WASN'T STUCK IN THAT FORM. THAT WAS INTERESTING TO KNOW.
by DEVLIN EMMERT
Special to the Astro City Rocket
[PRINCE GEORGE] After a fierce battle at the Gottfredson Mining Company's Williston
THE COPS CAME AROUND, OF COURSE. THEY SNIFFED AROUND EVEN AT THE BEST OF TIMES.
AND WITH THE LATEST "SUPER-VILLAIN" BEING HIS BROTHER-IN-LAW, THEY'D COME EVEN IF HE HAD A STRAIGHT JOB. BUT HE DIDN'T GIVE THEM ANYTHING, AND APPARENTLY NEITHER DID WILSON.
NO, CORDERO. AS BIG A SURPRISE TO ME AS TO YOU.
WE CAN REACH OUT TO HIM, THOUGH. SEE IF HE'D BE UP FOR MAKING SOME SERIOUS CASH WITH THOSE POWERS, ONCE HE'S COOLED A LITTLE.
CORDERO TOO. HE COULD HEAR IT IN THE MAN'S VOICE, HE WAS NERVOUS ABOUT JEROME HAVING A CONNECTION TO THAT KIND OF POWERHOUSE.
LET HIM SWEAT. IT ONLY MADE THATCHER MORE VALUABLE TO THE DEACON, SO CORDERO WOULDN'T DO ANYTHING.
AND THEN THERE WAS CASS.
SHE WAS PRETTY SHOOK UP, AND IT WAS A GOOD THING SHE HADN'T BEEN HOME WHEN WILSON HAD RETURNED. BUT THERE WERE NO KIDS, AND THE MARRIAGE -- IT HAD BEEN ON SHAKY GROUND ANYWAY.
HE'D FIND HER A JOB, FUNNEL HER SOME STEADY MONEY. SHE WAS HIS SISTER -- HE'D TAKE CARE OF HER EVEN IF HE WASN'T RESPONSIBLE.

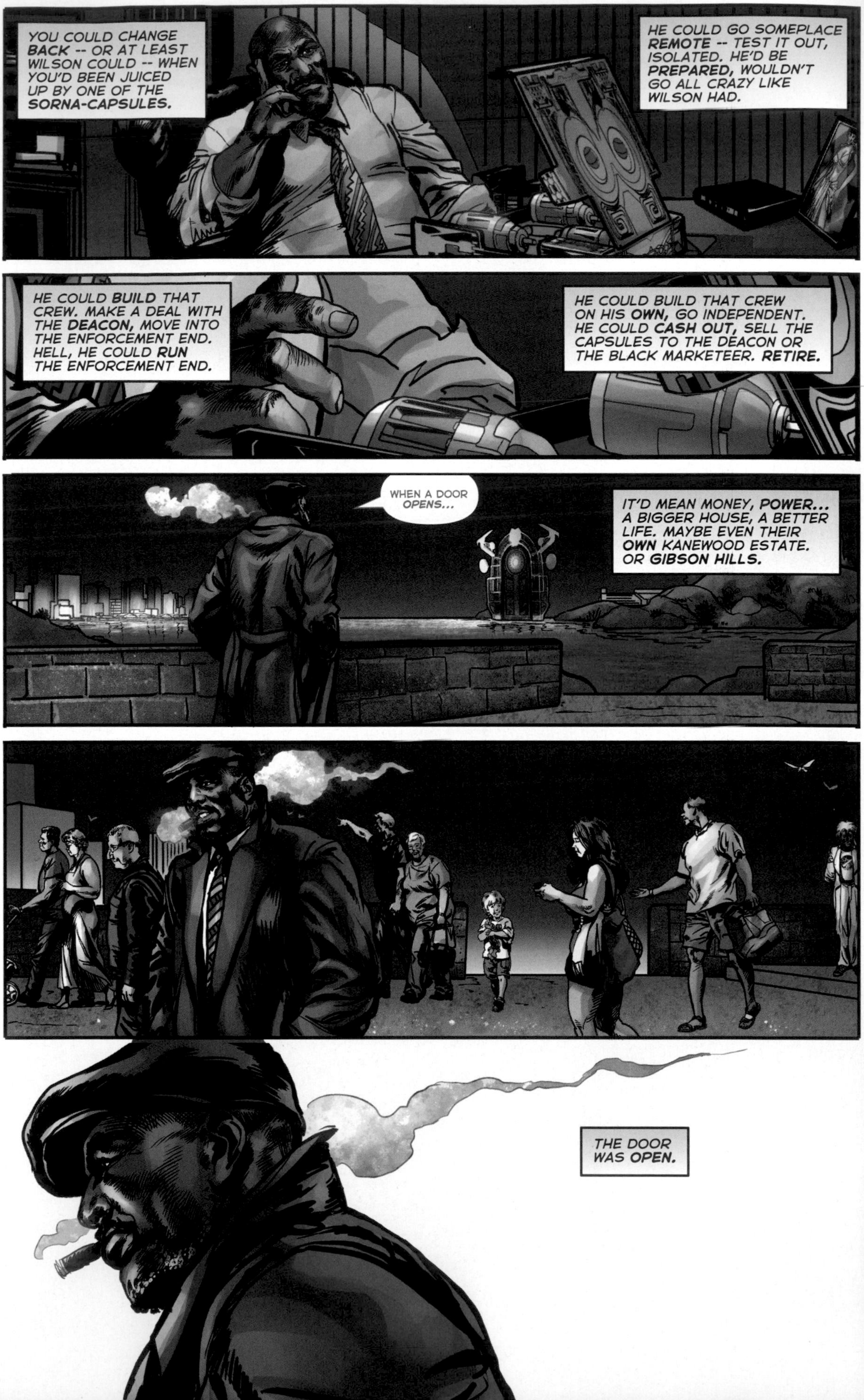
YOU COULD CHANGE BACK -- OR AT LEAST WILSON COULD -- WHEN YOU'D BEEN JUICED UP BY ONE OF THE SORNA-CAPSULES.
HE COULD GO SOMEPLACE REMOTE -- TEST IT OUT, ISOLATED. HE'D BE PREPARED, WOULDN'T GO ALL CRAZY LIKE WILSON HAD.
HE COULD BUILD THAT CREW. MAKE A DEAL WITH THE DEACON, MOVE INTO THE ENFORCEMENT END. HELL, HE COULD RUN THE ENFORCEMENT END.
HE COULD BUILD THAT CREW ON HIS OWN, GO INDEPENDENT. HE COULD CASH OUT, SELL THE CAPSULES TO THE DEACON OR THE BLACK MARKETEER. RETIRE.
WHEN A DOOR OPENS...
IT'D MEAN MONEY, POWER... A BIGGER HOUSE, A BETTER LIFE. MAYBE EVEN THEIR OWN KANEWOOD ESTATE. OR GIBSON HILLS.
THE DOOR WAS OPEN.

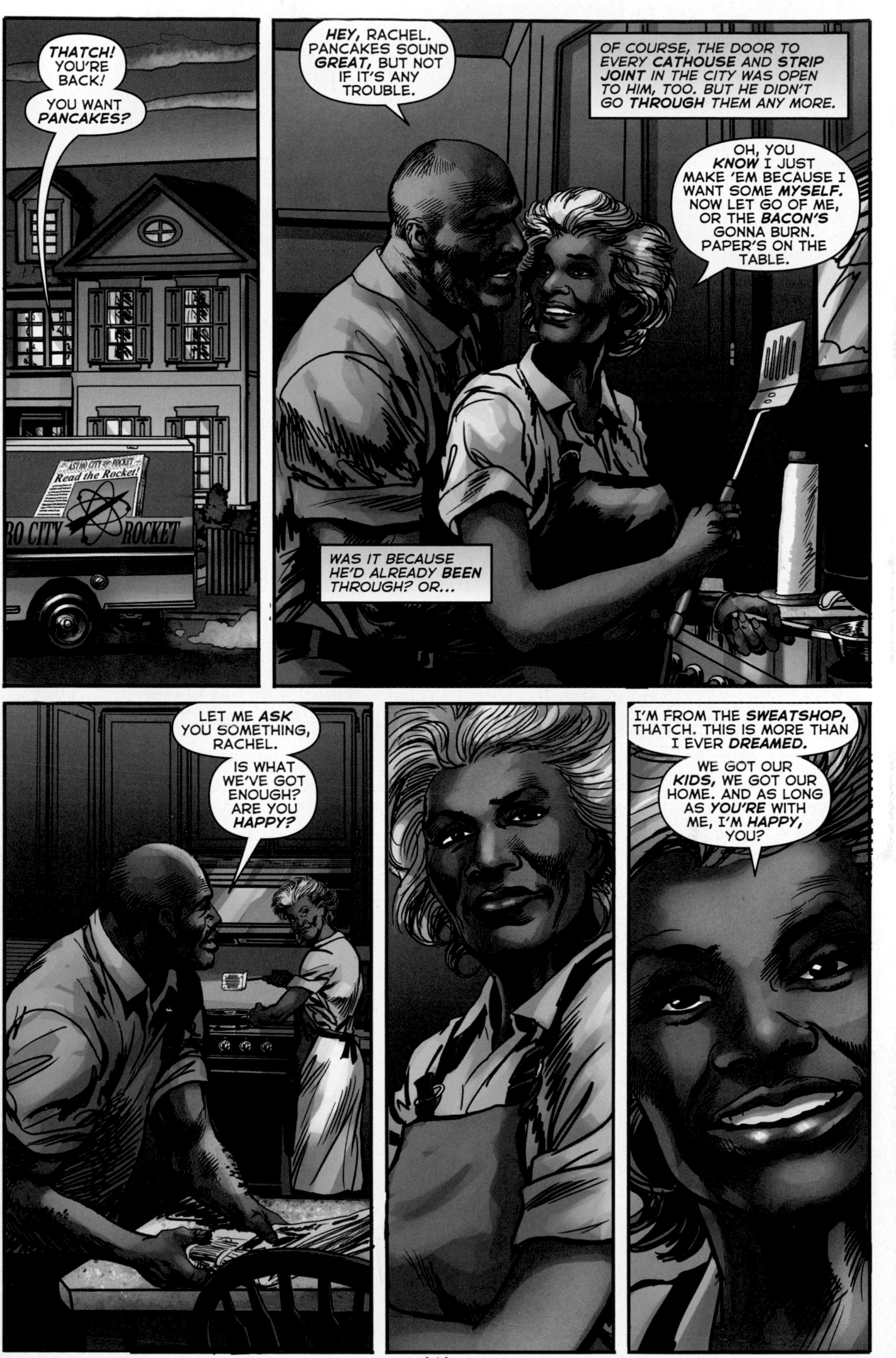
THATCH! YOU'RE BACK!
YOU WANT PANCAKES?
ASTRO CITY ROCKET
Read the Rocket!
RO CITY ROCKET
HEY, RACHEL. PANCAKES SOUND GREAT, BUT NOT IF IT'S ANY TROUBLE.
OF COURSE, THE DOOR TO EVERY CATHOUSE AND STRIP JOINT IN THE CITY WAS OPEN TO HIM, TOO. BUT HE DIDN'T GO THROUGH THEM ANY MORE.
OH, YOU KNOW I JUST MAKE 'EM BECAUSE I WANT SOME MYSELF. NOW LET GO OF ME, OR THE BACON'S GONNA BURN. PAPER'S ON THE TABLE.
WAS IT BECAUSE HE'D ALREADY BEEN THROUGH? OR...
LET ME ASK YOU SOMETHING, RACHEL.
IS WHAT WE'VE GOT ENOUGH? ARE YOU HAPPY?
I'M FROM THE SWEATSHOP, THATCH. THIS IS MORE THAN I EVER DREAMED.
WE GOT OUR KIDS, WE GOT OUR HOME. AND AS LONG AS YOU'RE WITH ME, I'M HAPPY, YOU?

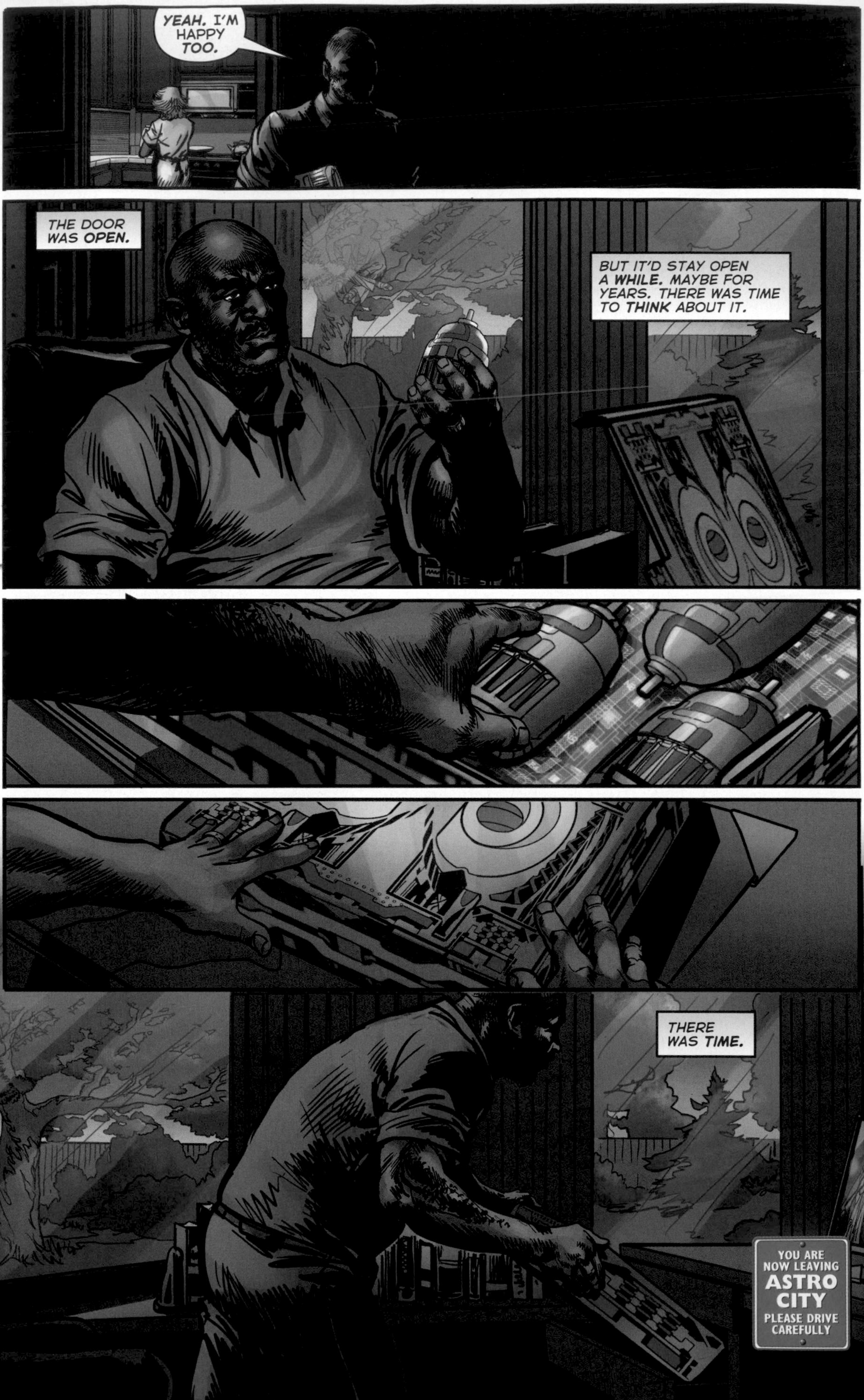
YEAH. I'M HAPPY TOO.
THE DOOR WAS OPEN.
BUT IT'D STAY OPEN A WHILE. MAYBE FOR YEARS. THERE WAS TIME TO THINK ABOUT IT.
THERE WAS TIME.
YOU ARE NOW LEAVING ASTRO CITY PLEASE DRIVE CAREFULLY

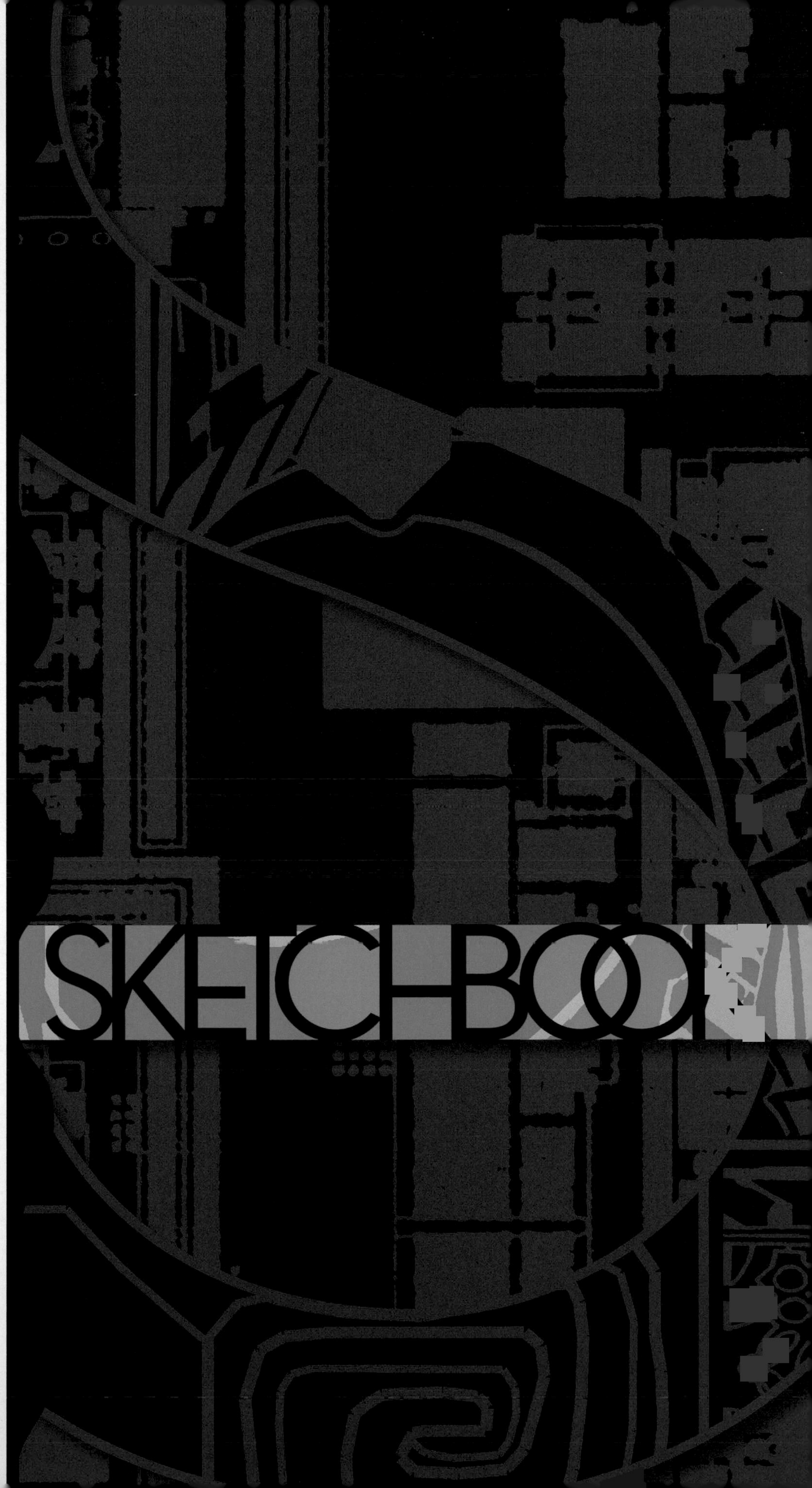
SKETCHBOO

AMBASSADOR

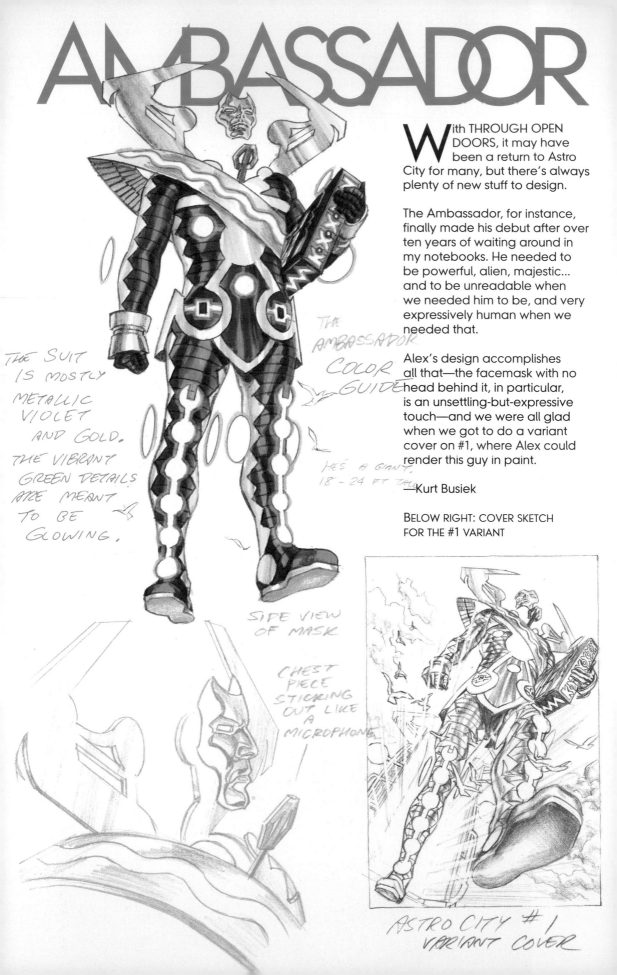

With THROUGH OPEN DOORS, it may have been a return to Astro City for many, but there's always plenty of new stuff to design.

The Ambassador, for instance, finally made his debut after over ten years of waiting around in my notebooks. He needed to be powerful, alien, majestic... and to be unreadable when we needed him to be, and very expressively human when we needed that.

Alex's design accomplishes all that—the facemask with no head behind it, in particular, is an unsettling-but-expressive touch—and we were all glad when we got to do a variant cover on #1, where Alex could render this guy in paint.

—Kurt Busiek

BELOW RIGHT: COVER SKETCH FOR THE #1 VARIANT

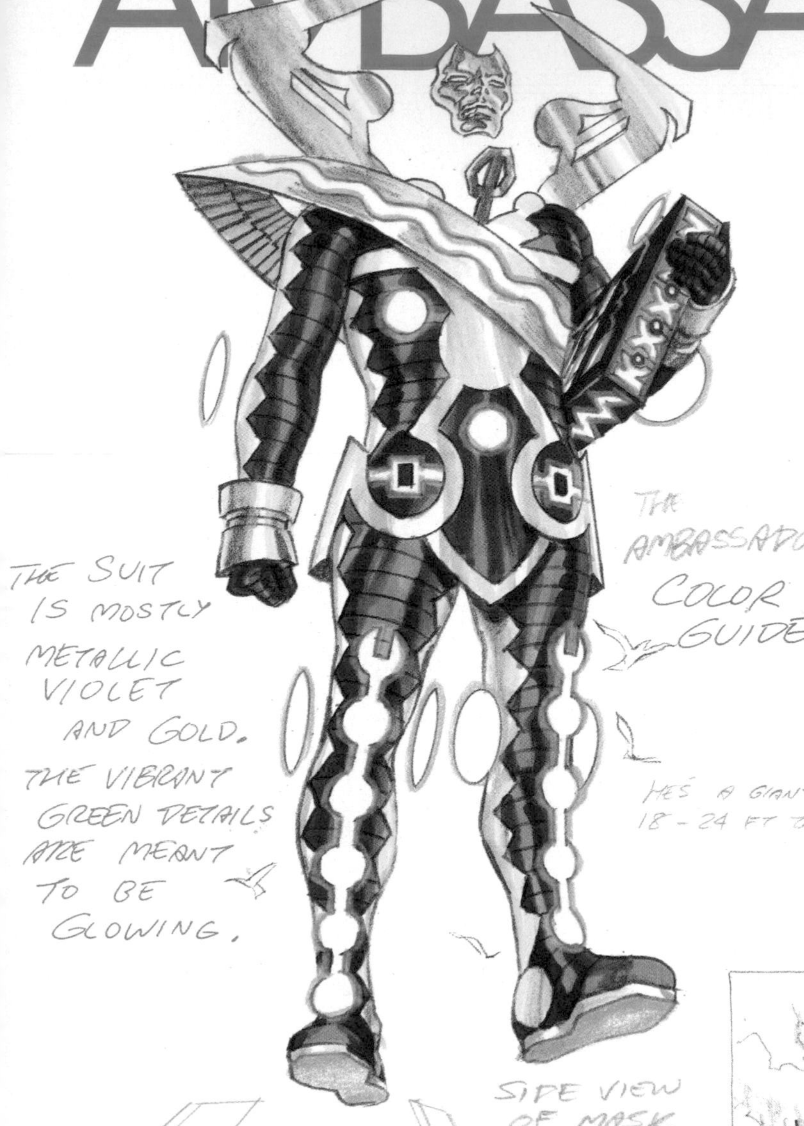
THE AMBASSADOR COLOR GUIDE
THE SUIT IS MOSTLY METALLIC VIOLET AND GOLD. THE VIBRANT GREEN DETAILS ARE MEANT TO BE GLOWING.
HE'S A GIANT. 18 - 24 FT TALL

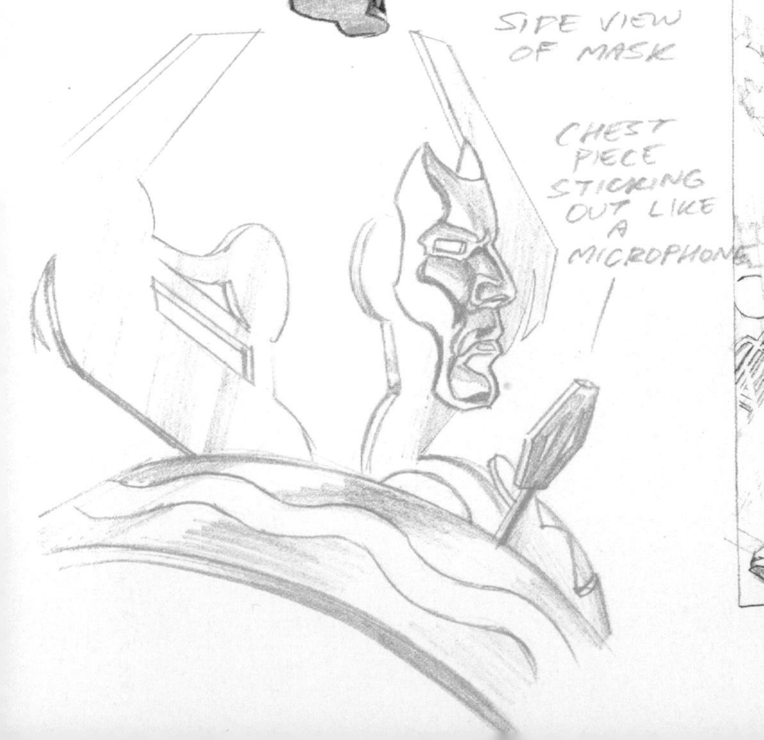
SIDE VIEW OF MASK
CHEST PIECE STICKING OUT LIKE A MICROPHONE

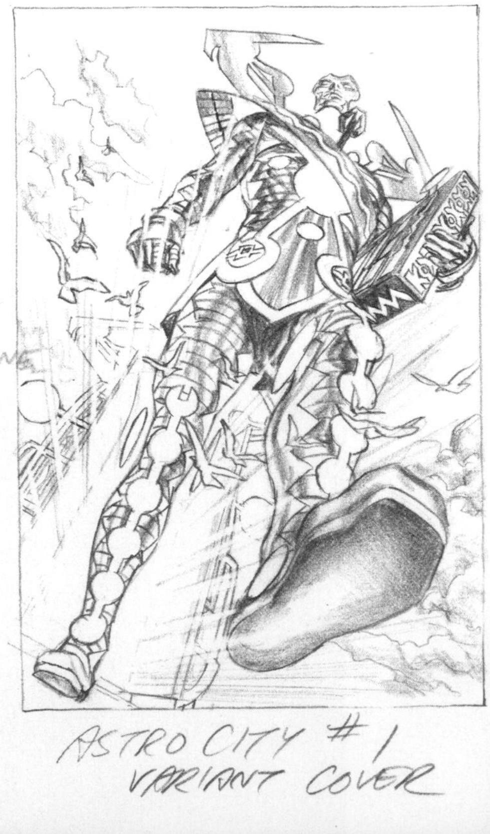
ASTRO CITY #1 VARIANT COVER

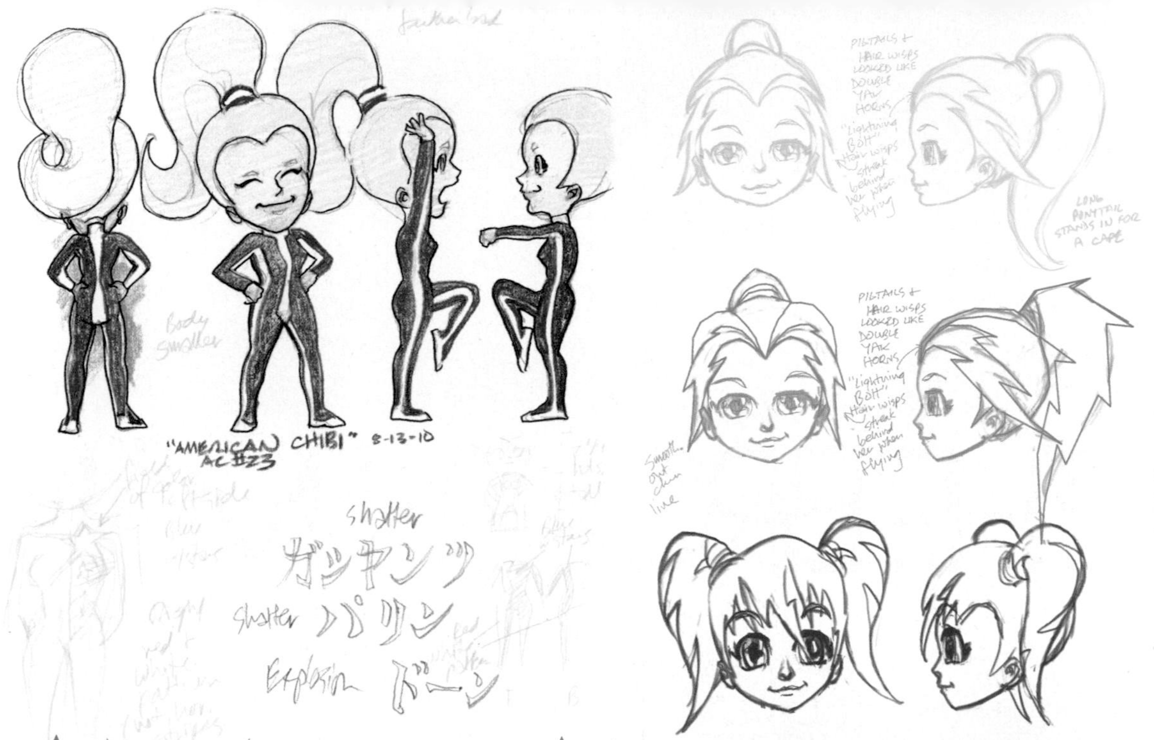
Body smaller
"AMERICAN CHIBI" 8-13-10
AC #23
PIGTAILS + HAIR WISPS LOOKED LIKE DOUBLE YAK HORNS
"Lightning Bolt" hair wisps streak behind her when flying
LONG PONYTAIL STANDS IN FOR A CAPE
shatter
shatter
Explosion

AMERICAN CHIBI

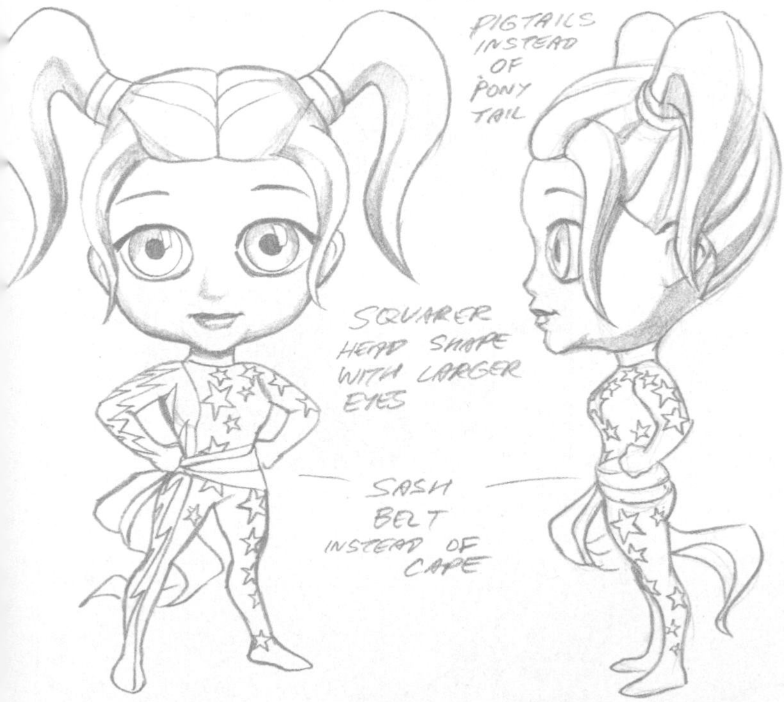
PIGTAILS INSTEAD OF PONY TAIL
SQUARER HEAD SHAPE WITH LARGER EYES
SASH BELT INSTEAD OF CAPE

Originally inspired by my old friend Scott McCloud drawing a chibi version of himself on a napkin, which led to us discussing the term "American chibi" and me deciding there had to be an Astro City hero of that name…

Designing her was a lot of work, figuring out the right head shape, hairstyle, eye size and more, and a lot of scans went back and forth between us. We'd better get her back on stage soon, after all that!

Top left: Brent's initial design.
Middle: Alex's revision.
Top right and bottom: Brent trying out hairstyles and colors.

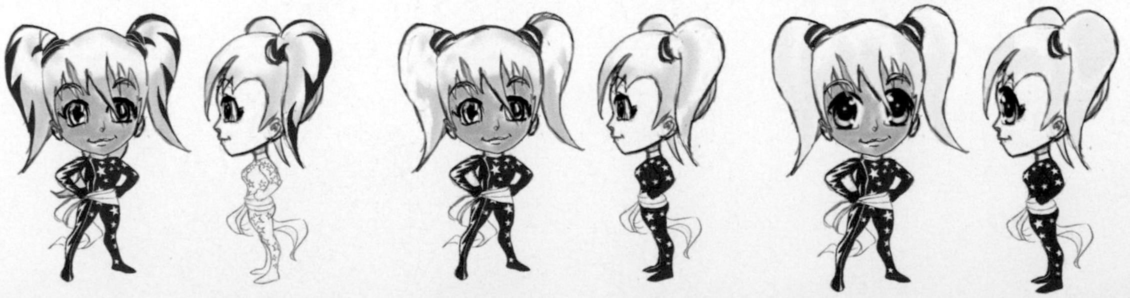

THE BROKEN MAN

A lot of people assume he was added as a nod to our becoming a Vertigo series, but #1 was written and drawn two years before the book joined Vertigo. And as you can see from Brent's notes, we were inspired by the Englehart/Rogers take on the Joker from DETECTIVE COMICS in the 1970s, as much or more than anything else.

Plus, the Broken Man's (secret) history goes almost all the way back to our very first issue, as you'll eventually discover...

More cartoony attitude!

M.Rogers' Joker attitude
Theatrical + ring master

Less insistent — more cool

White color

OUTLINE DESIGNS

The 13 clocks thing

"The Broken Man"
AC #23 8-12-10

NEGATIVE STYLE

BASIC COLOR STYLE

THE IRON LEGION

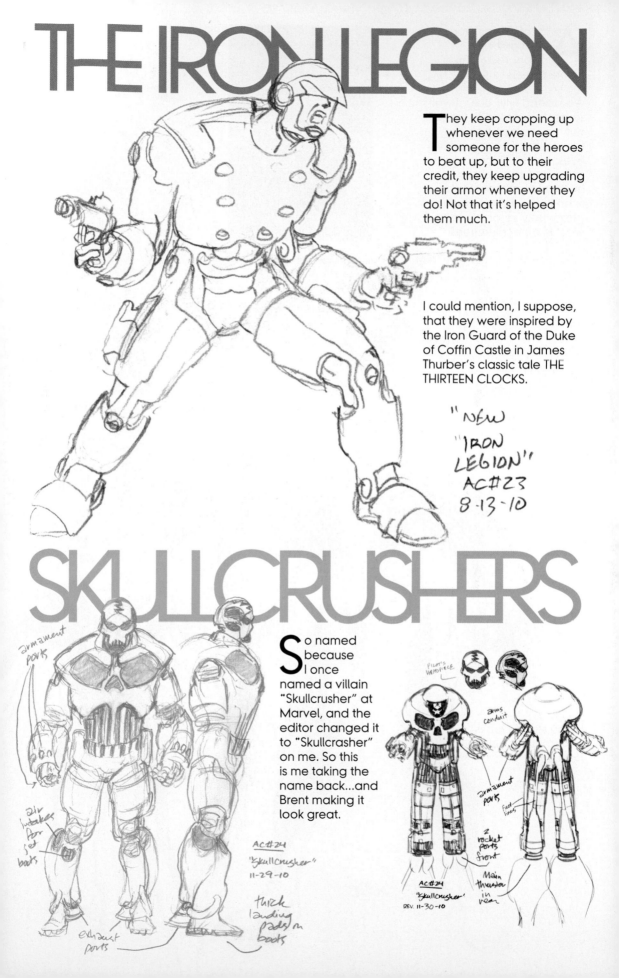

They keep cropping up whenever we need someone for the heroes to beat up, but to their credit, they keep upgrading their armor whenever they do! Not that it's helped them much.

I could mention, I suppose, that they were inspired by the Iron Guard of the Duke of Coffin Castle in James Thurber's classic tale THE THIRTEEN CLOCKS.

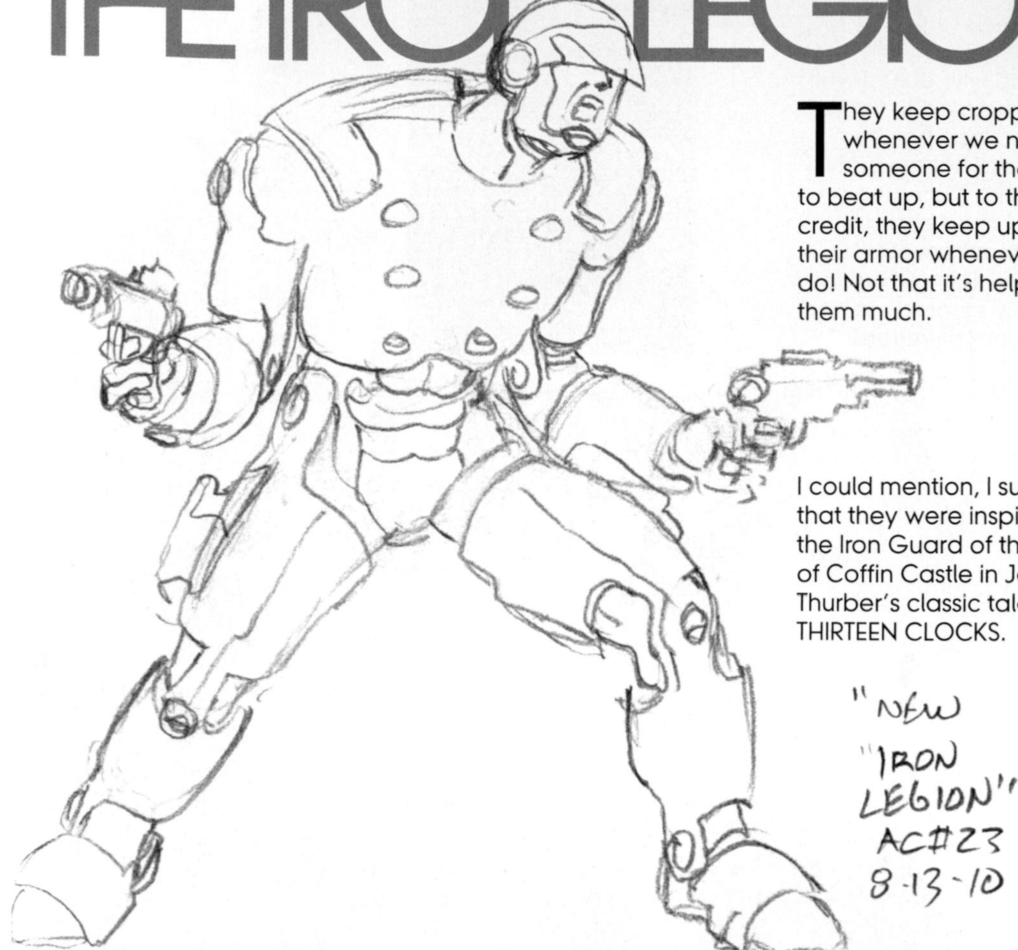
"NEW "IRON LEGION"
AC#23
8-13-10

SKULLCRUSHERS

So named because I once named a villain "Skullcrusher" at Marvel, and the editor changed it to "Skullcrasher" on me. So this is me taking the name back...and Brent making it look great.

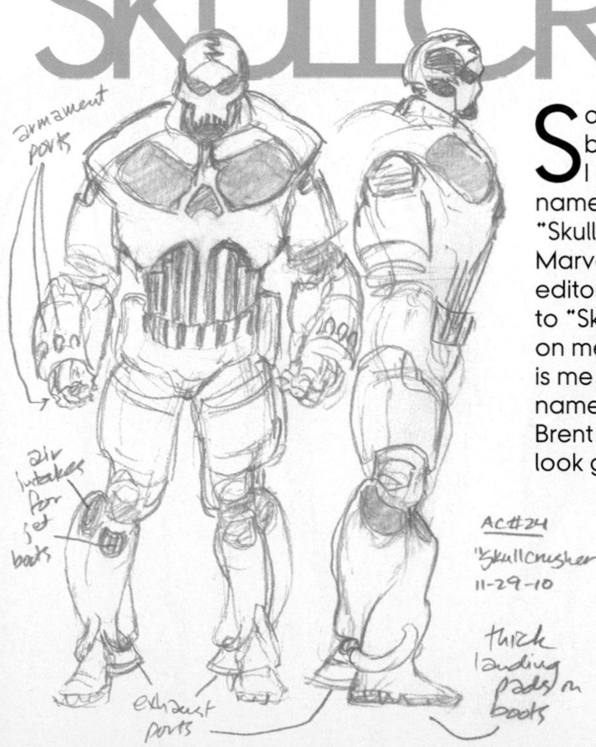
armament ports
air intakes for jet boots
exhaust ports
thick landing pads on boots
AC#24
"Skullcrusher"
11-29-10

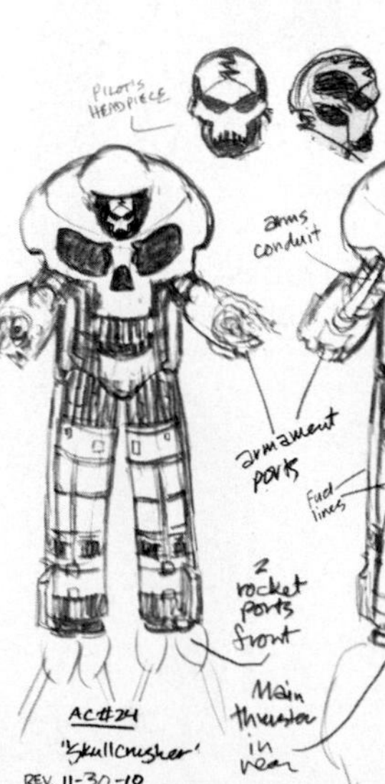
PILOT'S HEADPIECE
arms conduit
armament ports
fuel lines
2 rocket ports front
Main thruster in rear
AC#24
"Skullcrusher"
REV. 11-30-10

A lot of design work for a guy who's appeared in three whole panels so far!

We started with actual wolf spiders, and tried to figure out how to incorporate those tufts of hair and extra eyes. My first stabs at a mask and chest emblem built around them can be seen to the right, whereupon Alex wisely ignored me and went in other directions...

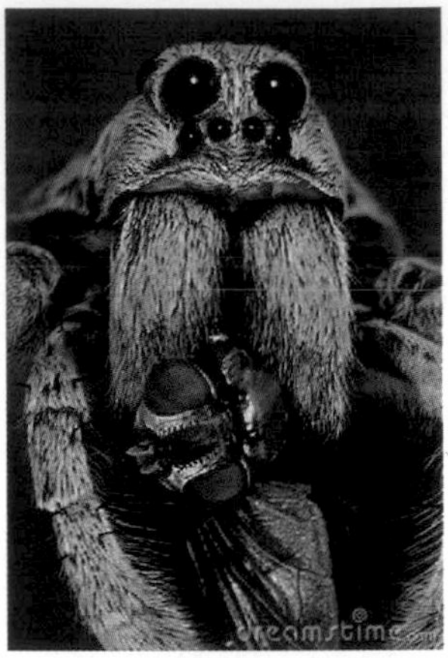

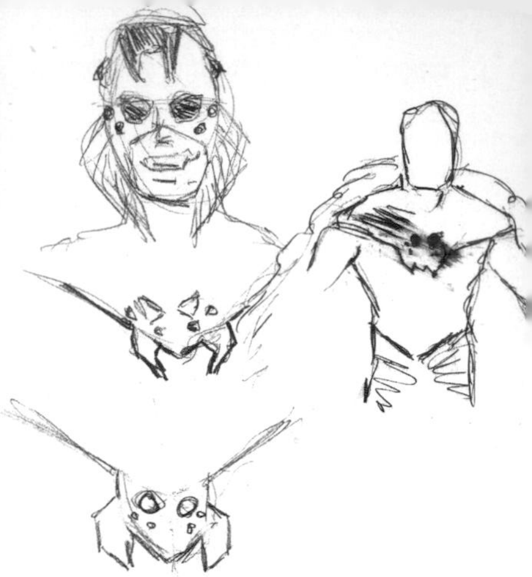

WOLFSPIDER

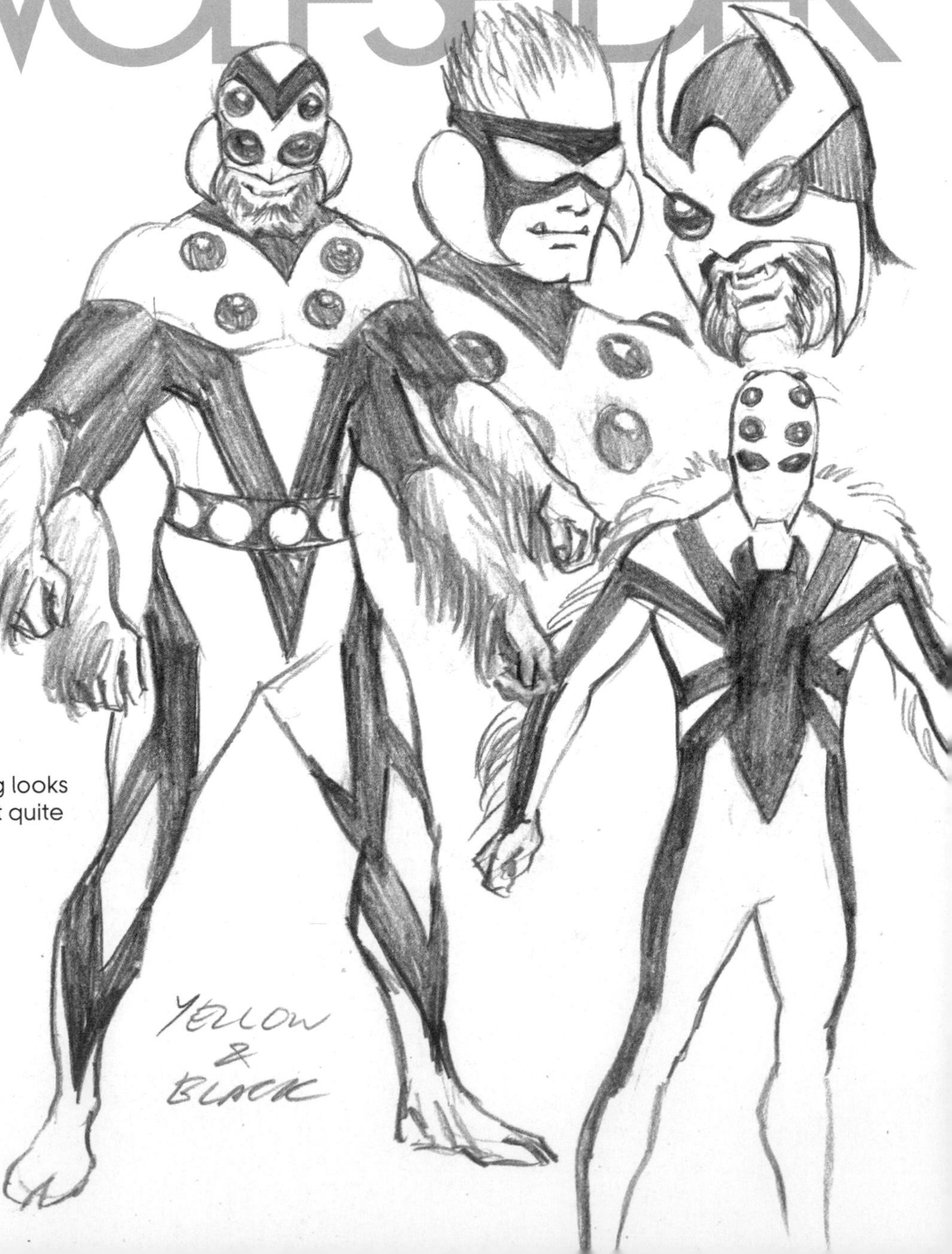
YELLOW
&
BLACK

Some striking looks here, but not quite right yet...

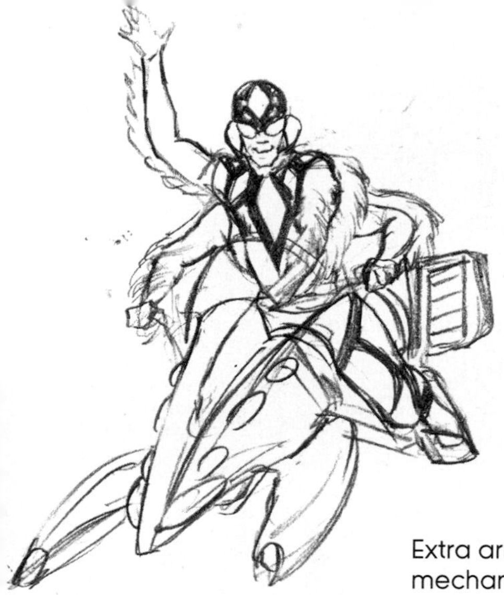

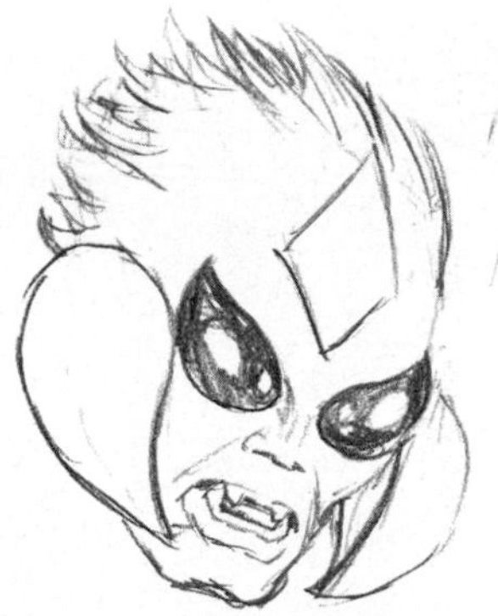

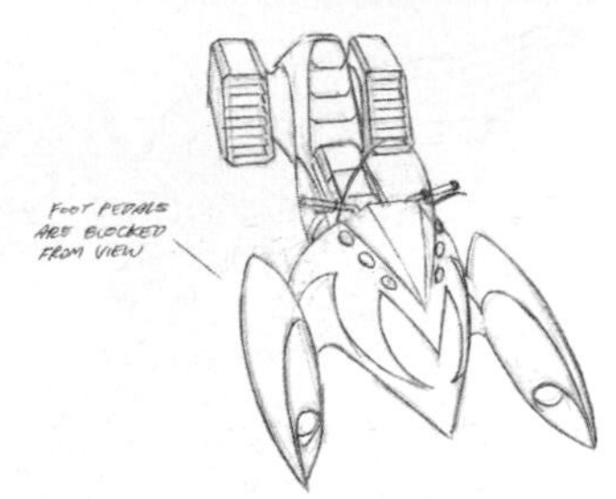
FOOT PEDALS ARE BLOCKED FROM VIEW

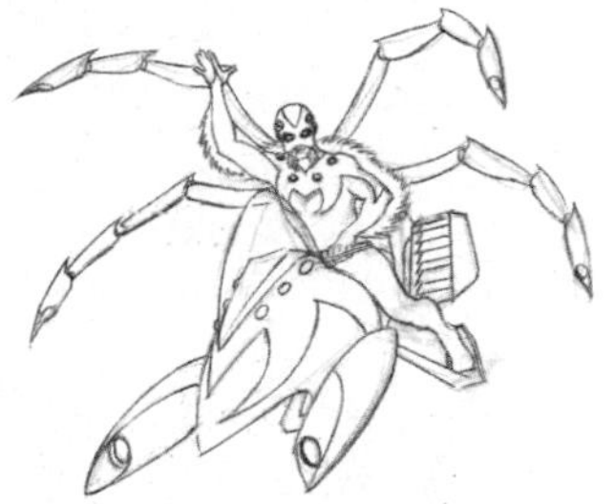

Extra arms: Real? Or mechanical? We ultimately settled on mechanical.

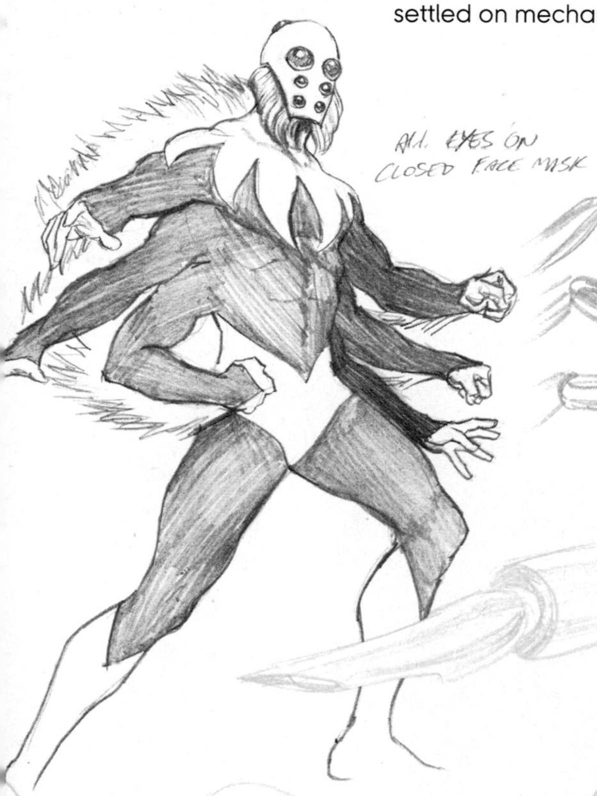
ALL EYES ON CLOSED FACE MASK

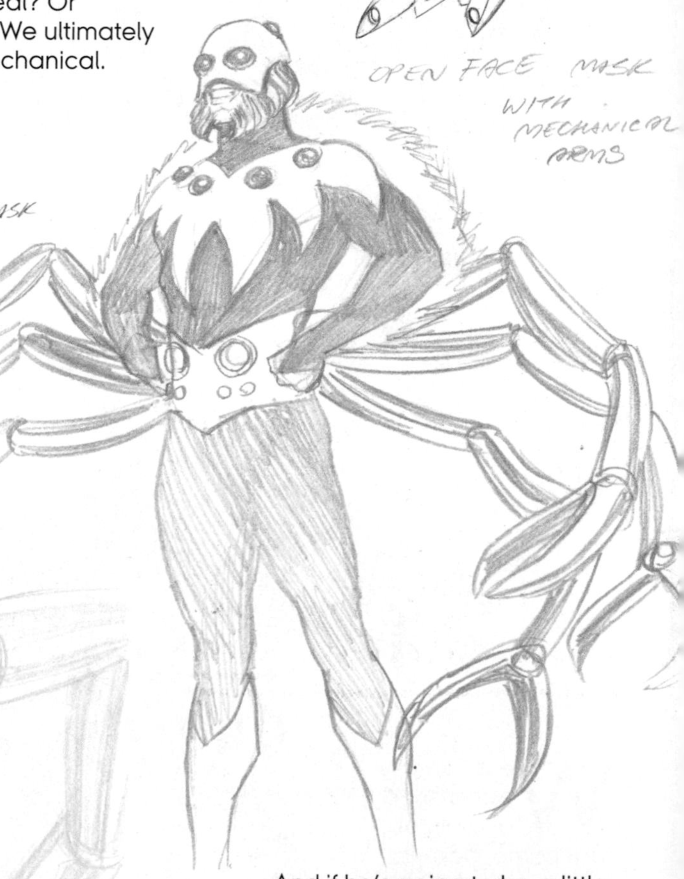
OPEN FACE MASK WITH MECHANICAL ARMS

And if he's going to be a little guy, he needs transportation!

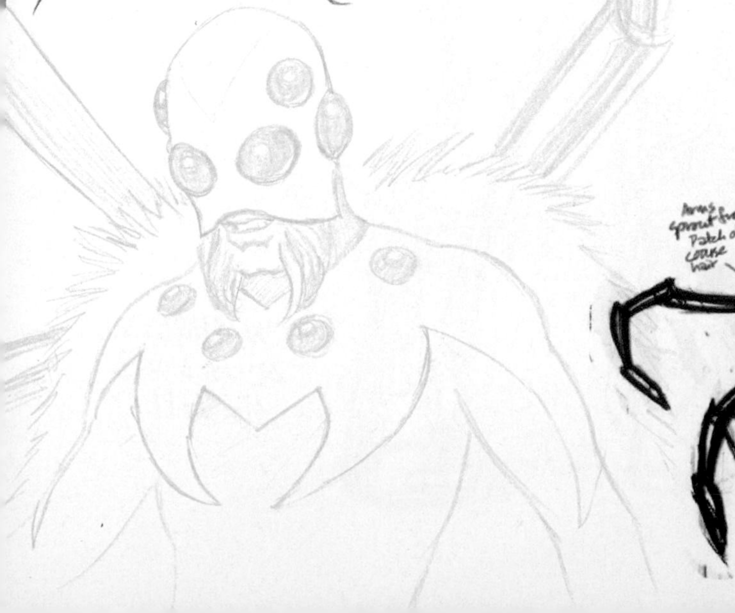

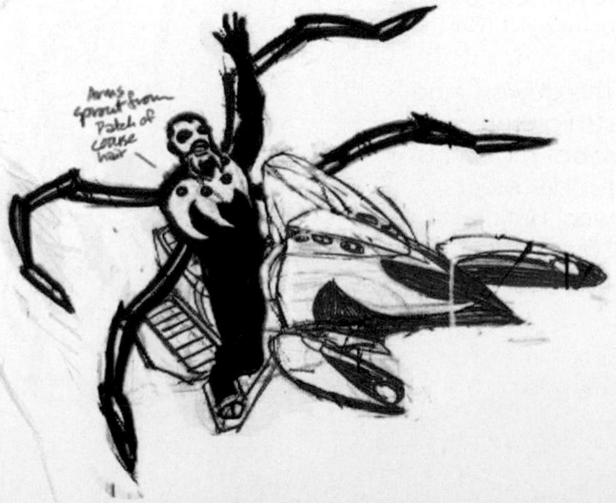
Arms sprout from Patch of coarse hair

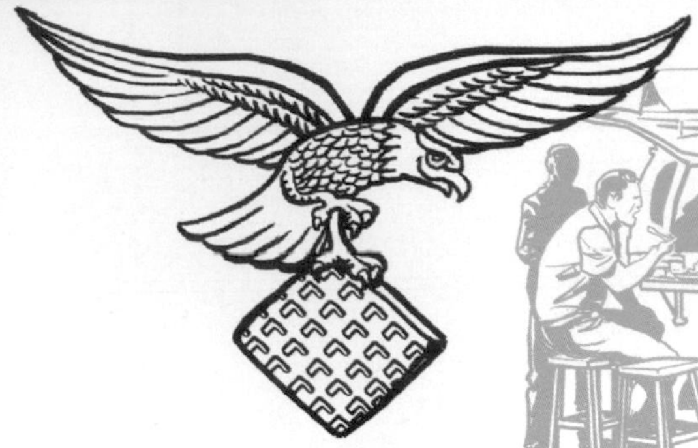

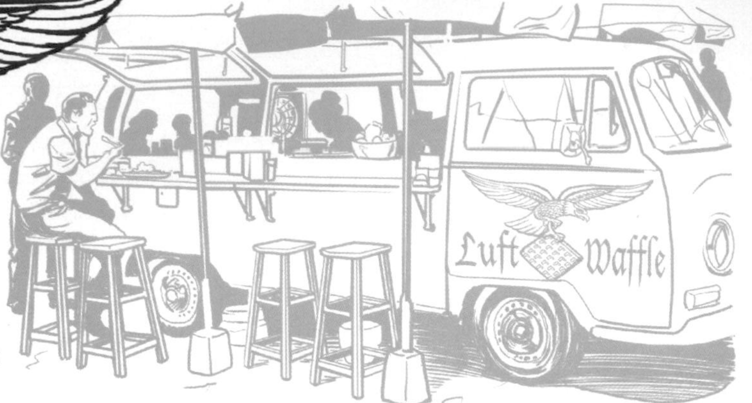
Luft Waffle

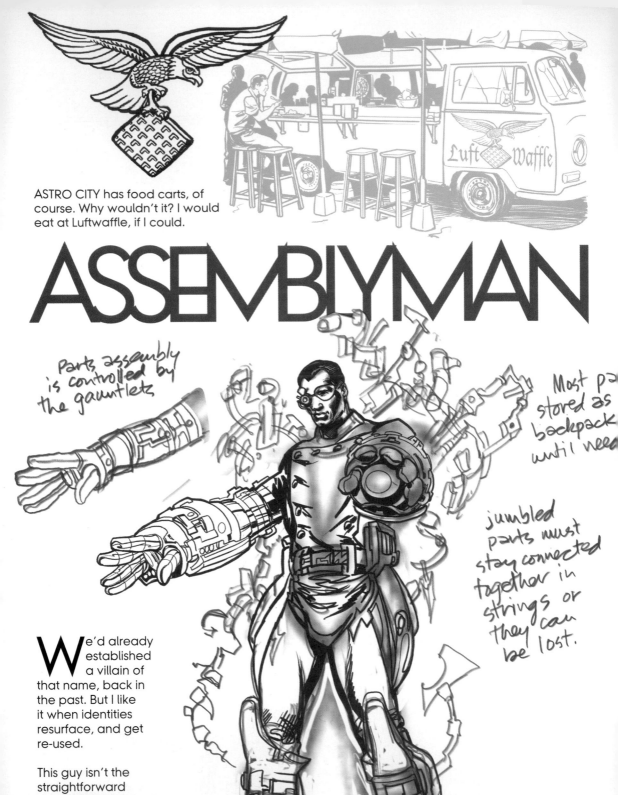

ASTRO CITY has food carts, of course. Why wouldn't it? I would eat at Luftwaffle, if I could.

ASSEMBLYMAN

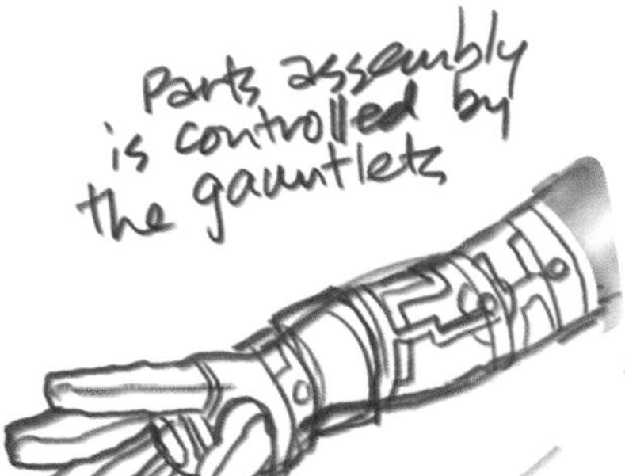
Parts assembly
is controlled by
the gauntlets

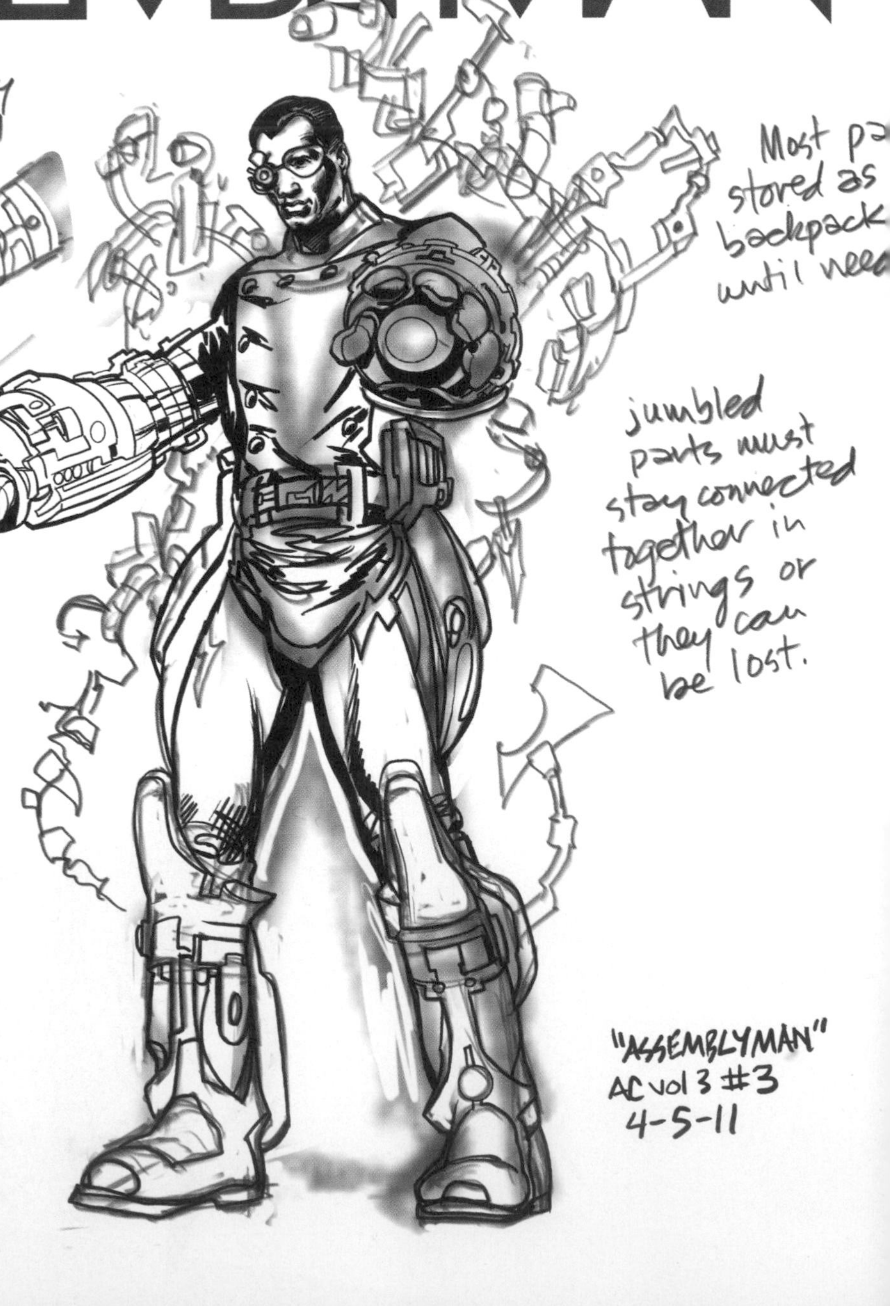
Most pa
stored as
backpack
until nee
jumbled
parts must
stay connected
together in
strings or
they can
be lost.
"ASSEMBLYMAN"
AC vol 3 #3
4-5-11

We'd already established a villain of that name, back in the past. But I like it when identities resurface, and get re-used.

This guy isn't the straightforward robot-maker his predecessor was, but he still "assembles" things.

How do you design a character who's got attitude and bluster, but who really doesn't have the chops to make it in the super-villain world?

He had to look good enough to be perceived as a threat when he first showed up, but when the tables get turned on him, the comedy has to work, too. So he needs to be, essentially, an imitation villain—looks good on the surface, but nothing beneath it.

Brent did a great job assembling a collection of "master-villain" clichés—the armor, the cloak, the goatee, the boots—that project the right flavor but don't really add up to anything specific. And the crowning touch, the oversized, glowing monocle, is both dramatic and slightly foolish, a nice sign that this guy is perhaps playing dress-up. Serving the outfit rather than the outfit serving him.

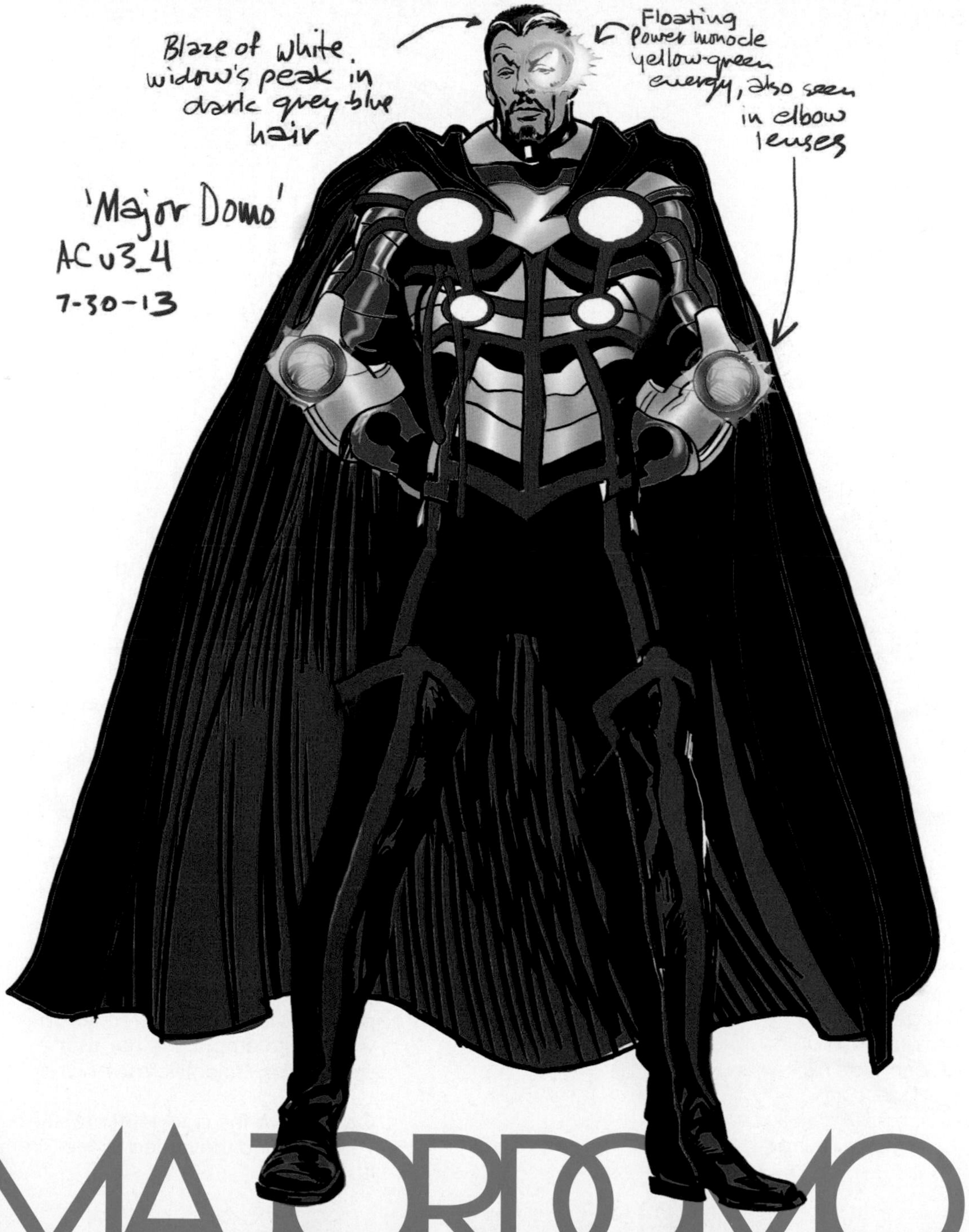
Blaze of white widow's peak in dark grey-blue hair
Floating Power monocle yellow-green energy, also seen in elbow lenses
'Major Domo'
ACv3_4
7-30-13

MAJORDOMO

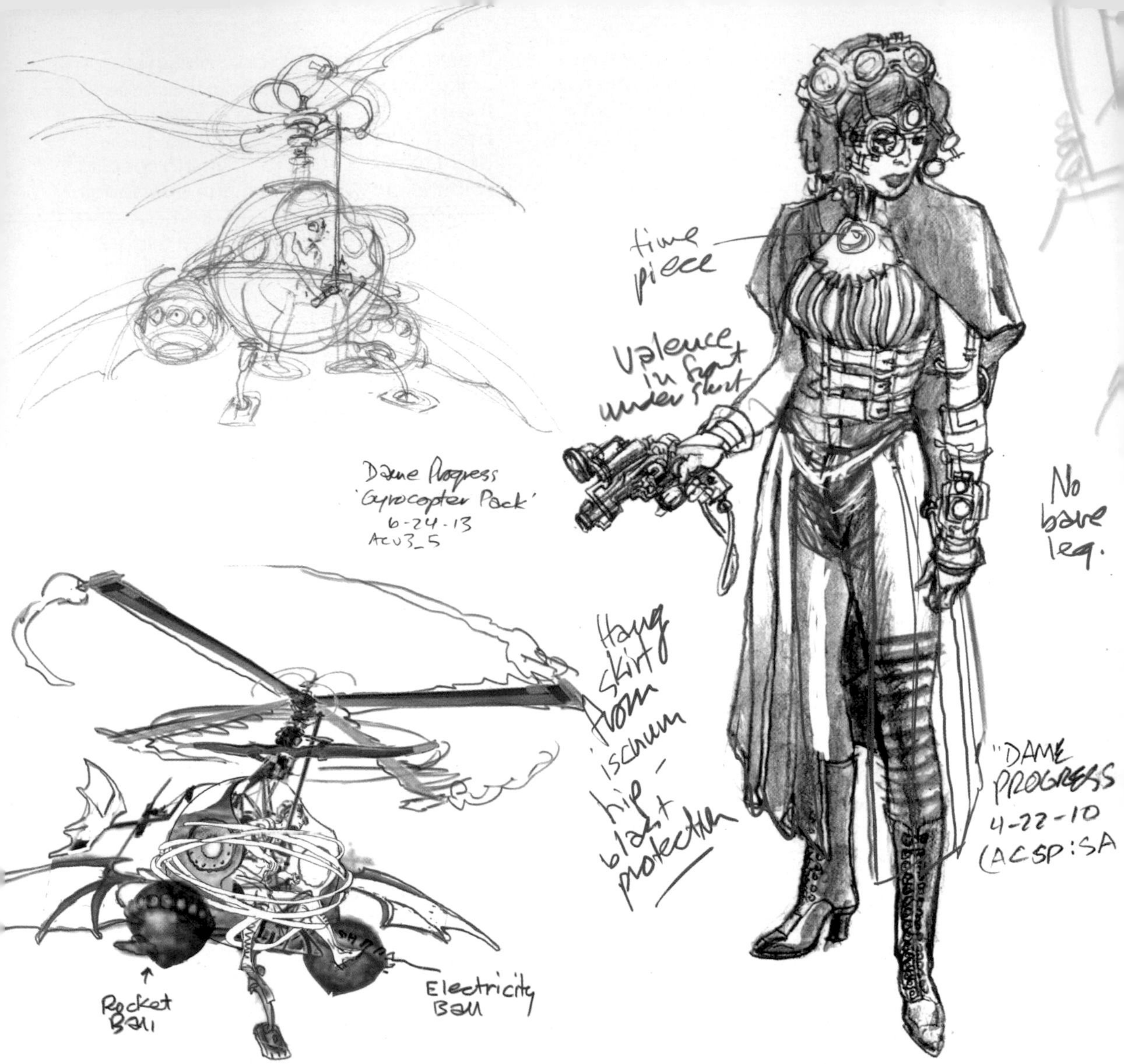
time piece
Valence in front under skirt
Dame Progress
'Gyrocopter Pack'
6-24-13
Acv3_5
No bare leg.
Hang skirt from ischium hip - blast protection
"DAME PROGRESS
4-22-10
(ACSP:SA
Rocket Ball
Electricity Ball

DAME PROGRESS

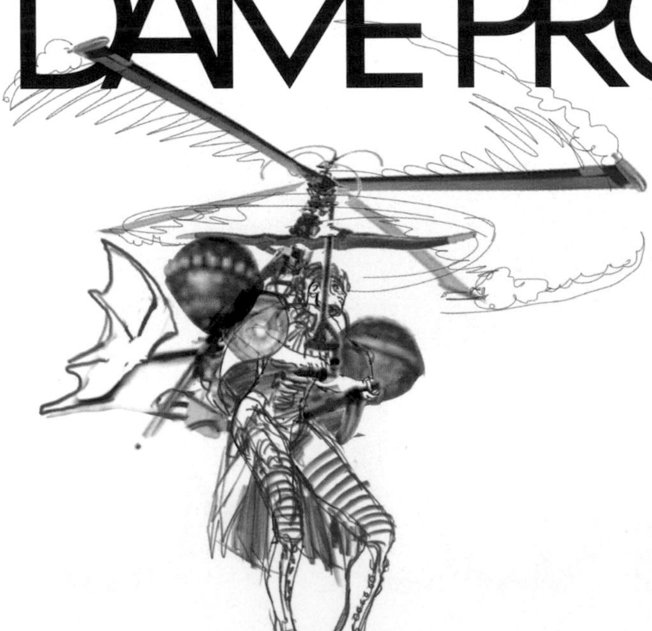

We saw the above sketch last volume, but here it is with Brent's additions, as we refined our approach.

She's not a superhero—she predates the concept, really—so we tried to emphasize her as a steampunk "scientific adventurer."

Gotta have the gadgetry and the vehicles, and they need to feel like it's 1903…

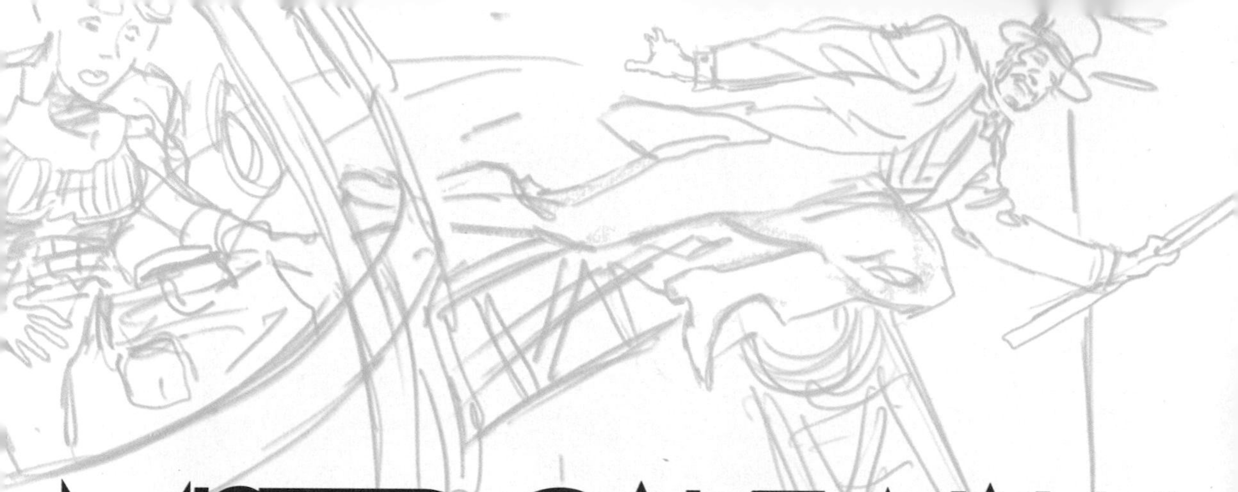

MISTER CAKEWALK

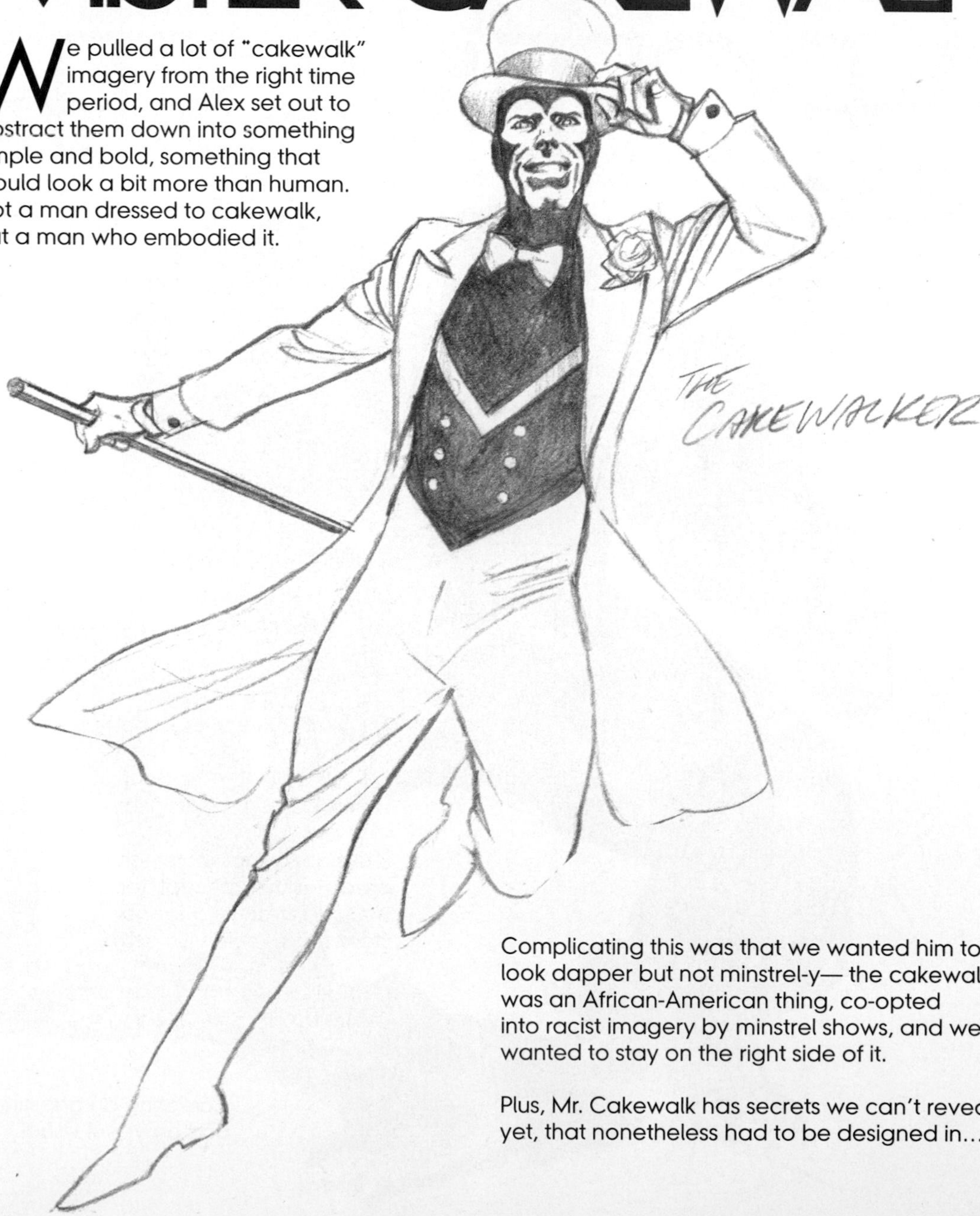
THE CAKEWALKER

We pulled a lot of "cakewalk" imagery from the right time period, and Alex set out to abstract them down into something simple and bold, something that would look a bit more than human. Not a man dressed to cakewalk, but a man who embodied it.

Complicating this was that we wanted him to look dapper but not minstrel-y— the cakewalk was an African-American thing, co-opted into racist imagery by minstrel shows, and we wanted to stay on the right side of it.

Plus, Mr. Cakewalk has secrets we can't reveal yet, that nonetheless had to be designed in...

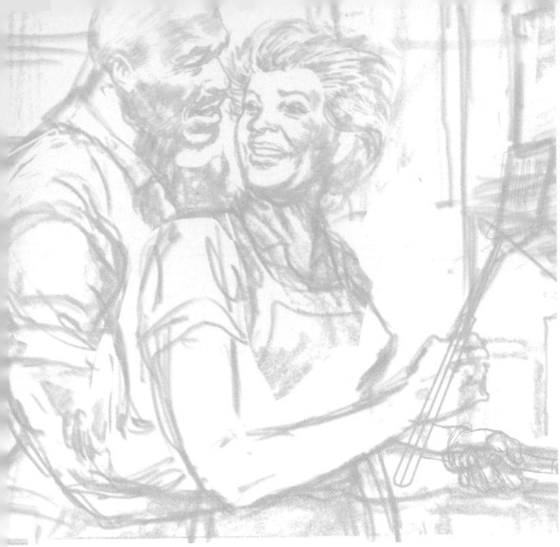

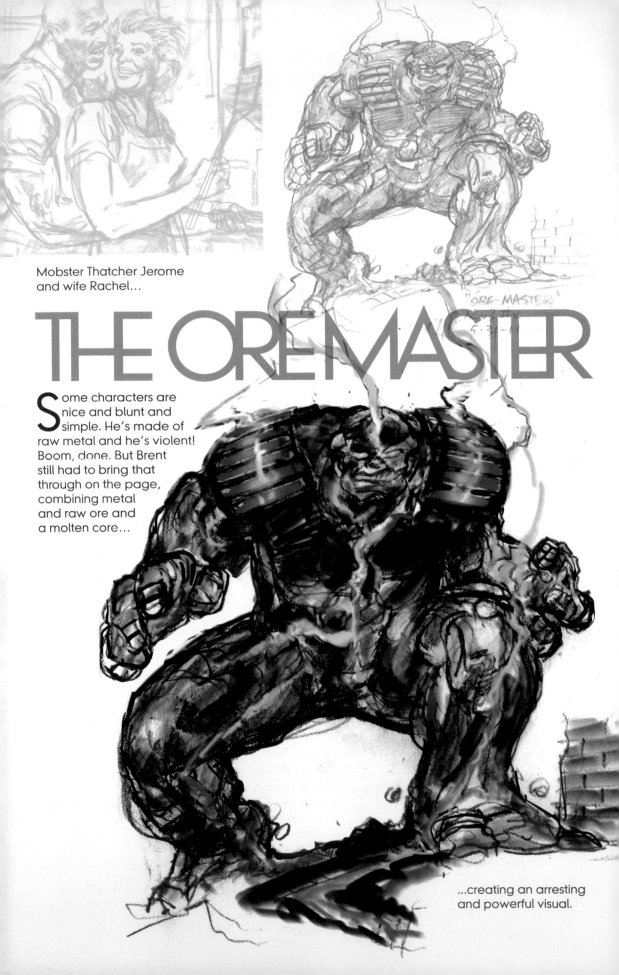

Mobster Thatcher Jerome and wife Rachel...

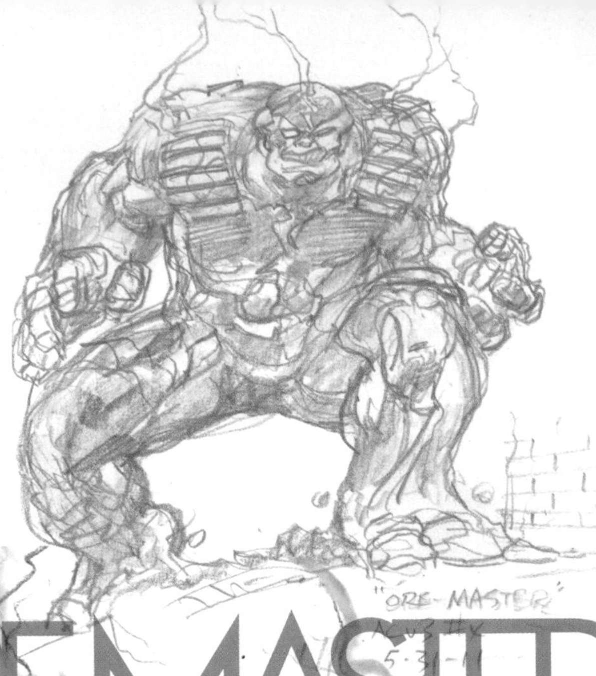
"ORE-MASTER"

THE ORE MASTER

Some characters are nice and blunt and simple. He's made of raw metal and he's violent! Boom, done. But Brent still had to bring that through on the page, combining metal and raw ore and a molten core...

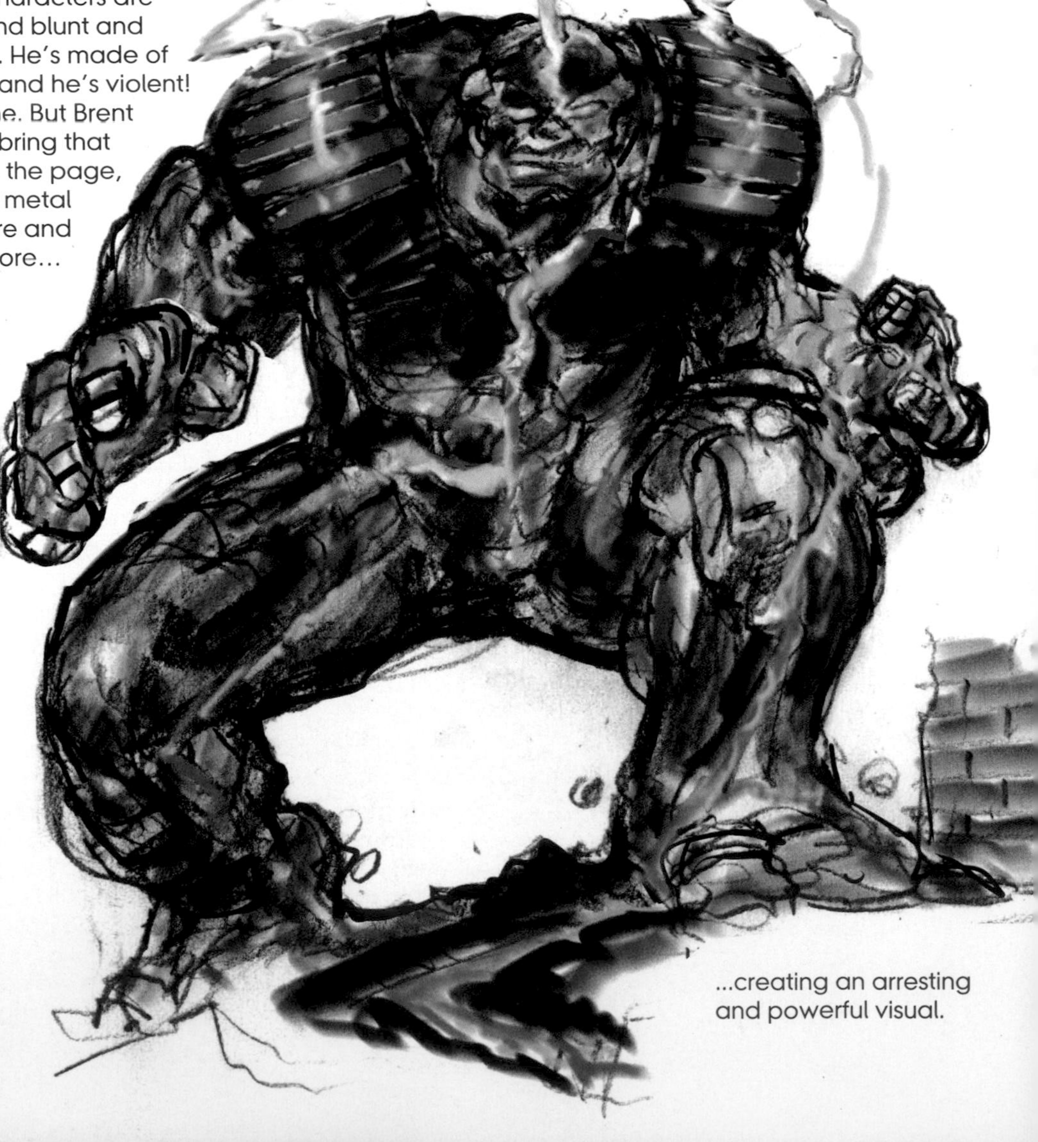

...creating an arresting and powerful visual.

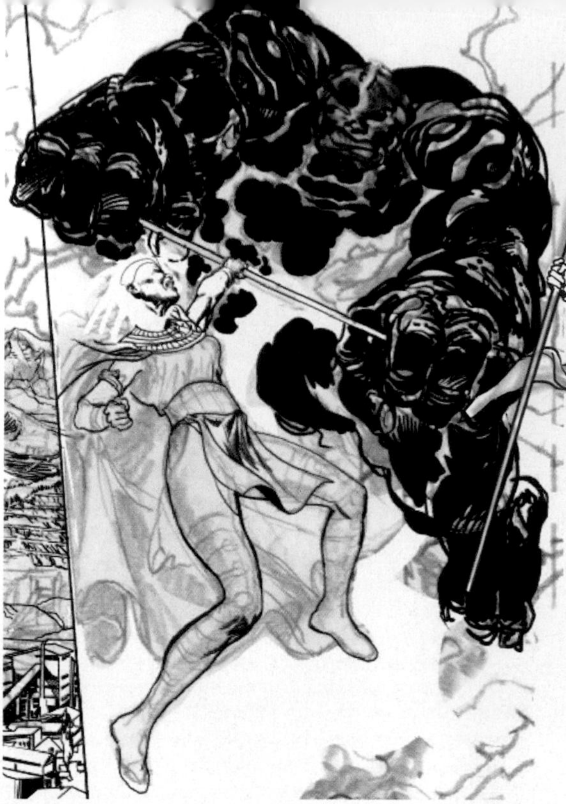

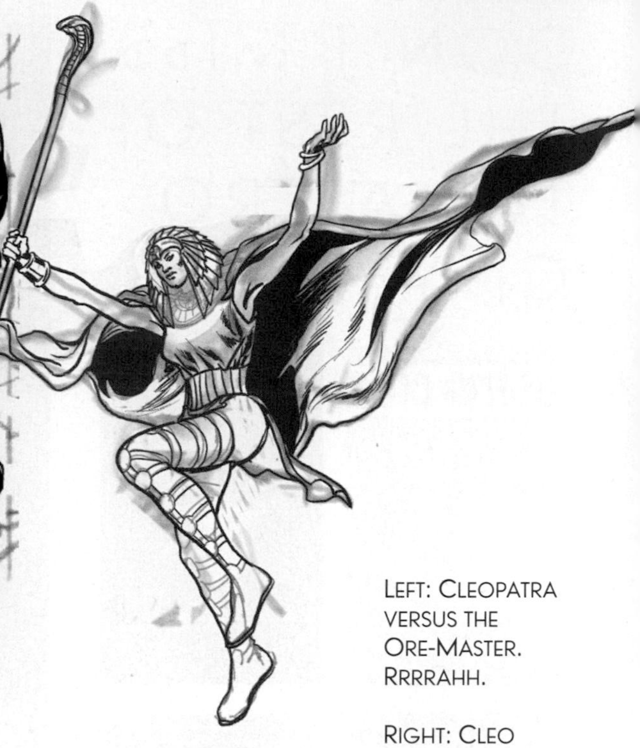

Left: Cleopatra versus the Ore-Master. Rrrrahh.

Right: Cleo takes to the air.

BOX O' SORNA

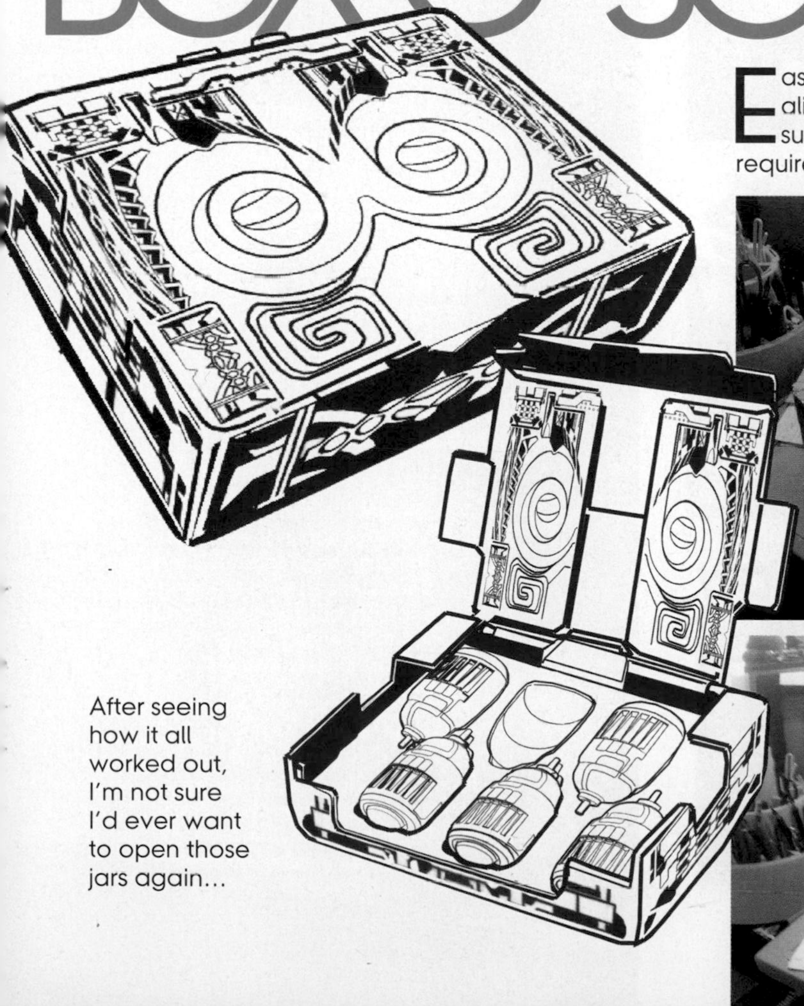

Easy enough to describe a hi-tech alien carrying case, but making sure it looks right sometimes requires making a model.

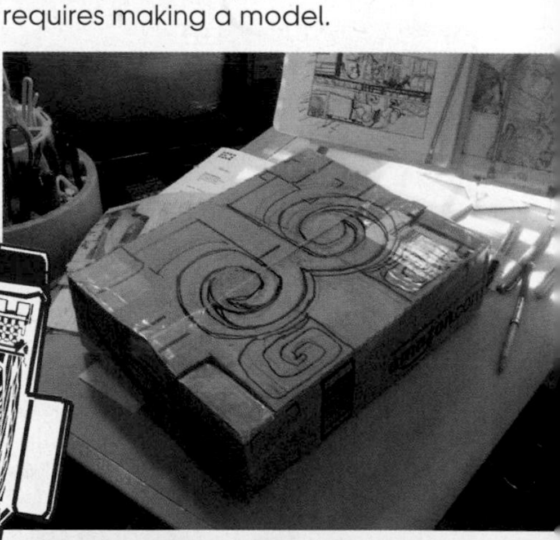

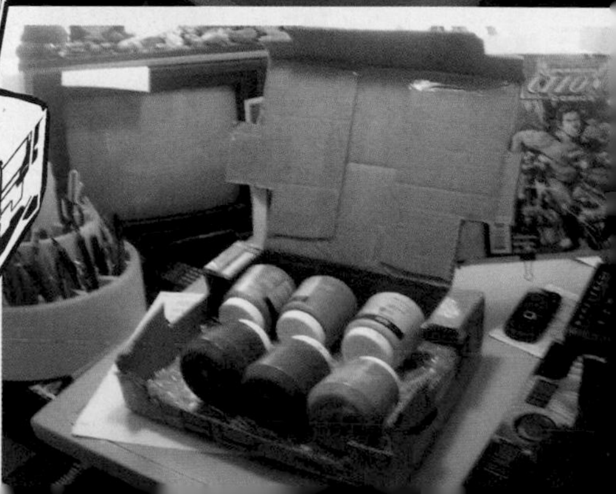

After seeing how it all worked out, I'm not sure I'd ever want to open those jars again...

DON'T MISS THE REST OF THE ASTRO CITY SERIES:

astro city
life in the big city
KURT BUSIEK • BRENT ANDERSON • ALEX ROSS

KURT BUSIEK'S
Astro City
BUSIEK • ANDERSON • BLYBERG
SINCLAIR • ROSS • COMICRAFT
Confession
Introduction by NEIL GAIMAN

ASTRO CITY
Family Album
BUSIEK • ANDERSON • BLYBERG
ROSS • SINCLAIR • COMICRAFT

KURT BUSIEK'S
Astro City
The
TARNISHED
ANGEL

ASTRO CITY
LOCAL HEROES

ASTRO CITY
THE DARK AGE
1: BROTHERS & OTHER STRANGERS
BUSIEK
ANDERSON
ROSS
SINCLAIR
COMICRAFT

ASTRO CITY
THE DARK AGE
2: BROTHERS IN ARMS
BUSIEK
ANDERSON
ROSS
SINCLAIR
COMICRAFT

astro city
SHINING
STARS
BUSIEK • ANDERSON • ROSS • SINCLAIR • COMICRAFT

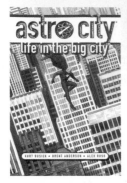

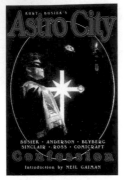

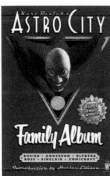

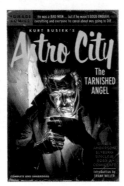

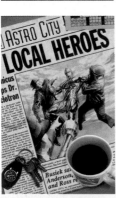

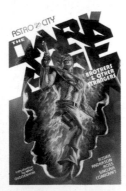

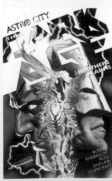

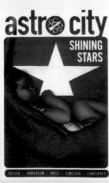

ABOUT THE CREATORS

KURT BUSIEK broke into comics in 1982, selling stories to both DC and Marvel within weeks of finishing college. Since then, he's been an editor, a literary agent, a sales manager and more, but is best known as the multiple-award-winning writer of ASTRO CITY, MARVELS, SUPERMAN, CONAN, ARROWSMITH, SUPERSTAR, SHOCKROCKETS and many others. He lives in the Pacific Northwest with his family.

BRENT ANDERSON began writing and drawing his own comics in junior high school and graduated to professional work less than a decade later. He's drawn such projects as KA-ZAR THE SAVAGE, X-MEN: GOD LOVES MAN KILLS, STRIKEFORCE: MORITURI, SOMERSET HOLMES, RISING STARS and, of course, ASTRO CITY, for which he's won multiple Eisner and Harvey Awards. He makes his home in Northern California.

ALEX ROSS worked on TERMINATOR: THE BURNING EARTH and Clive Barker's HELLRAISER before his breakout series, MARVELS, made him an overnight superstar. Since then, he's painted, plotted and/or written such series as KINGDOM COME, SUPERMAN: PEACE ON EARTH, JUSTICE, EARTH X, AVENGERS/INVADERS and PROJECT SUPERPOWERS, and won over two dozen industry awards.

ALEX SINCLAIR has colored virtually every DC Comics character in existence, and more besides. Best known for his award-winning work with Jim Lee and Scott Williams, he's worked on such books as BATMAN: HUSH, SUPERMAN: FOR TOMORROW, BLACKEST NIGHT, BATMAN & ROBIN, ASTRO CITY, JLA, IDENTITY CRISIS, ARROWSMITH and more.

WENDY BROOME was a longtime member of the coloring staff at WildStorm Studios, before going freelance in 2004. She's made a specialty of coloring large-cast books, including WILDCATS 3.0, THE AUTHORITY, GEN13, THE END LEAGUE, THUNDERCATS, WETWORKS and TOP10 as well as pitching in as needed on ASTRO CITY.

JOHN G. ROSHELL joined Comicraft in 1992, helping propel the lettering/design studio to its dominant position in the industry. As Senior Design Wizard, he's lettered thousands of comics pages, along with creating logos and fonts, designing book editions and more. He also writes the series CHARLEY LOVES ROBOTS, which appears in ELEPHANTMEN.

RICHARD STARKINGS dimly remembers working on some BATMAN project... THE KILLING JOKE? People insist that he did letter it with a tool not unlike a computer... but too many lattes and British chocolate has wiped his recollections of anything prior to Illustrator 5. He currently writes ELEPHANTMEN.